MW00388816

Table of Contents

Paul Taylor – Winger
Paul Laine – Danger Danger, The Defiants
PJ Farley – Trixter
Bruno Ravel – Danger Danger
Mark Gus Scott – Trixter
Stacey Blades – L.A. Guns, Electric Radio Kings
Steve Blaze – Lillian Axe
Ted Poley – Danger Danger, Tokyo Motor Fist
Terry Dunn – Banshee
Tod Howarth – Loudness, Frehley's Comet
Tony Cardenas Montana – Great White, Shadow and the Thrill
Tony Harnell – TNT, Skid Row, Starbreaker
Danny Vaughn – Tyketto, Waysted
Junkyard
Jason McMaster – Dangerous Toys, Broken Teeth
Tommy Richard – Vain, Orchid
Dito Godwin – producer, Motley Crue, Great White

Why?

That's the question I was asked most often. Why spend thousands of hours listening to old songs from no-hit wonders that flamed out in the 80s? Why interview rock musicians that haven't had a Billboard hit in 30 years? Why spend years working on this hair metal music project? My only answer was to shrug my shoulders, give a sly smile, and say...because the music was so good, the musicians were so interesting, and they all deserve to have their stories told and shared.

Today's rock fans need to know who Joey C. Jones is. The Wild Boyz deserve to be remembered. We all know about Motley Crue and Guns N' Roses. But what about Junkyard and Tora Tora? There were a hundred great bands that released some really fantastic music without the publicity and fanfare that bands like Bon Jovi and Def Leppard received. And guys like Lanny Cordola and Dennis Ogle deserve to have their stories told.

This isn't a book about Nikki Sixx and Tommy Lee partying with Ozzy. Or about Axl and Slash feuding. We didn't just go to Wiki and copy the same popular stories you've all read a thousand times.

The "why" started off with a flight on a jet. I browsed through Amazon to try and find a couple books on the hair metal/hair band era to read during my flight. And couldn't really find anything. So then I tried to update my IPod so I'd have some new music to listen to on the plane. I've heard Ratt's "Round and Round" a million times so I tried to find a website that would list more than just the same 100 anthems that we've all grown accustomed to. And I couldn't really find anything. Finally, I then tried to find a list of current bands that were trying to keep that hair metal style alive. Once again – nothing.

So at that point I decided to do something about it. That's what this book is. It is a true LABOR OF LOVE. This is the music I love, played by the bands I grew up loving. I tried to go deeper than any other books or websites on the subject to give fans like myself a one-stop place where they can get their fill of the wonderful and fantastic music we all grew up loving. The music that was the soundtrack of our youth.

And for the record – there was a LOT of research. I literally listened to every single album I could find that had any connection to the genre. Starting in 1981 and going through today. Thanks to YouTube, I was able to discover hundreds of bands that I had never even heard of in spite being a hair metal addict back in the day. It is a safe bet to say that I've listened to more hair metal bands than anybody alive. I spent a year just listening to music and watching music videos. I listened to a lot of bands that only released one album back in the late 80s and then disappeared forever. Did I miss some? No doubt. But I did the best I could!

There is a section in the book that lists the top 1,000 songs of the genre. It is broken down to the top 650 rock songs top 350 ballads. That should help you fill up your IPod.

I also interviewed more than 50 musicians for the project. From Billy Sheehan to Jay Jay French to Ted Poley to Marq Torien....and everybody in between! Their input was invaluable for the book.

Finally....I am a one-man show. I did all the research, all the writing, all the editing – everything. I've edited and revised and read every sentence in this book a hundred times. But being a one-man show there are NO doubt going to be errors. Bad grammar. Mistakes on names or years. Misspelled words. I spent a couple thousand hours of my own time on this book trying to get it as interesting – and accurate – as possible. I had zero money to spend on a professional writer or a professional editor. Every time I read the book I find a couple new errors. One of the rock stars I have become friends with (through writing the book) told me "dude, just stop and release it. It's rock 'n' roll – there are supposed to be a few mistakes, it isn't supposed to be perfect." So you will find mistakes, I apologize for that.

So, fellow music fans – here it is. My take on the fantastic hair metal and hair band music era. If you love the music as much as I do, then hopefully you'll find something enjoyable in here. Maybe you'll discover a new band or a couple new songs that you weren't aware of.

Please....enjoy!!!!

P.S.
The biggest complaint will be the label. "My favorite band wasn't a hair metal band." I get it. Some people hate the label. And that's OK! But at the end of the day, it's just a label that signifies a specific time period and semi-style of music. Ask yourself this question: If a friend invited you to their birthday party and said the theme was "hair metal music"....what type of music would you expect to hear?

At the end of the day, it is all just rock music. For the purpose of this book hair metal and hair band are just terms to describe the music that was mainly popular between 1985-1992. Hair metal is essentially just hard rock, hair band is basically just pop rock. It's really that simple.

Sebastian Bach turned down our interview request, saying it was an "embarrassment" to include him in the hair metal category. We told that story to another musician (he's interviewed in this book) and he laughed and said "Love Bach, he's a great guy. But when I hear the term hair metal – him and Skid Row are the first band I think of." Point is – it's all relative. And again, it's just a label that describes a certain type of music that was popular during a certain era of music. Guns N' Roses weren't hair metal? I'll show you pictures of them in complete make-up, hair teased and wearing spandex. And even a band like Cinderella, that plays a rock-blues style of music. Take a look at some of their pictures. Teased hair, make-up, purple outfits.

For me, the breakdown is pretty simple. The more straight forward hard rock bands are considered hair metal. GnR, Skid Row, Ratt, Dangerous Toys, Tesla. Those are the bands that have more of a sleazy metal style. The bands that are a bit lighter and prettier with a more polished pop rock sound– those bands I would classify in the hair band genre. The Bon Jovi and Poison type bands. Lol, then we have bands like Def Leppard who are firmly established in both groups. Their first three albums are pure hard rock magic. Then Hysteria came along and they went down the hair band road.

All we ask is don't be one of those dorks that get caught up in the name. Guys that actually get angry over the term hair metal. "It's an insult to all bands"....all we can say is: bro, it's just rock n roll music. The music is what matters, not what people call it. Life it too short to throw fits of rage over a simple label.

It's all rock n roll music......and we love almost all of it!!!!! So let's celebrate the music we all grew up loving!!!

1981-2017

In these opening chapters, we offer a breakdown of the entire hair metal and hair band genre. We will sometimes refer to it as HM/HB. Starting in the early 80s by bands like Dokken, Whitesnake, Def Leppard and Twisted Sister. And then joining the fray and dominating the late 80s and early 90s were bands like Guns N' Roses and Bon Jovi. For a good 5-6 year stretch, the HM/HB genre was the premier music style out there. MTV and rock radio was flooded by the above mentioned bands. Teenagers and young adults couldn't get enough of the feel-good, party inducing anthems that hair bands had to offer.

It's a common theme within the hard rock circles that grunge killed off the hair metal/hair band genre. But that's not necessarily the truth. The bottom line is this: hair metal was killing itself. Record labels were more to blame than grunge.

By 1990, the HM/HB (hair metal/hair band) market was saturated with so many bands that it turned into a huge overkill. As a teenager, every week I loved going to the record store and picking out an album or two. Every CD release day featured 3-4 potential great albums. But a few short years later when I went to college, the saturation of HM/HB by generic, faceless bands had taken over. So then when I went to the record store, there wasn't 3-4 major releases. There would be 30 new albums. By bands that all looked the same, sounded the same, that used z instead of s, and that released a video of the band in full make-up playing a song in an airplane hangar. The drummers made the same faces, the guitar players did all the same poses and the singers all had bandanas on their heads and microphone stands.

Fans still wanted great HM/HB music. They still wanted to buy the albums and go to the shows. But the greediness and short sidedness of the major labels flooded the market with so much mediocre fluff, that fans were simply overwhelmed. Imagine receiving a massage. It feels great. That was the major deathblow to the genre.

But grunge did play a part in the change of musical tide in the 90s. A generation of new kids weren't as happy as the prior generation. Life wasn't a big party...now it was about being morose and hating life. These kids didn't want to go to a party and drink, dance, have fun and share dreams of becoming millionaires. They wanted to drink, smoke weed and talk about how evil corporate America was. The drug of choice was a perfect example. One group sniffed cocaine so they could stay up for days partying. The other group wanted to shoot heroin so they could black out for days.

The definition of music was also changing. Originally there was heavy metal. That diverged into different genres like glam metal, thrash metal, pop metal, hard rock, pop rock, soft rock. Then those genres got diluted even more and some merged with other genres. Fans started to gravitate to certain styles of music. In my area there was a split between the thrash metal heads and the rock heads. Once upon a time we where all together, united as the metal militia. Now we had taken up arms against each other. Believe it or not, there was a time where Poison was considered a metal band! Today, Slayer fans would kick your ass if you claimed Poison or Warrant were metal bands.

But regardless of what the haters might think.....hair metal is far from dead!!! 2017 was one of the best years of the genre in the last twenty years! Guns N' Roses is breaking touring records. Hell, their 1987 release Appetite for Destruction has literally just charted as one of the top 10 billboard albums of the week – in 2018. That's incredible. Bands like Bon Jovi and Def Leppard are selling out their tours. Bands like Whitesnake, Poison and Telsa can sell out 5,000 seat venues without a problem. HM/HB might not be back like it's 1987....but it is back in full force. Great 80s/90s bands are releasing music, doing strong tours and the weekend festivals are off the charts. The Monsters of Rock Cruise is easily the most popular music cruises out there, and it isn't even close.

The Beginning

'Cum On Feel the Noize' is generally considered the song that kicked off the Hair Metal music era. While the Quiet Riot classic was definitely a game-changer and the album *Metal Health* was the genre's first number one album, the legendary Don Dokken should be credited for the initial hair metal song and album.

But before we show you baby pictures and brag about how cute the baby is or share videos of his first step, first we have to delve back into a little family history. Who are the baby's parents? Grandparents? Did he have any famous aunts and uncles? Don Dokken didn't just wake up one day and create an entire new genre. Here is where that baby's lineage falls.

Our favorite genre is the baby of a lot of different musical styles. Mix Alice Cooper in with some Van Halen and Queen and add a huge touch of Kiss. Toss in some Led Zeppelin. Oh yea, don't forget to top it off with a bunch of glam rock. To be honest, an entire book could be written about the influences of hair metal music. We could pull up hundreds of songs, dozens of bands, and weave our way back all the way to Chuck Berry and Johnny Be Goode.

The problem with a project like that is that every body – including you, the reader – has a different opinion on what bands and songs should be considered hair bands or hair metal. Are he Scorpions hair metal – or was just a portion of their career? Y&T? Fastway? WASP? Should Kiss, Van Halen and Cooper be listed? Everybody has a different list or set of guidelines. So compiling an accurate list of what bands/albums influenced those bands is an impossible task. If we can't agree on which bands fit into the genre, how can we agree on what bands influenced them?

With that said, using our own list and guidelines, we've came up with some key songs that you can reasonably trace back to being huge influences for "our" version of the genre. Below are ten songs and an album that obviously supplied the basic groundwork to what would become our favorite era of music. We've only gone back through the 1970s, with the thought that HB/HM officially kicked off in the early 80s. So the 70s would have been the teen years for our favorite stars.

Rock and Roll – Led Zeppelin, 1972
Schools Out – Alice Cooper, 1972
Dream On – Aerosmith, 1973
Come On Feel The Noize – Slade, 1973
You Ain't Seen Nothing Yet – BTO, 1974
Walk This Way – Aerosmith, 1975
Rock N Roll All Night – Kiss, 1975
More Than a Feeling – Boston, 1976
We Will Rock You – Queen, 1977
Van Halen – Van Halen, entire album, 1978
Train In Vain – The Clash, 1979

Slap these songs on a CD, well, on cassette, and presto: hair band and hair metal music was born.

In 1980, British rock band Whitesnake released their third album, titled *Ready an' Willing*. It was a hit in the United Kingdom and featured a song called Fool For Your Loving, which would end up being revised and later released on the smash 1989 album Slip Of The Tongue. But in 1980, David Coverdale and the boys were a pure blues based hard rock band.

For all intensive purposes, hair metal and hair band era official began in 1981. Three bands can take the glory for being the originators, even though two of their debut albums weren't released on major labels and their success came in following years.

The band that started the clichés that were copied by a hundred different of their peers – and wannabe peers – were a group of rag tag LA musicians named Motley Crue. On April 1st, 1981 singer Vince Neil decided to leave his band Rock Candy to join Nikki Sixx, Mick Mars and Tommy Lee. Amazingly, just nine short months later (November) Motley released the album *Too Fast For Love* on their own label – Leathur Records. Fans snapped up every copy of TFFL, the Crue were the toast of the Sunset Strip, and Tom Zutaut and Electra Records quickly signed the band to a major publishing deal.

Just one month after officially forming, in May of 1981 Motley Crue released two pure 100% hair metal songs. Again, it was on their own label, but the Toast of the Town and Stick To Your Guns releases were the first time American fans could hear a taste of what would become HB/HM. To this day, 36 years later, some people still say the solo in Toast of the Town is the best thing Mars has ever done.

English rockers Def Leppard released their second album – *High 'n' Dry* - in the summer of 1981. Mutt Lange came on board to fine tune the band, which was primary known as a heavy metal group. Leppard's first album – *On Through The Night* – was heavy enough that it earned the band a tour with AC/DC.

Lange came in and produced *High 'n' Dry*, which still featured a raw and dirty rock sound but was a little lighter and more radio friendly than their debut.

High 'n' Dry's contribution to the entire history of hair metal music comes down to three main points.

*The Lange/Leppard partnership, which would eventually propel Def Leppard into the rock upper stratosphere.
*The genre's first power ballad – 'Bringing On The Heartbreak'. Still holds up today.
*'Let It Go' – an underrated gem that influenced most of the heavier genre songs that dominated the charts for the next decade. Listen to 'Let It Go' and you can hear shades of Cinderella, Skid Row, Quiet Riot and even Guns N' Roses. Some people say that Cinderella owes their entire discography to the first ten seconds of 'Let It Go'.

The third significant release came from the legendary Don Dokken and his self-titled band. Dokken released *Breakin' The Chains* in 1981, but overseas on the French label Carrere Records. Dokken signed with Electra, which worked the band to fine-tune and tidy up the album and then released it in America in 1983.

But one of the band's most famous tunes and one of the genre's top 50 songs was featured on the France album: 'Breakin' The Chains'. Though it didn't become a hit in the United States until 1983, rock fans in the know were rocking out to 'Breakin' the Chains' way back in 1981. That's right. Two years before 'Cum On Feel The Noize' blew up and kicked off a music revolution, 'Breakin' The Chains' was already out there kicking ass. Love him or hate him, respect is certainly due. Dokken's 'Breakin' the Chains' is probably the first significant hair metal song ever released.

The HB/HM revolution hadn't started yet. But thanks to Dokken and 'Breakin' the Chains', Whitesnake and 'Fool for Your Lovin' and Def Leppard's 'Bringing on the Heartbreak" – the foundation was set.

1982
The prior year's start didn't really gain momentum and traction until 1983. *Too Fast For Love* was officially released, but didn't light up the charts or the rock world. Though today many fans still view *TFFL* as Motley's best and most creative album, it was a slow grinding ride to reach that point. Beating the crowd to the punch again was Whitesnake, releasing an early version of 'Here I Go Again' on their *Saints & Sinners* album.

A young singer named Jon Bon Jovi was trying to get his start in the music world. His song Runaway was drawing a lot of regional interest in the New Jersey area, but he hadn't signed with a major label let.

1983

The year all hell broke loose. Quiet Riot's *Metal Health* became the first metal album to top the Billboard charts and featured the legendary song 'Cum On Feel the Noize'. Kevin DuBrow's raspy vocals and MTV putting metal videos into heavy rotation turned the Slade song into a hair metal classic.

Metal Health deserves its Hall of Fame status. And the title song is probably the best rock tune that DuBrow ever wrote. But Quiet Riot's real success came on the backs of two cover songs – both coincidently by Slade.

The two albums that really skyrocketed the careers of two of the Mt Rushmore bands of HB/HM were released in 1983. And rock would never be the same. Two classic albums highlighted 1983 and really cemented Motley Crue and Def Leppard as legends of the genre.

Pyromania is one of the top rock albums of all time. And – along with *Metal Health* – really brought hair metal to the masses. While Def Leppard's sound was slowly mellowing from their heavy metal roots and turning into a pop-rock band, when *Pyromania* came out they were still considered a hard rock band. New guitar player Phil Collen and producer/writer Lange are either credited or loathed for their influence on Leppard's sound.

Not only did Def Leppard release the genre's first hair metal power ballad (1981's 'Bringing On the Heartbreak'), but *Pyromania* also featured the first hit song of the genre with another power ballad 'Photograph'. 'Photograph' topped the Billboard Rock chart and reached #12 on the Hot 100 chart. It was also released five months before 'Cum On Feel The Noize', which topped out at #5 on the Hot 100 and #7 on the Rock chart.

Pyromania also featured a lot more depth than *Metal Health*, which helped the album reach #2 status on the Billboard 200. Along with 'Photograph', the album contained classic songs like 'Rock of Ages', 'Foolin' and 'Too Late For Love'.

Completing the trilogy and sparking the glam side of the revolution were the Motley Crue boys with their "safe" devil-worshiping album *Shout At The Devil*. Motley came out with the big hair, make-up, pentagrams, fire and semi-dark lyrics....but one could tell that the band put as much time into their image and stage performance as they did their actual music.

The album wasn't as commercially successful as *Pyromania* and *Metal Health*. But young teens flocked to the safer heavy metal image that Motley Crue portrayed as opposed to real metal acts like Judas Priest and Ozzy.

1980-1983 Lists
Top Songs:
1. Photograph – Def Leppard
2. Cum On Feel the Noize – Quiet Riot
3. Shout at the Devil – Motley Crue
4. Rock of Ages – Def Leppard
5. Breaking the Chains – Dokken
6. Let It Go – Def Leppard
7. Looks That Kill – Motley Crue
8. Metal Health – Quiet Riot
9. Live Wire – Motley Crue
10. Fool for Your Loving – Whitesnake
11. Too Fast for Love – Motley Crue
12. Foolin' – Def Leppard
13. Too Young to Fall in Love – Motley Crue
14. Too Late for Love – Def Leppard
15. On Your Knees – Great White
16. Say What You Will – Fastway
17. Lady Strange – Def Leppard
18. You Can't Stop Rock 'n' Roll – Twisted Sister
19. Paris is Burning – Dokken
20. Out of the Night – Great White
21. Rock! Rock! (Till You Drop) – Def Leppard

Top Ballads:
1. Bringing On the Heartbreak – Def Leppard
2. Here I Go Again – Whitesnake
3. On with the Show – Motley Crue
4. For Shame – Kix
5. You're Not Alone – Twisted Sister
6. Thunderbird – Quiet Riot

Albums
1. Pyromania – Def Leppard
2. Too Fast for Love – Motley Crue
3. Shout at the Devil – Motley Crue
4. Metal Health – Quiet Riot
5. High 'n' Dry – Def Leppard
6. Breaking the Chains - Dokken
7. Saints and Sinners – Whitesnake
8. You Can't Stop Rock 'n' Roll – Twisted Sister
9. Ready an' Willing – Whitesnake
10. Fastway – Fastway
11. Out of the Night – Great White (EP)
12. Cool Kids – Kix
13. Killer Dwarfs – Killer Dwarfs

1984 – Two More Legends

HM/HB continued it's slow and steady ride in 1984, adding a couple more Hall of Fame acts and albums.

Bon Jovi was the biggest name to join the scene, but Ratt and Dokken released the year's best albums. And again, MTV's willingness to play hard rock bands in full rotation certainly helped propel the genre into the mainstream. Who can forget Milton Berle chilling with the Ratt boys at dinner?

Stephen Pearcy's unique voice and Warren DeMartini's shredding skills helped Ratt's *Out Of The Cellar* reach number seven on the Billboard 200, where it stayed in the top 200 for 56 weeks. *Out Of The Cellar* featured three standout tracks, 'Round and Round', 'Wanted Man' and 'Back for More'. 'Round and Round' is generally considered one of the top 10 songs of the genre. It just missed out on being a top 10 song on Billboard, topping out at #12 on the Hot 100.

Before going full pop rock, Bon Jovi started off as a pure hard rock act. Their self-titled album only made it's way to #43 on the Billboard 200, though the songs 'Runaway' and 'She Don't Know Me' were minor hits, cracking the top 50 on the Hot 100. At this point nobody was predicting BJ would end as the most commercially successful band of the genre.

Dokken and Whitesnake, two bands that pre-dated the break through but didn't garner the recognition of Def Leppard, Motley Crue and Quiet Riot, finally received public glory in 1984.

Dokken released *Tooth and Nail*, which included the year's best power ballad in 'Alone Again'. 'Into The Fire' was a great rock song and George Lynch's solos and overall guitar player thrust his name into the conversation of top rock guitar players alive.

More than any of the bands mentioned so far, road warriors David Coverdale and Whitesnake paid their dues in the industry before breaking out in 1984. Whitesnake released five albums before *Slide It In* established them as a popular mainstream American act. *Slide It In* topped out at #40 on the Billboard 200.

Twisted Sister is another fascinating band. They reached mainstream conscious partially because of a catchy song – 'We're Not Gonna Take It' – but also because of the look of lead singer Dee Snider. Today, Twisted Sister is a band that gets downgraded as a novelty act whose success was based on Snider's crazy clown look. But in reality, Snider is a highly intelligent guy and his band was one of the harder rocking bands of the era. Their early work is more metal than rock.

The Scorpions also posed an interesting conundrum. Klaus Meine and company are clearly a rock and roll band. But, during the HM/HB era they released a couple albums that fit squarely into the genre. So we feel you can't classify them solely as a hair metal band, but two of their albums were clearly the Scorpions attempt to stay relevant in the popular music type of the time. So those two albums will be ranked in the genre. *Love at First Sting* is a great album.

Again, a catchy song teamed up with a funny MTV video, and a genre legend was created. 'Rock You Like a Hurricane' is one of those rare hair metal songs that is still respected today by casual rock fans. Punch in 'Hurricane' the next time you are at a bar and watch people start playing air guitar and bopping their heads.

Top Songs:
1. Round and Round – Ratt
2. Rock You Like a Hurricane – Scorpions
3. We're Not Gonna Take It – Twisted Sister
4. Runaway – Bon Jovi
5. Slow an' Easy – Whitesnake
6. Back for More – Ratt
7. Boulevard of Broken Dreams – Hanoi Rocks
8. Slide it In – Whitesnake
9. Into the Fire – Dokken
10. Wanted Man – Ratt
11. Turn Up the Radio – Autograph
12. Big City Nights – Scorpions
13. Tooth and Nail – Dokken
14. I Wanna Rock – Twisted Sister
15. Mama Weer All Crazee Now – Quiet Riot
16. She Don't Know Me – Bon Jovi
17. Just Got Lucky - Dokken
18. Send Her to Me - Autograph

Ballads:
1. Alone Again – Dokken
2. Don't You Ever Leave Me – Hanoi Rocks
3. Still Loving You – Scorpions
4. The Price – Twisted Sister
5. It's Up to You – Icon
6. Life Is Too Lonely – Stone Fury
7. Without Your Love – TnT
8. This Time – Y&T
9. Open Your Heart – Europe
10. You Won't be Lonely – Stryper
11. Love Lies – Bon Jovi

12. I Can Do Without You – TKO

Albums That You Must Own:
Out of the Cellar – Ratt
Tooth and Nail – Dokken
Love at First Sting – Scorpions
Slide it In – Whitesnake
Bon Jovi – Bon Jovi
Two Steps from the Move – Hanoi Rocks
Stay Hungry – Twisted Sister
Great White – Great White
Sign in Please - Autograph

Other albums of interest:
Quiet Riot – Conditional Critical
Hanoi Rocks – All Those Wasted Years
Europe – Wings of Tomorrow
Stryper – The Yellow and Black Attack
Lizzy Borden – Give 'Em the Axe
TnT – Knights of the New Thunder
TnT – TnT (EP)
Keel – Lay Down the Law
Fastway – All Fired up
Lita Ford – Out for Blood
Icon – Icon
Rose Tattoo – Southern Stars
Rough Cutt – Rough Cutt
Zebra – No Tellin' Lies – September
Y&T – In Rock We Trust
Wrathchild – Stakk Attakk
Black 'n Blue – Black 'n Blue
Stone Fury - Burns Like a Star

1985 - Dokken

Ratt and Dokken took a step forward, Motley Crue struggled to find their sound and completely changed things up, throwing their fans for a loop.

Now we know that Motley Crue liked to change their style and look for each album. But back in the beginning days their drastic sound and looks change was quite a shock for those teen metal boys who were rebelling with the Crue. Motley went from pentagrams and shouting at the devil to pink eye shadow, pink scarfs and going full glam. To this day, most diehard fans list *Theatre of Pain* as their least favorite Crue album (until the band's final three outputs).

While abandoning their teen angst based, pop-orientated rock songs like 'Smoking In The Boys Room' and 'Home Sweet Home' did bring them their first real taste of chart success. *Theatre of Pain* climbed all the way to #6 on the album charts, the highest charting HM/HB album of the year. 'Home Sweet Home' made it up to #37, again the highest from the era. 'Smoking in the Boys Room' was the highest ranked song on the Rock Charts, making it all the way to #7.

Ratt and Dokken built on the success of their 1984 albums with extremely solid follow-ups.

Ratt's *Invasion of Privacy* is the band's highest charting album, reaching all the way up to #7 on Billboard and staying on the charts for 42 weeks. Key songs included 'Lay it Down', 'You're in Love' and 'Closer to My Heart'.

A year after releasing the year's best power ballad, Dokken followed by releasing 1985's best rocker! 'In My Dreams' is classic Dokken. It's catchy, Don Dokken's vocals are on point and the George Lynch solo is pure hair metal delight.

Bon Jovi released *7800 Fahrenheit*, which mirrored their first album with its hard rock sound. *Fahrenheit* made it to 37 on the Billboard 200, where it remained for an impressive 85 weeks.

Other notable releases include Kix with *Midnight Dynamite*, displaying a heavier sound than what they are now most known for. Keel, Y&T and Stryper also produced albums that charted.

Top Songs
1. In My Dreams – Dokken
2. Lay it Down – Ratt
3. Broken Heart – White Lion
4. You're in Love – Ratt

5. Smokin' in the Boy's Room – Motley Crue
6. It's Not Love – Dokken
7. The Hunter – Dokken
8. In and Out of Love – Bon Jovi
9. Summertime Girls – Y&T
10. Cold Shower – Kix
11. Crazy Nights – Loudness
12. Unchain the Night - Dokken
13. Tonight – Motley Crue
14. City Boy Blues – Motley Crue

Ballad
1. Home Sweet Home – Motley Crue
2. Love You to Pieces – Lizzy Borden
3. I Believe in You – Y&T (Open Fire, 1985)
4. Closer to My Heart – Ratt
5. You Keep Breaking My Heart – Rough Cutt
6. Frozen Tears – Icon
7. Silent Night – Bon Jovi
8. Jaded Heart – Dokken
9. Never Change Your Mind – Loudness
10. Walkin' Away – Kix
11. Slippin' Away – Dokken
12. I Believe in You – Twisted Sister
13. Together as One - Stryper

Must Own Albums
Under Lock and Key – Dokken
Invasion of Your Privacy – Ratt
Theatre of Pain – Motley Crue
Midnite Dynamite – Kix
7800 Fahrenheit – Bon Jovi

Other Albums of Interest:
Loudness – Thunder in the East
Keel - The Right to Rock
Y&T – Open Fire & Down for the Count
White Lion - Fight to Survive
Europe – On the Loose
Lizzy Borden - Love You to Pieces
Dad – Standing on the Never Never
Stryper - Solders Under Command

London – Non-stop Rock
Prophet – Prophet – (Ted Poley on vocals and drums)
Autograph – That's the Stuff
Fastway - Waiting for the Roar
Twisted Sister – Come Out and Play

1986 – Bon Jovi

While the HM/HB genre was laying its foundation and trying to figure out its place in the rock world, Bon Jovi officially declared to the masses that the genre was not only real – but it was about to dominate the music world.

After releasing two solid albums, Bon Jovi made three key personnel changes that literally changed the landscape of an entire music genre. Desmond Child was brought it to write a couple songs with the band. Bruce Fairbairn produced the album. Bob Rock mixed it. The results? Like Def Leppard would also do the following year, Bon Jovi mellowed their sound and went for a more mainstream rock approach and the change paid off in spades.

Slippery When Wet roared up the album charts, becoming the second genre record to hit number one. While *Metal Health* spent one week topping the album chart and a total of 81 weeks charting, *Slippery When Wet* spent an incredible eight weeks at #1 and stayed on Billboard for more than two years.

Slippery also produced two songs that went to number one – 'You Give Love a Bad Name' and 'Livin' on a Prayer'. 'Wanted Dead or Alive' also cracked the top 10, reaching #7.

Bon Jovi's acoustic performance at the 1989 MTV Music Awards singlehandedly started the rock acoustic craze of the 1990s.

While Bon Jovi's success can be tied to Richie Sambora's smooth guitar player and brilliant backing vocals, and to Jon's voice and movie star good looks, one cannot overlook the role that songwriter Child played in the band's success. Child co-wrote 'You Give Love a

Bad Name' and 'Living on a Prayer', as well as the underrated ballad 'I'd Die For You'.

While 1986 was the year of Bon Jovi, several other Hall of Fame bands made huge contributions. Leading the way were Cinderella, Poison, Tesla, White Lion and Europe. Meanwhile, Ratt continue their impressive three-year run with another great album.

For the third year in a row Ratt released an album that charted on Billboard. *Dancing Undercover* climbed all the way to #26 and produced the rock hit 'Dance' as well as killer songs 'Slip of the Lip' and 'Body Talk'.

Two bands with completely different styles jumped onto popularity in 1986. And both lead singers are still packing venues today. Cinderella and Poison burst onto the scene and helped shape the genre by splitting it into two categories: hair music and hair metal.

There is nothing glam or hair band about Tom Keifer and Cinderella. Unfortunately, the boys donned a little makeup, teased their hair and wore some funky clothes to support *Night Songs*. But if you listen to the album without looking at the pictures then you wouldn't attach the word glam to the band, even with a name like Cinderella.

A blues-based hard rock attack with Keifer's gravely voice produced one of the greatest albums of the entire genre. 'Shake Me', 'Somebody Save Me' and 'Nobody's Fool' still hold up today as great rock songs.

Meanwhile, completely across the spectrum on the other side of the room, Poison popped in with *Look What the Cat Dragged In*. The album cover features the four band member's faces in complete full-fledged theatre style makeup, looking more like women than men.

The lyrics were cheesy, singer Brett Michaels' voice is mediocre and none of the band members have ever been accused of being aficionados of their field. But the fans absolutely love them. It was a slow grind, but by the middle of the following year *Look What the Cat Dragged In* climbed all the way up to #3 on Billboard and fans –

mainly female – couldn't get enough of 'Talk Dirty To Me', 'I Won't Forget You' and 'I Want Action'.

The other major emergence from 1986 was Tesla, a band that would have been successful no matter what year, decade or what rock style was popular at the time. Jeff Keith's very distinct vocals and a killer guitar attack from guitarists Frank Hannon and Tommy Skeoch separated Tesla from most of their peers of the era. At heart, Tesla is a guitar-driven rock band that just happens to also make some kick-ass ballads to along with their large catalog of kick-ass rock songs.

Mechanical Resonance was released in December of 1986 and most of the singles in 1987, but for continuity sake, everything will be listed in the release year.

Europe's *The Final Countdown* is much maligned today. But back in 1986 fans were digging the smooth polished Europe sound. 'The Final Countdown' and power ballad 'Carrie' were huge MTV staples.

Top Songs

1. Livin' on a Prayer – Bon Jovi
2. You Give Love a Bad Name – Bon Jovi
3. Shake Me – Cinderella
4. Talk Dirty to Me – Poison
5. Little Suzi – Tesla
6. Somebody Save Me – Cinderella
7. The Final Countdown – Europe
8. Slip of the Lip – Ratt
9. Modern Day Cowboy - Tesla
10. Wild in the Streets – Bon Jovi
11. Dance – Ratt
12. Rock the Night – Europe
13. Body Talk – Ratt
14. Getting' Better – Tesla
15. Boyz are Gonna Rock – Vinnie Vincent Invasion
16. Night Songs - Cinderella
17. After Midnight – Fastway
18. Let it Go – Loudness
19. EZ Come EZ Go – Tesla
20. Shot in the Dark – Great White

21. The Wild and the Young – Quiet Riot

Top Ballad
1. Nobody's Fool – Cinderella
2. Wanted Dead or Alive – Bon Jovi
3. Never Say Goodbye – Bon Jovi
4. I Won't Forget You – Poison
5. Honestly – Stryper
6. Carrie – Europe
7. Tears of Fire – Keel
8. Love You Forever – Giuffria

Albums You Must Own
Slippery When Wet – Bon Jovi
Night Songs – Cinderella
Mechanical Resonance – Tesla
Look What the Cat Dragged In – Poison
Dancing Undercover - Ratt
The Final Countdown – Europe
To Hell with the Devil – Stryper
Vinnie Vincent Invasion – Vinnie Vincent Invasion
Shot in the Dark – Great White
Stand Tall – Killer Dwarfs
Lightning Strikes – Loudness

Other notable releases:
Quiet Riot – QR III
Guns n Roses – Live ?!*@ Like a Suicide
Lizzy Borden – Ultra violence & Menace to Society
Fastway – Trick or Treat
D.A.D. – Call of the Wild
Stage Dolls – Commandos
Black n' Blue – Nasty Nasty
Keel – The Final Frontier
King Cobra – Thrill of a Lifetime
London – Don't Cry Wolf
Rose Tattoo – Beats from a Single Drum
Rough Cutt -- Wants You
Shark Island – S'cool Buss
Zebra – 3.V
White Tiger – White Tiger
Tuff – Knock Yourself Out

Treat – The Pleasure Principle
Hericane Alice – Hericane Alice
Giuffria – Silk + Steel

1987 - Guns N' Roses

Two of the greatest albums of the genre were released in 1987. One
by a band that had already reached legendary status...but that
completely revamped their sound. And one by a band that redefined
the genre and simply blew every other band out of the conversation
as to who was the best band alive.

Def Leppard continued their trend from being a heavy metal/hard
rock band to a pop-rock act. In 1987 it paid off to the tune of their
album *Hysteria* selling more than 25 million copies, reaching #1 on
Billboard 200 and staying on the charts for 133 weeks. Six songs from
Hysteria made their way into the Billboard singles chart top 20.
Power ballad 'Love Bites' made it all the way to #1, while anthem
'Pour Some Sugar on Me' topped out at #2.

The fascinating talking point of *Hysteria* for fans revolve around Mutt
Lange's influence on Def Leppard's overall sound. To this day some
fans still pine for the Def Leppard that appeared to be on track to
become one of the world's greatest hard rock bands. While others are
happy with the more pop orientated sound the band shifted to once
Lange became involved in the writing and producing. Dudes love the
first three albums, chicks love everything since.

Then Axl Rose, Slash, Duff McKagan and Steven Adler changed
everything. *Appetite for Destruction* was released in July of 1987.
Before the album flamed out it would spend four weeks at #1 on the
Billboard 200. And wouldn't leave the charts for 147 weeks. Combine
those two numbers with the more than 30 million copies sold and
Guns N' Roses released the most successful album of the entire genre.
And one of the top 10 rock albums every released. To top it off, today
(2018) Appetite actually climbed back into the album top 10 chart.

The hair metal and hair band genre really exploded in 1987. Even without the classic GnR and Def Leppard records, the year still would have been one of the best collection of releases of the era.

Motley Crue redeemed themselves to their core fan base with the release of the rocking *Girls, Girls, Girls*. Instead of wearing a pound of makeup and playing piano ballads, *Girls, Girls, Girls* saw the boys dressed in leather, riding motorcycles and hanging out in strip clubs. They went from being a hair band and back to being a metal group. And the results were glorious. The album peaked at #2 on Billboard and stayed charting for almost a full year. The title track and 'Wild Side' were standouts, as well as the underrated ballad 'You're All I Need', which MTV refused to air.

In almost any other year - except maybe 1991 - Whitesnake's self-titled album would have easily been the year's top rated release. The record made it all the way to #2 on the Billboard 200, while the song 'Here I Go Again' was a #1 smash hit. 'Is This Love' made it all the way to #2. The riff from 'Still of the Night' is one of the most classic guitar epics of the entire genre.

In total, 12 of 1987 releases cracked the Billboard 200. Along with *Appetite for Destruction, Hysteria, Whitesnake, Girls, Girls, Girls*, also charting were Europe's *The Final Countdown* (8), Dokken's *Back for the Attack* (13), Great White's *Once Bitten* (23), Stryper's *To Hell with the Devil* (32), Tesla's *Mechanical Resonance* (32), Twisted Sister's *Love is for Suckers* (74), Keel's self-titled album(79) and the self-titled album from Faster Pussycat (97).

Great White copied the Def Leppard and Bon Jovi blueprint, bringing in an outside writer to give their sound a more friendly rock radio feel. Alan Niven co-wrote Great White classic's 'Rock Me' and 'Lady Red Light'. Lead singer Jack Russell teamed up with writer Jerry Lynn Williams to write their legendary ballad 'Save Your Love'.

Top Songs
1. Welcome to the Jungle – Guns N' Roses
2. Pour Some Sugar on Me – Def Leppard
3. Still of the Night – Whitesnake

4. Sweet Child O' Mine – Guns N' Roses
5. Rock Me – Great White
6. Girls, Girls, Girls – Motley Crue
7. Wild Side – Motley Crue
8. Dream Warriors – Dokken
9. Wait – White Lion
10. Paradise City – Guns N' Roses
11. Bathroom Wall – Faster Pussycat
12. Lady Red Light – Great White
13. Heaven Sent – Dokken
14. Nightrain – Guns N' Roses
15. Rocket Queen – Guns N' Roses
16. Armageddon It – Def Leppard
17. Tell Me – White Lion
18. It's So Easy - Guns N' Roses
19. Give Me All Your Love – Whitesnake
20. My Michelle – Guns N' Roses
21. Women – Def Leppard
22. Bad Boys – Whitesnake
23. All Over Now – Great White
24. Edge of a Broken Heart – Bon Jovi
25. Rocket – Def Leppard
26. Me Against the World – Lizzy Borden
27. Temptation – Y&T
28. Somebody's Waiting – Keel
29. Animal – Def Leppard
30. Down & Dirty - Autograph

Ballads

1. Save Your Love – Great White
2. Hysteria – Def Leppard
3. Here I Go Again – Whitesnake
4. You're All I Need – Motley Crue
5. Is This Love –Whitesnake
6. When the Children Cry – White Lion
7. Love Bites – Def Leppard
8. Everytime I Dream – Autograph
9. Strange Wings – Savatage
10. Fall in Love Again – Tigertailz
11. Eye of the Storm – Pretty Maids
12. Left to be Alone – Icon
13. Share a Dream - Leatherwolf

Albums You Must Own
Appetite For Destruction – Guns N' Roses
Hysteria – Def Leppard
Girls, Girls, Girls – Motley Crue
Whitesnake - Whitesnake
Once Bitten – Great White
Faster Pussycat – Faster Pussycat
Pride – White Lion
Back For the Attack – Dokken
Tell No Tales – TNT
Loud and Clear - Autograph

Other Albums of Interest:
Twisted Sister - Love is For Suckers
Lizzy Borden – Me Against the World/Den of Thieves/Visual Lies
Tora Tora – To Rock to Roll
Keel – Keel
D.A.D. – D.A.D. Draws a Circle
Icon – More Perfect Union
Britny Fox – In America
EZO – EZO
Sleeze Beez – Look Like Hell
Union – More Perfect Union
Lion – Dangerous Attraction
Loudness – Hurricane Eyes
Return – To the Top
Tigertailz – Young and Crazy
Y&T – Contagious & Forever
Treat – Dream Hunter
Leatherwolf – Leatherwolf
Lillian Axe – Lillian Axe
Michael Monroe - Nights are so Long

1988 – Bon Jovi
The depth of 1988 was outstanding as numerous classic bands
released very solid albums. But the class of the year was Bon Jovi,
who released the record-breaking album *New Jersey*.

Fans wondered how Bon Jovi could top or even come close to
matching *Slippery When Wet*. With ease apparently! *New Jersey*

quickly went to #1 on the Billboard 200 and stayed there for four weeks. The album still holds the record as the only hard rock album to have five singles reach the top 10 of the Billboard hot singles chart. Two of the songs – 'Bad Medicine' and 'I'll Be There for You' – reached number one.

Four debut albums elevated the 1988 class to rival 1987's overall strength. Officially breaking out were Winger, The BulletBoys, L.A. Guns and Kingdom Come. Two female groups also debuted with solid albums – Vixen and Femme Fatale. HM/HB was such a major force that even Britny Fox had a top 40 album.

Fans might be surprised to see that Kingdom Come had the most commercially successful album from the mentioned rookie outputs. Their self-titled album climbed all the way to #12 on the Billboard. The song 'Get It On' made it to #4 on the Billboard rock chart. Many dismissed Kingdom Come as a Led Zeppelin clone due to leader singer Lenny Wolf's vocals sounding very similar to Robert Plant.

L.A. Guns has had more lineup changes than any band in music history. But in 1988 the core group of Tracii Guns, Mick Cripps, Phil Lewis, Kelly Nickels and Steve Riley created a classic album. Their self-titled debut managed to peak at #50 on Billboard and produced classic songs like 'Sex Action', 'One More Reason' and 'Electric Gypsy'. Like a lot of L.A. Guns future albums, this one didn't produce a major billboard hit but it was a quality album from top-to-bottom.

Two words describe The BulletBoys: Marq Torien. He danced, pranced, strutted and also shredded on the guitar (he once auditioned for Ozzy as a guitar player). Every time Torien steps on stage he puts on a show. Their debut album made it all the way to #34 on Billboard thanks to fantastic songs 'Smooth Up in Ya' and cover of 'For the Love of Money'. 'Smooth Up In Ya' is absolutely classic hair metal, from the riff to the melody to the chorus and down to Torien's vocal performance. One of the all time great songs.

Winger's self-titled debut album peaked at #21 on Billboard. Reb Beach was a monster on guitar. Combine Beach with Kip Winger's model looks and the band managed to overcome juvenile lyrics to release a couple rock hits in 'Seventeen', 'Madalaine', 'Hungry' and 'Headed for a Heartbreak'.

Vixen and Femme Fatale joined Lita Ford as the genre's prominent female led bands. Ford's album *Lita* was her highest charting output, reaching #29 on the Billboard 200. Vixen's big hits were 'Edge of a Broken Heart' and 'Cryin'. Lorraine Lewis and Femme Fatale released classics 'Waiting For the Big One' and 'In And Out of Love'.

1988 wasn't just about Bon Jovi and newcomers. Several legendary bands also contributed very strong albums. Kix had their breakthrough record, Poison had another strong release, Cinderella continue to improve, while Ratt, Scorpions and Guns N' Roses all shared quality music.

Kix lightened their metal sound and went more commercial with *Blow My Fuse*. The change was a smashing success as 'Cold Blood' and the power ballad 'Don't Close Your Eyes' were as good as anything released in 1988.

Cinderella cemented themselves as one of the top bands of the era. *Long Cold Winter* peaked at #10 on Billboard and stayed charting for 66 weeks. Power ballads were becoming the norm but Cinderella managed to take ballads to an entirely different level. Some people still list 'Don't Know What You Got' as the top power ballad of all time. 'Coming Home' was also better than 99% of ballads released.

Hair band legend's Poison released their most successful album *Open Up and Say...Ahh!* The album climbed all the way to #2 on the album chart and had the band's only number one hit with 'Every Rose Has Its Thorns'.

Guns N' Roses wanted to keep their *Appetite* momentum going before their next full album so they released the EP *Lies*. It was a huge hit, selling more than five million copies and producing the hit ballad 'Patience'.

Veteran rockers Scorpions had a huge hit with their album Savage Amusement, which topped out at #5 on the Billboard 200.

Top Songs

1. Smooth Up in Ya – BulletBoys
2. Cold Blood – KIX
3. Electric Gypsy – L.A. Guns
4. Nothin' but a Good Time – Poison
5. Gypsy Road – Cinderella
6. Bad Medicine – Bon Jovi
7. One More Reason – L.A. Guns
8. I Want a Woman – Ratt
9. Kiss Me Deadly – Lita Ford
10. Way Cool Jr. – Ratt
11. For the Love of Money – BulletBoys
12. Seventeen – Winger
13. Blow My Fuse – KIX
14. Rhythm of Love – Scorpions
15. Get it On – Kingdom Come
16. Passion Rules the Game – Scorpions
17. Sex Action – LA Guns
18. Lay Your Hands On Me – Bon Jovi
19. Edge of a Broken Heart – Vixen
20. Bad Seamstress Blues – Cinderella
21. Girlschool – Britny Fox
22. Hungry – Winger
23. Fallen Angel – Poison
24. Waiting for the Big One – Femme Fatale
25. The Last Mile – Cinderella
26. Falling In and Out of Love – Femme Fatale
27. Can't Take My Eyes Off You – Dirty Looks
28. Superstitious – Europe
29. Love Made Me – Vixen
30. No Easy Way Out – Roxx Gang
31. That Time Of Year – Vinnie Vincent Invasion
32. Reckless Life – Guns N' Roses
33. Born to Be My Baby – Bon Jovi
34. Used To Love Her – Guns N' Roses
35. All I Want – D'Molls
36. Feel the Shake - Jetboy
37. Stay with Me Tonight – Quiet Riot
38. Tell Me Please – Killer Dwarfs
39. I Wanna Be Loved – House of Lords
40. Make Some Noise – Jetboy

Ballads
1. Don't Know What You Got – Cinderella
2. Don't Close Your Eyes - Kix
3. Coming Home – Cinderella
4. Patience – Guns N' Roses
5. Walk Away – Dokken
6. Every Rose Has Its Thorns – Poison
7. I'll Be There for You – Bon Jovi
8. Love Kills – Vinnie Vincent Invasion
9. Stick to Your Guns – Bon Jovi
10. Close My Eyes Forever – Lita Ford/Ozzy Osbourne
11. I Want to Love You Tonight – Ratt
12. Living In Sin – Bon Jovi
13. Long Cold Winter – Cinderella
14. Red Rose – Roxx Gang
15. Headed for a Heartbreak – Winger
16. What Love Can Be – Kingdom Come
17. Without the Night – Winger
18. Wild is the Wind – Bon Jovi
19. Save the Weak – Brtny Fox
20. Love Don't Lie – House of Lords
21. D'Stroll – D'Molls

Albums You Must Own:
New Jersey – Bon Jovi
Long Cold Winter – Cinderella
Blow My Fuse – Kix
Open Up and Say...Ahh! – Poison
L.A. Guns – L.A. Guns
Savage Amusement - Scorpions
Winger – Winger
Kingdom Come – Kingdom Come
Lita - Lita Ford
Reach for the Sky - Ratt
Out of This World - Europe
In God We Trust - Stryper, 1988
BulletBoys – BulletBoys
Lies – Guns N' Roses
All Systems Go – Vinnie Vincent Invasion
Vixen – Vixen
D'Molls – D'Molls

Big Deal – Killer Dwarfs
Femme Fatale – Femme Fatale
Britny Fox – Britny Fox
House of Lords – House of Lords
Feel the Shake – Jetboy
Cool From the Wire – Dirty Looks
Beast from the East – Dokken

Other Albums of Interest:
Motley – Raw Tracks
Quiet Riot – QR
Fastway – On Target
Black N Blue – In Heat
Brighton Rock – Take a Deep Breath
King Kobra – King Kobra III
Lillian Axe – Lillian Axe
Return – Attitudes
Roxx Gang – Things You've Never Done Before
Smashed Gladys – Social Intercourse
Wrathchild – The Biz Suxx

1989 – Skid Row

The arrival of Skid Row, evolution of Motley Crue and debut of Jani Lane and Warrant highlighted 1989. Several new bands also debuted, further diversifying the entire sound of the genre. Junkyard, Dangerous Toys, Tora Tora, Enuff Z'Nuff and Vain sounded nothing alike, but turned in high quality albums.

The biggest story of the year was the debut album from New Jersey rocker's Skid Row. Iconic vocalist Sebastian Bach unleashed one of the greatest rock voices in history on the self-titled album, which went all the way to #6 on the Billboard and had three singles chart: 'Youth Gone Wild', '18 and Life' and the incredible power ballad 'I Remember You'. Skid Row was the real deal. A band that toured with Bon Jovi and Aerosmith and blew the legends off the stage.

Motley Crue was often criticized for being more concerned with their image, partying and banging hot chicks than taking their career seriously. *Dr. Feelgood* showed what the boys were capable when sober and putting forth 100% effort. *Feelgood* is the band's masterpiece, topping the Billboard 200 and having four singles crack the top 30 of the Hot 100 song chart: 'Dr. Feelgood' (6), 'Without You' (8), 'Don't Go Away Mad' (19) and 'Kickstart My Heart' (27).

The third biggest release of the year was *Dirty Rotten Filthy Stinking Rich* by Warrant. Warrant was somewhat unique in the genre as singer Lane is still considered as one of the best songwriters of the entire genre. And live Warrant was more of a hard rock or almost metal band even though most of their studio output fell into the pop-rock category. *DRFSR* cracked the Billboard top 10, while hit songs included 'Down Boys', 'Sometimes She Cries' and the classic power ballad 'Heaven'.

Great White also released their band's top selling album with *Twice Shy,* which finished as the third highest charting album of the year. *Twice Shy* went as high as #9 on Billboard. 'Once Bitten, Twice Shy' was played on MTV seemingly every hour. The cover song reached the top five on the Hot 100.

The final album of the year to crack the top 10 album chart came from seasoned vets Whitesnake. The album was a little more popish than typical Whitesnake fare, but still produced four mainstream rock hits. 'Fool For You Lovin' and 'The Deeper The Love' both cracked the top 40 on the Billboard Hot 100.

Tesla released another strong album – *The Great Radio Controversy* – highlighted by the best power ballad of the entire genre: 'Love Song'.

Of the newbies, Tora Tora's *Surprise Attack* led the way on Billboard, reaching the top 50 on the album chart. Anthony Corder's blues voice differentiated Tora Tora from all the other hair bands. Junkyard was a mix of punk and classic rock. Dangerous Toys was the closet thing to a rawer sounding Guns N' Roses. Enuff Z'Nuff were channeling their inner-Beatles. And Vain sounded like a version of L.A. Guns but with the unique vocal style of Davey Vain.

Pretty Boy Floyd also released the glam classic Electric Boyz with Electric Toyz.

Top Songs

1. 18 and Life – Skid Row
2. Dr. Feelgood – Motley Crue
3. Youth Gone Wild – Skid Row
4. Don't Go Away Mad – Motley Crue
5. Hollywood – Junkyard
6. Kickstart My Heart – Motley Crue
7. Once Bitten, Twice Shy – Great White
8. Down Boys – Warrant
9. Someone Like You – Bang Tango
10. New Thing – Enuff Z'Nuff
11. Sleeping My Day Away – D-A-D
12. Walkin' Shoes – Tora Tora
13. Bang Goes the Bell – Babylon A.D.
14. Never Enough – L.A. Guns
15. Piece of Me – Skid Row
16. Beat the Bullet – Vain
17. Wait for You – Bonham
18. Naughty Naughty – Danger Danger
19. Scared – Dangerous Toys
20. Bang Bang – Danger Danger
21. Simple Man – Junkyard
22. Teas'n Pleas'n – Dangerous Toys
23. Mista Bone – Great White
24. Fly High Michelle – Enuff Z'Nuff
25. S.O.S. – Motley Crue
26. No Respect – Vain
27. Little Fighter – White Lion
28. Queen of the Nile – Dangerous Toys
29. Big Guns – Skid Row
30. Do You Like It – Kingdom Come
31. Your Momma Won't Know – Pretty Boy Floyd
32. Girl Nation – D-A-D
33. I Wanna Be Your Man – L.A. Guns
34. Poison Ivy – Faster Pussycat
35. I Wanna Be With You – Pretty Boy Floyd
36. Gotta Go – Kingdom Come
37. Guilty – Tora Tora
38. The Way it Is – Tesla
39. Who's Watching You – Vain
40. Addicted to That Rush – Mr. Big
41. Radar Love – White Lion

42. Blooze – Junkyard
43. All Lips and Hips – Electric Boys
44. Big Talk – Warrant
45. Inside Out – XYZ
46. Hang Tough – Tesla
47. Guilty – Bonham
48. Tonight I'm Falling – TnT
49. Hideaway – Leatherwolf
50. Shake It – Beau Nasty
51. Born to Burn – Heavy Pettin'
52. Ready to Rock – Melidian
53. The Kid Goes Wild – Babylon A.D.
54. Paris Calling – Shark Island
55. Rock and Roll (Is Gonna Set the Night on Fire) – Pretty Boy Floyd

Top Ballads
1. Love Song – Tesla
2. I Remember You – Skid Row
3. Heaven – Warrant
4. Wild Angels – Pretty Boy Floyd
5. House of Pain – Faster Pussycat
6. Desperate – Babylon A.D.
7. The Ballad of Jayne – L.A. Guns
8. Phantom Rider – Tora Tora
9. Forever Free – Wasp
10. Being There – Tora Tora
11. Anything for You – Mr. Big
12. Please Dear – Faster Pussycat
13. Without You – Vain
14. Baby Blue – Princess Pang
15. The Angel Song – Great White
16. Sometimes She Cries – Warrant
17. The Deeper the Love – Whitesnake
18. Feels Like a Hammer – Dangerous Toys
19. One Step From Paradise – Danger Danger
20. Without You – Motley Crue
21. Souvenirs' - XYZ
22. End of the Line – TnT
23. What Keeps Me Loving You – XYZ
24. The Way I feel – Leatherwolf
25. After the Love Has Gone – Shy
26. After the Rain – XYZ

27. Time For Change – Motley Crue
28. Paradise in the Sand – Beau Nasty
29. House of Broken Love – Great White
30. Make a Wish – Beau Nasty
31. Lost Without Your Love – Loudness
32. Broken Dreams – Fifth Angel
33. Missing You – Banshee
34. Every Sunrise – Cats in Boots
35. Can't Get Her Out of My Head – Silent Rage
36. Broken Home – White Lion

Albums You Must Own
Skid Row – Skid Row
Dr. Feelgood – Motley Crue
Junkyard – Junkyard
Enuff Z'Nuff – Enuff Z'Nuff
Cocked & Loaded – L.A. Guns
... Twice Shy – Great White
Dirty Rotten Filthy Stinking Rich – Warrant
Dangerous Toys – Dangerous Toys
No Respect – Vain
Big Game – White Lion
The Great Radio Controversy – Tesla
Surprise Attack – Tora Tora
Danger Danger – Danger Danger
Babylon A.D. – Babylon A.D.
Leather Boyz with Electric Toyz – Pretty Boy Floyd
Wake Me When It's Over – Faster Pussycat
In Your Face – Kingdom Come
Slip of the Tongue - Whitesnake
Mr. Big – Mr. Big
Psycho Café - Bang Tango
Intuition - TnT
No Fuel Left for the Pilgrims – D-A-D
Badlands - Badlands
The Disregard of Timekeeping – Bonham
XYZ - XYZ
Dirty, But Well Dressed – Beau Nasty
Funk-O-Metal Carpet Ride – Electric Boys
Love + War – Lillian Axe

Other Albums of Note:

Britny Fox - Boys In Heat
Gorky Park - Gorky Park
Shotgun Messiah – Shotgun Messiah
Princess Pang – Princess Pang
Leatherwolf – Street Ready
Lizzy Borden – Master of Disguise
Icon – Right Between the Eyes
EZO – Fire Fire
Icon – Right Between The Eyes
Little Caesar – Name Your Poison
Lion – Trouble in Angel City
Lord Tracy – Deaf Gods of Babylon
Loudness – Soldier of Fortune
Nitro – O.F.R.
Return – Straight Down the Line
Sea Hags – Sea Hags – April
Shark Island – Law of the Order
Wrathchild – Delirium
Winter Rose – Winter Rose
Treat – Organized Crime
Michael Monroe - Not Fakin' It
Banshee – Race Against Time
Cry Wolf – Cry Wolf
Heavy Pettin' – Big Bang
Melidian – Ready to Rock

1990 – Cherry Pie

HM/HB's momentum came to a halt in 1990. Only six albums cracked the Billboard album's top 20, with Poison and Warrant releasing the only real hit albums. Just 12 albums cracked the top 100.

Warrant's second album – *Cherry Pie* - was a pretty good capsulation of the entire genre. It had the big anthem song with the stripper friendly 'Cherry Pie'. It had the one serious song in 'Uncle Tom's Cabin'. And the underrated rocker that still holds up today in 'Mr. Rainmaker'. Plus the required ballads in 'I Saw Red' and 'Blind Faith'. Warrant also drew raves for their live performances. The album peaked at #7 on the Billboard 200.

Poison's *Flesh and Blood* was the year's most successful album. An interesting output as Brett Michaels tried to rev up his songwriting skills and depart a bit from the glam sugary pop from their previous albums. Michaels showed his skills on songs like 'Something To Believe in' (#4 on the singles chart) and 'Ride the Wind' (#38). But the band's opening single was pure cheese and a song that doesn't hold up well at all today. 'Unskinny Bop' was a hit for the band, reaching all the way up to #3 on Billboard. 'Life Goes On', a really fantastic ballad, also broke the top 40.

The year's big breakout debut came from high-pitched vocalist and ex-Vinnie Vince Invasion singer Mark Slaughter. His band's debut album – *Stick It To Ya* - featured two songs that would become classics. *Stick It To Ya* reached all the way to #18 on the Billboard albums charts where it remained for 85 weeks.

Cinderella released another strong album even though it didn't produce the amount of classic songs as their first two. Singer Tom Keifer often sites *Heartbreak Station* as his favorite Cinderella output. *Heartbreak Station* cracked the Billboard albums top 20 chart, peaking at #19. 'Shelter Me', 'Heartbreak Station' and 'The More Things Change' were really strong songs.

Newcomers FireHouse released their signature album. The self-titled disc was pure hair band gold, featuring 'Don't Treat Me Bad', 'Shake & Tumble' and the power ballad 'Love of a Lifetime'.

Winger, Ratt and Stryper also released albums that didn't perform as well as past outputs. Each album had a couple good songs, but as a whole didn't set the world on fire.

There were some interesting songs though. Tesla released an acoustic album that featured the hit song 'Signs'. Salty Dog channeled their inner-GnR with the album *Every Dog Has Its Day*. 'Come Along' sounded like nothing else released in 1990. Lynch Mob highlighted ex-Dokken guitar player George Lynch's massive skills. The song 'Wicked Sensation' still sounds good today. Steelheart showcased the out-of-this-world vocal skills of Miljenko Matijevic on their power ballad 'I'll Never Let You Go'.

Top Songs

1. Cherry Pie – Warrant
2. Up All Night – Slaughter
3. Uncle Tom's Cabin – Warrant
4. Shelter Me – Cinderella
5. Signs – Tesla
6. Don't Treat Me Bad – FireHouse
7. Mr. Rainmaker – Warrant
8. Come Along – Salty Dog
9. Shake & Tumble – FireHouse
10. Wicked Sensation – Lynch Mob
11. Doesn't Matter – Killer Dwarfs
12. Mad About You – Slaughter
13. Givin' Yourself Away – Ratt
14. Knockin' On Heaven's Door – Guns N' Roses
15. Lovin' You's a Dirty Job – Ratt
16. Dirty Love – Thunder
17. Ride the Wind – Poison
18. Tease Me Please Me - Scorpions
19. Living a Lie – Don Dokken
20. Is It Love – Paul Laine
21. Unskinny Bop – Poison
22. Spend My Life – Slaughter
23. Last Laugh – Killer Dwarfs
24. One in a Million – Trixter
25. Stomp It – Jetboy
26. Crash N Burn – Don Dokken
27. Give it to Me Good – Trixter
28. Switchblade Serenade – Spread Eagle
29. Let it Slide – Hurricane
30. Easy Come Easy Go – Winter
31. All She Wrote – Firehouse
32. Chain of Fools – Little Caesar
33. Can't Get Enuff – Winger
34. Stranger Than Paradise – Sleeze Beez
35. Life Loves a Tragedy - Poison
36. No More Tears – Julliet
37. Waitin' For The Man – Beggars & Thieves
38. Wild Young and Crazy – Hericane Alice
39. Bad Bad Girls – Fastway
40. I Was Made For Rock 'n' Roll – Tindrum

Ballads

1. Never Let You Go – Steelheart
2. I Saw Red – Warrant
3. Fly to the Angels – Slaughter
4. Love of a Lifetime – Firehouse
5. Something To Believe In – Poison
6. Sacrifice Me – Salty Dog
7. Life Goes On – Poison
8. Blind Faith – Warrant
9. Heartbreak Station – Cinderella
10. Love Can Make You Blind – Every Mother's Nightmare
11. Dream Girl – Hericane Alice
12. Miles Away – Winger
13. She's Gone – Steelheart
14. Too Late – Hericane Alice
15. Stick To Your Guns – Sweet F.A.
16. Just Like a Woman – Salty Dog
17. I Don't Love You Anymore – The Quireboys
18. Never Say Goodbye – Guardian
19. Wind of Change – Scorpions (Crazy World, 1990)
20. Can't Find My Way Home – House of Lords
21. In Your Arms – Little Caesar
22. Bed of Roses – Warrant
23. After the Rain – Paul Laine
24. The Time It's Love – D'Molls
25. I Wish it Would Rain – Little Caesar
26. Giving Yourself Away – Ratt
27. Too Late – Jetboy
28. What's On Your Mind – Blonz
29. Heart of Gold – Sweet F.A
30. Kill Me – Beggars & Thieves
31. Long Hard Road – Cry Wolf
32. Forever and a Day – Guardian
33. In Your Heart – Little Caesar
34. Love Walked In – Thunder
35. This Time – Sleeze Beez
36. Love is a Killer – Vixen
37. Heaven – Tigertailz
38. Lady – Stryper

Albums You Must Own
Cherry Pie – Warrant
Heartbreak Station – Cinderella

Flesh & Blood – Poison
Stick it to Ya – Slaughter
Don Dokken - Up from the Ashes
Every Dog Has Its Day – Salty Dog
FireHouse – FireHouse
In the Heart of the Young - Winger
Detonator - Ratt
Dirty Weapons – Killer Dwarfs
Against the Law - Stryper
Wicked Sensation – Lynch Mob
Rev it Up - Vixen
Steelheart – Steelheart
Trixter - Trixter
Five Man Acoustical Jam – Tesla
Stick to Your Guns - Sweet F.A.
Beggars & Thieves – Beggars & Thieves
Warped – D'Molls
Tear the House Down – Hericane Alice
Crazy World – Scorpions
Little Caesar – Little Caesar
Screwed Blued & Tattooed – Sleeze Beez

Other Albums of Note:
Cry Wolf - Crunch
The Quireboys – a bit of what you fancy
Hurricane – slave to the thrill
Cry Wolf - Crunch
Paul Laine – Stick it in Your ear
Motley – Raw Tracks
Quiet Riot – Winners Take all
Fastway – Bad Bad Girls
LA Guns – I Wanna Be Your Man
D.A.D. – Osaka After Dark
Mr. Big – Raw Like Sushi
Blue Tears – Blue Tears
Every Mother's Nightmare – Every Mother's Nightmare
House of Lords – Sahara
Jetboy – Damned Nation
D'Priest – Playa Del Rock
Love/Hate – Blackout in the Red Room
London Quireboys – A Bit of What You Fancy
Tigertailz – Bezerk

Y&T – Ten
Guardian – Fire and Love
Lita Ford - Stiletto
Spread Eagle – Spread Eagle
Blonz – Blonz
Thunder – Backstreet Symphony
Tindrum – Cool, Calm and Collected

1991 – Guns N' Roses

And just when fans thought that the HM/HB era might have peaked along came Guns N' Roses and Skid Row with monster outputs that kicked the entire music world in the ass.

GnR released two albums in 1991. *Use Your Illusion II* went to #1 on Billboard and charted for 106 weeks. *Use Your Illusion I* went to #2 and remained on the charts for 108 weeks. GnR became the first band to ever have the Billboard #1 and #2 album at the same time. GnR released eight singles from the two albums, dominating the music world for several years. 'Estranged', the last single, came out in 1994.

Some fans say GnR could have created one of the best rock albums in history if they would have cut out the fat and combined the two albums into one. But one of the reasons Axl and GnR were so great is because of their excess and that they didn't give AF what anybody else thought.

Classic songs from *Illusions* included power ballad 'November Rain', which is closing in on a billion views on YouTube. Yes, a billion views. Standouts include 'You Could Be Mine', 'Don't Cry', 'Estranged', 'Civil War' and covers 'Knocking On Heaven's Door' and 'Live and Let Die'.

Joining Guns N' Roses on tour and as the only hair metal acts to have a number one album in 1991 was Skid Row, whose album *Slave To The Grind* was the heaviest HM/HB album of the year. Bach took his vocal range to the next level on rockers like 'Monkey Business' and 'Slave to the Grind' and on top-notch power ballads 'Wasted Time', 'In a Darkened Room' and 'Quicksand Jesus'. Clearly one of the best hair metal albums of all time.

While GnR and Skid Row dominated the year, 1991 featured an extreme amount of talented outputs. Putting out strong albums were classic bands Tesla, L.A. Guns, Great White, Kix, White Lion, Danger Danger, Dangerous Toys, Enuff Z'Nuff, and Mr. Big.

Motley Crue released a compilation album that featured five new songs/covers, greatest hits and a couple live performances. *Decade of Decadence* featured a couple cool new songs with 'Primal Scream' and a strong cover of 'Teaser'.

Tesla's *Psychotic Supper* showed a definite divide between them and the typical hair band of the era. While a lot of albums of the genre featured a couple cool rockers, a power ballad and then numerous fillers, Tesla albums are routinely strong from top to finish. *Psychotic Supper* was more of the same. It did well on Billboard, going as high as #13 on the album chart, making it the fifth highest charter of the year. Five songs from *PS* charted on the Mainstream Rock chart, led by 'What You Give' which peaked at #7. 'Stir It Up' is one of their coolest releases.

Great White's *Hooked* was the final album to crack Billboard's top 20 album chart. *Hooked* came in at #18 in spite of not producing any "hit" songs. The albums best two outputs were covers – 'Can't Shake It' and 'Afterglow'.

Top Songs
1. You Could Be Mine – Guns N' Roses
2. Slave to the Grind – Skid Row
3. Stir it Up – Tesla
4. Civil War – Guns N' Roses
5. Monkey Business – Skid Row
6. It's Over Now – L.A. Guns
7. Primal Scream – Motley Crue
8. Green-Tinted Sixties Mind – Mr. Big
9. Kiss My Love Goodbye – L.A. Guns
10. Edison's Medicine – Tesla
11. I Do U – KINGOFTHEHILL
12. Roll the Dice – Wild Boyz
13. Yesterdays – Guns N' Roses
14. Riot Act – Skid Row

15. Can't Shake It – Great White
16. Beat the Bullet – Danger Danger
17. Angel N U – Dangerous Toys
18. Don't Blame It on Love – Danger Danger
19. Pretty Tied Up – Guns N' Roses
20. Desert Moon – Great White
21. Live and Let Die – Guns N' Roses
22. Blue Island – Enuff Z'Nuff
23. Out with the Boys – White Lion
24. All the Time in the World – Junkyard
25. Call it What You Want – Tesla
26. Dancing On Coals – Bang Tango
27. Coma – Guns N' Roses
28. Love Don't Come Easy – White Lion
29. Hollywood Ya – Enuff Z'Nuff
30. Forever Young – Tyketto
31. Hang On St. Christopher – BulletBoys
32. Heartbreak Blvd – Shotgun Messiah
33. Whisky Dusk – Badlands
34. Tainted Angel – SouthGang
35. Talk to Your Daughter – BulletBoys
36. Don't Damn Me – Guns N' Roses

Ballads

1. November Rain – Guns N' Roses
2. Time to Let You Go – Enuff Z'Nuff
3. Don't Cry – Guns N' Roses
4. To Be With You – Mr. Big
5. I Still Think About You – Danger Danger
6. If I Say – KINGOFTHEHILL
7. Wasted Time – Skid Row
8. Estranged – Guns N' Roses
9. Forever – Wild Boyz
10. Slippin' Away – Junkyard
11. Laugh 'N' a ½ - D-A-D
12. Wake Me Up – Tuff
13. Love Ain't Enough – SouthGang
14. You're All I Need – White Lion
15. Afterglow – Great White
16. Best of Friends – Dangerous Toys
17. Just Take My Heart – Mr. Big
18. Place in My Heart - KINGOFTHEHILL

19. Tear Down the Walls – Kix
20. In a Darkened Room – Skid Row
21. Your Love – Sweet FA
22. Still the One – Brighton Rock
23. I Hate Kissing You Good-Bye – Tuff
24. Free – Shotgun Messiah
25. Only Time Will Tell – Poison
26. Clean the Dirt – Junkyard
27. Prettiest Ones – Backboard Jungle
28. Slowly Slipping Sway – Harem Scarem
29. Standing Alone – Tyketto
30. Best of Friends – Blackeyed Susan
31. Love Don't Bother Me – Stage Dolls
32. I Found You – L.A. Guns
33. Honestly – Harem Scarem
34. Ride With Me – Blackeyed Susan
35. When I Find Love – XYZ
36. Over and Out – Britny Fox
37. Since You Been Gone – Tangier

Albums You Must Own

Use Your Illusion II – Guns N' Roses
Slave to the Grind – Skid Row
Psychotic Supper – Tesla
Use Your Illusion I – Guns N' Roses
Screw It – Danger Danger
Lean into It – Mr. Big
Hooked – Great White
Hollywood Vampires – L.A. Guns
Mane Attraction – White Lion
Hot Wire – Kix
Hellacious Acres – Dangerous Toys
KINGOFTHEHILL – KINGOFTHEHILL
Strength – Enuff Z'Nuff
Freakshow – BulletBoys
Voodoo Highway – Badlands
What Comes Around Goes Around – Tuff
Unleashed! – Wild Boyz
Sixes, Sevens, and Nines – Junkyard
Bite Down Hard – Britny Fox
Electric Rattlebone - Blackeyed Susan
Second Coming - Shotgun Messiah

Don't Come Easy – Tyketto
Tainted Angel - SouthGang
Fire and Love - Guardian

Other Albums of Interest:
Kingdom Come – Hands of Time
Motley – Decade of Decadence
Bon Jovi - Hard & Hot
Great White – The Blue EP
Blackboard Jungle - I Like it A lot
Lita Ford – Dangerous Curves
Stage dolls - Stripped
Ratt – Ratt & Roll 81-91
Europe – Prisoners in Paradise
Stryper – Can't Stop the Rock – July 20
Helix – The Early Years
LA Guns – Holiday Foreplay
D.A.D. – Riskin' it All
Contraband – Contraband –
Bang Tango – Dancin' on Coals
Brighton Rock – Love machine
Britny Fox – Bite Down Hard
Contraband – Contraband
Kik Tracee – No Rules
Lillian Axe – Out of the Darkness – Into the Light
Loudness – On The Prowl
Nitro – Nitro II: H.W.D.W.S.
Return – Four play
Return – V
Return – Replay
Saigon Kick – Saigon Kick
Tigertailz – Banzai!
XYZ – Hungry
Sweet FA - Temptation

1992 - Warrant
Warrant's best album and CDs from stalwarts Bon Jovi and Def
Leppard highlight what was probably the last year that HM/HB was
the dominant genre of the music world.

Adrenalize from Def Leppard topped the Billboard album chart and produced two top 20 songs – 'Have You Ever Needed Somebody So Bad' and 'Let's get Rocked'. But in terms of the Lep's career chain, *Adrenalize* was definitely a step down from success of the band's prior two albums *Pyromania* and *Hysteria*.

Like *Adrenalize*, *Keep The Faith* by Bon Jovi was a commercial success reaching #5 on Billboard. But it was also a step down from their prior two albums that had reached #1.

Bon Jovi went back to their roots a bit with *Keep The Faith*, producing a more hard rock orientated sound. 'Keep The Faith' was a great rock song and the album also had a couple strong ballads.

The year's two most interesting albums came from Warrant and newcomers from Canada Slik Toxik. Warrant's *Dog Eat Dog* made it to #25 on Billboard. *Doin' The Nasty* from Slik Toxik earned the band numerous band, album and song awards in their home country.

Continuing with the trend, *Dog Eat Dog* was less commercially successful than the band's prior two albums. Which is crazy as most critics and fans cite *Dog Eat Dog* as Warrant's best overall album. Lane was at his writing peak with *DED*, which features the entire spectrum of styles. From metal to rock to pop to a couple killer ballads, *Dog Eat Dog* had it all.

Slik Toxik's sound was similar to early Skid Row. Lead singer Nick Walsh sounded a lot like legendary Sebastian Bach. *Don' The Nasty* didn't break though at a high level in America. But songs like 'Sweet Asylum', 'Helluvatime', 'By The Fireside' and 'White Lies, Black Truth' were better than 99% of music released in the entire genre.

Slaughter's *The Wild Life* was the surprise hit album of 1992. The band's second album climbed all the way up to #8 on the Billboard 200 even though it had no songs landing into the singles top 50.

Tora Tora showed their debut success wasn't a fluke with a really strong album in *Wild America*.

Top Songs

1. Helluvatime – Slik Toxik
2. Keep The Faith – Bon Jovi
3. The Hole In My Wall – Warrant
4. Sweet Asylum – Slik Toxik
5. Wild America – Tora Tora
6. Tonight – Def Leppard
7. Nonstop to Nowhere – Faster Pussycat
8. Real Love – Slaughter
9. Amnesia – Tora Tora
10. You're So Vain – Faster Pussycat
11. Bridges are Burning – Warrant
12. No Matter What – Lillian Axe
13. The Wild Live – Slaughter
14. Machine Gun – Warrant
15. White Lies, Black Truth – Slik Toxik
16. Drop in the Ocean – Kik Tracee
17. Reach for the Sky – FireHouse
18. Hang On Lucy – Wildside
19. Nowhere to Go But Down – Tora Tora
20. Hair of the Dog – Wildside
21. True Believer – Lillian Axe
22. She's Into Something Heavy – Electric Boys
23. Let's Get Rocked – Def Leppard
24. Hard Luck Town – Killer Dwarfs
25. We Will Rock You – Warrant

Ballads

1. Sad Theresa – Warrant
2. Days Gone Bye – Slaughter
3. Andy Warhol Was Right – Warrant
4. By the Fireside – Slik Toxik
5. Love is on the Way – Saigon Kick
6. The Bitter Pill – Warrant
7. As Time Goes By – Tora Tora
8. Friends – Faster Pussycat
9. Love is a Lie – Great White
10. Let it Rain – Warrant
11. Have You Ever Needed Someone So Bad – Def Leppard
12. Bed of Roses – Bon Jovi
13. When I Look Into Your Eyes – FireHouse
14. Looks Like Love – Wildside

15. So Far Away – Pretty Wicked
16. I Don't Want to Live Without You – Sleeze Beez
17. Driftin' Back – Killer Dwarfs
18. Nobody Knows – Roxy Blue
19. I Want You – Bon Jovi
20. A Better Man – Thunder
21. Kiss the Love Goodbye – Wildside
22. Mama Don't You Cry – Steelheart
23. As the Candle Burns – Trixter
24. See You Someday – Lillian Axe
25. What's Forever For – House of Lords
26. All Your Love – Steelheart
27. Can't Find My Way – Hardline
28. Hold the Dream – FireHouse
29. Turn it On – Heavy Bones
30. Times Are Changin' – Roxy Blue
31. Nothin' Great About a Heartache – Bad4Good
32. So Savage the Heart – Babylon A.D.
33. Don't Go - Nitro

Albums You Must Own
Doin' The Nasty – Slik Toxik
Dog Eat Dog – Warrant
Adrenalize – Def Leppard
The Wild Life – Slaughter
Keep The Faith – Bon Jovi
Wild America – Tora Tora
Lynch Mob – Lynch Mob
Whipped! – Faster Pussycat
Poetic Justice – Lillian Axe
Psycho City – Great White
Hold Your Fire – FireHouse
Under the Influence - Wildside
Method to the Madness – Killer Dwarfs
The Lizard – Saigon Kick
Tangled in Reigns - Steelheart

Other Albums of Note:
Heavy Bones – Heavy Bones
Bad4good – Refuge
Beggars & Thieves – Look What You Create
Twisted Sister – Big Hits and Nasty Cuts

White Lion – The Best of White Lion – September 15
Faster Pussycat – Belted, Buckled and booted
TnT – Realized Fantasies
Lita Ford – The Best of Lita Ford
LA Guns – Cuts
Bonham – Mad Hatter
Skid Row – B-Side Ourselves
Babylon A.D. – Nothing Sacred
Sleeze Beez – Powertool
House of Lords – Demons Down
Kik Tracee – Field Trip
Little Caesar - Influence
Love/Hate – Wasted in America
Shotgun Messiah – I Want More
SouthGang – Group Therapy
TNT – Realized Fantasies
T-Ride T-Ride – may 19
Trixter – Hear!
Treat – Treat
Roxy Blue Want Some
Nitro II: H.W.D.W.S
Pretty wicked – Pretty wicked
Hardline – Double Eclipse
Electric Boys - Groovus Maximus
Banshee – Take 'Em By Storm

1993 – Vince Neil, Stephen Pearcy

A pretty decent year for power ballads. But overall, a clear signal that the HM/HB era was essentially finished.

Vince Neil's solo album *Exposed* and Poison's *Native Tongue* were the only new material albums to even break Billboard's top 50 on the album charts. *Exposed* was a pretty solid album, peaking at #13. But it only stayed on the charts for a total of 13 weeks. *Native Tongue* reached #16 before quickly dropping off the chart.

The year's two biggest charting albums were a cover's output from Guns N' Roses – *The Spaghetti Incident* (#4) and *RetroActive* from Def Leppard (#9).

After being fired from Motley Crue, Neil worked with stalwarts Jack Blades, Tommy Shaw and Steve Stevens and produced the year's best album. 'You're Invited' was the best rock song of the year. *Exposed* had the feel of a more polished Motley album than what the band usually released.

Stephen Pearcy (Ratt) and Fred Coury (Cinderella) teamed up to form Arcade. The debut album was one of the more interesting rock albums of the year. 'Mother Blues" is a brilliant ballad, one of the best releases in Pearcy's career.

Top Songs

1. You're Invited (But Your Friend Can't Come) – Vince Neil
2. Nothing To Lose - Arcade
3. Spinning Wheel – Love/Hate
4. Living is a Luxury – Vince Neil
5. Little Wild Thing – Kingdom Come
6. Fractured Love – Def Leppard
7. Stand – Poison
8. Can't Have Your Cake – Vince Neil
9. Wait All Night – Joey C. Jones and the Glory Hounds
10. Shoeshine Johnny – Guardian
11. These Daze – Enuff Z'Nuff
12. House of Pain – Every Mother's Nightmare
13. Black Rain – Enuff Z'Nuff
14. Sister of Pain – Vince Neil

Top Ballads

1. Mother Blues – Arcade
2. Wild World – Mr. Big
3. Roses on Your Grave – Alleycat Scratch
4. Cry No More – Arcade
5. Cry – Sic Vikki
6. Forever – Vince Neil
7. Sweet Mystery - Guardian
8. Hard to Say Goodbye – Stage Dolls
9. Two Steps Behind – Def Leppard
10. Faith – Spread Eagle
11. Ain't Seen Love Like That – Mr. Big
12. Friends – Kingdom Come
13. It's Over – Triumph

14. Who's The One – Winger
15. Miss You in a Heartbeat– Def Leppard

Albums You Must Own
Exposed – Vince Neil
Arcade – Arcade
Animals With Human Intelligence – Enuff Z'Nuff
Bad Image – Kingdom Come
RetroActive – Def Leppard
Miracle Mile - Guardian
Bump Ahead – Mr. Big
Pull – Winger
Native Tongue – Poison
Deadboys in Trash City - Alleycat Scratch
The Spaghetti Incident – Guns N' Roses

Other Albums of interest:
Quiet Riot – Terrified
Quit Riot – The Randy Rhoads Years
Tesla – Last Action Hero – Music from the Original Motion Picture
Poison – Native Tongue – February 8
Enuff Z'Nuff – Animals With Human Intelligence
BulletBoys – Za-Za
Stage Dolls – Stories we Could Tell
Every Mother's Nightmare – Wake Up Screaming
Lillian Axe – Psychoschizophrenia
Love/Hate – Let's Rumble
London Quireboys – Bitter Sweet & Twisted
Saigon Kick – Water
Shotgun Messiah – Violent New Breed
Gorky Park – Moscow Calling
Spread Eagle – Open to the Public
Triumph – Edge of Excess
Cry – Sic Vikki

1994 – Tesla, Bang Tango
It wasn't a great year in terms of quantity, but a few classic bands put out some top-notch albums to help 1994 be a definite step-up from 1993. Quality over quantity was the theme for 1994

Three albums broke into the Billboard top 20. Motley Crue replaced Vince Neil with John Corabi. Their album – *Motley Crue* – led the way peaking at #7. Bon Jovi put out a greatest hits album with two new songs. *Cross Road* topped in at #8. Tesla's incredible album *Bust A Nut* rounded out the trio, making it all the way to #20.

Motley Crue's album was one of the most talked about and debated releases in the history of the entire genre. Corabi's voice, writing style and stage presence were 100% the polar opposite of Vince Neil's. Corabi gave Motley a much heavier rock sound. Some fans hated it and wouldn't accept Crue without Vince. While others still claim to this day that *MC94* is Motley's finest hour. Nikki Sixx has recently came out and said he wished they would have released the album under a different band name. Regardless of all that, we rate it as one of the best albums of 1994. 'Hooligan's Holiday' and 'Misunderstood' are great rockers and 'Driftaway' is the best ballad Motley Crue ever released – sorry 'Home Sweet Home' fans.

In spite of the juvenile name, Tesla's *Bust A Nut* is a shining accomplishment from a band that has an outstanding discography. *BAN* arguably has the best rocker and the best power ballad of the year. 'Need Your Loving', 'Mama's Fool', 'Games People Play' and all kicked your ass on the rock side. Power ballad 'Try So Hard' is one of the best songs of Tesla's career.

Bang Tango released a killer album – *Love After Death* – but only released it overseas after the label refused an American release. Definitely pick it up if you can find a copy online as it rocks!

We haven't listed a lot of band's Greatest Hits compilations (or live albums) in our roundup. But Bon Jovi's *Cross Road* featured two brand new songs, one that turned into being their most successful song in the band's storied history. The ballad 'Always' went to #2 on the Billboard Mainstream Top 40 and stayed in the top 10 for an incredible full six months.

Great White, Dangerous Toys, L.A. Guns and Cinderella didn't find much commercial success in 1994, but they released strong albums.

Top Songs

1. Need Your Loving – Tesla
2. Screamin' For More – Dangerous Toys
3. Hooligan's Holliday – Motley Crue
4. Sail Away – Great White
5. Don't Count Me Out – Bang Tango
6. Misunderstood – Motley Crue
7. Ready to Believe – Electric Boys
8. Mama's Fool – Tesla
9. Why Ain't I Bleeding – L.A. Guns
10. Get Up – Vain
11. Sympathy For the Devil – Guns N' Roses
12. Games People Play – Tesla
13. Nothing Better to Do – L.A. Guns
14. Room With a View – Arcade
15. Someday I'll Be Saturday Night – Bon Jovi
16. Hard Luck Champion – Dangerous Toys
17. Bad Attitude Shuffle – Cinderella

Top Ballads

1. Driftaway – Motley Crue
2. Try So Hard – Tesla
3. Always – Bon Jovi
4. Babe I'm Gonna Leave You – Great White
5. Through the Rain – Cinderella
6. Mother's Eyes – Great White
7. A Thousand Goodbyes – Bang Tango
8. Kiss of Death – L.A. Guns
9. When I'm Gone - Arcade
10. No Second Time – Enuff Z'Nuff
11. Promise the Moon – Dangerous Toys
12. Hard to Find The Words – Cinderella
13. Crystal Eyes – L.A. Guns
14. Gone With the Wind – Great White
15. 10,000 Miles Away – Motley Crue

Albums You Must Own:

Bust a Nut – Tesla
Motley Crue – Motley Crue
Sail Away – Great White
Still Climbing – Cinderella
Vicious Circle – L.A. Guns

Love After Death – Bang Tango
Pissed – Dangerous Toys
A/2 – Arcade
Freewheelin' – Electric Boys
Cross Road – Bon Jovi

Other Albums of Note:
Motley – Quaternary
Bone Machine - Dogs
Lizzy Borden – Best of Lizzy Borden
Enuff Z'Nuff – 1985
Sleeze Beez – Insanity Beach
Vain – Move On It
Tuff – Fist First
Trixter - Undercovers
Tyketto – Strength in Numbers

1995 – Bon Jovi

Bon Jovi released what was arguably the last great album from the original HM/HB era. *These Days* is the darkest and most adult album Bon Jovi has ever released. Many fans praise it as the band's best work. *These Days* topped out at #9 on Billboard, but the album was hugely successful overseas going to #1 in most major markets.

The real strength in *These Days* is in its depth of quality material. When so many albums have 3-4 strong singles and then nothing but filler songs, *These Days* is considered a complete album. Reminiscence of the old days when listening to an entire album was a musical experience from start to finish, as opposed to today when people just pick out a couple songs that they add to their iPods.

Skid Row also released their heaviest album – *Subhuman Race* – which fans seemed to either love or hate. It was the last release featuring singer Sebastian Bach. *Subhuman Race* is almost pure heavy metal at times, though the best song on the album is the amazing ballad 'Breakin' Down'.

Dokken's *Dysfunctional* cracked the top 50 on the Billboard album chart, coming in at #47, which was a bit of a surprise and a feather in the cap for Don and the boys.

Warrant, Slaughter, Vince Neil & FireHouse released decent albums.

Jani Lane said that 'Stronger Now' is the best song he'd ever written. It's a great power ballad. *Ultraphobic* was Warrant trying to modernize their sound and for the most part fans didn't dig it. But the album produced a couple pretty strong songs that still hold up today. 'Ultraphobic', 'Family Picnic' and 'Stronger Now' are great tunes.

Neil's second solo album couldn't match the friendly pop-rock sound of his first. Like so many others, Neil attempted to follow the grunge and grittier sound and it didn't really work. He did hit a home run on the power ballad 'Skylar's Song', which was dedicated to his daughter who tragically passed the way from cancer at just four-years old.

Top Songs
1. These Days – Bon Jovi
2. Ultraphobic – Warrant
3. Searchin' – Slaughter
4. Hearts Breaking Even – Bon Jovi
5. One Less Mouth to Feed – Vince Neil
6. If That's What it Takes – Bon Jovi
7. Family Picnic – Warrant
8. Down to the Bone – Quiet Riot
9. Steppin' Over – Tesla
10. The Maze – Dokken
11. Nobody Cares – Danger Danger
12. Quick Step to Love – Vain
13. Love is a Dangerous Thing – FireHouse

Top Ballads
1. Stronger Now – Warrant
2. Breakin' Down – Skid Row
3. Skylar's Song – Vince Neil
4. I Live My Life for You – FireHouse
5. Nothing Left to Say – Dokken
6. Letting You Go – Bon Jovi
7. No Regrets – Y&T
8. Here For You – FireHouse
9. If You Run Around – Kix
10. Yesterday's Gone – Slaughter

11. When Love and Hate Collide – Def Leppard

Album You Must Own
These Days – Bon Jovi
Ultraphobic – Warrant
Subhuman Race – Skid Row
Fear No Evil – Slaughter
Dysfunctional – Dokken
3 - Firehouse
Show Business - Kix
Carved in Stone – Vince Neil

Other Albums of Interest:
DL – Vault
Quiet Riot – Down to the Bone
Lita Ford – Black – February 14
D.A.D. – Helpyourselfish
D.A.D. – Good Clean Family Entertainment You Can Trust
Danger Danger – Dawn
Enuff Z'Nuff – Tweaked
BulletBoys – Acid Monkey
Icon – An Even More Perfect Union
Kingdom Come – Twilight Cruiser
London Quireboys – From Tooting to Barking
Roxx Gang – The Voodoo You Love
Saigon King – Devil in the Details
Tigertailz – Wazbones!
Wildside - Wildside
Y&T – Musically Incorrect
XYZ – Take What You Can Live
Vain – Fade
Tuff – Religious Fist
Tyketto – Shine
Kingdom Come – Twilight Cruiser

1996 – Jack Russell

Jack Russell was everywhere in 1996. Great White released a great album in *Let it Rock* featuring the best ballad of the year with 'Miles Away'. But Russell also released a solo album – *Shelter Me* – that was pretty incredible as well. Russell ended up singing on the 2nd and 3rd best albums of the year.

Def Leppard got rid of mega producer Mutt Lange and completely changed their sound on the album *Slang*. The album climbed up to number #14 on Billboard but quickly dropped off the charts. It was interesting to hear Def Leppard experiment musically, but as of today there are officially only seven people in the world who list *Slang* as their favorite album from the band.

Warrant had a couple good songs from their *Best Of* album and industrial sounding *Belly To Belly*. Great White's *Let It Rock* produced a couple quality ballads.

Top Songs
1. Thin Disguise – Warrant
2. If That's What it Takes – Mr. Big
3. Nobody Else – Warrant
4. Letter to a Friend – Warrant
5. Hey Bulldog – Jack Russell
6. Work it Out – Def Leppard
7. Shelter Me – Jack Russell
8. Little Mistake – Mr. Big
9. Stare – Gorky Park
10. We Will Rock You – Warrant
11. We All Die Young – Steelheart

Top Ballads
1. Miles Away – Great White
2. All I Want is Everything – Def Leppard
3. You'll Lose a Good Thing – Jack Russell
4. Where is the Love – Great White
5. When I Look Into Your Eyes – Jack Russell
6. Goin' Where the Wind Blows – Mr. Big
7. Not One Night – Mr. Big

Albums You Must Own:
Hey Man – Mr. Big
Let it Rock – Great White
Shelter Me – Jack Russell
Belly to Belly – Warrant
Slang – Def Leppard

Other Albums of Interest:
Bone Machine – Disappearing, Inc
Great White – Stage
TnT – Till Next Time
Warrant – Rocking Tall
LA Guns – American Hardcore
Firehouse – Good Acoustics
Steelheart - Wait
Enuff Z'Nuff – Peach Fuzz
Tigertailz – You Lookin' At Me
Tuff – Decade of Disrespect
Gorky Park – Stare
Michael Monroe - Peace of Mind

1997 – D-A-D

Vince Neil returned to Motley Crue and Whitesnake and Slaughter put out decent albums. But the most interesting album of 1997 was the re-emergence of Danish rockers D-A-D.

Generation Swine traveled all the way to #4 on Billboard, but mainly road the coattails of people being excited to have Neil back in the band. In a later interview, Neil himself called the album "terrible" and said the band was experimenting too much.

David Coverdale and Whitesnake put out a pretty strong album in *Restless*. 'No More Tears' is a great ballad, suiting Coverdale's maturing voice perfectly.

D-A-D had been around since the 80s and found intermediate small success in the United States. Their album *Simpatico* started a new run of material that showed just how talented the band is. Jesper Binzer has a great voice.

Danger Danger released *Four The Hard Way*, their second with singer Paul Laine. A change back to their pop-rock sound worked well, as *Four The Hard Way* was a fairly solid release. Slaughter's *Revolution* didn't have the depth of some of their earlier work, but featured several solid songs.

Top Songs

1. Empty Heads – D-A-D
2. What's Going On – Beggars & Thieves
3. Still Kickin' – Danger, Danger (Paul Laine)
4. Get Up My Friend – Kingdom Come
5. Mad Days – D-A-D
6. So Sad to See You – Enuff Z'Nuff
7. Crying – Whitesnake
8. You're My Everything – Slaughter
9. Hello, Hello (I'm Back Again) – Y&T
10. Glitter – Motley Crue
11. Everybody Needs A Hero – Pretty Boy Floyd
12. Afraid – Motley Crue

Top Ballads
1. Too Many Tears – Whitesnake
2. Jealous Guy – Enuff Z'Nuff
3. Can't Go On – Whitesnake
4. Hard to Say Goodbye – Slaughter
5. Now or Forever – D-A-D
6. Don't Fade Away – Whitesnake

Albums You Must Own:
Restless Heart – Whitesnake
Simpatico – D-A-D
Four The Hard Way – Danger Danger
Revolution – Slaughter
Master Seven – Kingdom Come
Endangered Species – Y&T
Generation Swine – Motley Crue

Other Albums of Interest:
Autograph – Missing Pieces
Dokken – Shadowlife
Beggars & Thieves – Look what you create
TnT – Firefly
LA Guns – Hollywood Rehearsal
Danger Danger – Four The Hard Way
Enuff Z'Nuff – Seven
Stage Dolls – Dig
D'Molls – Beyond D'Valley of D'Molls
Jetboy – A Day in the Glamorous Life
Pretty Boy Floyd – A Tale of Sex, Designer Drugs and the Death of Rock

London Quireboys – A Bit of What you Fancy/Bitter Sweet & Twisted
Roxx Gang – Love 'Em and Leave 'Em
Tuff – Regurgitation

1998 - Hardcore Superstar

The highlight of the year was the debut album from Swedish rockers Hardcore Superstar - *It's Only Rock 'n' Roll*. Highlights include the brilliant hard rock song 'Someone Special' that would have been a huge hit in 1988. 'Right Here, Right Now' is also great.

Junkyard's *Joker* had a hard route to go, but was the second best overall album of the year.

Motley Crue's *Greatest Hits* produced their finest post-*Dr. Feelgood* song with 'Bitter Pill'.

Top Songs
1. Someone Special – Hardcore Superstar
2. Bitter Pill – Motley Crue
3. Right Here, Right Now – Hardcore Superstar
4. Hello/Goodbye – Hardcore Superstar
5. All Those Bad Things – Junkyard
6. Wasted – L.A. Guns
7. Enslaved – Motley Crue
8. Tears Don't Mean a Thing – Junkyard
9. Ridin' On – Little Caesar
10. Forever – Skid Row
11. The River – Badlands
12. Rock 'N' Roll – Sebastian Bach
13. I Don't Think So – Phil Lewis

Ballads
1. Tell Me That You Love Me – Little Caesar
2. Holdin' On – Junkyard
3. Hangin' Round With My Dreams – Junkyard

Albums You Must Own:
It's Only Rock 'n' Roll – Hardcore Superstar
Joker - Junkyard
This Time It's Different – Little Caesar

Other Albums of Interest:
FireHouse – Category 5
Great White – Rock Me
Keel – Keel VI: Back in Action
Phil Lewis - More Purple than Black
L.A. Guns - Wasted
D.A.D. – Psychopatico
Badlands – Dusk
Little Caesar – The Time it's Different
Pretty Boy Floyd – Porn Stars
Roxx Gang – Mojo Gurus
Saigon Kick – Moments from the Fringe
Vixen – Tangerine
Stevie Rachelle – Who The Hell Am I?
Gorky Park – Protivofazza
Lynch Mob – Syzygy (EP)

1999 – Great White

Def Leppard released the only charting album and Great White came through with a really great set of songs.

Euphoria from Def Leppard was a step-up from their last release – *Slang* – and more of a step-back to their familiar arena rock sound. Leppard brought back their muse Mutt Lange for a couple songs. One being 'Promises', which was the album's most successful tune. 'Promises' topped the Billboard Rock chart.

Great White never received some of the accolades their peers did in the late 80s and early 90s, but Jack Russell and the boys continued to put out quality albums after the HM/HB era slowly faded away.

Can't Get Their From Here features several good songs, really showcasing Russell's voice. 'Ain't No Shame' is a great rock song, 'Rolling Stoned' made the Billboard Rock chart top 10 and 'Silent Night' and 'In the Tradition' are great ballads.

L.A. Guns released an album – *Shrinking Violet* – with Jizzy Pearl on vocals. Pearl helped produce the best ballad of the year in

'Dreamtime'. Slaughter, Enuff Z'Nuff, Dokken and Ratt all put out pretty decent records, showing that the "old guys" can still rock.

Top Songs
1. Ain't No Shame – Great White
2. Rollin' Stoned – Great White
3. Oh My God – Guns N' Roses
4. Killin' Time – Slaughter
5. Promises – Def Leppard
6. Bringing Me Down – FireHouse
7. Someday – Enuff Z'Nuff
8. Erase the Slate – Dokken
9. Backseat Action – Shameless
10. Ain't It Funny – Enuff Z'Nuff
11. Because I Love You – TNT
12. Don't Call it Love – Beggars & Thieves
13. Luv Sick – Ratt
14. Hole In The Sun – Mr. Big
15. So Good, So Fine – Ratt

Top Ballads
1. Dreamtime – L.A. Guns
2. Silent Night – Great White
3. Nothin' Left to Lose – Slaughter
4. On My Own – Slaughter
5. My New Religion – Mr. Big
6. Goodbye – Def Leppard

Albums You Must Own:
Can't Get There from Here – Great White
Back to Reality – Slaughter
Paraphernalia – Enuff Z'Nuff
Erase the Slate – Dokken
Ratt – Ratt
Euphoria – Def Leppard
Shrinking Violet – L.A. Guns
Back to Reality - Slaughter

Other Albums of Interest:
Motley – Supersonic and Demonic Relics
Great White – Great Zeppelin: A Tribute to Led Zeppelin
Twisted Sister – Club Daze Volume 1: The Studio Sessions

TnT – Transistor
Warrant – Greatest & Latest
Firehouse – Category 5
Mr. Big – Get Over It
Michael Monroe - Life Gets You Down
Beggars & Thieves – The Grey Album
Jetboy – Make Some More Noise
Jetboy – Lost & Found
King Kobra – The Lost Years
Lillian Axe – Fields of Yesterday
Saigon Kick – Bastards
Shameless – Backstreet Anthems
Lynch Mob – Smoke This

2000 - Shameless

New albums by heavyweight's Bon Jovi and Motley Crue highlighted 2000.

Motley Crue lost drummer Tommy Lee, but their album *Tattoo You* still managed to reach #41 on the Billboard album chart and produced a top 13 hit on the Billboard Rock charts with 'Hell on High Heels'. The album featured a few songs that sounded like older classic Crue, but also featured several flat-out clunkers.

Bon Jovi came back strong with their first album in five years. *Crush* was a continuation of the more polished and pop side of the band, which brought their music to a newer and "older" audience that is lovingly referred to as the "soccer mom" crowd. Real rock fans had hoped they would continue down the harder rock side ala *These Days*. But *Crush* sold a couple million copies and went to #9 on the Billboard 200.

Some of the lower tiered HM/HB came through with quality albums and breathed some unexpected life into the genre. Babylon A.D., Danger Danger and Every Mother's Nightmare impressed the fan base with a couple really strong albums.

An interesting band to break through in 2000 was the super-group Shameless with their second album titled *Queen 4 a Day*. The band is a hodgepodge of musicians from several famous bands. Musicians on the album included members of Tuff, Pretty Boy Floyd, L.A. Guns, Guns N' Roses, Big Bang Babies, Kiss and Warrant. Their album *Queen 4 a Day* is pretty entertaining album, filling up our top songs of the year list with four selections. We've picked 'Far Away' as one of the best ballads of all time.

Top Songs
1. It's My Life – Bon Jovi
2. Liberation – Hardcore Superstar
3. Please Me Tease Me - Shanghai
4. Queen 4 a Day – Shameless
5. I Wanna Live – Babylon A.D.
6. Six Million Dollar Man – Danger, Danger
7. Hollywood Ending – Motely Crue
8. Free Your Mind – Kingdom Come
9. Pray – Every Mother's Nightmare
10. Say it Isn't So – Bon Jovi
11. New Tattoo – Motley Crue

Top Ballads
1. Far Away – Shameless
2. Don't You Ever Leave Me – Hardcore Superstar
3. The Sky's Falling – Babylon A.D.
4. I Don't Think I Love U – Shameless
5. Somehow – Every Mother's Nightmare
6. Don't Hide Your Heart - Shanghai
7. A Place Where Love Can't Go – Shameless

Albums You Must Own:
Crush – Bon Jovi
American Blitzkrieg – Babylon A.D.
Bad Sneakers and a Pina Colada – Hardcore Superstar
Queen 4 a Day – Shameless
The Return of the Great Gildersleeves – Danger, Danger
Smokin' Delta Voodoo – Every Mother's Nightmare
Take Another Bite - Shanghai
New Tattoo – Motley Crue

Other Albums of Interest:
Melodica – Long Way From Home
Great White – Latest & Greatest

Poison – Crack a Smile….and More
Poison – Power to the People
Lizzy Borden – Deal with the Devil
LA Guns – Black City Breakdown
Junkyard – Shut Up – We're Trying to Practice
D.A.D. – Everything Glows
D.A.D. – The Early Years
Firehouse – 02
BulletBoys – Burning Cats and Amputees
Babylon A.D. – American Blitzkrieg
Kingdom Come – Too
Lizzy Borden – Deal With The Devil
London Quireboys – Lost in Space
Rock City Angeles – Rock City Angeles
Roxx Gang – Drink' T.N.T. and Smokin' Dynamite
Stevie Rachelle – Sixty-Six
Enuff Z'Nuff – 10
Kingdom Come - Too

2001 – Danger Danger

A rather boring year other than a fascinating situation with the band Danger Danger.

Ted Poley recorded the album *Cockroach* with Danger Danger back in 1993. But before its release Poley left the band and was replaced by Paul Laine. The band re-recorded the album with Laine's vocals. Poley sued DD and both versions of Cockroach were caught in the crossfire and shelved. Until 2001, that is, when the label took the unique stance of releasing it as a 2-CD set including both singer's version.

In our opinion, the musical tone of the album seems to fit Poley's voice better, so we'll give Ted the win in this battle. His version of 'Still Kickin' is our pick for the second best song of 2001. We also prefer Poley's take on the ballad 'Afraid Of Love'. Laine did a great job too, as we loved his version of 'Good Time'.

Warrant's *Under the Influence* featured one original song and what an amazing one it was. *Face* is one of the best songs Jani Lane ever wrote.

Hardcore Superstar, L.A. Guns and Mr. Big released decent albums.

Top Songs
1. Face – Warrant
2. Still Kickin' – Danger Danger (Ted Poley)
3. Shame – Hardcore Superstar
4. Beautiful – L.A. Guns
5. Lost in America – Mr. Big
6. Good Time – Danger Danger (Paul Laine)
7. Wimpy Sister – Hardcore Superstar
8. Sick Little Twisted Mind – Danger Danger (Ted Poley)
9. American Hair Band – Tuff
10. Wake Up – Mr. Big
11. Shine – Mr. Big

Ballad
1. Love Has its Reasons - Shanghai
2. Nothing Like it in the World – Mr. Big
3. Mother's Love – Hardcore Superstar
4. Afraid of Love – Danger Danger (Ted Poley)
5. Through These Eyes – Shanghai
6. I Don't Want to Be Happy – Mr. Big
7. Searching – The Quireboys
8. Don't Call Me Crazy – L.A. Guns
9. Don't Break My Heart Again – Danger Danger (Ted Poley)
10. Happy Everyday – Penny Black (Russ Graham)

Albums You Must Own:
1. *Actual Size* – Mr. Big
2. *Cockroach* – Danger Danger (Ted Poley)
3. *Man in the Moon* – L.A. Guns
4. *Thank You* – Hardcore Superstar
5. *Bombs Away* – Shanghai
6. *Cockroach* – Danger Danger (Paul Laine)
7. *Penny Black* – Russ Graham

Other Albums of Interest:
Melodica - LoveMetal
Babylon Bombs – Then Things You Can't Live Without
Faster Pussycat – Between the Valley of the Ultra Pussy
Warrant – Under the Influence
Every Mother's Nightmare – Back Traxx

King Kobra – Hollywood Trash
London Quireboys – This is Rock 'n' Roll
London Quireboys – Rock Champions
Roxx Gang – Bodacious Ta Tas
Blackeyed Susan – Dedicated to the Ones We Love

2002 – L.A. Guns

Bon Jovi continued their pop trend but easily had the most successful album of the year. *Bounce* made it all the way to #2 on the Billboard 200. *Bounce* had a couple great pop-rock songs, but also featured several ballads and lots of keyboards, leaving some fans disappointed - but some fans thrilled.

Classic rockers L.A. Guns and Dokken roared back to prominence with great albums. Especially *Waking the Dead* by L.A. Guns, which was founder and guitar player Tracii Guns last album before leaving the band for several years. In our opinion, *Waking The Dead* is the band's second best overall album.

Dokken's *Long Way Home* might have the creepiest cover in genre history, especially with a song called 'Little Girl' on the album. You can definitely tell that George Lynch isn't on the album, as it's a little softer and pop orientated than most of Dokken's work. But in terms of quality, *Long Way Home* is pretty polished and features some pretty good pop songs.

D-A-D's *Soft Dogs* is another strong outing from the band, who continue to put out solid album after solid album.

Shameless tightened up their lineup, sticking with more of a core group and released a decent album called *Splashed*. The real highlight of the record are ballads 'She's Not Coming Home Tonight' and 'Operator' which spotlight Steve Summer's voice to perfection.

Top Songs
1. Don't You Cry – L.A. Guns
2. Everyday – Bon Jovi
3. Between You and Me – D-A-D
4. City of Angeles – L.A. Guns

5. Any Kinda Love – Jack Russell
6. Little Girl – Dokken
7. Misunderstood – Bon Jovi
8. Revolution – L.A. Guns
9. Torn to Shreds – Def Leppard
10. The Distance – Bon Jovi
11. A Day Late, a Dollar Short – Hanoi Rocks
12. What's The Matter – D-A-D
13. You're So Beautiful – Def Leppard
14. So What? – D-A-D
15. Everyday – Def Leppard

Best Ballads
1. Long, Long Way to Go – Def Leppard
2. She's Not Coming Home Tonight – Shameless
3. Goodbye My Friend – Dokken
4. Whatever it Takes – Jack Russell
5. Sacred Place – Paul Shortino's The Cutt
6. Operator – Shameless
7. I've Found – Dokken
8. In My Darkest Moment – Hanoi Rocks

Albums You Must Own:
Waking the Dead – L.A. Guns
Bounce – Bon Jovi
Twelve Shots on the Rocks – Hanoi Rocks
Soft Dogs – D-A-D
For You – Jack Russell
Long Way Home – Dokken
X – Def Leppard
Splashed – Shameless

Other Albums of Interest:
Poley/Pichler - Big
Great White – Recover
Stephen Pearcy – Social Intercourse
Poison – Hollyweird
Every Mother's Nightmare – Deeper Shade of Grey
Jetboy – One More for Rock N' Roll
Kingdom Come - Independent
Rose Tattoo – Pain
Rough Cutt – Sacred Place

2003 – Junkyard

Hardcore Superstar continued to establish themselves as one of the world's premier hard rock bands. *No Regrets* featured really great hard rocking songs – 'Still I'm Glad' and 'Honey Tongue'. Every album HCSS releases has 4-5 quality songs. They are also incredible live.

Junkyard put out an EP called *Tried and True*, and even though it only contained six songs it was easily one of the best releases of 2003. The title track is a great ballad and 'Waste of Time' is a fantastic rocker.

Like a lot of other fans, we didn't give Skid Row's *Thickskin* much of a chance when it came out. Replacing legendary singer Sebastian Bach just didn't seem feasible. But on repeated listens over the years and taking out our Bach-bias, we have to admit that *Thickskin* is actually a pretty good album. *Thickskin* is a little more radio friendly than the final two Skid Row releases with Bach. Judging them as a new band, *Thickskin* is a pretty decent album. 'See You Around' is a great song.

Top Songs
1. Still I'm Glad –Hardcore Superstar
2. Lovin' a Girl Like You – Danger Danger
3. Honey Tongue – Hardcore Superstar
4. See You Around – Skid Row
5. Tonight – Motley Crue (Too Fast For Love Reissue Bonus Track, 2003)
6. United – XYZ
7. Good Times – Enuff Z'Nuff
8. Waste of Time – Junkyard
9. Amazing – BulletBoys
10. Lonely Ones – Britny Fox

Best Ballads
1. Tried and True – Junkyard
2. Where R U – Pretty Boy Floyd

Albums You Must Own:
No Regrets – Hardcore Superstar
Tried and True – Junkyard

Thickskin – Skid Row
Welcome to Blue Island – Enuff Z'Nuff

Other Albums of Interest:
Autograph - Buzz
Autograph – More Missing Pieces
Donnie Vie – Just Enough
Bon Jovi – This Left Feels Right – Nov 4
Bon Jovi – Bon Jovi – Target EP
Britny Fox – Springhead Motorshark
TnT – Give Me a Sign
TnT - Taste
Junkyard – Tried and True
Firehouse – Prime Time
Danger Danger – Rare Cuts
BulletBoys – Sophie
Pretty Boy Floyd – Tonight Belongs to the Young
Tigertailz – Original Sin
Zebra – Zebra IV
Y&T – Unearthed Vol 1
XYZ – Letter to God
Lynch Mob – Revolution
Shugaazer - Shift
Michael Monroe - Whatcha Want

2004 - Tesla

Tesla released what was easily the best genre album of what was a very interesting year.

Guns N' Roses released a *Greatest Hits* album – with no new songs on it – that would go on to become one of the best selling GH albums of all time. The album became one of only seven albums to spend 400 weeks on the Billboard 200 charts. It has also sold more than 6 million copies to date. The world still craves GnR music, even if Axl doesn't like sharing his work!

A couple foreign-based bands and old classic artists also came through with strong albums or great songs. Norwegian's Wig Wam's debut album *667.. The Neighbour of the Beast* sounded like it was lifted straight out of 1989. Finland's Private Line's *21ˢᵗ Century Pirates* contained the year's best ballad – 'Selflove-Sick'.

Classic bands Dokken, TnT, Bang Tango and the Stage Dolls all released albums that contained a couple of strong tracks. Roxx sounds like they were living on the Sunset Strip.

After taking a break from releasing new music for a decade, Tesla roared back with *Into The Now*, which charted as high as #31 on the Billboard 200. 'Caught in a Dream' is the best song of 1994. Any fan of the HM/HB era must own this record.

Top Songs
1. Caught in a Dream – Tesla
2. Word's Can't Explain – Tesla
3. Mine All Mine – Wig Wam
4. She Needs Me – TnT
5. The Last Goodbye – Dokken
6. Bleed – Private Line
7. Look @ Me – Tesla
8. Give Up Your Heart – Roxx

Best Ballad
1. Selflove-Sick – Private Line
2. Tell Me Where To Go – Wig Wam
3. Only You – Tesla
4. Most Important Thing – Bang Tango
5. Too Late For Love – Stage Dolls
6. Perfectly – TnT
7. Someone Like You – Stage Dolls

Albums You Must Own:
Into the Now – Tesla
667... The Neighbour of the Beast – Wig Wam
Start from the Dark – Europe
My Religion – TnT
Greatest Hits – Guns N' Roses

Other Albums of Interest:
Donnie Vie – This & That
Dokken – Hell to Pay – July 13
Dokken – Change the World: An Introduction Date
Bon Jovi - 100,000,000 BJ Fans Can't be Wrong

Warrant – Then and Now
LA Guns – Rips the Covers Off
LA Guns – Hollywood Raw: The Original Sessions
Enuff Z'Nuff - ?
Enuff Z'Nuff – Favorites
Stage Dolls – Get a Life
Bang Tango – Ready to Go
House of lords – The Power and the Myth
Kingdom Come – Perpetual
Pretty Boy Floyd – Dirty Glam
Pretty Boy Floyd – The Greatest Collection: The Ultimate Pretty Boy Floyd
London Quireboys – Well Oiled
TNT – My Religion
Y&T – Unearthed Vol 2
Private Line – 21st Century Pirates
Kingdom Come – Perpetual
Wildside – The Wasted Years
The Last Vegas - Lick 'Em and Leave 'Em

2005 - KINGOFTHEHILL

Bon Jovi released another top five album but the real stars of 2005
were a rising band and one that had a brief taste of success back in
the day.

Hardcore Superstar continued to establish themselves as one of the
premier hard rock bands of the 2000s. Their self-titled album
featured three of the top five songs of the year, including 2005's best
'We Don't Celebrate Sundays'. This album simply kicks ass.

The big surprise came from funk rockers KINGOFTHEHILL with their
killer album *Unreleased*. Frankie Muriel is one of the most underrated
singers of the genre and he shines on what should have been the
follow-up to their self-titled album from 1991. 'What Kind of Man' has
the groove of a rock-Prince song.

Motley Crue put out another greatest hits album, but *Red, White &
Crue* contained one really fantastic new tune – 'If I Die Tomorrow'.
We would have loved an entire album filled with this style of rock.

Bon Jovi's *Have a Nice Day* went to #2 on the Billboard 200 and had two songs chart on the Singles chart – 'Who Says You Can't Go Home' at #23 and 'Have a Nice Day' #53. We haven't ranked the album/songs as high on our lists as their Billboard success would indicated they should be, but *Have a Nice Day* was another step from the band in their transformation from a rock band to a pop/country/adult contemporary act. At this point, BJ is more country than rock.

Swedish glam rockers Crashdiet released a very strong debut album in *Rest in Sleaze*.

Top Songs
1. We Don't Celebrate Sundays – Hardcore Superstar
2. What Kind of Man – KINGOFTHEHILL
3. If I Die Tomorrow – Motley Crue
4. Wild Boys – Hardcore Superstar
5. Allright – D-A-D
6. Standing on the Verge – Hardcore Superstar
7. Who Says You Can't Go Home – Bon Jovi
8. It's a Miracle – Crashdiet
9. Have a Nice Day – Bon Jovi
10. Save it for Yourself – KINGOFTHEHILL
11. Long Way Home – Blue Tears
12. Mama – KINGOFTHEHILL
13. Knokk 'em Down – Crashdiet
14. Dream Seque – KINGOFTHEHILL
15. Crucify – Babylon Bombs
16. So Free Now – Vain
17. Hollywood's Burning – L.A. Guns
18. King of Cool – Big Cock

Best Ballads
1. Tonite – KINGOFTHEHILL
2. You Filled My Head – D-A-D
3. Rainy Days – XYZ

Albums You Must Own:
Hardcore Superstar – Hardcore Superstar
Unreleased – KINGOFTHEHILL
Rest in Sleaze – Crashdiet

Have a Nice Day – Bon Jovi
Scare Yourself – D-A-D
Tales from the Strip – L.A. Guns

Other Albums of Interest:
Def Leppard – Rock of Ages
Babylon Bombs – Cracked Wide Open and Bruised
Motley – Red, White & Crue
Hanoi Rocks – Another Hostile Takeover
Big Cock – Year of the Cock
White Lion – Rocking the USA
Stryper – Reborn
TnT – All the Way to the Sun
L.A. Guns – Black List
Enuff Z'Nuff – One More For the Road
Blue Tears – Mad, Bad and Dangerous
Blue Tears – Dancin' On The Back Streets
King Kobra – Number One
Return – Return
Rock City Angels – Young Man's Blues
TNT – All the Way to the Sun
XYZ – Rainy Days
XYZ – Forbidden Demos
Vain - On the Line
The Last Vegas - Seal the Deal

2006 – Wig Wam

One of the most fascinating stories of the entire genre came through in 2006. Joey C. Jones is the poster boy for the "should have been huge" comments that so many fans make about bands they feel didn't receive the success they deserved back in the day.

Jones has the magical voice. Has played in a couple great bands. He helped create some fantastic songs. Labels were offering them record deals – famously, Sweet Savage turned down a record deal that Poison ended up taking. And, Jones was best buddies with the legends of the era during the height of the HM/HB years. Dude even lived, wrote and recorded with C.C. DeVille!!! He partied with Stephen Pearcy, Eddie Van Halen and Sam Kinison. But for whatever the reason....Jones never reached the stardom of his counterparts.

The fascinating part is that Jones was finally able to release a bunch of the songs he recorded back in the late 80s and early 90s. It was more than a decade after the heyday of the genre – but Jones is finally getting the rewards that he so justly deserves. *Melodies for the Masses* is easily the best album of the year. It is full of songs that transport you right back to cracking a beer, cruising in your Camaro and partying with hot girls wearing spandex and having big hair.

Also buy the Wig Wam album, check out Kingdom Come's *Ain't Crying For the Moon* and you are good until 2007. 'Slip Away' is a great ballad from Babylon Bombs.

Top Songs
1. Summer Song – Joey C. Jones
2. Friends in Spirit – Kingdom Come
3. Slave to Your Love – Wig Wam
4. Set It Off – Vains of Jenna
5. Blue Skies – Shark Island
6. Always the Pretender – Europe
7. Breaking All the Rules – Wig Wam
8. Rock Hard – Big Cock
9. (Heads Up!) Look Out Below! – Ted Poley

Best Ballads
1. Slip Away – Babylon Bombs
2. At the End of the Day – Wig Wam
3. I Believe – Tigertailz
4. Picture Yourself – Joey C. Jones
5. Save Yourself – Blue Tears

Albums You Must Own:
Melodies for the Masses – Joey C Jones
Wig Wamania – Wig Wam
IV – Winger
Lit Up/Let Down – Vains of Jenna
Ain't Crying for the Moon – Kingdom Come

Other Albums of Interest:
Alleycat Scratch – Last Call
Babylon Bombs – Doin' You Nasty
Def Leppard – Yeah!

Ted Poley – Collateral damage
Quiet Riot – Rehab – October 3
Big Cock - Big Cock
Stephen Pearcy - Fueler
Twisted Sister – A Twisted Christmas
Europe – Secret Society
Faster Pussycat – The Power and the Glory Hole
D.A.D. – Scare Yourself Alive
Steelheart – Just a Taste
Skid Row – Revolutions per Minute
Babylon A.D. – In the Beginning, Persuaders Recordings
Bang Tango – From the Hip
Blue Tears – The Innocent Ones
House of Lords – World Upside Down
Shark Island – Gathering of the Faithful
Tigertailz – Bezerk 2.0
Warrant – Born Again
Blackeyed Susan – Step Inside
Donnie Vie – DvieD-EP
Europe – Secret Society

2007 – Sebastian Bach

Bon Jovi's *Lost Highway* went to #1 on the Billboard 200, but the band's crossover to a mixture of a country and adult contemporary band didn't resonate well with fans who were hoping for Bon Jovi to return to their hard rock roots.

How do you propel yourself out of the shadow of being the front man of a legendary band? Easy, you invite your buddy Axl Rose to come sing on your first studio solo album and you also utilize the writing skills of longtime Bon Jovi hit maker Desmond Child. Sebastian Bach made a huge statement with his album *Angel Down*, showing ex-Skid Row members the enormous talent they had kicked out of the band. With a little help from his friend's Axl and Child, Bach delivered the best rock album of 2007.

Legend Rose lent his singing chops on a couple songs, the highlight being a cover of Aerosmith's 'Back in the Saddle'. Rose also added vocals to 'Love is a Bitchslap' and 'Stuck Inside'. Some say Rose's vocals on 'Stuck Inside' are some of his best of his career since Appetite.

But the true standout track is Bach's ballad 'By Your Side'. It's easily the best ballad of the year and certainly stands toe-to-toe with the slower stuff from his Skid Row days.

Hardcore Superstar released another kick-ass hard rock album, highlighted by the song 'Dreamin' In a Casket'. Hands down, the second best rock album of 2007.

After an eight-year album break, Great White came back strong with *Back to the Rhythm*. It's classic sounding Great White - rock anthems with blues choruses and heart-warming power ballads.

Swedish glam band Crazy Lixx released a strong debut album in *Loud Minority*. Tesla released two covers albums with their own unique stripped down rock style and a GH/alternative recordings EP. Shameless released another strong album, highlighted by L.A. Guns frontman Phil Lewis providing vocals on 'Better Off Without You'. Hanoi Rocks and Crashdiet also released solid albums.

Top Songs
1. Dreamin' in a Casket – Hardcore Superstar
2. Better Off Without U – Shameless
3. Back to the Rhythm – Great White
4. Love is a Bitchslap – Sebastian Bach
5. Heroes are Forever – Crazy Lixx
6. Everything I Own – Tesla
7. Falling Rain – Crashdiet
8. Fashion - Hanoi Rocks
9. Blue Eyed Soul – Sweet FA
10. Sensitive to the Light – Hardcore Superstar
11. Famous 4 Madness – Shameless
12. Teenage Revolution – Hanoi Rocks
13. You Don't Understand – Sebastian Bach
14. Complications – Shameless
15. Man About Town – Rose Tattoo
16. Stuck Inside – Sebastian Bach

Best Ballads
1. By Your Side – Sebastian Bach
2. Just Yesterday – Great White
3. Falling Into You – Sebastian Bach
4. You Want to Make a Memory – Bon Jovi
5. Walk Away – Tyketto
6. Milez Away – Tigertailz
7. I Love You – Tesla
8. Rolling Stone – Sweet FA

Albums You Must Own:
Angel Down – Sebastian Bach
Dreamin' in a Casket – Hardcore Superstar
Street Poetry – Hanoi Rocks
Back to the Rhythm – Great White
Famous 4 Madness – Shameless
Blood Brothers – Rose Tattoo
Reel to Reel I & II – Tesla
Loud Minority – Crazy Lixx
Lost Highway – Bon Jovi
A Peace of Time - Tesla

Other Albums of Interest:
Ted Poley - Smile
Donnie Vie – Extra Strength
Crashdiet - The Unattractive Revolution
Poison – Poison'd!
Lizzy Borden – Appointment with Death
TnT – The New Territory
BulletBoys – Behind the Orange Curtain
Jetboy – The Glam Years
Lillian Axe – Waters Rising
Tigertailz – Thrill Pistol
TNT – The New Territory
Tyketto – The Last Sunset
Sweet FA – The Lost Tapes
Lillian Axe – Waters Rising

2008 – Chinese Democracy
Holy Cow – was this 1988 or 2008? Three albums made it all the way
to the top 5 on the Billboard album charts, and there were releases

from legendary bands like Guns N' Roses, Motley Crue, Def Leppard, Whitesnake, Dokken, Tesla, Junkyard, Steelheart, TnT and White Lion.

The most interesting and controversial album came from iconic frontman Axl Rose. Rose lost his entire classic Guns N' Roses lineup of Slash, Duff, Izzy and Steven Adler and then took a reported (depending on the source) 13 years and spent $13 million dollars to create *Chinese Democracy*, which reached #3 on the Billboard 200.

Let's be clear, *Chinese Democracy* is a great album on its own. The issue that most can't detach from is that CD is that is the only output from Axl since 1993's Spaghetti Incident. And it doesn't have Slash/Duff/Izzy/Adler on it. This is the album Axl let the original band breakup over? Was this album worth waiting 13 years for? Is this album worth $13 million dollars? The answer to all that is no. Looking at all that transpired, no album could hold up to those losses/attachments. Not even *Appetite*. We firmly belief that if Axl had also released CD2, CD3 and a fourth album, Chinese Democracy wouldn't be judged so harshly. But as it stands, *CD* has had the carry the weight of the entire GnR breakup on its shoulders.

We are just judging CD as a stand-alone album. Regardless of the cost, musicians, extra baggage. And we have to tell you – it's pretty outstanding.

'Better' is an absolutely fantastic rock song. 'Street of Dreams', 'Madagascar', 'Prostitute', 'Catcher in The Rye', 'Sorry' and 'TWAT' all sound like classic Guns N' Roses. If they had been released on a 1994 Guns N' Roses album fans would hailed them as brilliant GnR material. We also love that Axl expanded his normal hard rock/Queen/Elton John style and experimented with a few different styles. 'Shackler's Revenge' and 'Scraped' were Nine Inch Nails inspired, 'Riad' is pure Led Zeppelin meets heavy metal, 'IRS' is pure pop rock. 'If The World' is classic James Bond theme music. 'This I Love'....well, you just have to listen to it.

Motley Crue's *Saints of Los Angeles* was hyped as being the band's return to their roots. Fans were eager to check it out and bought enough copies to send it to #4 on Billboard. But most of the songs felt forced and the like the band was trying too hard to capture their sound from the 1980s. Motley is one of our favorite bands of all time and we had high hopes for Saints.

While Axl simply didn't give a rat's ass and did his own thing and Motley Crue tried to reproduce their 80s sounds, it's hard to quantify what Def Leppard was trying to do. Without Mutt Lange, the song writing and lyrical content was definitely subpar. Case in point – they actually have a song called 'Bad Actress' with lyrics like:
You can't sing can't dance
Can't fit in your pants
You're a bad actress
You can't run can't walk gotta learn how to talk
You're a bad actress
Does that scream "rock n' roll" to you?
Further proof, the lead single featured country singer Tim McGraw. The band then performed live with Taylor Swift.
Songs from the *Sparkle Lounge* did make it all the way to #5 on Billboard, so some fans did buy the album.

But let's get back to the positive. Whitesnake's *Good to be Bad* is their best album since the early 90s. 'Lady Down Your Love' and 'Summer Love' are almost good as the band's classic songs. *GTOB* is a strong album from top to bottom, full of great tunes.

Tesla continued their consistent run of great albums. *Forever More* featured the best ballad of the year – 'Fallin' Apart'.

Top Songs
1. Better – Guns N' Roses
2. Lay Down Your Love – Whitesnake
3. Forever More – Tesla
4. TWAT – Guns N' Roses
5. Can You Hear the Wind Blow – Whitesnake
6. Standing On the Outside – Dokken
7. So What – Tesla
8. All For Love – Whitesnake
9. Give Me A Reason – Dokken
10. Breaking' Free – Tesla
11. Catcher in the Rye – Guns N' Roses

12. Buried Unkind – Steelheart
13. Hello, Hello – TnT
14. Riad N' the Bedouins – Guns N' Roses
15. By By Johnny – Return
16. Dream – White Lion
17. Tomorrow – Def Leppard
18. This Ain't a Love Song – Motley Crue
19. Saints of Los Angeles – Motley Crue

Best Ballads
1. Fallin' Apart – Tesla
2. Summer Rain – Whitesnake
3. Street of Dreams – Guns N' Roses
4. All I Want All I Need – Whitesnake
5. Take Me Home – White Lion
6. Madagascar – Guns N' Roses
7. Me and Dad – TnT
8. I Remember – Dokken
9. The Missing Kind – TnT
10. Never Let You Go – White Lion
11. Just in Case – Tesla
12. Good 2B Alive – Steelheart
13. I Won't Cry – Pleasure Dome (Ted Poley)
14. Don't Ask Me to be Faithful – Big Cock

Albums You Must Own:
Chinese Democracy – Guns N' Roses
Forever More – Tesla
Good to be Bad – Whitesnake
Lighting Strikes Again – Dokken
Atlantis – TnT
Good 2B Alive – Steelheart
Return of the Pride – White Lion
Saints of Los Angeles – Motley Crue
Songs From The Sparkle Lounge – Def Leppard

Other Albums of Interest:
The Last Vegas – The Last Vegas
Pleasure Dome – For Your Personal Amusement
Poley/Rivera – Only Human
Big Cock - Motherload
Junkyard – Put it on Ten and Pull the Knobs Off

D.A.D. – Monster Philosophy
House of Lords – Come to my Kingdom
London Quireboys – Homewreckers & Heartbreakers
Return – Best of Both Worlds
Rock City Angels – Use Once & Destroy
Tora Tora – The Warehouse…20 years later
Don Dokken – Solitary

2009 – The Last Vegas

Bon Jovi's *The Circle* went to #1 on the Billboard album chart and was marketed as a return to their roots. But we weren't impressed and didn't feel the album had any memorable songs after 'Thorn In My Side'.

The real standout tracks of the year come from old-timer's Great White on the rock side while The Last Vegas had the best ballad of the genre in almost a decade.

The Last Vegas's major label debut – *Whatever Gets You Off* – had a powerhouse producing crew behind it – Motley Crue's Nikki Sixx, guitar player DJ Ashba and legendary writer/producer Marti Frederiksen. The album is a refreshing throwback to the good old days of hard rock bands. It's got heavy songs, songs with an anthem chorus and the standard power ballad. 'Apologize' is the best ballad released in the HM/HB genre since 2000's 'Far Away' from Shameless.

Great White released their last album with iconic front man Jack Russell. *Rising* didn't tickle the fancy of rock critics, but we think the band put out a really strong album. It's a bit mellow and relaxed, but still sounds like classic Great White. We chose 'I Don't Mind' as the best rock song of the year.

The biggest surprise of the year came from the band Europe, who produced some classic genre songs even though 'Carrie' and 'The Final Countdown' are sometimes mocked as cheese rock. Anybody expecting cheese rock on *Last Look at Eden* will be pleasantly surprised. The album rocks hard, led by the bad-ass song 'Gonna Get Ready' and a fantastic ballad in 'New Love in Town'.

Hardcore Superstar continued with their string of really strong albums. *Beg For It* is chalked full of hard rocking goodness.

Top Songs
1. I Don't Mind – Great white
2. Gonna Get Ready – Europe
3. Shades of Grey – Hardcore Superstar
4. Babylon's Burning – Babylon Bombs
5. Paper Heart – Vains of Jenna
6. Nervous Breakdown – Hardcore Superstar
7. Last Look at Eden – Europe
8. I'm Bad – The Last Vegas
9. Thorn in My Side – Bon Jovi
10. Hearts on the Highway – Danger Danger
11. Get it On – Vains of Jenna
12. Resurrection Love – Babylon's Bombs
13. Big World Away – Winger

Best Ballads
1. Apologize – The Last Vegas
2. My Sanctuary – Great White
3. It's Alright – Babylon Bombs
4. B-Song – Tora Tora
5. New Love in Town – Europe
6. Words Don't Count – White Lion
7. Who Am I To Blame – Tora Tora
8. Tonite – Tora Tora
9. After All This Time – Winger
10. Redemption – Little Caesar
11. Better Off Alone – Vains of Jenna
12. Always Within Me – Winger
13. My Love – Stryper

Albums You Must Own
Rising – Great White
Last Look at Eden – Europe
Babylon's Burning – Babylon Bombs
Whatever Gets You Off – The Last Vegas
Beg for It – Hardcore Superstar
Karma – Winger
Lost Tracks, Demos and Oddities – White Lion

The Art of Telling Lies – Vains of Jenna
Miss B Haven – Tora Tora
10c Billionaire - Bulletboys

Other Albums of Interest:
Bon Jovi – The Circle
Stryper - Murder by Pride
Ted Poley – Greatestits Vol. 1
Faster Pussycat – Front Row for the Donkey Show
Lita Ford – Wicked Wonderland
D.A.D. – The Overmuch Box
D.A.D. – Behind the Seen
Danger Danger – Revolve
House of Lords – Cartesian Dreams – Sept 18
Kingdom Come – Magnified
Lillian Axe – Sad Day on Planet Earth
Little Caesar – Redemption
Pretty Boy Floyd – Glam as Fuck
London Quireboys – Halfpenny Dancer
Tora Tora – Bombs Away: The Unreleased Surprise Attack Recordings
Vandal – Better Days
Hawk – Let The Metal Live
Lynch Mob – Smoke and Mirrors

2010 - Ratt
Ratt came through with one of the best albums of their career and
Vince Neil took a song written by Nikki Sixx to the top of our charts!

Showing how fickle the music world is, just a few months after
releasing their best album in 20 years the Ratt lineup that released
Infestation – which went all the way to #30 on Billboard – went on an
"indefinite hiatus" and the band stopped touring. 'Best of Me', 'As
Good as it Gets' and 'Garden of Eden' are all tremendous rock songs.

Vince Neil's *Tattoos & Tequila* cracked the top 60 on Billboard and
produced the best overall song of 2010 in 'Another Bad Day'.
Interesting note, 'Another Bad Day' was written by a who's who of the
rock music scene. Tracii Guns, James Michael, Kevin Kadish and Sixx
share writing credits. Reportedly the song was written for Motley

Crue but Tommy Lee didn't find it worthy enough for inclusion. That decision worked out well for Neil, who turned the song into a hit.

Hardcore Superstar continued their streak of top notch-albums. *Split Your Lip* might be their best overall release. 'Moonshine', 'Last Call for Alcohol', 'Run To Your Mamma' and 'Here Comes That Sick Bitch Again' make *Split Your Lip* one of the best rock albums of the decade.

Vain, Enuff Z'Nuff and Jetboy had decent albums. Overseas rockers had a strong year, Reckless Love, Wig Wam, Crashdiet and Crazy Lixx all had strong releases.

Top Songs
1. Another Bad Day – Vince Neil
2. Best of Me – Ratt
3. Moonshine – Hardcore Superstar
4. As Good as it Gets – Ratt
5. Save Her – Crash Diet
6. Don't Forget Me When I'm Gone – Alleycat Scratch
7. Love Drug - Vain
8. Do You Want to Taste It – Wig Wam
9. Lazy Day – Enuff Z'Nuff
10. Touch – Bad City
11. Push & Pull – Keel
12. Love Machine – Reckless Love
13. Perfectly Wrong – Jetboy
14. Last Call for Alcohol – Hardcore Superstar
15. Take Me For a Ride – Bad City
16. 21 'Till I Die – Crazy Lixx
17. Tangled Up – Treat
18. Showdown in Central Park – Bad City

Best Ballads
1. What Do You Got – Bon Jovi
2. Run to Your Mama – Hardcore Superstar
3. Here Comes that Sick Bitch Again – Hardcore Superstar
4. What of Our Love – Crazy Lixx
5. Man in the Moon – Wig Wam
6. Shouldn't Cry – Vain
7. Here Comes Lonely – Vain
8. Fire in the Pouring Rain – Bad City

9. Beautiful Pain – Crashdiet

Albums You Should Own:
Infestation – Ratt
Split Your Lip – Hardcore Superstar
All Those Strangers – Vain
Welcome to the Wasteland – Bad City
Tattoos & Tequila – Vince Neil
Dissonance – Enuff Z'Nuff
Off Your Rocker – Jetboy
New Religion – Crazy Lixx
Streets of Rock & Roll – Keel
Generation Wild – Crashdiet
Non Stop Rock'n Roll – Wig Wam
Reckless Love – Reckless Love

Other Albums of Interest:
Cry Wolf – Twenty Ten
Alleycat Scratch – Last Call
TnT – A Farewell to Arms
Keel – Streets of Rock & Roll
Stage Dolls – Always
Beggars & Thieves – Stone Alone EP
Lillian Axe – Deep Red Shadows
Y&T – Facemelter
Treat – Coup de Grace

2011 - Whitesnake

Does David Coverdale ever age? Like fine wine, Whitesnake seems to get better over time. Guitar players Rob Beach and Doug Aldrich's blistering guitar attack and Brian Tichy's drum attack make *Forevermore* sound like it was a classic album from the late 80s or early 90s. *Forevermore* is the must own album from 2011.

Classic veterans added some punch to the year's best album list and also made 2011 one of the deepest years in recent memory. There are 40 songs you should add to your iPod playlist. And if you are fans of the bands that released albums this year, that number could easily push past 50 songs.

Ballads ruled the day. Some incredible love songs were released, highlighted by 'Shelter From the Rain' from Tora Tora, 'Have You Seen Her' from Bang Tango, 'We All Fall Down' from D-A-D, 'One of These Days' from Whitesnake and 'Better Off Without You' from Tesla.

D-A-D continues to put out high quality albums. *Dic-Nil-Lan-Daft-Erd-Ark* is the second best album of the year, featuring the fantastic song 'We All Fall Down'.

Bass player Jerry Dixon flexed his songwriting skills and new singer Robert Mason breathed some life back into Warrant. *Rockaholic* isn't an 80s throwback album – like Whitesnake successfully did – but is more of the sound of a band creating a new identity. And it's definitely worth your time to check it out.

Tesla released *Twisted Wires & The Acoustic Session*, a throwback to their 'Signs' days. '2nd Street' is our choice for the best overall song of the year.

The most pleasant surprise of the year came from old-timer's Fastway. New singer Toby Jepson helped Fastway release what we feel is the best album of their entire career. *Eat Dog Eat* is strong from top to finish.

Veteran's Tora Tora, Vain, Shameless and Bang Tango all released strong albums. Def Leppard released another live album, but the standout of *Mirror Ball, Live & More* is new song 'Undefeated' which is the best rocker Leppard has released in a decade.

Top Songs
1. 2nd Street – Tesla
2. Undefeated – Def Leppard
3. Steal Your Heart Away – Whitesnake
4. Deliver Me – Fastway
5. Undertow – Mr. Big
6. Rock Down This Place – Hell in the Club
7. Animal Attraction – Reckless Love
8. Living a World Away – Tora Tora

9. All Out of Luck – Whitesnake
10. Last Time in Neverland – D-A-D
11. My Own Worst Enemy – Sebastian Bach
12. Bring on the World – Bang Tango
13. Greener – Vain
14. Goodbye 2 U – Shameless
15. Unforgiven – Mr. Big
16. I Need You – Whitesnake
17. Innocence is No Excuse – Shameless
18. Snake – Warrant
19. I Want What She's Got – D-A-D
20. Vain – Vain
21. Blue Trees – Kingdom Come
22. Big Money – House of Lords
23. We Come Undone – Beggars & Thieves

Best Ballads
1. Shelter From the Rain – Tora Tora
2. Have You Seen Her – Bang Tango
3. We All Fall Down – D-A-D
4. One of These Days – Whitesnake
5. Star – Hell in the Club
6. Better Off Without You – Tesla
7. Dead and Gone – Fastway
8. Rescue Me – Tora Tora
9. Fantasy – Reckless Love
10. Home – Warrant
11. Stranger in My Life – Mr. Big
12. Candle and the Stone – Tora Tora
13. Tears in the City – Warrant
14. Kings of the World – Def Leppard
15. Cryin' Turns to Rain – King Kobra
16. Forevermore – Whitesnake

Albums You Should Own:
Forevermore – Whitesnake
Dic-Nil-Lan-Daft-Erd-Ark – D-A-D
Rockaholic – Warrant
Revolution Day – Tora Tora
Eat Dog Eat – Fastway
Enough Rope – Vain
Twisted Wires & The Acoustic Sessions – Tesla

Let the Games Begin – Hell in the Club
Kicking & Screaming – Sebastian Bach
Pistol Whipped in the Bible Belt – Bang Tango
Animal Attraction – Reckless Love
Dial S for Sex – Shameless
Stakkattakktwo – Wrathchild
We Are the Brokenhearted – Beggars &Thieves
What If... - Mr. Big

Other Albums of Interest:
House of Lords – Big Money
Kingdom Come – Rendered Waters
Tryx – Dayz Gone By
Stage Dolls – Always
King Kobra - King Kobra
Electric Boy And Them Boys Done Swang
Sensory Overdrive – Michael Monroe
Stryper – The Covering
Vains of Jenna - Reverse Trip

2012 – L.A. Guns

Though original and founding member Tracii Guns wasn't involved, Phil Lewis's version of L.A. Guns released the Sunset Strip homage album that Motley Crue wishes *Saints of Los Angeles* would have been.

Guitar player Stacy Blades more than held his own as a shredder on the *Hollywood Forever* album, which was L.A. Guns first album since 2005. It's also the last album the band released before Guns rejoined the group in 2017.

Like almost all L.A. Guns albums *Hollywood Forever* is solid from start to finish. Key songs include the amazing power ballad 'Underneath the Sun', as well as rockers like 'You Better Not Love Me' and the title track 'Hollywood Forever'.

Another classic band with a major lineup change came up big in 2012. Great White without Jack Russell didn't seem feasible. Russell has such a unique voice it's hard to imagine the band without him. To combat the comparisons, Great White didn't just hire a Russell clone but instead went for a different sound with former XYZ singer Terry Ilous who possesses a voice full of bluesy-rasp.

Great White's *Elation* featured two really fantastic songs with the rocking 'Something For You' and the soulful ballad 'Hard to Say Goodbye'.

The other four worthwhile albums in 2012 came from the newer crowd. The Last Vegas, Crazy Lixx, Harry Hess and Wig Wam all put out fun rock albums.

Top Songs
1. Bag of Bones – Europe
2. Something for You – Great White
3. Evil Eyes – The Last Vegas
4. Hollywood Forever – L.A. Guns
5. Prisoner of Love – Little Caesar
6. Downtown – Crazy Lixx
7. The Bigger the Better – Wig Wam
8. You Better Not Love Me – L.A. Guns
9. Slow Drag – Lynch Mob
10. For the Last Time – Dokken
11. Sweet, Bad and Beautiful – Crazy Lixx
12. You Are the One – The Last Vegas
13. Queenie – L.A. Guns
14. Dig in Deep – Tyketto

Best Ballads
1. I Live For You – Harry Hess
2. Hard to Say Goodbye – Great White
3. Underneath the Sun – L.A. Guns
4. Good Night – The Last Vegas
5. The Coolest Thing – Trixter
6. Don't Leave Me – Harry Hess
7. Only the Dead Know – Crazy Lixx

Albums You Should Own:
Hollywood Forever – L.A. Guns
Elation – Great White
Bad Decisions – The Last Vegas
Living in Yesterday – Harry Hess

Riot Avenue – Crazy Lixx
Wall Street – Wig Wam
Bag of Bones - Europe

Other Albums of Interest:
Donnie Vie – Wrapped Around My Middle Finger
Banshee - Mindslave
Dokken – Broken Bones
Bon Jovi – Inside Out
Lita Ford – Nobody's Child
Little Caesar – American Dream
Pretty Boy Floyd – Special Edition 4 Track EP
Tuff – What Comes Around Goes Around ....Again
Trixter – New Audio Machine
Tyketto – Dig In Deep
Lynch Mob – Sound Mountain Sessions (EP)

2013 – Tom Keifer

The HM/HB genre made a bit of a comeback in 2013 with three albums landing on the Billboard album top 40 chart. Bon Jovi led the way with *What About Now* occupying the #1 spot, Def Leppard's *Viva! Hysteria* going to #24 and Stryper's *No More Hell to Pay* coming in strong at #35.

But the real standout album of the year came from former Cinderella front man Tom Keifer. One of the disappointments from the era was the small output of music from the original lineups of major bands like Cinderella, Guns N' Roses, Kix and Skid Row. Cinderella only released four studio albums, the last coming in 1994.

It was a long draught but Keifer did his part to make up for the wait with his brilliant solo album *The Way Life Goes*. On its own, *The Way Life Goes* is the top album of 2013. But the backstory makes it even more amazing. Between Cinderella's 1994 release and *The Way Life Goes* Keifer saw his band break up, lost his voice and had to undergo multiple throat surgeries, his mother died and he went through a divorce. You can feel every ounce of that turmoil in songs like 'It's Not Enough', 'The Flower Song' and 'You Showed Me'.

The second best album of the year is another fascinating story. Skid Row's created an amazing EP of music – *United World Rebellion Chapter One* – but also couldn't hide from the question that was on all music fan's minds. Imagine how good this album would have been with Sebastian Bach on vocals. Instead, Johnny Solinger handled the vocals and did an admirable job. Today, Solinger is releasing country rock albums.

Former Hanoi Rocks legend Michael Monroe put out a very good album – *Horns and Halos*, featuring the brilliant song 'Stained Glass Heart'. Santa Cruz debuted to an American audience with *Screaming for Adrenaline*, which some fans compared to a mix of Guns N' Roses and Van Halen.

Top Songs
1. It's Not Enough – Tom Keifer
2. I'm With You – Bon Jovi
3. Stained Class Heart – Michael Monroe
4. Taste of It – Like an Army
5. One More Minute – Hardcore Superstar
6. Aiming High – Santa Cruz
7. Stitches – Skid Row
8. Night on Fire – Reckless Love
9. Lonely Road – Killer Dwarfs
10. Kings of Demolition – Skid Row
11. Cocaine Cowboys – Crashdiet
12. Sweet Sensation – Santa Cruz
13. The Flower Song – Tom Keifer
14. Angel Falling – Reckless Love
15. The Way Life Goes – Tom Keifer
16. No More Hell to Pay - Stryper

Best Ballads
1. Long Time No See – Hardcore Superstar
2. The is Killing Me – Skid Row
3. You Showed Me – Tom Keifer
4. Hot Rain – Reckless Love
5. Home – Like an Army
6. Thick and Thin – Tom Keifer
7. Dying To Live – Reckless Love

Albums You Should Own:
The Way Life Goes – Tom Keifer
United World Rebellion Chapter One – Skid Row
C'mon Take on Me – Hardcore Superstar
Screaming for Adrenaline – Santa Cruz
Spirit – Reckless Love
Horns and Halos – Michael Monroe

Other Albums of Interest:
Bon Jovi - What About Now
Killer Dwarfs – Start @ One
Stryper – Second Coming
Stryper – No More Hell to Pay
King Kobra – King Kobra II
Kingdom Come – Outlier
London Quireboys – Beautiful Cures
Tigertailz – Knives
Shameless – Beautiful Disaster
Crashdiet - The Savage Playground
The Circus – Coming For You

2014 - Kix

Kix showed a new generation of rock fans why they were heavyweights of the genre with *Rock Your Face Off*, their first album in almost 20 years. Tesla, Mr. Big and Winger added solid albums to their discography.

Tesla's *Simplicity* was the second best album of the year. It rose all the way to #24 on the Billboard 200 and produced the year's best song in 'So Divine' and second best ballad with 'Cross My Heart'.

Fans had been waiting 19 years since Kix's last album and *Rock Your Face Off* certainly didn't disappoint. 'Inside Outside Inn' is a fantastic ballad, the best of the year and the band's second best of all-time after 'Don't Close Your Eyes'. Rocker 'You're Gone' sounds like classic Kix: arena rock with a bit of humor tossed in.

Skid Row did it again, releasing another EP that had a couple really great songs on it. 'Give it to the Gun' and 'Catch Your Fall' are the highlights of *Rise of the Damnation Army Chapter Two*.

Sebastian Bach also put out a pretty decent album. *Give 'Em Hell* lacks that signature standout song, but all in all it's 53 minutes of quality music. Guns N' Roses legend Duff McKagan plays bass on the album.

Hannon Tramp released the best ballad with 'How Many Times'.

Top Songs
1. So Divine – Tesla
2. You're Gone – Kix
3. Muse – Hell in the Club
4. Love Me with Your Top Down – Kix
5. Outlaw – Crazy Lixx
6. Devil on My Shoulder – Hell in the Club
7. Give it the Gun – Skid Row
8. Temptation – Sebastian Bach
9. Love Blind – Babylon A.D.
10. Miss You – The Last Vegas
11. Gotta Love the Ride – Mr. Big
12. Take It – Hannon Tramp
13. Time Bomb – Tesla
14. Sweet Salvation – The Last Vegas
15. Better Days – Darkhorse (Paul Laine)
16. Sound of the Loud Minority – Crazy Lixx
17. Fragile – Mr. Big

Best Ballad
1. How Many More Times – Hannon Tramp
2. Inside Outside Inn – Kix
3. Cross my Heart – Tesla
4. Catch Your Fall – Skid Row
5. Other Than Me – Tesla
6. Had Enough – Sebastian Bach
7. The Man Who Has Everything – Mr. Big
8. Love is a Mystery – Babylon A.D.
9. Strong – Darkhorse (Paul Laine)
10. Just Let Your Heart Decide – Mr. Big
11. Lonely – Hannon Tramp
12. East/West – Mr. Big
13. Out of This World – Winger

Albums You Should Own:
Rock Your Face Off – Kix
Simplicity – Tesla
...The Stories We Could Tell – Mr. Big
Hannon Tramp – Hannon Tramp
Better Days Comin' – Winger
Rise of the Damnation Army United World Rebellion Chapter Two – Skid Row
Give 'Em Hell – Sebastian Bach
Sweet Salvation – The Last Vegas
Crazy Lixx – Crazy Lixx
Devil on My Shoulder – Hell in the Club

Other Albums of Interest:
Donnie Vie – Goodbye: Enough Z'Nuff
Donnie Vie – The White Album
Quiet Riot – Quiet Riot 10
Electric Boys – Starflight United
D.A.D. – Disn30land Af30r D30k
Skid Row – United World Rebellion: Chapter Two – August 5
Enuff Z'Nuff – Covered in Gold
Babylon A.D. – Lost Sessions/Fresno, Ca 93
House of Lords – Big Money
Lynch Mob – Sun Red Sun

2015 - Stryper
Bon Jovi and Def Leppard released Billboard top 10 albums, but the best overall rock album came from Hardcore Superstar. Stryper's *Fallen* was the band's 7th album to reach the Billboard 200.

Hardcore Superstar continued to release amazing albums. Some longtime fans felt *HCSS* didn't have the same energy has past albums. We disagreed and felt it contained a handful of outstanding tracks, just like every album of their discography. 'Touch The Sky' features popular singer Etzia sharing vocals. The band toured North America with Michael Monroe, a fascinating combination of bands. Monroe helped start the HM/HB era, while Hardcore Superstar might currently be the best of the genre.

Finish rockers Santa Cruz also released a kick-ass album with their self-titled release. Non-ballad and straight old fashion hard rock and roll songs helped Santa Cruz earn the second spot of the year. 'We Are The Ones to Fall' is a classic.

Ex-Wig Wam singer Sten Nilsen put together a Norwegian all-star band Ammunition. Their debut album *Shanghaied* kicks nothing but ass. Santa Cruz and Ammunition would have fit squarely into the GnR/Skid Row vein of 1989.

Hall of Famer's Bon Jovi's *Burning Bridges* (#3) and Def Leppard's self-titled album (#10) weren't as strong as the work they released in their prime. But both bands took top spots in our 2015 list. 'We Don't Run' is Bon Jovi's best rocker since the *These Days* era, and tops out list for the best song of the year. Def Leppard's 'Blind Faith' was our choice as the year's best power ballad.

Top Songs
1. We Don't Run – Bon Jovi
2. Touch the Sky – Hardcore Superstar
3. We Are The Ones to Fall – Santa Cruz
4. Party 'Til I'm Gone – Hardcore Superstar
5. Give Me a Sign - Ammunition
6. Sea of Love – Def Leppard
7. Don't Mean Shit – Hardcore Superstar
8. Faded - Junkyard
9. Life is Beautiful – Bon Jovi
10. Bonafide Heroes – Santa Cruz
11. Symphony – BulletBoys
12. Testify – Lynch Mob
13. Bye Bye Babylon – Santa Cruz
14. Saturday Night Gave Me Sunday Morning – Bon Jovi
15. Rock' to The Edge of the Night – Trixter

Best Ballads
1. Blind Faith – Def Leppard
2. Praise You – Europe
3. Road to Babylon - Ammunition
4. All Over Again – Stryper
5. Blown Away – Every Mother's Nightmare
6. Deep in Her Heart – Mark Slaughter

Albums You Should Own:
HCSS – Hardcore Superstar

Santa Cruz – Santa Cruz
Shanghaied - Ammunition
Burning Bridges – Bon Jovi
Reflections in a Rear View Mirror – Mark Slaughter
Human Era – Trixter
Def Leppard – Def Leppard

Other Albums of Interest:
Whitesnake – The Purple Album
Europe – War of Kings
Stryper – Fallen
BulletBoys – Elefante
Every Mother's Nightmare – Grind (EP)
House of Lords – Indestructible
London Quireboys – St Cecilia and the Gypsy Soul
Tigertailz – Lost Reelz
Michael Monroe - Blackout States
Lynch Mob – Rebel

2016 – The Last Vegas

The Last Vegas dominated 2016, releasing the year's best album, best rock song and best power ballad. Unlike the following year, 2016 was almost completely void of big-name bands except for Bon Jovi's *This House is Not For Sale*, which went to #1 on Billboard.

Top Songs
1. Hard to Get Over (You're So) – The Last Vegas
2. We Are the Weekend – Reckless Love
3. The Life & Death of Mr. Nobody – Hell in the Club
4. Keep it Up All Night – Reckless Love
5. I Need it Now - Tyketto
6. Along For the Ride – The Last Vegas
7. Monster – Reckless Love
8. Let's Get Cracking – Reckless Love
9. Touch of Grey – Bon Jovi

Best Ballads
1. Anything it Takes – The Last Vegas
2. Naked – Hell in the Club
3. Scream - Tyketto
4. Real Love – Bon Jovi

5. Love's Got Nothing on Me – The Last Vegas
6. Universe & You – The Last Vegas

Albums You Should Own:
Eat Me – The Last Vegas
Shadow of the Monster – Hell in the Club
Invader – Reckless Love
Reach – Tyketto
Boutique Sound Frames - PJ Farley

Other Albums of Interest:
Donnie Vie - !
Autograph - Louder
Ted Poley – Beyond the Fade
Bon Jovi – This House is Not for Sale
Lita Ford – Time Capsule
Tigertailz - Blast
Vain – Rolling with The Punches
Stevie Rachelle– best sTuff
Treat – Ghost of Graceland
Enuff Z'Nuff – Clowns Lounge
Femme Fatale – One More for the Road

2017 – The Giants Return
While 2016 was devoid of star power, the heavyweights of the genre came out in full force in 2017. L.A. Guns, Jack Russell, Mark Slaughter, Stevie Rachelle, Stephen Pearcy, Babylon A.D. , Mr. Big, Babylon A.D., Warrant and Vain all came out with top shelf albums, making 2017 an exciting year for the HM/HB genre.

D-A-D was always on the very far ledge of being added to this book. In reality, they are more of a rock band than hair metal band. But a couple of their more popular songs fit squarely into the genre. And they are such an awesome band we figured it was better to include them. With that said, the solo album from singer Jesper Binzer is more of a rock album than HB/HM so we aren't going to include it in our rankings. BUT – and this is a Rosanne Barr size butt – Binzer's *Dying Is Easy* is hands down, without a doubt the best album of 2017. Do yourself a favor and go buy it.

The Missing Peace featured the return of the classic L.A. Guns duo of Tracii Guns and Phil Lewis. And what a return it was. 'The Devil Made Me Do It' is the best rock song of the year and *The Missing Peace* is the best album of 2017. It is classic L.A. Guns.

Jack Russell came back strong with the fantastic *He Saw it Comin'*.

Tuff and Shameless singer Rachelle continues his impressive hot streak by joining another standout band – Tales From the Porn. Danger Danger legendary singer Ted Poley found his way back into our top list with the band Tokyo Motor Fist.

At the very least there are 14 bands that deserve your $15. For what the music scene is today, that's a pretty impressive accomplishment for the HM/HB genre.

Top songs
1. The Devil Made Me Do It – L.A. Guns
2. Young Blood Rising – Santa Cruz
3. Love Don't Live Here – Jack Russell
4. Cut From the Same Cloth – Junkyard
5. Music Man - Warrant
6. Down and Dirty – Deaf, Dumb & Blond
7. Girls Wanna Party – Tales From the Porn
8. Forevermore – Mark Slaughter
9. Speed – L.A. Guns
10. Ten Miles Wide – Stephen Pearcy
11. Fool on Fire – Babylon A.D.
12. Damn I'm in Love Again – Mr. Big
13. Rolling With the Punches – Vain
14. You Got Me Twisted - Steelheart
15. Blame it on the Night – Jack Russell
16. Faded - Warrant
17. Hell or High Water - Junkyard
18. Perfect Love – Tales From the Porn
19. Get Off Your Ass- Autograph
20. Mean to Me – Mr. Big
21. Godspeed – Jack Russell
22. Don't Let it Happen to You – Vain
23. We Got the Power – Pretty Boy Floyd
24. She's All Coming Back to Me Now – Mr. Big

25. Styrofoam Cup - Junkyard
26. The Flood's the Fault of the Rain – L.A. Guns
27. Rain – Stephen Pearcy
28. Running Wild – L.A. Cobra
29. Wild Child – Craxy Lixx
30. Love Me Insane – Tokyo Motor Fist
31. Can't Get Enough - Shameless
32. Blown Away – Every Mother's Nightmare
33. Never Let You Down – Great White
34. Done to Me – Tokyo Motor Fist
35. Walk the Earth - Europe

Best Ballad
1. Get Me Out of California – Santa Cruz
2. Anything For You – Jack Russell
3. U in My Life - Warrant
4. Disposable – Mark Slaughter
5. Let Me In – Great White
6. It Can't be That Bad – Shameless (Ft: Frankie Muriel)
7. We Can't Bring Back Yesterday – Pretty Boy Floyd
8. Christine – L.A. Guns
9. Lips of Rain - Steelheart
10. Pictures – Europe
11. All I Own - Autograph
12. Days are Through – Every Mother's Nightmare
13. Get You Off My Mind – Tokyo Motor Fist

Albums You Should Own:

1. The Missing Peace – L.A. Guns
2. Rolling With the Punches – Vain
3. He Saw it Comin' – Jack Russell
4. Defying Gravity – Mr. Big
5. Revelation Highway – Babylon A.D.
6. High Water – Junkyard
7. Louder Harder Faster – Warrant
8. Through Worlds of Stardust - Steelheart
9. Smash – Stephen Pearcy
10. Halfway There - Mark Slaughter
11. Bad Blood Rising – Santa Cruz
12. H.M.M.V – Tales From the Porn
13. L.A. Days - Deaf, Dumb & Blond

14. Shotgun Slinger – L.A. Cobra

Other Albums of Interest:
Every Mother's Nightmare – Grind
Autograph - Get Off Your Ass
Great White - Full Circle
Pretty Boy Floyd - Public Enemies
Europe – Walk the Earth
Shameless – The Filthy 7
Quiet Riot – Wasted
Tokyo Motor Fist – Love Me Insane
Adrenaline – Blackout Express

HAIR METAL BOOKS

Below is a ranking of what we feel are the 35 most interesting books written about the Hair Metal/Hair Band era. Some of them you've no doubt already read. Hopefully we have presented a few unknowns that you can pick up and add to your collection.

We didn't just pick our personal favorites or the ones about our favorite bands. We factored in the writing styles, if the book had a quality editing team, how interesting the story was and if the book appeared to have heart/soul behind it or if it was just written to cash in on a popular band's success.

We personally read every book on the list. But then also searched through as many reviews as possible to get a feel for how others felt. We read personal reviews from rock media critics as well as reading all the comments from fans on sites like Amazon and in comment sections on the critic's reviews.

Our biggest complaint is that there simply aren't enough band books. Bios on Guns N' Roses, Motley Crue and Bon Jovi dominate the genre, making up well over half of the releases. Maybe the second and third tier bands don't have enough of a history for their own full-length books. But it would be an awesome to have some in-depth stories on some of the colorful characters of the genre.

Other downfalls are the lack of editing for most of these books. As well as musicians trying to impress us – the fans – with the constant stories of "I got drunk with Ozzy then banged 12 chicks at once."

Motley Crue's The Dirt: Confessions of the World's Most Notorious Rock Band is our selection as the best overall book of the HM/GB genre. Released in 2001, written by Neil Strauss and the members of Motley Crue.

The Dirt is a great title, as each member of the band opens up and tells you their thoughts about each other, the band and their lives. They all give you the full dirt – warts, scratches, scars, blood, the good and the absolute worst moments of the band's history. Nothing is spared, feelings and pride are left behind, and no story/stone is left unturned. Copious amounts of sex, drugs, violence and rock n' roll. Decadence at every level and aspect of their career. These guys lived the life that the teenage boys in all of us could only dream about.

The Dirt really shows the four different and unique personalities of Mick, Vince, Tommy and Nikki. It's amazing look into their lives and how different these guys were from another. It's really quite amazing that Motley Crue lasted as long as they did.

The Dirt is the standard for the genre. An absolute must own. Just the Mick Mars sections make it a must own.

2.
Hollywood Rocks – and accompanying four-CD (2007)
Simon Toon, Michael Rocchio and Jason Splat.
The best picture book released on the genre. Hollywood Rocks features fantastic unreleased photos of all the major bands and future superstars during their Sunset Strip days, as well as pictures of old ticket stubs and flyers. The book also gives recognition to all the popular Sunset Strip bars.

Be sure and make sure you also order the 4-CD set, which features some great songs from the Sunset Strip bands, including unreleased material, demos and B-sides. If you grew up during the hair metal music scene, Hollywood Rocks is the yearbook that you must own.

3.
Slash (2007)
Slash, Anthony Bozza

If you are looking for a GnR book that bashes Axl Rose and reveals the gory details of the band's breakup, you will be disappointed with Slash's book. But if you are interesting in learning about Slash's journey from a young bike rider to a hard rock guitar God, insights on his time with GnR and Velvet Revolver, and his struggles with addictions then this is the book for you!

Slash comes off as a pretty mellow dude who really just wanted to avoid drama and do drugs, party, bang chicks and make the best hard rock music possible. He strips back the layers of himself and his own life, revealing all his dirty secrets and vices. But he stays pretty respectful when talking about his famous Guns N' Roses band mates. Seemingly wanting to tell their mutual story to the best of his ability and memory – but without ruffling any feathers. Several times while telling a story Slash mentions that he is just writing what he remembers and that his band mates probably have a different recollection of the events.

Depending on your reason for reading Slash you'll be happy or sad that the book is authentic forage into Slash's life with his time in GnR just being a part of the bigger story. If you were hoping for a GnR tell-all and you don't care about the band member's childhood stories....you might be disappointed. Especially considering the book's almost 500-page length.

The book is filled with a pretty top-notch picture collection that is clearly one of the book's highlights. A low light would definitely be the editing, which is below mediocre at best. Misspellings, grammar mistakes and factual errors. The factual errors can be expected, after all, the stories are taken from the memories of a self-confessed drug addict who spent years in a daze. But the book's co-writer could have spent a day fact-checking and cleared up 99% of the mistakes. Why this wasn't done for a book of this stature is a mystery.

Better editing and shortening the book by 50 pages would have made it an all-time classic. But as it stands, Slash is still one of the better rock biographies out there. Fans of GnR, Slash, hair metal, guitar and those who suffer from drug and alcohol addiction should definitely pick up this book.

4.
Shut Up and Give Me the Mic (2012)
Dee Snider

If you're looking for another hard rock tale of sex with groupies, copious amounts of drugs and debauchery, you can go read virtually every other genre related book. Shut Up and Give Me the Mic is a refreshing change from the typical rock star book. Dee Snider is one of the rare rock stars that doesn't drink, smoke or do drugs.

The book details Dee's career, his personal life, as well as a great overview of how the music business works. Dee is extremely arrogant and narcissistic and that will turn off a few readers. But he is also extremely intelligent and open with the mistakes he has made.

Younger fans will be surprised to learn that Snider was more than just a tall dude dressed in clown make-up. He is actually one of the more intelligent musicians alive, he helped kick off the hair metal genre and he was a major factor in fighting Tipper Gore's PMRC.

5.
It's So Easy: and Other Lies (2011)
Duff McKagan

One of the better written books related to the genre. Duff McKagan is a talented writer and is clearly one of the more intelligent and hardworking musicians to come from the Sunset Strip.

This isn't the history of GnR, but is the life story of one member of the band, a dude who doesn't just define himself as being the bass player in a rock band. But if you want to read a fascinating tale of a musician from one of the most popular rock bands of all time talk about how he overcame an addiction to alcohol (he almost died) and got his life back on track, then you should most definitely purchase Duff's memoirs.

McKagan does touch on key moments in GnR history and does share interactions with Slash, Axl and the rest of the band, as well as issues the band went through on their way to the top – as well as the trials and tribulations that came along with being the most popular rock band alive.

Duff seems to be one of the rare superstars of the era whose sole purpose was to make music and give the fans a great live rock show, as opposed to those whose main reason for rocking was to score hot chicks and do as much drugs as possible. He is also very faithful and dedicated to his wife and children, which was nice to read. We guarantee you will have a new-found respect for Duff after reading It's So Easy.

6.
The Heroin Diaries: A Year in the Life of a Shattered Rock Star (2007)
Nikki Sixx, Ian Gittins
If you are a huge Motley Crue fan, or more specifically a huge fan of Nikki Sixx, then you should most definitely give The Heroin Diaries a read. If you are a Sixx worshipper and think the Crue bass player is a "Rock God" then you'll think HD is a courageous work of art. You'll rail on about how brave Sixx is for sharing insights on his drug addiction during a very traumatic time of his life.

If you aren't a big Crue fan or Sixx worshipper then the book will seem more sizzle than actual steak. Sixx comes off as a bit of a self-entitled whiner with a "look at me" complex. And there are a group of rock fans out there that think Sixx grossly exaggerated his drug use in an attempt to pimp his image as a rock n' roll bad boy. But that's always been the downfall of Sixx. While rockers like Tommy Lee or Slash or Ozzy simply went balls-deep into debauchery, Sixx couldn't hang with those dudes but desperately wanted fans to think he could. Instead of enjoying his drug-fueled haze – he was apparently coherent enough to keep a detailed diary of his day's activities.

There are some interesting parts in Heroin Diaries. It's worth a read if you are a Crue fan or a fan of the hair metal genre. But only if you've already read The Dirt, which is a thousand times more compelling. HD probably would have worked better as a long magazine article - a feature extensive piece in Rolling Stone or Playboy. But as a full-length book it gets a bit repetitive, the colors are a bit annoying and the comments from Nikki's friends are often bit weird.

With all that said, Sixx is definitely one of the legends of the HMHB era. He is a great songwriter, his band is an all time great, and fans of the era should definitely read this book.

7.
The Big Book of Hair Metal: The Illustrated Oral History of Heavy Metal's Debauched Decade (2014)
Martin Popoff
A must own for anybody who considers themselves a die-hard fan of the hair metal genre. Popoff draws on a lot of his own past interviews with key players of the era. The book is filled with a lot of cool pictures, memorabilia and really gives an impressive time line of the history of HM/HB music.

Popoff does a year-by-year introspect and really tries to give information on the bands that mattered as well as the bands that were around, but barely made a dent in the scene.

8.
Killer Show (2012)
John Barylick
Amazon Description by Author:
"On February 20, 2003, the deadliest rock concert in U.S. history took place at a roadhouse called The Station in West Warwick, Rhode Island. That night, in the few minutes it takes to play a hard-rock standard, the fate of many of the unsuspecting nightclub patrons was determined with awful certainty. The blaze was ignited when pyrotechnics set off by Great White, a 1980s heavy-metal band, lit flammable polyurethane "egg crate" foam sound insulation on the club's walls. In less than 10 minutes, 96 people were dead and 200 more were injured, many catastrophically. The final death toll topped out, three months later, at the eerily unlikely round number of 100.

The story of the fire, its causes, and the legal and human aftermath is one of lives put at risk by petty economic decisions—by a band, club owners, promoters, building inspectors, and product manufacturers. Any one of those decisions, made differently, might have averted the tragedy. Together, however, they reached a fatal critical mass.

Killer Show is the first comprehensive exploration of the chain of events leading up to the fire, the conflagration itself, and the painstaking search for evidence to hold the guilty to account and obtain justice for the victims."

Anyone who has entered an entertainment venue and wondered, "could I get out of here in a hurry?" will identify with concertgoers at The Station. Fans of disaster nonfiction and forensic thrillers will find ample elements of both genres in Killer Show.

9.
Dirty Rocker Boys (2013)
Bobbie Brown, Caroline Ryder

Bobbie Brown and Tawny Kitaen. It's impossible to think about the hair metal genre without bringing up the era's two hottest video vixens. Brown was not only every teenage boy's fantasy woman, but she also had the same control over rock stars and movie stars as well.

If you think Brown's book is going to be vapid and shallow – think again. Dirty Rocker Boys is extremely well written and Brown shows that she is a highly intelligent and thoughtful person. IE: - more than just the pretty face and hot body we all remember.

Bobbie is brutally honest with her story, which is even more crazy and out-of-control than you imagined it would be. She shares her substance issues, affairs with famous rockers and actors and most interestingly (at least to us) her marriage and life with Jani Lane.

Dirty Rocker Boys is an extremely fun and interesting read. We highly recommend it.

10.
Sex, Drugs, Ratt & Roll: My Life in Rock (2013)

Stephen Pearcy, Sam Benjamin
Pearcy's book is really fantastic if you want to learn the history of Mickey Ratt and about Pearcy's younger days and all the sex he's had thanks to being a hair metal legend. But if you are interested in the creative process with Ratt, his relationship and thoughts about Ratt band mates and his opinions on all the band's breakups and changing members, you'll be sorely disappointed.

Sex, Drugs, Ratt & Roll is well written and the non-sex sections are very interesting and make for easy reading. But it could have moved up a notch if Pearcy had left off 50% of the sex talk and added 50 more pages of Ratt behind the scenes stories, studio insights and spilled the dirt on his relationship with band members.

This is a great book about Stephen Pearcy. But Ratt fans will be a little disappointed if they were hoping for more of a Ratt biography.

11.
18 and Life on Skid Row (2016)
Sebastian Bach
Reading 18 and Life on Skid Row is probably similar to an experience of spending a weekend with Sebastian Bach. A roller coaster ride of emotions and thoughts. Some amazing, some crazy, some parts didn't make sense and some of it was annoying.

Bach deserves props for writing the book without a ghostwriter or co-writer. But it's extremely obvious that no editor was used. There are continuity issues, some terrible grammar usage and often the book reads like it was published without having anybody give it a second look.

It was interesting to read about Bach's childhood and strong relationship with his father. The book contains the usual rock star partying stories, lots of drugs, drinking and sex with groupies. Bach spent a lot of time partying with some of the biggest rock stars of the era – most notably Axl Rose. But at times it seems like more bragging than sharing stories.

The biggest bummer of the book was the lack of information and insight about his time in Skid Row and his eventual split from the band. One wonders if he left that alone in hopes of eventually rejoining Skid Row.

All in all, if you are a fan of Skid Row, Bach or the hair metal genre, 18 and Life on Skid Row is an entertaining book. But like partying and having fun on Friday night, remember that Saturday morning brings in a hangover and headache.

12
Tommyland (2004)
Anthony Bozza, Tommy Lee

Like a lot of books in this genre, whether you enjoy Tommyland or not will determine how much you like Tommyland. Tommy fans will love it, those who think Tommy is obnoxious and annoying will hate it. He has parts in the book that are – not kidding - his dick talking. That sums up a lot about this book.

Tommyland goes deep into Tommy's life and childhood, which we found to be extremely interesting. And spends a lot of time lamenting about his past loves – especially Pam Anderson. It's always fascinating to see what kind of childhood our idols had and lives these rock superstars live when they aren't onstage. Dude is an open book – for better or worse. And shares everything.

The penis parts are pretty juvenile and distract from the overall story. But I suppose if you are a huge Tommy Lee fan you might think that it's a funny aspect. You might be grossed out or think parts of this book are pretty juvenile. But you will be entertained.

13
Adrenalized (2014)
Phil Collen, Chris Epting

Phil Collen's book – Adrenalized – pretty much mimics the last 25 years of Def Leppard's career. Safe, by the numbers and nothing controversial.

Like so many other autobiographies this is the Phil Collen life story and not the history of Def Leppard. We learned a lot about his side projects and music background.

There aren't a lot of stories of band debauchery or in the studio secret nuggets. Though Collen seems to know he has to fill one rock star book cliché and he shares a lot of stories about all the women he's bedded. The last chapter is a little out of place, but you'll have to read it to see why.

All in all a decent read. Collen seems like a solid dude and he probably doesn't get as much credit as he should in the rock world. We enjoyed reading Adrenalized.

14.
My Appetite for Destruction: Sex & Drugs & Guns N' Roses (2010)
Steven Adler, Lawrence J. Spagnola
Steven Adler seems like a really fun loving guy who wears his heart on his sleeve. He's a really solid drummer, famous for his hard rock groove and genuinely appears to love pounding the kit – whether it's in front of 50 people at a club or 50,000 fans in a stadium.

Unfortunately though, the title of his book pretty much sums up his career and downfall. Sex & Drugs come before Guns N' Roses. If Stevie had put GnR first on his list he might still be touring with GnR.

Adler's book is a quick and fun read. He gives some cool GnR stories, lets us into his childhood and struggles with addiction. But often Adler deflects blame for his own mishaps and failures to other people or to simple bad luck. He doesn't seem to accept the fact that his career is where it's at because of his life choices.

15.
Tattoos & Tequila: To Hell and Back with One of Rock's Most Notorious Frontmen (2010)
Vince Neil, Mike Sager
We found Neil's book to be a fun read and a pretty good biography about his life and who he is as a person. Whether that is a good thing or not....that's not our place to judge.

There isn't a lot here that Motley Crue fans don't already know. But it is interesting to hear Neil's opinions on various band members and his time in Motley Crue. His parts on his beautiful daughter Skylar are very touching. Neil clearly loved her with all his heart. Losing a child is a tragedy that no parent should have to suffer.

But a lot of the book is Vince trashing numerous people for their shortcomings while not admitting the part he played in any of the wrongdoing. He complains about his ex-wives but doesn't feel bad about cheating on them with groupies and strippers.

Definitely worth a read if you are a Motley fan or HM/HB fan.

16.
American Hair Metal (2006)
Steven Blush
Blush's book is a really fun read. Not an in-depth history of the era, but a book full of fantastic pictures and humorous quotes from the stars that we all grew up listening to and admiring. Blush doesn't just focus on the legends, he also features pictures/stories from the lessor known groups of the era. Nitro is on the cover – enough said.

17, 18
Eddie Trunk's Essential Hard Rock and Heavy Metal Volumes I & II (2011, 2013)
Eddie Trunk
Eddie Trunk has lived the life that most fans can only dream about. He's interviewed and hung out with every hair metal superstar out there. As a fan of hard rock music, metal and hair metal, you probably should own both volumes of Trunk's book. But just know you are not getting in-depth information on the bands we love. You are getting brief info along with Eddie's thoughts (or stories) about the band.

These books aren't rated in our upper echelon of HM/HB books though, as our favorite genre is just a portion of the book's content.

19.
Living Like a Runaway: A Memoir (2014)
Lita Ford

If you want to hear Lita brag about how great and innovative of a guitar player she is and how many guys she slept with – you'll love Living Like a Runaway. If you were hoping to learn more information about the Runaways or with her ongoing feud with her famous ex-husband – you might want to skip it.

Ford is a talented guitar player and no doubt helped break the barrier for other female rock guitar players. But her sense of her contribution to the hard rock world is vastly over inflated.

20.
Tales of a Ratt: Things You Shouldn't Know (2010)
Bobby Blotzer, Jim Clayton
As long as you go in knowing what to expect, Tales of a Ratt is an entertaining read.

The grammar is abysmal. And not just spelling and grammar errors, but Blotzer also misspells other rocker's names. It's also a little hard to keep track of what is going on as Blotzer constantly jumps around from different time periods with no real transition. And he often doesn't supply the ending to a story...but will then repeat the same basic story three chapters later.

If you can get past all that the book feels like you are sitting beside Blotzer at a bar, balls deep into a bottle of Jack Daniels and he is just randomly telling you stories about his life. A lot of it is probably exaggerated, Blotzer clearly has an ego, and he seems pretty bitter about his time in Ratt.

But like I said, if you can get past all that it's sort of an enjoyable book to read. Some of the stories are pretty funny and entertaining.

21.
Rocker's Road: A Journey Through the Fading Days of 80s Metal (2015)
Ben Want
Not the most exciting book we've ever read, but feel it deserves a place on the list as instead of the rock star tales listed above Rocker's

Road is the story of a young musician who traveled to Los Angeles to try and make it.....and didn't.

It's interesting to read about the trials and tribulations of a rocker who didn't go onto become a member of Motley Crue or Poison.

Other Books Worth Checking Out:

GUNS N' ROSES

Guns N' Roses: The Life and Times of a Rock N' Roll Band (2017) Paul Elliott

This GnR biography has slid in a bit under the radar amongst the plethora of GnR books. British rock journalist Paul Elliott has been writing about the band for 30 years and his knowledge of the band really shows. It's refreshing to read a history about the band without having the author's bias towards specific band members bleeding through. Elliott also includes a pretty nice group of pictures.

Reckless Road: Guns N' Roses and the Making of Appetite for Destruction (2008) Marc Canter, Jason Porath

Canter was a friend of the band before they broke big and delivers a book full of amazing pictures of GnR from the early days, as well as stories from the band and people loosely associated with GnR on the Sunset Strip in its heyday.

Last of the Giants: The True Story of Guns N' Roses (2016) Mick Wall

Not a bad book about the legendary band. Wall gives a solid timeline and band history, covering all the major points. It's nice to see Izzy get some coverage and interesting to read what Alan Niven had to say. Nothing really new and exciting here, but a good overview of the band. You can tell that Wall is a huge Axl Rose fan.

Welcome to My Jungle: An Unauthorized Account of How a Regular Guy Like Me Survived Years of Touring with Guns N'

Roses, Pet Wallabies, Crazed ... One of the Greatest Rock Bands of All Time
Craig Duswalt
Duswalt seems like a really nice guy who had a really fun job. But if you bought this book because of the title – Welcome to My Jungle – then you will be sorely disappointed by the content.
Duswalt did spend a couple years working with GnR and no doubt has some great stories to share. Unfortunately in this book, he comes off as more of a public relations staff member of Axl's. Buy this book if you are interested in Duswalt's career – but don't buy it if you are looking for unknown stories about GnR.

Appetite for Dysfunction: A Cautionary Tale (2016)
Vicky Hamilton
A detailed look at Hamilton's life and career. The title of the book is a little misleading, seeming to take advantage of her time with Guns N' Roses. Fans expecting hundreds of pages of inside stories on Axl and Company will be disappointed.
It's an interesting read. A bit of a look at what went on during the Sunset Strip glory days of HM/HB music. But there is also a bit of woe-is-me and you have to wonder how a book gets published with so many typos.

W.A.R. The Unauthorized Biography of William Axl Rose (2008)
Mick Wall
Wall does a great job detailing Axl's younger years and does give some insight on Axl and his fellow GnR band mates during the band's heyday. But you also have to keep in mind that the title is 100% accurate. W.A.R. is an "unauthorized" biography, and it was written by an author who had a falling out with Axl.
So while Wall doesn't sugarcoat or kiss Axl's ass, he also sometimes seems to go a bit far with criticizing the legendary frontman. But you can also tell that Wall did a lot of research into making sure he got the bones of the story correct.

Guns N' Roses FAQ: All That's Left to Know About the Bad Boys of Sunset Strip (2017)
Rich Weidman

Weidman seems to be a fan of the band and is a competent enough writer. This isn't a bad book by any means, but there is nothing new here that GnR fans didn't already know and he does make some factual mistakes. We list it here though as there is a ton of information about GnR.

BON JOVI

Bon Jovi: The Story (2016)
Bryan Reesman
Reesman's book features some great photos and he interacted with the band for the book's text. Hardcore Bon Jovi fans will love this coffee table book. On the downside, a lot of the pictures are from the last decade and there really isn't much meat to the story, it's more of a public relationships piece on why Bon Jovi is so great. There are no "Dirt" type stories.

Jon Bon Jovi: The Biography (2005)
Laura Jackson
Well written, gives a pretty good timeline of Jon Bon Jovi's life. Written more for fans that don't already know JBJ's life story. No sordid gritty details – you can tell the writer is a huge fan of Jon. A bit of a fluff piece, but worth owning if you love Bon Jovi.

Bon Jovi: When We Were Beautiful (2009)
Bon Jovi
Basically a written documentary on the band highlighting how "great" the band is. On the plus side, the pictures are top notch and you get to read insights from all band members. On the downside you can read it in a day and the information isn't really that telling. Basically it's the exact opposite of The Dirt. You can tell the band is trying to protect its image.

If you love Bon Jovi then definitely buy the book. If you aren't a fan of the band then skip it. Some would see the comment and go "duh, it's like that with any band biography" but that's simply not the case. We've read a lot of books about bands/artists that we didn't really personally like, but knew they have lived interesting lives and wanted to read their tales. All the Bon Jovi books are basically just public relations outputs to make sure the band's image stays squeaky clean.

Let it Rock: The Story of Bon Jovi's Slippery When Wet (2014)
Neil Daniels
Daniels churns out rock biographies at the same rate Bon Jovi releases albums! In spite of the name, this book also digs into other albums and time frames of Bon Jovi's career.
If you are a Bon Jovi fan or are interested in how a legendary album was recorded then check it out.

MOTLEY CRUE

This is Gonna Hurt: Music, Photography and Life Through the Distorted Lens of Nikki Sixx (2013)
Nikki Sixx
Only die-hard Nikki Sixx fans will enjoy this book. If you don't like Sixx, you'll like him even less after reading it.

Motley Crue: A Visual History, 1983-2005 (2009)
Neil Zlozower
What you get:
This is a coffee table sized book documenting photographer Neil Zlozower's collection of Motley Crue pics. The pictures are high quality and adequately cover 83-05 as the title says. Photos are typical in the photography studio, staged live performances, actual live performances, and some candid shots. Shout, Theatre, Girls, Dr. Feelgood and New Tattoo are represented. Interspersed are page length commentaries from other photographers, clothing designers, industry types, and Nikki, Vince, and Mick.

Kickstart My Heart: A Motley Crue Day-by-Day (2015)
Martin Popoff
There are some cool pictures and memorabilia items, a well as interesting insights from people not in the band. But if you've read The Dirt and all the autobiographies from band members, there isn't a lot of new information here.

MUTT and DESMOND

We all know who Bon Jovi and Def Leppard are. We know what they look like, sound like, we know the band's history. We know their popular albums from front-to-back and the songs word-for-word.

But if you aren't a total die-hard fan of the bands there are two names you might not be familiar with. And without these two guys, two hair metal legends might not have grown beyond being opening acts or small arena level bands.

Desmond Child
From Livin' La Vida Loca to I Hate Myself For Loving You

Whatever your favorite Bon Jovi song is, Child most likely had a hand in writing it. He collaborated with the band on 28 different tunes, including their biggest and most legendary hits.

You Give Love a Bad Name – check.
Livin' on a Prayer – check.
Bad Medicine – check.
Keep the Faith – check.
Born to be My Baby – check.
Hearts Breaking Even – check.
And the list continues to include 22 other classic songs.

Child was more than just a scribe for the New Jersey rockers. He is also a master songwriter for many different artists in several different genres. In the rock world, he has written hits for Aerosmith (Dude Looks Like a Lady, Crazy and What it Takes), Poison by Alice Cooper, Lovin' You's a Dirty Job and Givin' Yourself Away by Ratt and several songs for Kiss, including I Was Made for Loving You, Heaven's on Fire and Let's Put the X in Sex.

Child also wrote songs for Vince Neil and Sebastian Bach.

Outside of the genre, Child wrote hit songs for artists like Ricky Martin, Cher, Joan Jett, Dream Theatre, Selena Gomez and Kelly Clarkson. He is in the Songwriters Hall of Fame, earning that honor after writing more than 70 songs that have charted on the Billboard top 40. His songs have appeared on albums that have sold more than 300 million copies.

Child got his first big break in 1979 when he co-wrote the song I Was Made for Loving You for Kiss on their Dynasty album. To this day, it still ranks as one of the band's most successful songs.

Paul Stanley passed Child's number and information on to fellow musicians Jon Bon Jovi and Richie Sambora. Child reportedly joined JBJ and Sambora in the basement of Richie's parent's house. The three quickly penned You Give Love a Bad Name which would go on to become Bon Jovi's first number one hit. Two more number one smashes soon followed – Livin' on a Prayer and Bad Medicine – and the rest is history.

"The Desmond you don't know about," says Jon Bon Jovi, "is the one who not only taught me the next level of songwriting, but so many of the true aspects of friendship: truth, honor and loyalty. We've been through a lot together – the ups and the downs...and the ups again." (Desmond Child Wikipedia Page).

With Child's help, Bon Jovi is considered one of the Mt. Rushmore artists of the hair metal genre. Without his help they possibly fall down to the LA Guns and Winger level.

The Success of Def Leppard

While Bon Jovi was still able to write, record and release several billboard hits and albums on their own merits, Mutt Lange has been the engine behind the Def Leppard train of success.

Lange's career has been off the charts. Unparalleled in the industry, Lange might be the most successful writer/producer in music history.

Def Leppard released two of the most iconic rock albums in music history: *Pyromania* in 1983, followed up by *Hysteria* in 1987.

Pyromania was one of the albums that really kicked off the hair metal era and its 10-million plus in sales has landed it as many rock fans favorite DL album. Lange co-wrote every song on the album, including classics like Photograph and Rock of Ages.

Lange secured his role as the ultimate hair metal songwriter on Leppard's follow-up album *Hysteria*. Lange was scheduled to produce *Hysteria* but had to drop out do to physical exhaustion. DL brought another producer on but the band couldn't ever get on the same page with the new guy. So Lange came back to save the day. And did he ever. Lange co-wrote every song on *Hysteria*, which went on to sell more than 25 million copies. Key songs include Pour Some Sugar on Me and the hit ballads Love Bites and the title track Hysteria.

Lange also produced two more Def Leppard albums. The critically acclaimed *High' N' Dry* (1981) and *Adrenalize* (also co-wrote most songs) in 1992, which sold several million copies and went to number one on the Billboard album charts. Lange co-wrote a couple songs for the 1999 album *Euphoria*, including the song Promises which went to #1 on the rock charts.

History

Lange received his big break while working with AC/DC. In 1979 the band wasn't happy with their current producer so they brought Lange in to see what he could do. Not only did he produce an album generally considered a rock masterpiece, but Lange also helped singer Bon Scott improve his studio vocals. And, just for fun, Lange also sang backup on several songs. *Highway to Hell* went on to sell approximately 10 million copies and was the band's breakthrough album.

Unfortunately, Scott ended up passing away after the album's release. AC/DC decided to carry on, hiring new singer Brian Johnson and bringing Lange back into the studio for the follow-up to *Highway to Hell*.

Lange and the Young brothers turned their game up to even a higher level. Lange worked his studio magic with Johnson's vocals and pushed the rest of the band to create the best album they were capable of writing and recording. The result? *Back in Black*, released in 1980, which went on to sell more than 50 million copies and is the 2nd highest selling album of all time.

Lange produced one more album for the Australian rockers, their 1981 release – *For Those About to Rock* – which went on to occupy the number one album spot on Billboard. In spite of the overwhelming success that Lange brought to the band, AC/DC chose to go with other producers for the rest of their career, wanting to get back to the more "raw" sound the band had before Lange helped turned them into a more polished sounding hard rock band. AC/DC have released eight albums since moving on from Lange. Those eight albums combined sales are less than *Back in Black's* number of albums sold.

Lange's work with Def Leppard and AC/DC is enough to earn him a spot in the Rock and Roll Hall of Fame – as a writer and producer. But Lange proved he wasn't just a hard rock savant.

Lange's third member of his mighty trilogy is country singer Shania Twain. He produced and co-wrote her 1997 album *Come On Over*, which turned into the top selling country music album of all time, top selling studio album by a female with 40 million copies, the top selling album of the 1990s and the 9th best selling album in US history.

Lange also produced and co-wrote Twain's 1995 album *The Woman In Me* that sold more than 20 million copies. And 2002's *Up* which sold more than 15 million copies.

Not only did Lange work on one of the best hair metal albums of all time, one of the best rock albums of all time, and one of the best country albums of all time, but he also wrote and produced songs/albums for such artists as:
- Bryan Adams (co-wrote I Do It For You – which spent 16 weeks at #1 on the UK Billboard chart)

- Foreigner – 4
- The Cars – Heartbeat City
- Billy Ocean
- Michael Bolton
- Nickelback
- Maroon 5 – Hands All Over
- Muse - Drones
- Dionne Warwick
- Tina Turner – What's Love Got to Do With It
- Celine Dion
- Backstreet Boys – Backstreet's Back and Millennium
- Britney Spears – Oops!...I Did It Again
- Lady Gaga – Born This Way

Some of the most popular songs Lange wrote or co-work include:
*All For Love – Rod Stewart/Sting/Bryan Adams
*It's Gotta Be You – Backstreet Boys
*Said I Loved You But I Lied – Michael Bolton
*All I Wanna do Is Make Love To You – Heart
*Do You Believe in Love – Huey Lewis and the News
*Lovin' Every Minute of It – Loverboy
*Who Are You – Carrie Underwood
*Get Out of My Dreams, Get Into My Car – Billy Ocean

Lange has five Grammy Awards on his resume.

DUDES WHO DESERVE MORE CREDIT

While lead singers get all the glory and adoration, below we've listed band members that have been instrumental to their band's success. Some have received more recognition than others, but this is the list of the dudes who were the real heart and soul of their bands.

Slash and Izzy - Guns N' Roses
It's hard to make your mark when the most high profile singer in the business - Axl Rose - fronts your band. But for Guns N' Roses, there is no denying the important of guitar players Slash and Izzy Stradlin.

Slash is obviously recognized as a guitar God not just in the hair metal genre, but in relation to all guitar players in rock history. He has written and shared numerous iconic guitar riffs and solos, while also co-writing several GnR classics like "You're Crazy", "Civil War", "Coma" and "Perfect Crime."

Izzy is a decent guitar player, but his main contribution to GnR comes from his impressive song-writing skills. Stradlin wrote or is listed as a co-writer on more than half of GnR's pre-Chinese Democracy catalog. His biggest hits include "Used to Love Her", "Don't Cry" and "You Could Be Mine".

Paul Gilbert and Billy Sheehan – Mr. Big

Talent wise it doesn't get much better than Mr. Big's Gilbert and Sheehan. Gilbert is a guitar virtuoso, easily one of the five best players in the genre. He co-wrote about half of Mr. Big's catalog, including being the sole writer of the great song "Green Tinted Sixties Minds".

Sheehan is also one of the best bass players in HM/HB genre's history. Like Gilbert, he also is listed as co-writer on about half of Mr. Big's song catalog.

Nikki Sixx – Motley Crue

Sixx is obviously one of the most well known figures in Hair Metal history. But the remarkable part is that his bass playing is the lowest ranked part of his legendary status.

Sixx wrote or co-wrote all of Motley's catalog. He has essentially been the band's agent, promoter, manager, public relations agent, etc. Sixx is essentially the engine that drove Motley Crue to worldwide success. Without Sixx there wouldn't have been a Motley Crue.

DiMartini/Crosby

Stephen Pearcy has that mistakable voice. But many think the real heart and soul of Ratt was the guitar duo of Warren DeMartini and Robbin Crosby. DiMartini is a monster on the guitar, one of the best shredders of the genre. Crosby teamed up with DiMartini to give Ratt a potent guitar-attack, as he was also an upper tier lead player.

The Ratt duo were also proficient writers. The two have co-writing credits on the majority of Ratt's songs – especially all the hits. Crosby on "Round and Round", "Wanted Man", "Lay it Down" and "Body Talk". DiMartini also on "Round and Round" and "Lay it Down" as well as "Slip of the Lip", "Way Cool Jr." and "Loving You's a Dirty Job".

Donnie Purnell

Purnell was the main songwriter for Kix until his falling out with the band in the mid-90s. Bass player Purnell wrote or co-wrote all of the band's hits, including Blow My Fuse, Cold Blood and Don't Close Your Eyes.

Purnell also co-produced the band's most successful album – Blow My Fuse.

Steve Clark

A lot of fans feel like Def Leppard lost their balls as a hard rock band after guitar player Clark passed away.

Clark was an amazing guitar player, able to effortlessly switch back from being lead or rhythm. Clark was also an excellent songwriter, sharing co-writing credits on 90% of all Def Leppard songs through the *Hysteria* album, including all the band's major hits.

Bolan and Sabo

Sebastian Bach has that magical voice. But the guys who wrote the songs that propelled Skid Row to stardom were bass player Rachel Bolan and guitar player Dave Sabo.

Bolan wrote or co-wrote virtually every Skid Row song, including all the classics: "Youth Gone Wild", "I Remember You", "Monkey Business" and "18 and Life". Bolan, along with being an accomplished musician and writer, has also produced several songs and albums for other bands. Sabo doesn't have quite the same number as writing credits as Bolan, but he does own the sole writing credit on "Breakin' Down", which is the best Skid Row song released since the band's *Slave to the Grind* album.

Fred Coury

Coury is the top-ranked drummer on the list. While most known for his drumming and producing skills with Cinderella, Coury has also played with Guns N' Roses and Night Ranger, as well as produced songs and albums for numerous other bands.

Coury is also an award-winning composure, scoring for TV series like The Night Shift and The Wall.

Mark Kendall

Kendall has done it all for Great White. He helped start the band, has co-wrote the majority of their songs, co-produce the *Once Bitten* album and is a top-notch guitar player.

Dana Strum

While not being the most liked musician in the genre, bass player Strum has had a remarkable career. In his early days, he has been credited with introducing both Randy Rhoads and Jake E Lee to Ozzy.

Strum then joined the Vinnie Vincent Invasion and was listed as co-producer for both the band's albums. Joined Mark Slaughter in the band Slaughter, and was a co-writer on 100% of the band's first three albums, which he also co-produced.

Strum has also played with the Vince Neil band, as well as producing albums for other artists, most notably Kik Tracee's 1991 *No Rules*.

Gilby Clarke

To a lot of people, Gilby is that dude who replaced Izzy Stradlin in GnR. But for those of us in the know, the GnR gig was just 1% of Clarke's career!

Gilby's resume is extremely impressive. He has played with, worked with or produced albums/songs with: Guns N' Roses, Heart, Slash's Snakepit, Nancy Sinatra, LA Guns and virtually ever other hair metal star from the late 80s and early 90s.

Honorable Mention:

George Lynch: legendary guitar player and co-wrote a lot of Dokken's discography. Also the driving force behind the critically acclaimed Lynch Mob.

Jeff Pilson: Co-wrote almost every song for Dokken. Wrote "Dream Warriors" with George Lynch. Great backup singer, great piano player, and played acoustic guitar on some Dokken songs.

Frank Hannon: phenomenal guitar player, co-wrote most of Tesla's popular material.

John Sykes: Writing credits on almost every song of Whitesnake's 1987 signature album. Also wrote, produced and played lead guitar on three blue Murder albums. Very underrated talent.

Richie Sambora: Bon Jovi was more than just their lead singer. Sambora is a well-respected guitar player, but he also co-wrote and helped produced a number of Bon Jovi legendary songs and albums. Had three solo albums that he wrote and produced.

Reb Beach: extremely versatile guitar player. There is a reason that he has been chosen to play with Winger, Dokken. Danger Danger and Whitesnake, Twisted Sister as well as Fiona and The Bee Gees.

Keri Kelli: Dude has played in more well known bands than anybody in the genre. Has played with: Pretty Boy Floyd, Slash's Snakepit, Shameless, Warrant, Jani Lane solo, L.A. Guns, Big Bang Babies, Alice Cooper, Adler's Appetite, Stephen Pearcy solo, Tuff and Night Ranger.

Bruno Ravel/Steve West: wrote almost all of Danger Danger's songs. Both have producing credits as well as being very talented musicians. And for fun, they also sang backup vocals on

THE LISTS

Below are lists of what I feel are the top 1,000 songs and 350 albums from the hair metal / hair band music era.

I know you won't fully agree with my lists….nobody will agree 100% with it (or with any "best of" list. I really just want you to understand that this isn't a list of my 1,000 favorite songs and 350 favorite albums. These lists took two years to put together. They were constantly being revised and revamped. A couple times I thought I was finished, but then randomly discovered a new band that put out an album in the early 90s that had a really great song it. It was a never ending cycle and in all honesty, I could probably keep doing deep research, discovering more bands, and revising the lists. But at some point I had to stop.

Let me stress this, as people love to trash any list made regarding music. "This list is crap, song X should have been number 27 and where is song Y?" People tend to compare lists to "their" favorite song ranking. These lists are NOT that. These lists aren't my personal favorite song lists.

I used a bunch of criteria to come up the rankings. Billboard success – how many copies did the album sell, how high did the individual song rank on the charts? How long did the song/album stay ranked? I looked at other charts, like Dial MTV or how the song/album did on Headbanger's Ball. I looked at rock music critic's lists. How did Rolling Stone rank the albums? How iconic was the song? How iconic was the album or band? Welcome to the Jungle is played at every major sporting event in the world – that means something. How "good" is the actual song – was it just thrown together to cash in on the popularity of hair bands? Or is the band filled with upper level musicians and the songs were clearly worked on and crafted to perfection?

I know you won't agree 100% with them…but I hope you do respect the time and effort that went into me trying to get them as accurate as possible.

Top Rock Songs
1. Welcome to the Jungle – Guns N' Roses (Appetite for Destruction, 1987)
2. Photograph – Def Leppard (Pyromania, 1983)

3. Cum on Feel the Noize – Quiet Riot (Metal Health, 1983)
4. Round and Round – Ratt (Out of the Cellar, 1984)
5. Rock You Like a Hurricane – Scorpions (Love at First Sting, 1984)
6. Livin' on a Prayer – Bon Jovi (Slippery When Wet, 1986)
7. Pour Some Sugar on Me – Def Leppard (Hysteria, 1987)
8. 18 and Life – Skid Row (Skid Row, 1989)
9. Still of the Night – Whitesnake (Whitesnake, 1987)
10. Shout at the Devil – Motley Crue (Shout at the Devil, 1983)
11. Smooth Up in Ya – BulletBoys (BulletBoys, 1988)
12. Cherry Pie – Warrant (Cherry Pie, 1990)
13. Dr. Feelgood – Motley Crue (Dr. Feelgood, 1989)
14. Sweet Child O' Mine – Guns N' Roses (Appetite for Destruction, 1987)
15. Youth Gone Wild – Skid Row (Skid Row, 1989)
16. Cold Blood – Kix (Blow My Fuse, 1988)
17. Electric Gypsy – L.A. Guns (L.A. Guns, 1988)
18. Rock of Ages – Def Leppard (Pyromania, 1983)
19. Breaking the Chains – Dokken (Breaking the Chains, 1981/83)
20. Let it Go – Def Leppard (High 'n' Dry, 1981)
21. You Give Love a Bad Name – Bon Jovi (Slippery When Wet, 1986)
22. Helluvatime – Slik Toxik (Doin' the Nasty, 1992)
23. Rock Me – Great White (Once Bitten, 1987)
24. Looks That Kill – Motley Crue (Shout at the Devil, 1983)
25. Up All Night – Slaughter (Stick it to Ya, 1990)
26. Metal Health – Quiet Riot (Metal Health, 1983)
27. Uncle Tom's Cabin – Warrant (Cherry Pie, 1990)
28. Girls, Girls, Girls – Motley Crue (Girls, Girls, Girls, 1987)
29. In My Dreams – Dokken (Under Lock and Key, 1985)
30. Nothing but a Good Time – Poison (Open Up and Say...Ahh!, 1988)
31. Shake Me – Cinderella (Night Songs, 1986)
32. Talk Dirty to Me – Poison (Look What the Cat Dragged In, 1986)
33. Wild Side – Motley Crue (Girls, Girls, Girls, 1987)
34. Don't Go Away Mad – Motley Crue (Dr. Feelgood, 1989)
35. Gypsy Road – Cinderella (Long Cold Winter, 1988)
36. You Could Be Mine – Guns N' Roses (Use Your Illusion II, 1991)
37. Bad Medicine – Bon Jovi (New Jersey, 1988)
38. One More Reason – L.A. Guns (L.A. Guns, 1988)
39. Live Wire – Motley Crue (Too Fast for Love, 1981/82)
40. Fool For Your Loving – Whitesnake (Ready an' Willing, 1980)
41. Hollywood – Junkyard (Junkyard, 1989)
42. Foolin' – Def Leppard (Pyromania, 1983)
43. Kickstart My Heart – Motley Crue (Dr. Feelgood, 1989)

44. Monkey Business – Skid Row (Slave to the Grind, 1991)
45. Once Bitten, Twice Shy – Great White (Twice Shy, 1989)
46. Lay it Down – Ratt (Invasion of Your Privacy, 1985)
47. Down Boys – Warrant (Dirty Rotten Filthy Stinking Rich, 1989)
48. We're Not Gonna Take It – Twisted Sister (Stay Hungry, 1984)
49. Little Suzi – Tesla (Mechanical Resonance, 1986)
50. Dream Warriors – Dokken (Back for the Attack, 1987)
51. Too Fast for Love – Motley Crue (Too Fast for Love, 1981/82)
52. Someone Like You – Bang Tango (Psycho Café, 1989)
53. You're Invited (But Your Friend Can't Come) Vince Neil (Exposed, 1993)
54. Wait – White Lion (Pride, 1987)
55. New Thing – Enuff Z'Nuff (Enuff Z'Nuff, 1989)
56. Sleeping My Day Away – D-A-D (No Fuel for the Pilgrims, 1989)
57. Walkin' Shoes – Tora Tora (Surprise Attack, 1989)
58. Shelter Me – Cinderella (Heartbreak Station, 1990)
59. Paradise City – Guns N' Roses (Appetite for Destruction, 1987)
60. Bang Goes the Bell – Babylon A.D. (Babylon A.D., 1989)
61. Signs – Tesla (Five Man Acoustical Jam, 1990)
62. Broken Heart – White Lion (Fight to Survive, 1985)
63. Never Enough – L.A. Guns (Cocked & Loaded, 1989)
64. Somebody Save Me – Cinderella (Night Songs, 1986)
65. You're in Love – Ratt (Invasion of Your Privacy, 1985)
66. The Final Countdown – Europe (The Final Countdown, 1986)
67. These Days – Bon Jovi (These Days, 1995)
68. Slip of the Lip – Ratt (Dancing Undercover, 1986)
69. Too Young to Fall in Love – Motley Crue (Shout at the Devil, 1983)
70. Bathroom Wall – Faster Pussycat (Faster Pussycat, 1987)
71. Lady Red Light – Great White (Once Bitten, 1987)
72. Smokin' in the Boy's Room – Motley Crue (Theatre of Pain, 1985)
73. Too Late for Love – Def Leppard (Pyromania, 1983)
74. Piece of Me – Skid Row (Skid Row, 1989)
75. Beat the Bullet – Vain (No Respect, 1989)
76. It's Not Love – Dokken (Under Lock and Key, 1985)
77. Wait for You – Bonham (The Disregard of Timekeeping, 1989)
78. The Hunter – Dokken (Under Lock and Key, 1985)
79. Naughty Naughty – Danger Danger (Danger Danger, 1989)
80. Caught in a Dream – Tesla (Into the Now, 2004)
81. Don't Treat Me Bad – FireHouse (FireHouse, 1990)
82. Mr. Rainmaker – Warrant (Cherry Pie, 1990)
83. Slave to the Grind – Skid Row (Slave to the Grind, 1991)
84. Heaven Sent – Dokken (Back for the Attack, 1987)

85. Scared – Dangerous Toys (Dangerous Toys, 1989)
86. Runaway – Bon Jovi (Bon Jovi, 1984)
87. Come Along – Salty Dog (Every Dog has its Day, 1990)
88. Keep the Faith – Bon Jovi (Keep the Faith, 1992)
89. Stir it Up – Tesla (Psychotic Supper, 1991)
90. Bang Bang – Danger Danger (Danger Danger, 1989)
91. Need Your Lovin' – Tesla (Bust a Nut, 1994)
92. Simple Man – Junkyard (Junkyard, 1989)
93. I Want a Woman – Ratt (Reach For the Sky, 1988)
94. Teas'n Pleas'n – Dangerous Toys (Dangerous Toys, 1989)
95. Screamin' for More – Dangerous Toys (Pissed, 1994)
96. Civil War – Guns N' Roses (Use Your Illusion II, 1991)
97. On Your Knees – Great White (Out of the Night, 1983)
98. Say What You Will – Fastway (Fastway, 1983)
99. Modern Day Cowboy – Tesla (Mechanical Resonance, 1986)
100.   Lady Strange – Def Leppard (High 'n' Dry, 1981)
101.   Thin Disguise – Warrant – (Best Of, 1996)
102.   Slow an' Easy – Whitesnake (Slide It In, 1984)
103.   Nightrain – Guns N' Roses (Appetite for Destruction, 1987)
104.   Mista Bone – Great White (Twice Shy, 1989)
105.   You Can't Stop Rock 'n' Roll Twisted Sister (You Can't Stop
     Rock 'n' Roll, 1983)
106.   Back for More – Ratt (Out of the Cellar, 1984)
107.   Fly High Michelle – Enuff Z'Nuff (Enuff Z'Nuff, 1989)
108.   Rock! Rock! (Till You Drop) – Def Leppard (Pyromania,
     1983)
109.   Shake & Tumble – FireHouse (FireHouse, 1990)
110.   Paris is Burning – Dokken (Breaking the Chains, 1981/83)
111.   Kiss Me Deadly – Lita Ford (Lita, 1988)
112.   Boulevard of Broken Dreams – Hanoi Rocks - (Two Steps
     From the Move, 1984)
113.   Slide It In – Whitesnake – (Slide It In, 1984)
114.   The Hole in My Wall – Warrant (Dog Eat Dog, 1992)
115.   Wicked Sensation – Lynch Mob (Wicked Sensation, 1990)
116.   Into the Fire – Dokken – (Tooth and Nail, 1984)
117.   Way Cool Jr. – Ratt (Reach for the Sky, 1988)
118.   Someone Special – Hardcore Superstar (It's Only Rock 'n'
     Roll, 1998)
119.   It's Over Now – L.A. Guns – Hollywood Vampires, 1991
120.   S.O.S. – Motley Crue (Dr. Feelgood, 1989)
121.   Wild in the Streets – Bon Jovi (Slippery When Wet, 1986)
122.   No Respect – Vain (No Regrets, 1989)

123.   For the Love of Money – Bulletboys (BulletBoys, 1988)
124.   Seventeen – Winger (Winger, 1988)
125.   Blow My Fuse – Kix (Blow My Fuse, 1988)
126.   Summer Song – Joey C. Jones (Melodies for the Masses, 2006)
127.   Better – Guns N' Roses (Chinese Democracy, 2008)
128.   Sweet Asylum – Slik Toxik (Doin' the Nasty, 1992)
129.   Little Fighter – White Lion (Big Game, 1989)
130.   Another Bad Day – Vince Neil (Tattoos & Tequila, 2010)
131.   Wanted Man – Ratt (Out of the Cellar, 1984)
132.   Queen of the Nile – Dangerous Toys (Dangerous Toys, 1989)
133.   It's Not Enough – Tom Keifer (The Way Life Goes, 2013)
134.   Big Guns – Skid Row (Skid Row, 1989)
135.   Rhythm of Love – Scorpions (Savage Amusement, 1988)
136.   Get it On – Kingdom Come (Kingdom Come, 1988)
137.   Rocket Queen – Guns N' Roses (Appetite for Destruction, 1987)
138.   Doesn't Matter – Killer Dwarfs (Dirty Weapons, 1990)
139.   Do You Like It – Kingdom Come (In Your Face, 1989)
140.   Passion Rules the Game – Scorpions (Savage Amusement, 1988)
141.   Mad About You – Slaughter (Stick It To Ya, 1990)
142.   Out of the Night – Great White (Out of the Night, 1983)
143.   Sex Action – LA Guns (L.A. Guns, 1988)
144.   Your Momma Won't Know Pretty Boy Floyd (Leather Boyz with Electric Toyz, 1989)
145.   Dance – Ratt (Dancing Undercover, 1986)
146.   Lay Your Hands on Me – Bon Jovi (New Jersey, 1988)
147.   It's My Life – Bon Jovi (Crush, 2000)
148.   Best of Me – Ratt (Infestation, 2010)
149.   Givin' Yourself Away – Ratt (Detonator, 1990)
150.   Primal Scream – Motley Crue (Decade of Decadence, 1991)
151.   Knockin' On Heaven's Door – GNR (Days of Thunder 1990, Use Your Illusion 1991)
152.   Face – Warrant (Under the Influence, 2001)
153.   Green-Tinted Sixties Mind – Mr. Big (Lean Into It, 1991)
154.   Girl Nation – D-A-D (No Fuel Left for the Pilgrims, 1989)
155.   Lovin' You's a Dirty Job – Ratt (Detonator, 1990)
156.   Edge of a Broken Heart – Vixen (Vixen, 1988)
157.   Kiss My Love Goodbye – L.A. Guns (Hollywood Vampire, 1991)

158.   I Wanna be Your Man – L.A. Guns (Cocked and Loaded, 1989)

159.   Edison's Medicine – Tesla (Psychotic Supper, 1991)

160.   Poison Ivy – Faster Pussycat (Wake Me When It's Over, 1989)

161.   Rock the Night – Europe (The Final Countdown, 1986)

162.   Don't You Cry – L.A. Guns (Waking the Dead, 2002)

163.   Bad Seamstress Blues – Cinderella (Long Cold Winter, 1988)

164.   Body Talk – Ratt (Dancing Undercover, 1986)

165.   Bitter Pill – Motley Crue (Greatest Hits, 1998)

166.   I Wanna Be With You – Pretty Boy Floyd (Leather Boyz with Electric Toyz, 1989)

167.   I Do U – KINGOFTHEHILL (KINGOFTHEHILL, 1991)

168.   Getting' Better – Tesla (Mechanical Resonance, 1986)

169.   If That's What it Takes – Mr. Big (Hey Man, 1996)

170.   Armageddon It – Def Leppard (Hysteria, 1987)

171.   Girlschool – Britny Fox (Britny Fox, 1988)

172.   I'm With You – Bon Jovi (What About Now, 2013)

173.   Boyz Are Gonna Rock – Vinnie Vincent Invasion (Vinnie Vincent Invasion, 1986)

174.   Lay Down Your Love – Whitesnake (Good to be Bad, 2008)

175.   Hungry – Winger (Winger, 1988)

176.   Fallen Angel – Poison (Open Up and Say...Ahh!, 1988)

177.   Roll the Dice – Wild Boyz (Unleashed!, 1991)

178.   Night Songs – Cinderella (Night Songs, 1986)

179.   Wild America – Tora Tora (Wild America, 1992)

180.   Waiting for the Big One – Femme Fatale (Femme Fatale, 1988)

181.   Yesterdays – Guns N' Roses (Use Your Illusion II, 1991)

182.   Gotta Go – Kingdom Come (In Your Face, 1989)

183.   Tell Me – White Lion (Pride, 1987)

184.   Guilty – Tora Tora (Surprise Attack, 1989)

185.   The Last Mile – Cinderella (Long Cold Winter, 1988)

186.   Hooligan's Holiday – Motley Crue (Motley Crue, 1994)

187.   Riot Act – Skid Row (Slave to the Grind, 1991)

188.   Dirty Love – Thunder (Backstreet Symphony, 1990)

189.   Can't Shake It – Great White (Hooked, 1991)

190.   Ride the Wind – Poison (Flesh & Blood, 1990)

191.   The Way it Is – Tesla (The Great Radio Controversy, 1989)

192.   Beat the Bullet – Danger Danger (Screw It, 1991)

193.   Angel N U – Dangerous Toys (Hellacious Acres, 1991)

194. Falling In and Out of Love – Femme Fatale (Femme Fatale, 1988)
195. Ultraphobic – Warrant (Ultraphobic, 1995)
196. Don't Blame it on Love – Danger Danger (Screw It, 1991)
197. Sail Away – Great White – (Sail Away, 1994)
198. Who's Watching You – Vain (No Respect, 1989)
199. Can't Take My Eyes Off You – Dirty Looks (Cool From the Wire, 1988)
200. Searchin' – Slaughter (Fear No Evil, 1995)
201. Hearts Breaking Even – Bon Jovi (These Days, 1995)
202. Forever More – Tesla (Forever More, 2008)
203. Pretty Tied Up – Guns N' Roses (Use Your Illusion II, 1991)
204. Bag of Bones – Europe (Bag of Bones, 2012)
205. Desert Moon – Great White (Hooked, 1991)
206. I Don't Mind – Great White (Rising, 2009)
207. Stained Glass Heart – Michael Monroe (Horns and Halos, 2013)
208. In and Out of Love – Bon Jovi (7800 Fahrenheit, 1985)
209. Live and Let Die – Guns N' Roses (Use Your Illusion I, 1991)
210. Unchain the Night – Dokken (Lock and Key, 1985)
211. Blue Island – Enuff Z'Nuff (Strength, 1991)
212. So Divine – Tesla (Simplicity, 2014)
213. TWAT – Guns N' Roses (Chinese Democracy, 2008)
214. Turn Up the Radio – Autograph – (Sign in Please, 1984)
215. If That's What it Takes – Bon Jovi (These Days, 1995)
216. Big City Nights – Scorpions (Love at First String, 1984)
217. Moonshine – Hardcore Superstar (Split Your Lip, 2010)
218. Tooth and Nail – Dokken (Tooth and Nail, 1984)
219. As Good as it Gets – Ratt (Infestation, 2010)
220. Everyday – Bon Jovi (Bounce, 2002)
221. I Wanna Rock - Twisted Sister (Stay Hungry, 1984)
222. It's So Easy - Guns N' Roses (Appetite for Destruction, 1987)
223. Mama Weer All Crazee Now – Quiet Riot (Condition Critical, 1984)
224. Between You and Me – D-A-D (Soft Dogs, 2002)
225. Addicted to That Rush – Mr. Big (Mr. Big, 1989)
226. We Don't Celebrate Sundays – Hardcore Superstar (Hardcore Superstar, 2005)
227. Give Me All Your Love – Whitesnake (Whitesnake, 1987)
228. She Don't Know Me – Bon Jovi – (Bon Jovi, 1984)
229. Radar Love – White Lion (Big Game, 1989)
230. What Kind of Man – KINGOFTHEHILL (Unreleased, 2005)

231.   Tease Me Please Me – Scorpions (Crazy World, 1990)
232.   Just Got Lucky – Dokken (Tooth and Nail, 1984)
233.   If I Die Tomorrow – Motley Crue (Red, White & Crue, 2005)
234.   Blooze – Junkyard (Junkyard, 1989)
235.   All Lips N' Hips – Electric Boys (Funk-O-Metal Carpet Ride, 1989)
236.   Can You Hear the Wind Blow – Whitesnake (Good To Be Bad, 2008)
237.   Big Talk – Warrant (Dirty Rotten Filthy Stinking Rich, 1989)
238.   Out with the Boys – White Lion (Main Attraction, 1991)
239.   My Michelle – Guns N' Roses (Appetite for Destruction, 1987)
240.   Ain't No Shame – Great White (Can't Get There From Here, 1999)
241.   2nd Street – Tesla (Twisted Wires & The Acoustic Sessions, 2011)
242.   Inside Out – XYZ (XYZ, 1989)
243.   Nobody Else – Warrant – (Belly to Belly, 1996)
244.   Living a Lie – Don Dokken (Up From the Ashes, 1990)
245.   Women – Def Leppard (Hysteria, 1987)
246.   All the Time in the World – Junkyard (Sixes, Sevens, and Nines, 1991)
247.   Superstitious – Europe (Out of this World, 1988)
248.   Don't Count Me Out – Bang Tango (Love After Death, 1994)
249.   Empty Heads – D-A-D (Simpatico, 1997)
250.   Misunderstood – Motley Crue (Motley Crue, 1994)
251.   Save Her – Crashdiet (Generation Wild, 2010)
252.   Still I'm Glad – Hardcore Superstar (No Regrets, 2003)
253.   Hang Tough – Tesla (The Great Radio Controversy, 1989)
254.   Still Kickin' – Danger Danger (Cockroach, 2001)
255.   Lovin' a Girl Like You – Danger Danger (Rare Cuts, 2003)
256.   Love Made Me – Vixen (Vixen, 1988)
257.   Call it What You Want – Tesla (Psychotic Summer, 1991)
258.   Bad Boys – Whitesnake (Whitesnake, 1987)
259.   The Devil Made Me Do It – L.A. Guns (The Missing Peace, 2017)
260.   You're Gone – Kix (Rock Your Face Off, 2014)
261.   Tonight – Def Leppard (Adrenalize, 1992)
262.   We Don't Run – Bon Jovi (Burning Bridges, 2015)
263.   All Over Now – Great White (Once Bitten, 1987)
264.   No Easy Way Out – Roxx Gang (Things You've Never Done Before, 1988)

265.   Edge of a Broken Heart – Bon Jovi (Disorderlies, 1987)
266.   Words Can't Explain – Tesla (Into the Now, 2004)
267.   City of Angeles – L.A. Guns (Waking the Dead, 2002)
268.   Something for You – Great White (Elated, 2012)
269.   Letter to a Friend – Warrant – (Belly to Belly, 1996)
270.   Touch the Sky - Hardcore Superstar (HCSS, 2015)
271.   That Time of Year – Vinnie Vincent Invasion (All Systems Go, 1988)
272.   Dreamin' in a Casket – Hardcore Superstar (Dreamin' in a Casket, 2007)
273.   Gonna Get Ready – Europe (Last Look at Eden, 2009)
274.   We are the Ones to Fall – Santa Cruz (Santa Cruz, 2015)
275.   Rocket – Def Leppard (Hysteria, 1987)
276.   Reckless Life – Guns N' Roses (Lies, 1988)
277.   Better Off Without U – Shameless (Famous 4 Madness, 2007)
278.   Liberation – Hardcore Superstar (Bad Sneakers and a Pina Colada, 2000)
279.   Please Me Tease Me – Shanghai (Take Another Bite, 2000)
280.   Ready to Believe – Electric Boys (Freefallin, 1994)
281.   Born to be My Baby – Bon Jovi (New Jersey, 1988)
282.   Muse – Hell in the Club (Devil on My Shoulder, 2014)
283.   Mama's Fool – Tesla (Bust a Nut, 1994)
284.   Used to Love Her – Guns N' Roses (Lies, 1988)
285.   Back to the Rhythm – Great White (Back to the Rhythm, 2007)
286.   Honey Tongue – Hardcore Superstar (No Regrets, 2003)
287.   Rollin' Stoned – Great White (Can't Get There From Here, 1999)
288.   What's Going On –Beggars & Thieves (Look What You Create, 1997)
289.   Shades of Grey – Hardcore Superstar (Beg For It, 2009)
290.   Why Ain't I Bleeding – L.A. Guns (Vicious Circle, 1994)
291.   Babylon's Burning – Babylon Bombs (Babylon's Burning, 2009)
292.   Love Me with Your Top Down – Kix (Rock Your Face Off, 2014)
293.   Standing on the Outside – Dokken (Lightning Strikes Again, 2008)
294.   Mine All Mine – Wig Wam (667 The Neighbour of the Beast, 2004)
295.   Is it Love – Paul Laine (Stick It In Your Ear, 1990)

296. Friends in Spirit – Kingdom Come (Ain't Crying for the Moon, 2006)
297. Nonstop to Nowhere – Faster Pussycat (Whipped, 1992)
298. Get Up – Vain (Move on Out, 1994)
299. Nothin' to Lose – Arcade (Arcade, 1993)
300. Outlaw – Crazy Lixx (Crazy Lixx, 2014)
301. Paper Heart – Vains of Jenna (The Art of Telling Lies, 2009)
302. Real Love – Slaughter (The Wild Life, 1992)
303. Unskinny Bop – Poison (Flesh & Blood, 1990)
304. Taste of It – Like an Army (Single 2013)
305. Love is a Bitchslap – Sebastian Bach (Angel Down, 2007)
306. Slave to Your Love – Wig Wam (Wig Wamania, 2006)
307. Amnesia – Tora Tora (Wild America, 1992)
308. Don't Forget Me When I'm Gone – Alleycat Scratch (Last Call, 2010)
309. Me Against the World – Lizzy Borden (Visual Lies, 1987)
310. So What! – Tesla (Forever More, 2008)
311. Dancin' on Coals – Bang Tango (Dancin' on Coals, 1991)
312. Spend My Life – Slaughter (Stick it to Ya, 1990)
313. Love Drug – Vain (All Those Strangers, 2010)
314. Last Laugh – Killer Dwarfs (Dirty Weapons, 1990)
315. You're So Vain – Faster Pussycat (Whipped, 1992)
316. Guilty – Bonham (The Disregard of Timekeeping, 1989)
317. Bridges are Burning – Warrant (Dog Eat Dog, 1992)
318. One in a Million – Trixter (Trixter, 1990)
319. Coma – Guns N' Roses (Use Your Illusion, 1991)
320. No Matter What – Lillian Axe (Poetic Justice, 1992)
321. Love Don't Come Easy – White Lion (Main Attraction, 1991)
322. The Wild Life – Slaughter (The Wild Life, 1992)
323. Stomp It – Jetboy (Damned Nation, 1990)
324. Crash 'N Burn – Don Dokken (Up From the Ashes, 1990)
325. Shame – Hardcore Superstar (Thank You, 2001)
326. Give it to Me Good – Trixter (Trixter, 1990)
327. Beautiful – L.A. Guns (Man in the Moon, 2001)
328. Spinning Wheel – Love/Hate (Let's Rumble, 1993)
329. Tonight I'm Falling – TnT (Intuition, 1989)
330. Living is a Luxury – Vince Neil (Exposed, 1993)
331. Hollywood Ya – Enuff Z'Nuff (Strength, 1991)
332. Any Kinda Love – Jack Russell (For You, 2002)
333. All for Love – Whitesnake (Good to be Bad, 2008)
334. Queen 4 a Day – Shameless (Queen 4 a Day, 2000)
335. Lost in America – Mr. Big (Actual Size, 2001)

336.   Switchblade Serenade – Spread Eagle (Spread Eagle, 1990)
337.   Hideway – Leatherwolf (Street Ready, 1989)
338.   Hard to Get Over (You're So) – The Last Vegas (Eat Me, 2016)
339.   Summertime Girls – Y&T (Down for the Count, 1985)
340.   Let it Slide – Hurricane (Slave to the Thrill, 1990)
341.   Do You Want to Taste It – Wig Wam (Man in the Moon, 2010)
342.   Evil Eyes – The Last Vegas (Bad Decisions, 2012)
343.   Forever Young – Tyketto (Don't Come Easy, 1991)
344.   Little Girl – Dokken (Long Way Home, 2002)
345.   Easy Come Easy Go – Winger (In the Heart of the Young, 1990)
346.   Hang On St. Christopher – BulletBoys (Freakshow, 1991)
347.   All I Want – D'Molls (D'Molls, 1988)
348.   Heroes are Forever – Crazy Lixx (Loud Minority, 2007)
349.   Shake It – Beau Nasty (Dirty, But Well Dressed, 1989)
350.   After Midnight – Fastway (Trick or Treat, 1986)
351.   One More Minute – Hardcore Superstar (C'mon Take On Me, 2013)
352.   Heartbreak Blvd – Shotgun Messiah (Second Coming, 1991)
353.   Aiming High – Santa Cruz (Screaming for Adrenaline, 2013)
354.   All She Wrote – FireHouse (FireHouse, 1990)
355.   Whisky Dusk – Badlands (Voodoo Highway, 1991)
356.   Stitches – Skid Row (United World Rebellion Chapter One, 2013)
357.   Give Me a Reason – Dokken (Lighting Strikes Again, 2008)
358.   Little Wild Thing – Kingdom Come (Bad Image, 1993)
359.   Tainted Angel – SouthGang (Tainted Angel, 1991)
360.   Right Here, Right Now – Hardcore Superstar (It's Only Rock 'n' Roll, 1998)
361.   Chain of Fools – Little Caesar (Little Caesar, 1990)
362.   Fractured Love – Def Leppard (Retro Active, 1993)
363.   Hello/Goodbye – Hardcore Superstar (It's Only Rock 'n' Roll, 1998)
364.   Nervous Breakdown – Hardcore Superstar (Beg For It, 2009)
365.   Machine Gun – Warrant (Dog Eat Dog, 1992)
366.   Wasted – L.A. Guns (Wasted, 1998)
367.   Last Look at Eden – Europe (Last Look at Eden, 2009)
368.   See You Around – Skid Row (Thickskin, 2003)
369.   Talk to Your Daughter – BulletBoys (Freakshow, 1991)

370. White Lies, Black Truths – Slik Toxik (Doin' the Nasty, 1992)
371. Good Time – Danger, Danger (Paul Laine) (Cockroach, 2001)
372. One Less Mouth to Feed – Vince Neil (Carved in Stone, 1995)
373. Born to Burn – Heavy Pettin' (Big Bang, 1989)
374. Drop in the Ocean – Kik Tracee (Field Trip, 1992)
375. Lazy Day – Enuff Z'Nuff (Dissonance, 2010)
376. Misunderstood – Bon Jovi (Bounce, 2002)
377. We are the Weekend – Reckless Love (Invader, 2016)
378. Can't Get Enuff – Winger (In the Heart of the Young, 1990)
379. Games People Play – Tesla (Bust a Nut, 1994)
380. Young Blood Rising – Santa Cruz (Bad Blood Rising, 2017)
381. Reach for the Sky – FireHouse (Hold Your Fire, 1992)
382. Cold Shower – Kix (Midnight Dynamite, 1985)
383. Undefeated – Def Leppard (Mirror Ball – Live & More, 2011)
384. Touch – Bad City (Welcome To The Wasteland, 2010)
385. Set it Off – Vains of Jenna (Lit Up/Let Down, 2006)
386. I'm Bad – The Last Vegas (Whatever Gets You Off, 2009)
387. Revolution – L.A. Guns (Waking the Dead, 2002)
388. Hang on Lucy – Wildside (Under the Influence, 1992)
389. I Wanna Live – Babylon A.D. (American Blitzkrieg, 2000)
390. Crazy Nights – Loudness (Thunder in the East, 1985)
391. Stranger than Paradise – Sleeze Beez (Screwed Blued & Tattooed, 1990)
392. Nowhere to Go But Down – Tora Tora (Wild America, 1992)
393. I Was Made for Rock 'n' Roll – Tindrum (Cool, Calm and Collected, 1990)
394. Life Loves a Tragedy – Poison (Flesh and Blood, 1990)
395. Party Til' I'm Gone – Hardcore Superstar (HCSS, 2015)
396. Hair of the Dog – Wildside (Under the Influence, 1992)
397. Sympathy for the Devil – Guns N' Roses (Interview with a Vampire, 1994)
398. Tonight – Motley Crue (Too Fast For Love Reissue Bonus Track, 2003)
399. House of Pain – Every Mother's Nightmare (Wake Up Screaming, 1993)
400. Nothing Better to Do – L.A. Guns (Vicious Circle, 1994)
401. Family Picnic- Warrant (Ultraphobic, 1995)
402. True Believer – Lillian Axe (Poetic Justice, 1992)

403.   Breakin' Free – Tesla (Forever More, 2008)
404.   She Needs Me – TnT (My Religion, 2004)
405.   Room With a View – Arcade (A/2 1994)
406.   No More Tears – Julliet (Julliet, 1990)
407.   Hey Bulldog – Jack Russell (Shelter Me, 1996)
408.   Give Me a Sign – Ammunition (Shanghaied, 2015)
409.   Love Don't Live Here – Jack Russell (He Saw it Comin', 2017)
410.   Torn to Shreds – Def Leppard (X, 2002)
411.   Let it Go – Loudness (Lighting Strikes, 1986)
412.   Work it Out – Def Leppard (Slang, 1996)
413.   Cut From the Same Cloth – Junkyard (High Water, 2017)
414.   Push & Pull – Keel (Streets of Rock & Roll, 2010)
415.   Wild Boys – Hardcore Superstar (Hardcore Superstar, 2005)
416.   Still Kickin' – Danger, Danger (Four the Hard Way, 1997)
417.   Stand – Poison (Native Tongue, 1993)
418.   Down to the Bone – Quiet Riot (Down to the Bone, 1995)
419.   Ready to Rock – Melidian (Lost in the Wild, 1989)
420.   Music Man – Warrant (Louder Harder Faster, 2017)
421.   Allright – D-A-D (Scare Yourself, 2005)
422.   Standing on the Verge – Hardcore Superstar (Hardcore Superstar, 2005)
423.   Night on Fire – Reckless Love (Spirit, 2013)
424.   Send Her to Me – Autograph (Sign in Please, 1984)
425.   Can't Have Your Cake – Vince Neil (Exposed, 1993)
426.   Oh My God – Guns N' Roses (End of Days, 1999)
427.   Who Says You Can't Go Home – Bon Jovi (Have a Nice Day, 2005)
428.   Shoeshine Johnny – Guardian (Miracle Mile, 1993)
429.   Wait All Night – Joey C Jones (Melodies for the Masses, 2006)
430.   Get Up My Friend – Kingdom Come (Master Seven, 1997)
431.   All Those Bad Things – Junkyard (Joker, 1998)
432.   These Daze – Enuff Z'Nuff (Animals with Human Intelligence, 1993)
433.   Devil on My Shoulder – Hell in the Club (Devil on My Shoulder, 2014)
434.   Waitin' for the Man – Beggars & Thieves (Beggars & Thieves, 1990)
435.   Mad Days – D-A-D (Simpatico, 1997)
436.   Hollywood Forever – L.A. Guns (Hollywood Forever, 2012)

437. Six Million Dollar Man – Danger, Danger (The Return of the Gildersleeves, 2000)
438. Steppin' Over – Tesla (Times Makin' Changes, 1995)
439. Killin' Time – Slaughter (Back to Reality, 1999)
440. Temptation – Y&T (Contagious, 1987)
441. The Life & Death of Mr. Nobody – Hell in the Club (Shadow of the Monster, 2016)
442. Wild Young and Crazy – Hericane Alice (Tear the House Down, 1990)
443. Sea of Love – Def Leppard (Def Leppard, 2015)
444. Shelter Me – Jack Russell (Shelter Me, 1996)
445. She's Into Something Heavy – Electric Boys (Groovus Maximus, 1992)
446. Give it the Gun – Skid Row (United World Rebellion Chapter Two, 2014)
447. Blue Skies – Shark Island (Gathering of the Faithful, 2006)
448. Catcher in the Rye – Guns N' Roses (Chinese Democracy, 2008)
449. Feel the Shake – Jetboy (Feel the Shake, 1988)
450. The Kid Goes Wild – Babylon A.D. (Babylon A.D., 1989)
451. Bad Bad Girls – Fastway (Bad Bad Girls, 1990)
452. Down and Dirty – Deaf, Dumb & Blond (L.A. Days, 2017)
453. Promises – Def Leppard (Euphoria, 1999)
454. Don't Damn Me – Guns N' Roses (Use Your Illusion I, 1991)
455. Let's Get Rocked – Def Leppard (Adrenalize, 1992)
456. Black Rain – Enuff Z'Nuff (Animals With Human Intelligence, 1993)
457. Temptation – Sebastian Bach (Give 'Em Hell, 2014)
458. Steal Your Heart Away – Whitesnake (Forevermore, 2011)
459. It's a Miracle – Crashdiet (Rest in Sleaze, 2005)
460. Paris Calling – Shark Island (Law of the Order, 1989)
461. The Last Goodbye – Dokken (Hell to Pay, 2004)
462. The Distance – Bon Jovi (Bounce, 2002)
463. So Sad to See You – Enuff Z'Nuff (Seven, 1997)
464. Crying – Whitesnake (Restless Heart, 1997)
465. Lonely Road – Killer Dwarfs (Start @ One, 2013)
466. City Boy Blues – Motley Crue (Theatre of Pain, 1985)
467. Buried Unkind – Steelheart (Good 2B Alive, 2008)
468. Have a Nice Day – Bon Jovi (Have a Nice Day, 2005)
469. Hollywood Ending – Motley Crue (Tattoo You, 2000)
470. Wimpy Sister – Hardcore Superstar (Thank You, 2001)

471.   Rock and Roll – Pretty Boy Floyd (Leather Boyz with Electric Toyz, 1989)
472.   Deliver Me – Fastway (Eat Dog Eat, 2011)
473.   Always the Pretender – Europe (Secret Society, 2006)
474.   Everything I Own – Tesla (A Peace of Time, 2007)
475.   Undertow – Mr. Big (What If…, 2011)
476.   You're My Everything – Slaughter (Revolution, 1997)
477.   Love Blind – Babylon A.D. (Lost Sessions, 2014)
478.   Keep it Up All Night – Reckless Love (Invader, 2016)
479.   Little Mistake – Mr. Big (Hey Man, 1996)
480.   Don't Mean Shit – Hardcore Superstar (HCSS, 2015)
481.   Save it for Yourself – KINGOFTHEHILL (Unreleased, 2005)
482.   Rock Down This Place – Hell in the Club (Let the Games Begin, 2011)
483.   Stay with Me Tonight – Quiet Riot (QR, 1988)
484.   Animal Attraction – Reckless Love (Animal Attraction, 2011)
485.   Breaking All the Rules – Wig Wam (Wig Wamania, 2006)
486.   Somebody's Waiting – Keel (Keel, 1987)
487.   Falling Rain – Crashdiet (The Unattractive Revolution, 2007)
488.   Hello, Hello – TnT (Atlantis, 2008)
489.   Bleed – Private Line (21st Century Pirates, 2004)
490.   Fashion - Hanoi Rocks (Street Poetry, 2007)
491.   The Maze – Dokken (Dysfunctional, 1995)
492.   Bringing Me Down – FireHouse (Category 5, 1999)
493.   Blue Eyed Soul – Sweet FA (The Lost Tapes, 2007)
494.   Living a World Away – Tora Tora (Revolution Day, 2011)
495.   Nobody Cares – Danger Danger (Dawn, 1995)
496.   Look @ Me – Tesla (Into the Now, 2004)
497.   Kings of Demolition – Skid Row (United World Rebellion Chapter One, 2013)
498.   Faded – Junkyard (single, 2015)
499.   All Out of Luck – Whitesnake (Forevermore, 2011)
500.   Hello, Hello (I'm Back Again) - Y&T (Endangered Species, 1997)
501.   Sick Little Twisted Mind – Danger, Danger (Ted Poley) (Cockroach, 2001)
502.   Stare – Gorky Park (Stare, 1996)
503.   Miss You – The Last Vegas (Sweet Salvation, 2014)
504.   Tell Me Please – Killer Dwarfs (Big Deal, 1988)

505. Last Time in Neverland – D-A-D (Dic-Nil-Lan-Daft-Erd-Ark, 2011)
506. Thorn in My Side – Bon Jovi (The Circle, 2009)
507. Shot in the Dark – Great White (Shot in the Dark, 1986)
508. Sister of Pain – Vince Neil (Exposed, 1993)
509. My Own Worst Enemy – Sebastian Bach (Kicking & Screaming, 2011)
510. Prisoner of Love – Little Caesar (American Dream, 2012)
511. Riad N' the Bedouins – Guns N' Roses (Chinese Democracy, 2008)
512. A Day Late, A Dollar Short – Hanoi Rocks (Twelve Shots on the Rocks, 2002)
513. Life is Beautiful – Bon Jovi (Burning Bridges, 2015)
514. Cocaine Cowboys – Crashdiet (The Savage Playground, 2013)
515. Long Way Home – Blue Tears (Mad, Bad and Dangerous, 2005)
516. Downtown – Crazy Lixx (Riot Avenue, 2012)
517. Bring On The World – Bang Tango (Pistol Whipped in the Bible Belt, 2011)
518. Someday I'll Be Saturday Night – Bon Jovi (Cross Road, 1994)
519. Glitter – Motley Crue (Generation Swine, 1997)
520. Someday – Enuff Z'Nuff (Paraphernalia, 1999)
521. Sweet Sensation – Santa Cruz (Screaming for Adrenaline, 2013)
522. The Bigger the Better – Wig Wam (Wall Street, 2012)
523. Enslaved – Motley Crue (Greatest Hits, 1998)
524. Mama – KINGOFTHEHILL (Unreleased, 2005)
525. Symphony – BulletBoys (Elefante, 2015)
526. Sensitive to the Light – Hardcore Superstar (Dreamin' In a Casket, 2007)
527. Love Machine – Reckless Love (Reckless Love, 2010)
528. The Flower Song – Tom Keifer (The Way Life Goes, 2013)
529. Hard Luck Town – Killer Dwarfs (Method to the Madness, 1992)
530. Girls Wanna Party – Tales From The Porn (H.M.M.V., 2017)
531. Greener – Vain (Enough Rope, 2011)
532. Gotta Love the Ride – Mr. Big (The Stories We Could Tell, 2014)
533. Tears Don't Mean a Thing – Junkyard (Joker, 1998)
534. Goodbye 2 U – Shameless (Dial S for Sex, 2011)

535.　　Take It – Hannon Tramp (Hannon Tramp, 2014)
536.　　Testify – Lynch Mob (Rebel, 2015)
537.　　Angel Falling – Reckless Love (Spirit, 2013)
538.　　The Wild and the Young – Quiet Riot (III, 1986)
539.　　You Better Not Love Me – L.A. Guns (Hollywood Forever, 2012)
540.　　Hearts on the Highway – Danger Danger (Revolve, 2009)
541.　　Time Bomb – Tesla (Simplicity, 2014)
542.　　Hard Luck Champion – Dangerous Toys (Pissed, 1994)
543.　　Good Times – Enuff Z'Nuff (Welcome to Blue Island, 2003)
544.　　Bye Bye Babylon – Santa Cruz (Santa Cruz, 2015)
545.　　Forevermore – Mark Slaughter (Halfway There, 2017)
546.　　What's the Matter – D-A-D (Soft Dogs, 2002)
547.　　Slow Drag – Lynch Mob (Sound Mountain Sessions, 2012)
548.　　Unforgiven – Mr. Big (What If..., 2011)
549.　　American Hair Band – Tuff (History of Tuff, 2001)
550.　　United – XYZ (Letter to God, 2003)
551.　　The Way Life Goes – Tom Keifer (The Way Life Goes, 2013)
552.　　Speed – L.A. Guns (The Missing Piece, 2017)
553.　　Bad Attitude Shuffle – Cinderella (Still Climbing, 1994)
554.　　I Wanna Be Loved – House of Lords (House of Lords, 1988)
555.　　I Need You – Whitesnake (Forevermore, 2011)
556.　　Perfectly Wrong – Jetboy (Off Your Rocker, 2010)
557.　　Ten Miles Wide – Stephen Pearcy (Smash, 2017)
558.　　For the Last Time – Dokken (Broken Bones, 2012)
559.　　Ridin' On – Little Caesar (This Time It's Different, 1998)
560.　　Sweet Salvation – The Last Vegas (Sweet Salvation, 2014)
561.　　Innocence is No Excuse – Shameless (Dial S for Sex, 2011)
562.　　Get it On – Vains of Jenna (The Art of Telling Lies, 2009)
563.　　Famous 4 Madness – Shameless (Famous 4 Madness, 2007)
564.　　Saturday Night Gave Me Sunday Morning – Bon Jovi (Burning Bridges, 2015)
565.　　Better Days – Darkhorse (Let it Ride, 2014)
566.　　Fool on Fire – Babylon A.D. (Revelation Highway, 2017)
567.　　Snake – Warrant (Rockaholic, 2011)
568.　　Quick Step to Love – Vain – (Fade, 1995)
569.　　Damn I'm in Love Again – Mr. Big (Defying Gravity, 2017)
570.　　Make Some Noise – Jetboy (Feel the Shake, 1988)
571.　　Erase the Slate – Dokken (Erase the Slate, 1999)
572.　　Rolling with the Punches – Vain (Rolling With the Punches, 2017)
573.　　Sweet, Bad and Beautiful – Crazy Lixx (Riot Avenue, 2012)

574. Last Call for Alcohol – Hardcore Superstar (Split Your Lip, 2010)
575. You Got Me Twisted – Steelheart (Through Worlds of Stardust, 2017)
576. Knokk 'em Down – Crashdiet (Rest in Sleaze, 2005)
577. Blame it on the Night – Jack Russell (He Saw it Comin', 2017)
578. I Want What She's Got – D-A-D (Dic-Nil-Lan-Daft-Erd-Ark, 2011)
579. Sound of the Loud Minority – Crazy Lixx (Crazy Lixx, 2014)
580. Faded – Warrant (Louder Harder Faster, 2017)
581. Hell or High Water – Junkyard (High Water, 2017)
582. Forever – Skid Row (40 Seasons, 1998)
583. Teenage Revolution – Hanoi Rocks (Street Poetry, 2007)
584. You are the One – The Last Vegas (Bad Decisions, 2012)
585. Perfect Love – Tales From the Porn (H.M.M.V., 2017)
586. We Will Rock You – Warrant (Gladiator, 1992)
587. By By Johnny – Return (Best of Both Worlds, 2008)
588. Get Off Your Ass – Autograph (Get Off Your Ass, 2017)
589. You Don't Understand – Sebastian Bach (Angel Down, 2007)
590. Vain – Vain (Enough Rope, 2011)
591. Mean to Me – Mr. Big (Defying Gravity, 2017)
592. Resurrection Love – Babylon's Bomb (Babylon's Burning, 2009)
593. Free Your Mind – Kingdom Come (Too, 2000)
594. Godspeed – Jack Russell (He Saw it Comin', 2017)
595. The River – Badlands (Dusk, 1998)
596. Take Me for a Ride – Bad City (Welcome To The Wasteland, 2010)
597. Give Up Your Heart – Roxx (Outlaws, Fools & Thieves, 2004)
598. Don't Let it Happen to You – Vain (Rolling With the Punches, 2017)
599. Wake Up – Mr. Big (Actual Size, 2001)
600. Complications – Shameless (Famous 4 Madness, 2007)
601. Styrofoam Cup – Junkyard (High Water, 2017)
602. Dream – White Lion (Return of the Pride, 2008)
603. No More Hell to Pay – Stryper (No More Hell to Pay, 2013)
604. Queenie – L.A. Guns (Hollywood Forever, 2012)
605. Waste of Time – Junkyard (Tried and True, 2003)
606. We All Die Young – Steelheart (Wait, 1996)

607. Rock 'N' Roll – Sebastian Bach (Bring 'Em Back Alive, 1999)
608. Tomorrow – Def Leppard (Songs From the Sparkle Lounge, 2008)
609. Pray – Every Mother's Nightmare (Smokin' Delta Voodoo, 2000)
610. 21 'Till I Die – Crazy Lixx (New Religion, 2010)
611. I Need it Now – Tyketto (Reach, 2016)
612. Dream Seque – KINGOFTHEHILL (Unreleased, 2005)
613. Dig in Deep – Tyketto (Dig in Deep, 2012)
614. Along For the Ride – The Last Vegas (Eat Me, 2016)
615. Crucify – Babylon Bombs (Cracked Wide Open and Bruised, 2005)
616. This Ain't a Love Song – Motley Crue (Saints of Los Angeles, 2008)
617. You're So Beautiful – Def Leppard (X, 2002)
618. The Flood's the Fault of the Rain – L.A. Guns (The Missing Peace, 2017)
619. Rock Hard – Big Cock (Big Cock, 2006)
620. Everybody Needs a Hero – Pretty Boy Floyd (A Tale of Sex, 1997)
621. Say it Isn't So – Bon Jovi (Crush, 2000)
622. So What? – D-A-D (Soft Dogs, 2002)
623. Animal – Def Leppard (Hysteria, 1987)
624. Rain – Stephen Pearcy (Smash, 2017)
625. So Free Now – Vain (On the Line, 2005)
626. Monster – Reckless Love (Invader, 2016)
627. Backseat Action – Shameless (Backstreet Anthems, 1999)
628. Rock to the Edge of the Night – Trixter (Human Era, 2015)
629. Fragile – Mr. Big (The Stories we Could Tell, 2014)
630. Blue Trees – Kingdom Come (Rendered Waters, 2011)
631. Big World Away – Winger (Karma, 2009)
632. Tangled Up – Treat (Coup De Grace, 2010)
633. Saints of Los Angeles, Motley Crue (Saints of Los Angeles, 2008)
634. Shine – Mr. Big (Actual Size, 2001)
635. Running Wild – L.A. Cobra (Shotgun Slinger, 2017)
636. Big Money – House of Lords (Big Money, 2011)
637. Showdown in Central Park – Bad City (Welcome to the Wasteland, 2010)
638. Hollywood's Burning – L.A. Guns (Tales From the Strip, 2005)

639.   We Come Undone – Beggars and Thieves (We are the Brokenhearted, 2011)
640.   Let's Get Cracking – Reckless Love (Invader, 2016)
641.   (Heads Up!) Look Out Below! – Ted Poley (Collateral Damage, 2006)
642.   King of Cool – Big Cock (Return of the Cock, 2005)
643.   Man About Town – Rose Tattoo (Blood Brothers, 2007)
644.   Stuck Inside – Sebastian Bach (Angel Down, 2007)
645.   Touch of Grey – Bon Jovi (This House is Not For Sale, 2016)
646.   Amazing – BulletBoys (Sophie, 2003)
647.   Down & Dirty – Autograph (Loud and Clear 1987)
648.   Love is a Dangerous Thing – FireHouse (3, 1995)
649.   New Tattoo – Motley Crue (New Tattoo, 2000)
650.   Lonely Ones – Britny Fox (Springhead Motorshark, 2003)

Top Ballads:

1. Love Song – Tesla (The Great Radio Controversy, 1989)
2. November Rain – Guns N' Roses (Use Your Illusion I, 1991)
3. I Remember You – Skid Row (Skid Row, 1989)
4. Save Your Love – Great White (Once Bitten, 1987)
5. Don't Know What You Got – Cinderella (Long Cold Winter, 1988)
6. Hysteria – Def Leppard (Hysteria, 1987)
7. I'll Never Let You Go – Steelheart (Steelheart, 1990)
8. Bringing on the Heartbreak – Def Leppard (High 'n' Dry, 1981)
9. Here I Go Again – Whitesnake (Whitesnake, 1987; S&S, 1982)
10. Heaven – Warrant (Dirty Rotten Filthy Stinking Rich, 1989)
11. Home Sweet Home – Motley Crue (Theatre of Pain, 1985)
12. Don't Close Your Eyes – Kix (Blow My Fuse, 1988)
13. Time to Let You Go – Enuff Z'Nuff (Strength, 1991)
14. Coming Home – Cinderella (Long Cold Winter, 1988)
15. Stronger Now – Warrant (Ultraphobic, 1995)
16. Don't Cry – Guns N' Roses (Use Your Illusion I, 1991)
17. Wild Angels – Pretty Boy Floyd (Leather Boyz with Electric Toyz, 1989)
18. House of Pain – Faster Pussycat (Faster Pussycat, 1989)
19. To Be With You – Mr. Big (Lean Into It, 1991)
20. Every Rose Has Its Thorn – Poison (Open Up and Say...Ahh!, 1988)
21. The Ballad of Jayne – L.A. Guns (Cocked & Loaded, 1989)
22. Alone Again – Dokken (Tooth and Nail, 1984)
23. Nobody's Fool – Cinderella (Night Songs, 1986)
24. Wanted Dead or Alive – Bon Jovi (Slippery When Wet, 1986)
25. Apologize – The Last Vegas (Whatever Gets You Off, 2009)

26. I Saw Red – Warrant (Cherry Pie, 1990)
27. Never Say Goodbye – Bon Jovi (Slippery When Wet, 1986)
28. Patience – Guns N' Roses (Lies, 1988)
29. Desperate – Babylon A.D. (Babylon A.D., 1989)
30. Fly to the Angels – Slaughter (Stick it to Ya, 1990)
31. Far Away – Shameless (Queen 4 a Day, 2000)
32. You're All I Need – Motley Crue (Girls, Girls, Girls, 1987)
33. Walk Away – Dokken (Beast From the East, 1988)
34. Don't You Ever Leave Me – Hanoi Rocks – (Two Steps From the Move, 1984)
35. On with the Show – Motley Crue (Too Fast For Love, 1981/82)
36. Breakin' Down – Skid Row (Subhuman Race, 1995)
37. Phantom Rider – Tora Tora (Surprise Attack, 1989)
38. Driftaway – Motley Crue (Motley Crue, 1994)
39. I Still Think About You – Danger Danger (Screw It, 1991)
40. If I Say – KINGOFTHEHILL (KINGOFTHEHILL, 1991)
41. Love of a Lifetime – FireHouse (FireHouse, 1990)
42. I'll Be There for You – Bon Jovi (New Jersey, 1988)
43. Try So Hard – Tesla (Bust a Nut, 1994)
44. Wasted Time – Skid Row (Slave to the Grind, 1991)
45. Sad Theresa – Warrant (Dog Eat Dog, 1992)
46. Always – Bon Jovi (Cross Road, 1994)
47. Estranged – Guns N' Roses (Use Your Illusion II, 1991)
48. Something to Believe In – Poison (Flesh & Blood, 1990)
49. Still Loving You – Scorpions – (Love at First Sting, 1984)
50. Miles Away – Great White (Let it Rock, 1996)
51. For Shame – Kix (Cool Kids 1983)
52. Sacrifice Me – Salty Dog (Every Dog has its Day, 1990)
53. Forever – Wild Boyz (Unleashed!, 1991)
54. Love Kills – Vinnie Vincent Invasion (All Systems Go, 1988)
55. Days Gone Bye – Slaughter (The Wild Life, 1992)
56. By Your Side – Sebastian Bach (Angel Down, 2007)
57. Long Time No See – Hardcore Superstar (C'mon Take On Me, 2013)
58. Mother Blues – Arcade (Arcade, 1993)
59. Stick to Your Guns – Bon Jovi (New Jersey, 1988)
60. Laugh 'N' a ½ - D-A-D (Riskin' it All, 1991)
61. Dreamtime – LA Guns (Shrinking Violet, 1999)
62. I Believe in You – Y&T (Open Fire, 1985)
63. Close My Eyes Forever – Lita Ford/Ozzy Osbourne (Lita, 1988)
64. Skylar's Song – Vince Neil (Carved in Stone, 1995)
65. I Won't Forget You – Poison (Look What the Cat Dragged In, 1986)
66. Slippin' Away – Junkyard (Sixes, Sevens, and Nines, 1991)

67. Life Goes On – Poison (Flesh & Blood, 1990)
68. Blind Faith – Warrant (Cherry Pie, 1990)
69. Is This Love –Whitesnake (Whitesnake, 1987)
70. I Want to Love You Tonight – Ratt (Reach the Sky, 1988)
71. Silent Night – Great White (Can't Get There From Here, 1999)
72. Too Many Tears – Whitesnake (Restless Heart, 1997)
73. Heartbreak Station – Cinderella (Heartbreak Station, 1990)
74. When the Children Cry – White Lion (Pride, 1987)
75. Wild World – Mr. Big (Bump Ahead, 1993)
76. Andy Warhol Was Right – Warrant (Dog Eat Dog, 1992)
77. Don't You Ever Leave Me – Hardcore Superstar (Bad Sneakers and a Pina Colada, 2000)
78. Babe I'm Going to Leave You – Great White (Greatest Hits, 1994)
79. Living in Sin – Bon Jovi (New Jersey, 1988)
80. By the Fireside – Slik Toxik (Doin' the Nasty, 1992)
81. Love Bites – Def Leppard (Hysteria, 1987)
82. Long Cold Winter – Cinderella (Long Cold Winter, 1988)
83. Fallin' Apart – Tesla (Forever More, 2008)
84. Forever Free – Wasp (The Headless Children, 1989)
85. Love is on the Way – Saigon Kick (The Lizard, 1992)
86. You're Not Alone – Twisted Sister (You Can't Stop Rock 'n' Roll, 1983)
87. Honestly – Stryper (To Hell with the Devil, 1986)
88. Carrie – Europe (The Final Countdown, 1986)
89. Thunderbird – Quiet Riot (Metal Health, 1983)
90. Being There – Tora Tora (Surprise Attack, 1989)
91. Love Can Make You Blind – Every Mother's Nightmare (Every Mother's Nightmare, 1990)
92. Love You to Pieces – Lizzy Borden (Love You to Pieces, 1985)
93. Anything for You – Mr. Big (Mr. Big, 1989)
94. Anything it Takes – The Last Vegas (Eat Me, 2016)
95. Red Rose – Roxx Gang (Things You've Never Done Before, 1988)
96. Headed for a Heartbreak – Winger (Winger, 1988)
97. The Bitter Pill – Warrant (Dog Eat Dog, 1992)
98. What Love Can Be – Kingdom Come (Kingdom Come, 1988)
99. Please Dear – Faster Pussycat (Wake Me When It's Over, 1989)
100. Wake Me Up – Tuff (What Comes Around Goes Around, 1991)
101. As Time Goes By – Tora Tora (Wild America, 1992)
102. Love Ain't Enough – SouthGang (Tainted Angel, 1991)
103. Without the Night – Winger (Winger, 1988)
104. Friends – Faster Pussycat (Whipped, 1992)

105.   You're All I Need – White Lion (Main Attraction, 1991)
106.   Shelter From the Rain – Tora Tora (Revolution Day, 2011)
107.   Wild is the Wind – Bon Jovi (New Jersey, 1988)
108.   All I Want is Everything – Def Leppard (Slang, 1996)
109.   Long, Long Way to Go – Def Leppard (X, 2002)
110.   Without You – Vain (No Respect, 1989)
111.   Love is a Lie – Great White (Psycho City,1992)
112.   What Do You Got – Bon Jovi (Greatest Hits, 2010)
113.   Summer Rain – Whitesnake (Good to be Bad, 2008)
114.   Run to Your Mama – Hardcore Superstar (Split Your Lip, 2010)
115.   Through the Rain – Cinderella (Still Climbing, 1994)
116.   Roses on Your Grave – Alleycat Scratch (Deadboys in Trash City, 1993)
117.   Dream Girl – Hericane Alice (Tear the House Down, 1990)
118.   Miles Away – Winger (In the Heart of the Young, 1990)
119.   You'll Lose a Good Thing – Jack Russell (Shelter Me, 1996)
120.   She's Not Coming Home Tonight – Shameless (Splashed, 2002)
121.   Baby Blue – Princess Pang (Princess Pang, 1989)
122.   Have You Seen Her – Bang Tango (Pistol Whipped in the Bible Belt, 2011)
123.   Afterglow – Great White (Hooked, 1991)
124.   The Angel Song – Great White (Twice Shy, 1989)
125.   Best of Friends – Dangerous Toys (Hellacious Acres, 1991)
126.   Sometimes She Cries – Warrant (Dirty Rotten Filthy Stinking Rich, 1989)
127.   Just Take My Heart – Mr. Big (Lean Into It, 1991)
128.   How Many More Times – Hannon Tramp (Hannon Tramp, 2014)
129.   Place in My Heart – KINGOFTHEHILL (KINGOFTHEHILL, 1991)
130.   Love Has it's Reasons – Shanghai (Bombs Away, 2001)
131.   Tear Down the Walls – Kix (Hot Wire, 1991)
132.   The Deeper the Love – Whitesnake (Slip of the Tongue, 1989)
133.   She's Gone – Steelheart (Steelheart, 1990)
134.   Street of Dreams – Guns N' Roses (Chinese Democracy, 2008)
135.   In a Darkened Room – Skid Row (Slave to the Grind, 1991)
136.   Where is the Love – Great White (Let It Rock, 1996)
137.   Inside Outside Inn – Kix (Rock Your Face off, 2014)

138.   Slip Away – Babylon Bombs (Doin' You Nasty, 2006)
139.   Your Love – Sweet FA (Temptation, 1991)
140.   Souvenirs' – XYZ (XYZ, 1990)
141.   Still the One – Brighton Rock (Love Machine, 1991)
142.   Too Late – Hericane Alice (Tear the House Down, 1990)
143.   Here Comes that Sick Bitch Again – Hardcore Superstar
         (Split Your Lip, 2010)
144.   Stick to Your Guns – Sweet F.A. (Stick To Your Guns, 1990)
145.   Tried and True – Junkyard – (Tried and True, 2003)
146.   My Sanctuary – Great White (Risen, 2009)
147.   Cry No More – Arcade (Arcade, 1993)
148.   Cry – Sic Vikki (Kiss Me in French, 1993)
149.   Just Like a Woman – Salty Dog (Every Dog Has Its Day,
         1990)
150.   When I Look Into Your Eyes – Jack Russell (Shelter Me,
         1996)
151.   Selflove-Sick – Private Line (21st Century Pirates, 2004)
152.   The Price – Twisted Sister – (Stay Hungry, 1984)
153.   Closer to My Heart – Ratt (Invasion of Your Privacy, 1985)
154.   Let it Rain – Warrant (Dog Eat Dog, 1992)
155.   I Don't Love You Anymore – The Quireboys (A Bit of What
         You Fancy, 1990)
156.   Mother's Eyes – Great White (Sail Away, 1994)
157.   Forever – Vince Neil (Exposed, 1993)
158.   Have You Ever Needed Someone So Bad (Adrenalize, Def
         Leppard – 1992)
159.   A Thousand Goodbyes – Bang Tango (Love After Death,
         1994)
160.   I Hate Kissing You Good-Bye Tuff (What Comes Around
         Goes Around, 1991)
161.   Bed of Roses – Bon Jovi (Keep the Faith, 1992)
162.   It's Alright – Babylon Bombs (Babylon's Burning, 2009)
163.   Just Yesterday – Great White (Back to the Rhythm, 2007)
164.   Never Say Goodbye – Guardian (Fire and Love, 1990)
165.   The Sky's Falling – Babylon A.D. (American Blitzkrieg,
         2000)
166.   Get Me Out of California – Santa Cruz (Bad Blood Rising,
         2017)
167.   This is Killing Me – Skid Row (United World Rebellion
         Chapter One, 2013)
168.   We All Fall Down – D-A-D (Dic-Nil-Lan-Daft-Erd-Ark, 2011)
169.   Free – Shotgun Messiah (Second Coming, 1991)

170.	All I Want All I Need – Whitesnake (Good to be Bad, 2008)
171.	I Don't Think I Love U – Shameless (Queen 4 a Day, 2000)
172.	Nothing Like it in the World – Mr. Big (Actual Size, 2001)
173.	When I Look Into Your Eyes – FireHouse (Hold Your Fire, 1992)
174.	Naked – Hell in the Club (Shadow of the Monster, 2016)
175.	Only Time Will Tell – Poison (Swallow This Live, 1991)
176.	You Keep Breaking My Heart – Rough Cutt (Rough Cutt, 1985)
177.	Looks Like Love – Wildside (Under the Influence, 1992)
178.	Clean the Dirt – Junkyard (Sixes, Sevens, and Nines, 1991)
179.	Frozen Tears – Icon (Night of the Crime, 1985)
180.	Feels Like Hammer – Dangerous Toys (Dangerous Toys, 1989)
181.	Every Time I Dream – Autograph (Loud and Clear 1987)
182.	Silent Night – Bon Jovi (7800 Fahrenheit, 1985)
183.	So Far Away – Pretty Wicked (Pretty Wicked, 1992)
184.	B-Song – Tora Tora (Miss B Haven, 2009)
185.	One Step From Paradise – Danger Danger (Danger Danger, 1989)
186.	Going' Where the Wind Blows – Mr. Big (Hey Man, 1996)
187.	Falling Into You – Sebastian Bach (Angel Down, 2007)
188.	New Love in Town – Europe (Last Look at Eden, 2009)
189.	I Don't Want To Live Without You – Sleeze Beez (Powertool, 1992)
190.	Driftin' Back – Killer Dwarfs (Method to the Madness, 1992)
191.	Strange Wings – Savatage (Hall of the Mountain King, 1987)
192.	Kiss of Death – L.A. Guns (Vicious Circle, 1994)
193.	Tell Me That You Love Me – Little Caesar (This Time It's Different, 1998)
194.	You Showed Me – Tom Keifer (The Way Life Goes, 2013)
195.	Tell Me Where to Go – Wig Wam (667 The Neighbour of the Beast, 2004)
196.	Jaded Heart – Dokken (Under Lock and Key, 1985)
197.	Without You – Motley Crue (Dr. Feelgood, 1989)
198.	When I'm Gone – Arcade (A/2 1994)
199.	Nobody Knows – Roxy Blue (Want Some, 1992)
200.	Wind of Change – Scorpions (Crazy World, 1990)
201.	Fall in Love Again – Tigertailz (Young and Crazy, 1987)
202.	Cross My Heart – Tesla (Simplicity, 2014)
203.	Goodbye My Friend – Dokken (Long Way Home, 2002)
204.	I Want You – Bon Jovi (Keep the Faith, 1992)

205.	What of Our Love – Crazy Lixx (New Religion, 2010)
206.	A Better Man – Thunder (Laughing on Judgment Day, 1992)
207.	Can't Find My Way Home – House of Lords (Sahara, 1990)
208.	Eye of The Storm – Pretty Maids (Future World, 1987)
209.	Whatever it Takes – Jack Russell (For You, 2002)
210.	In Your Arms – Little Caesar (Little Caesar, 1990)
211.	Take Me Home – White Lion (Return of the Pride, 2008)
212.	Only You – Tesla (Into the Now, 2004)
213.	I Live For You – Harry Hess (Living in Yesterday, 2012)
214.	Prettiest ones – Blackboard Jungle (I Like it a lot, 1991)
215.	Slowly Slipping Sway – Harem Scarem (Harem Scarem, 1991)
216.	Bed of Roses – Warrant (Cherry Pie, 1990)
217.	Sweet Mystery – Guardian (Miracle Mile, 1993)
218.	Anything for You – Jack Russell (He Saw it Comin', 2017)
219.	Mother's Love – Hardcore Superstar (Thank You, 2001)
220.	Standing Alone – Tyketto (Don't Come Easy, 1991)
221.	After the Rain – Paul Laine (Stick it in Your Ear, 1990)
222.	U in My Life – Warrant (Louder Harder Faster, 2017)
223.	Hard to Say Goodbye – Stage Dolls (Stories We Could Tell, 1993)
224.	Kiss the Love Goodbye – Wildside (Under the Influence, 1992)
225.	Madagascar – Guns N' Roses (Chinese Democracy, 2008)
226.	Disposable – Mark Slaughter (Halfway There, 2017)
227.	The Time It's Love – D'Molls (Warped, 1990)
228.	End of the Line – TnT (Intuition, 1989)
229.	Two Steps Behind – Def Leppard (Retro Active, 1993)
230.	Mama Don't You Cry – Steelheart (Tangled in the Reigns, 1992)
231.	Best of Friends – Blackeyed Susan (Electric Rattlebone, 1991)
232.	Faith – Spread Eagle (Open to the Public, 1993)
233.	Love Don't Bother Me – Stage Dolls (Stripped, 1991)
234.	I Wish it Would Rain – Little Caesar (Little Caesar, 1990)
235.	Man in the Moon – Wig Wam (Non Stop Rock 'N Roll, 2010)
236.	Nothin' Left to Lose – Slaughter (Back to Reality, 1999)
237.	One of These Days – Whitesnake (Forevermore, 2011)
238.	Hot Rain – Reckless Love (Spirit, 2013)
239.	I Found You – L.A. Guns (Hollywood Vampires, 1991)
240.	Words Don't Count – White Lion (Lost Tracks, Demos and Oddities, 2009)

241. No Second Time – Enuff Z'Nuff (1985, 1994)
242. Love's Got Nothing on Me – The Last Vegas (Eat Me, 2016)
243. Save the Weak – Brtny Fox (Brtny Fox, 1988)
244. Giving Yourself Away – Ratt (Detonator, 1990)
245. Love Don't Lie – House of Lords (House of Lords, 1988)
246. What Keeps Me Loving You – XYZ (XYZ, 1989)
247. Honestly – Harem Scarem (Harem Scarem, 1991)
248. As the Candle Burns – Trixter (Hear!, 1992)
249. Scream – Tyketto (Reach, 2016)
250. Catch Your Fall – Skid Row (United World Rebellion Chapter Two, 2014)
251. Too Late – Jetboy (Damned Nation, 1990)
252. See You Someday – Lillian Axe (Poetic Justice, 1992)
253. Star – Hell in the Club (Let the Games Begin, 2011)
254. Ride With Me – Blackeyed Susan (Electric Rattlebone, 1991)
255. Over and Out – Britny Fox (Bite Down Hard, 1991)
256. Better Off Without You – Tesla (Twisted Wires & The Acoustic Sessions, 2011)
257. What's Forever For – House of Lords (Demons Down, 1992)
258. The Way I Feel – Leatherwolf (Street Ready, 1989)
259. Most Important Thing – Bang Tango (Ready To Go, 2004)
260. Holdin' On – Junkyard (Joker, 1998)
261. What's on Your Mind – Blonz (Blonz, 1990)
262. Shouldn't Cry – Vain (All Those Strangers, 2010)
263. On My Own – Slaughter (Back to Reality, 1999)
264. Real Love – Bon Jovi (This House is Not For Sale, 2016)
265. Jealous Guy – Enuff Z'Nuff (Seven, 1997)
266. Ain't Seen Love Like That – Mr. Big (Bump Ahead, 1993)
267. All Your Love – Steelheart (Tangled in Reigns, 1992)
268. Promise the Moon – Dangerous Toys (Pissed, 1994)
269. When I Find Love – XYZ (XYZ, 1991)
270. Hard to Find the Words – Cinderella (Still Climbing, 1994)
271. Friends – Kingdom Come (Bad Image, 1993)
272. Can't Find My Way – Hardline (Double Eclipse, 1992)
273. It's Up to You – Icon – (Icon, 1984)
274. No More Tears – Julliet (Julliet, 1990)
275. Hard to Say Goodbye – Great White (Elated, 2012)
276. At the End of the Day – Wig Wam (Wig Wamania, 2006)
277. Me and Dad – TnT (Atlantis, 2008)
278. Hold the Dream – FireHouse (Hold Your Fire, 1992)
279. I Live My Life for You – FireHouse (3, 1995)

280.   Kill Me – Beggars & Thieves (Beggars & Thieves, 1990)
281.   Dead and Gone – Fastway (Eat Dog Eat, 2011)
282.   Hangin' Round with My Dreams – Junkyard (XXX, 1998)
283.   Where R U – Pretty Boy Floyd (The Vault 2, 2003)
284.   Underneath the Sun – L.A. Guns (Hollywood Forever, 2012)
285.   Too Late for Love – Stage Dolls (Get a Life, 2004)
286.   Tonight – KINGOFTHEHILL (Unreleased, 2005)
287.   It's Over – Triumph (Edge of Excess, 1993)
288.   Tears of Fire – Keel (The Final Frontier, 1986)
289.   Long Hard Road – Cry Wolf (Crunch, 1990)
290.   Times are Changin' – Roxy Blue (Want Some, 1992)
291.   You Filled My Head – D-A-D (Scare Yourself, 2005)
292.   Rescue Me – Tora Tora (Revolution Day, 2011)
293.   I Remember – Dokken (Lighting Strikes Again, 2008)
294.   Heart of Gold – Sweet F.A. (Stick to Your Guns, 1990)
295.   Other Than Me – Tesla (Simplicity, 2014)
296.   You Want to Make a Memory – Bon Jovi (Lost Highway, 2007)
297.   Life is Too Lonely – Stone Fury (Burns Like a Star, 1984)
298.   Crystal Eyes – L.A. Guns (Vicious Circle, 1994)
299.   Who Am I To Blame – Tora Tora (Miss B Haven, 2009)
300.   Forever and a Day – Guardian (Fire and Love, 1990)
301.   Sacred Place – Paul Shortino's The Cutt (Sacred Place, 2002)
302.   Can't Go On – Whitesnake (Restless Heart, 1997)
303.   Had Enough – Sebastian Bach (Give 'Em Hell, 2014)
304.   Somehow – Every Mother's Nightmare (Smokin' Delta Voodoo, 2000)
305.   Afraid of Love – Danger, Danger (Ted Poley) (Cockroach, 2001)
306.   Operator – Shameless (Splashed, 2002)
307.   Without Your Love – TnT – 1984
308.   Nothin' Great About a Heartache – Bad4Good (Refuge, 1992)
309.   After the Rain – XYZ (XYZ, 1989)
310.   Nothing Left to Say – Dokken (Dysfunctional, 1994)
311.   Let Me In – Great White (Full Circle, 2017)
312.   The Man Who Has Everything – Mr. Big (The Stories We Could Tell, 2014)
313.   Gone With the Wind – Great White (Sail Away, 1994)
314.   Letting You Go – Bon Jovi (These Days, 1995)
315.   Fantasy – Reckless Love (Animal Attraction, 2011)

316.   Perfectly – TnT (My Religion, 2004)
317.   This Time – Y&T – (In Rock We Trust, 1984)
318.   So Savage the Heart – Babylon A.D. (Nothing Sacred, 1992)
319.   I Believe – Tigertailz (Bezerk 2.0, 2006)
320.   The Missing Kind – TnT (Atlantis, 2008)
321.   It Can't Be that Bad – Shameless FT: Frankie Muriel (The Filthy 7, 2017)
322.   Home – Like an Army (single release, 2013)
323.   Don't Hide Your Heart – Shanghai (Take Another Bite, 2000)
324.   Who's the One – Winger (Pull, 1993)
325.   Picture Yourself – Joey C. Jones (Melodies for the Masses, 2006)
326.   Good Night – The Last Vegas (Bad Decisions, 2012)
327.   Tonite – Tora Tora (Bombs Away, 2009)
328.   Never Let You Go – White Lion (Return Of The Pride, 2008)
329.   Hard to Say Goodbye – Slaughter (Revolution, 1997)
330.   Not One Night – Mr. Big (Best of Mr. Big, 1996)
331.   Through These Eyes – Shanghai (Bombs Away, 2001)
332.   Just in Case – Tesla (Forever More, 2008)
333.   No Regrets – Y&T (Musically Incorrect, 1995)
334.   D'Stroll – D'Molls (D'Molls, 1988)
335.   Time for Change – Motley Crue (Dr. Feelgood, 1989)
336.   Home – Warrant (Rockaholic, 2011)
337.   In Your Heart – Little Caesar (Little Caesar, 1990)
338.   My New Religion – Mr. Big (Get Over It, 1999)
339.   After All This Time – Winger (Karma, 2009)
340.   I Don't Want to be Happy – Mr. Big (Actual Size, 2001)
341.   10,000 Miles Away – Motley Crue (Quaternary, 1994)
342.   Paradise in the Sand – Beau Nasty (Dirty, But Well Dressed, 1989)
343.   Blind Faith – Def Leppard (Def Leppard, 2015)
344.   Now or Forever – D-A-D (Simpatico, 1997)
345.   Redemption – Little Caesar (Redemption, 2009)
346.   Love Walked In – Thunder (Backstreet Sympathy, 1990)
347.   Good 2B Alive – Steelheart (Good 2b Alive, 2008)
348.   Thick and Thin – Tom Keifer (The Way Life Goes, 2013)
349.   Better Off Alone – Vains of Jenna (The Art of Telling Lies, 2009)
350.   Stranger in My Life – Mr. Big (What If..., 2011)

Top Albums

1. Appetite for Destruction – Guns N' Roses – 1987
The album that shifted the genre from pretty-boy hair bands to hard rock hair metal bad boys, Guns N' Roses Appetite for Destruction is the quintessential album for everything that was good about the era.

Unlike many of their fellow rockers, there was nothing fake or manufactured about GnR or its music. Axl Rose's growling vocals, full of anger, angst and venom. Slash shredding on the guitar. Duff McKagan's punk rock bass lines. Steven Adler's Hollywood style feel good groove on the kit. And Izzy Stradlin's Rolling Stones inspire song writing (and look).

Throw all that together and it is no surprise the best overall rock band of the 80s would also release the best hair metal album of the entire genre. Appetite is still the greatest selling debut album of all time, clocking in at more than 30 million copies sold. It had one of the longest stays on the Billboard top album chart in rock history, staying listed for more than three years (172 total weeks) from its 1987 release date.

2. Pyromania – Def Leppard – 1983
The album that truly kicked off the entire genre. In the early 80s, bands like Judas Priest, Van Halen, Iron Maiden and Kiss were the leaders of the Metal scene. Crowds were digging their sound, but many were searching for something that was heavy but was also a little more pop friendly. A sound you could cruise around in your car too or having a beach kegger with your best friends. Rock with an edge – but friendly enough for your girlfriend to like. Pyromania was the album that brought hard rock back to the masses.

3. Slippery When Wet – Bon Jovi – 1986
The best pure hair band of all time came up with the best album of 1986 and helped define the genre for the next several years. Bon Jovi laid the groundwork for all future power ballads with their classic songs Wanted Dead or Alive and Never Say Goodbye.

4. Hysteria – Def Leppard – 1987

Hysteria was a legit contender for the number one spot as it spawned four top 10 hits and sold more than 25 million copies. Many hair band fans will proudly declare it as the best album in the genre's history. But it falls to number four due to Def Leppard seemingly altering their sound to cash in on the 80s popular music theme. With that said – they still did it better than almost everybody else.

Big hooks, great backing vocals, power ballads and arena anthems – Hysteria had them all.

5. Skid Row – Skid Row – 1989

The album that introduced the world to the man who might have had the best voice in the entire genre – Sebastian Bach. Brilliant songwriters Dave Sabo and Rachel Bolan contributed three tracks that are still revered today – Youth Gone Wild, 18 and Life and I Remember You.

Skid Row promoted this album opening for Aerosmith and Bon Jovi. Many still feel like the Skidders blew their more popular headliners off the stage.

6. Girls, Girls, Girls – Motley Crue – 1987

Vince Neil never sounded better. Motley Crue really hit their stride in 1987, shedding their makeup and teased hair for motorcycles and leather jackets. Girls, Girls, Girls went all the way to #2 on Billboard.

7. New Jersey – Bon Jovi – 1988

How do you follow up a number one album that sold almost 20 million copies? If your Bon Jovi, you release another number one album that featured five top 10 Billboard hits.

New Jersey produced two number one smashes – I'll Be There For You and Bad Medicine.

8. Use Your Illusion II – Guns N' Roses – 1991

Reached number one on Billboard and spent 106 weeks on the charts. Who can forget the Terminator video for You Could Be Mine? Axl's epic ballad Estranged is also featured on II.

9. Dr. Feelgood – Motley Crue – 1989

By 1989, Motley Crue were the older statesmen of the hair metal era. Growing as songwriters and musicians, Dr. Feelgood was the band's only number one album.

10. Slave to the Grind – Skid Row – 1991

The heaviest album of the entire genre. Also one of the best. Reached number one on Billboard album chart.

11. Long Cold Winter – Cinderella – 1988

The best blues-based rock album of the decade. Cinderella really came into their own as a powerhouse band with Long Cold Winter, which featured a couple Billboard top 20 power ballads

12. Night Songs – Cinderella – 1986

Reached top three on Billboard. Great debut album.

13. Whitesnake – Whitesnake – 1987

The album that made Tawny Kitaen famous. David Coverdale was masterful and the songs kicked ass. Still of the Night has one of the best opening riffs in rock history.

14. Blow My Fuse – Kix – 1988

The East Coast legends top selling and most critically revered album.

15. Too Fast for Love – Motley Crue – 1981

Still labeled as Motley's most honest album.

16. Open Up and Say...Ahh! – Poison – 1988

Glam rocker's most successful album, led by iconic power ballad Every Rose Has Its Thorns.

17. Out of the Cellar – Ratt – 1984

Their debut and best album. Reached #7 on the Billboard album chart. People still love Round and Round today.

18. Tooth and Nail – Dokken – 1984

George Lynch and Don Dokken were already feuding, but they still
created a guitar-heavy masterpiece.

19. Shout at the Devil – Motley Crue – 1983
Pyromania opened the door, but Motley jumped through that door
with middle fingers held high and invited fans to convert to the dark
side with Shout at the Devil.

20. Metal Health – Quiet Riot – 1983
Reached number one on Billboard. Produced the hair metal
masterpiece Cum On Feel the Noize.

21. Under Lock and Key – Dokken – 1985
22. L.A. Guns – L.A. Guns - 1988
23. Mechanical Resonance – Tesla - 1986
24. Love at First Sting – Scorpions - 1984
25. Once Bitten – Great White - 1987
26. Doin' The Nasty – Slik Toxik - 1992
27. Dog Eat Dog – Warrant – 1992
28. Cherry Pie – Warrant – 1990
29. Psychotic Supper – Tesla – 1991
30. Use Your Illusion I – Guns N' Roses – 1991
31. High 'N' Dry – Def Leppard – 1981
32. Junkyard – Junkyard - 1989
33. Enuff Z'Nuff – Enuff Z'Nuff – 1989
34. Heartbreak Station – Cinderella – 1990
35. Look What the Cat Dragged In – Poison – 1986
36. Cocked & Loaded – L.A. Guns - 1989
37. ... Twice Shy – Great White - 1989
38. Invasion of Your Privacy – Ratt – 1985
39. Bust A Nut – Tesla – 1994
40. These Days – Bon Jovi – 1995
41. Dirty Rotten Filthy Stinking Rich – Warrant - 1989
42. Waking the Dead – L.A. Guns - 2002
43. Dancing Undercover – Ratt – 1986
44. Savage Amusement – Scorpions – 1988
45. Faster Pussycat – Faster Pussycat - 1987
46. Dangerous Toys – Dangerous Toys – 1989
47. No Respect – Vain - 1989
48. Flesh & Blood – Poison – 1990
49. Breaking the Chains – Dokken – 1981/83

50. Winger – Winger - 1988
51. Pride – White Lion – 1987
52. Big Game – White Lion – 1989
53. Kingdom Come – Kingdom Come - 1988
54. Stick it to Ya – Slaughter – 1990
55. Screw It! – Danger Danger – 1991
56. Adrenalize – Def Leppard - 1992
57. Infestation – Ratt - 2010
58. The Final Countdown – Europe - 1986
59. The Great Radio Controversy – Tesla - 1989
60. Slide it In – Whitesnake - 1984
61. Theatre of Pain – Motley Crue – 1985
62. Surprise Attack – Tora Tora – 1989
63. Bon Jovi – Bon Jovi – 1984
64. The Wild Life – Slaughter – 1992
65. Danger Danger – Danger Danger - 1989
66. Babylon A.D. – Babylon A.D. – 1989
67. Motley Crue – Motley Crue – 1994
68. Back for the Attack – Dokken – 1987
69. Lita - Lita Ford – 1988
70. Keep the Faith – Bon Jovi – 1992
71. Sail Away – Great White – 1994
72. Reach for the Sky – Ratt – 1988
73. Two Steps from the Move – Hanoi Rocks - 1984
74. Stay Hungry – Twisted Sister – 1984
75. Chinese Democracy – Guns N' Roses - 2008
76. Leather Boyz with Electric Toyz – Pretty Boy Floyd - 1989
77. Midnite Dynamite – Kix - 1985
78. It's Only Rock 'n' Roll – Hardcore Superstar - 1998
79. Up From The Ashes – Don Dokken - 1990
80. Out of This World – Europe – 1988
81. Every Dog Has Its Day – Salty Dog – 1990
82. Lean Into It – Mr. Big – 1991
83. FireHouse – FireHouse – 1990
84. In God We Trust - Stryper, 1988
85. BulletBoys – BulletBoys - 1988
86. Hooked – Great White – 1991
87. Hollywood Vampires – L.A. Guns – 1991
88. Angel Down – Sebastian Bach – 2007
89. Wake Me When It's Over – Faster Pussycat – 1989
90. Exposed – Vince Neil – 1993
91. Eat Me – The Last Vegas – 2016

92. Restless Heart – Whitesnake – 1997
93. 7800 Fahrenheit – Bon Jovi – 1985
94. Mane Attraction – White Lion – 1991
95. In the Heart of the Young – Winger - 1990
96. Simpatico – D-A-D – 1997
97. Hot Wire – Kix – 1991
98. Wild America – Tora Tora – 1992
99. Hellacious Acres – Dangerous Toys - 1991
100. KINGOFTHEHILL – KINGOFTHEHILL – 1991
101. Detonator – Ratt – 1990
102. Arcade – Arcade – 1993
103. Forevermore – Whitesnake – 2011
104. Strength - Enuff Z'Nuff - 1991
105. Still Climbing – Cinderella – 1994
106. Dic-Nil-Lan-Daft-Erd-Ark – D-A-D - 2011
107. Bounce – Bon Jovi – 2002
108. Saints & Sinners – Whitesnake – 1982
109. No Regrets – Hardcore Superstar – 2003
110. Lies – Guns N' Roses - 1988
111. You Can't Stop Rock 'n' Roll – Twisted Sister - 1983
112. Twelve Shots on the Rocks – Hanoi Rocks- 2002
113. All Systems Go – Vinnie Vincent Invasion – 1988
114. Hardcore Superstar – Hardcore Superstar - 2005
115. Soft Dogs – D-A-D – 2002
116. Unreleased – KINGOFTHEHILL – 2005
117. Lynch Mob – Lynch Mob – 1992
118. Dirty Weapons – Killer Dwarfs - 1990
119. The Missing Peace – L.A. Guns - 2017
120. Whipped! – Faster Pussycat – 1992
121. Actual Size – Mr. Big – 2001
122. Vicious Circle – L.A. Guns – 1994
123. Against the Law - Stryper - 1990
124. Into the Now – Tesla – 2004
125. Wicked Sensation – Lynch Mob - 1990
126. Crush – Bon Jovi – 2000
127. Tried and True – Junkyard – 2003
128. Forever More – Tesla – 2008
129. Rising – Great White – 2009
130. In Your Face – Kingdom Come – 1989
131. Melodies for the Masses – Joey C. Jones - 2006
132. Split Your Lip – Hardcore Superstar – 2010
133. Freakshow – BulletBoys – 1991

176.   United World Rebellion Chapter One – Skid Row - 2013
177.   Long Way Home – Dokken - 2002
178.   Rolling with the Punches – Vain – 2017
179.   Big Deal – Killer Dwarfs - 1988
180.   Have a Nice Day – Bon Jovi – 2005
181.   Unleashed! – Wild Boyz - 1991
182.   Let the Games Begin – Hell in the Club - 2011
183.   Hey Man – Mr. Big – 1996
184.   Kicking & Screaming – Sebastian Bach - 2011
185.   Dissonance – Enuff Z'Nuff – 2010
186.   Can't Get There From Here – Great White - 1999
187.   He Saw it Comin' – Jack Russell - 2017
188.   Scare Yourself – D-A-D – 2005
189.   Four the Hard Way – Danger, Danger – 1997
190.   Off Your Rocker – Jetboy – 2010
191.   American Blitzkrieg – Babylon A.D. - 2000
192.   Cockroach – Danger, Danger (Ted Poley), 2001
193.   Pistol Whipped in the Bible Belt – Bang Tango - 2011
194.   To Hell with the Devil – Stryper - 1986
195.   Tell No Tales – TnT – 1987
196.   Bad Sneakers and a Pina Colada – Hardcore Superstar - 2000
197.   667 The Neighbour of the Beast – Wig Wam - 2004
198.   X – Def Leppard – 2002
199.   Animal Attraction – Reckless Love - 2011
200.   New Religion – Crazy Lixx – 2010
201.   Queen 4 a Day – Shameless – 2000
202.   Babylon's Burning – Babylon Bombs – 2009
203.   The Return of the Great Gildersleeves – Danger, Danger - 2000
204.   Let it Rock – Great White – 1996
205.   Shelter Me – Jack Russell - 1996
206.   Streets of Rock & Roll – Keel – 2010
207.   Whatever Gets You Off – The Last Vegas - 2009
208.   Start from the Dark – Europe – 2004
209.   Generation Wild – Crashdiet – 2010
210.   Under the Influence – Wildside – 1992
211.   Fastway – Fastway - 1983
212.   Bad Image – Kingdom Come – 1993
213.   Smokin' Delta Voodoo – Every Mother's Nightmare - 2000
214.   Rock Your Face Off – Kix - 2014
215.   Revolution – Slaughter – 1997

299.	Invader – Reckless Love – 2016
300.	The Lizard – Saigon Kick - 1992
301.	Louder Harder Faster – Warrant - 2017
302.	XYZ – XYZ – 1989
303.	Crazy World – Scorpions - 1990
304.	Don't Come Easy – Tyketto - 1991
305.	Saints of Los Angeles – Motley Crue – 2008
306.	Reckless Love – Reckless Love – 2010
307.	Through Worlds of Stardust – Steelheart - 2017
308.	Back to Reality – Slaughter - 1999
309.	What If… - Mr. Big – 2011
310.	Deadboys in Trash City - Alleycat Scratch – 1993
311.	Dirty, But Well Dressed – Beau Nasty - 1989
312.	Little Caesar – Little Caesar - 1990
313.	Smash – Stephen Pearcy – 2017
314.	Paraphernalia – Enuff Z'Nuff - 1999
315.	Bombs Away – Shanghai – 2001
316.	3 - FireHouse - 1995
317.	Human Era – Trixter – 2015
318.	Funk-O-Metal Carpet Ride – Electric Boys – 1989
319.	Screwed Blued & Tattooed – Sleeze Beez – 1990
320.	Cockroach – Danger Danger (Paul Laine) - 2001
321.	Tainted Angel - SouthGang – 1991
322.	Show Business – Kix – 1995
323.	Sign in Please – Autograph – 1984
324.	Penny Black – Russ Graham 2001
325.	Carved in Stone – Vince Neil – 1995
326.	Lit Up/Let Down – Vains of Jenna - 2006
327.	Halfway There – Mark Slaughter – 2017
328.	Erase the Slate – Dokken - 1999
329.	Ain't Crying for the Moon – Kingdom Come – 2006
330.	Songs From The Sparkle Lounge – Def Leppard – 2008
331.	Reach – Tyketto – 2016
332.	Ratt – Ratt – 1999
333.	Bad Blood Rising – Santa Cruz - 2017
334.	Thickskin – Skid Row – 2003
335.	Devil on My Shoulder – Hell in the Club - 2014
336.	Slang – Def Leppard – 1996
337.	Welcome to Blue Island – Enuff Z'Nuff - 2003
338.	Generation Swine – Motley Crue – 1997
339.	Bag of Bones – Europe – 2012
340.	Euphoria – Def Leppard – 1999

INTERVIEWS

These interviews are exclusive to this book. We conducted each and every one of them.

This section of the book was quite the process. A real mixture of emotions ranging from pure joy to extreme disappointment. The joy came when receiving a response from a musician that I've loved for 30-plus years. Getting an audio file from Marq Torien was surreal. Chatting with the legendary Billy Sheehan was a true highlight. Sheehan might be the best rock bass player alive today and is also one of the nicest and friendly guys around.

Several superstars went out of their way to share their valuable time with me. Guys like Jeff Pilson, Mark Kendall, Jay Jay French, Ted Poley, Mark Knight and Mike Tramp went above and beyond what they needed to do for an interview request. I'm still in awe that I got to interview Joey Allen from Warrant. I hate to single anybody out because more than 50 musicians blessed me with interviews. I owe SO MUCH to them all. I cannot thank these guys enough.

I do have to give a really big shout out to Drew Fortier of Bang Tango and Zen From Mars. Drew is also an actor, documentary maker and book writer. He has recently released his autobiography "Dark, Depressing and Hilarious." I highly suggest you purchase it. It's not listed in our "books chapter" but that's only because we were past our publishing deadline when Drew's fantastic book was released.

Fortier took the time from his extremely busy schedule to answer question after question after question.....and then a week later, ten more questions! As a writer, musician, and documentarian, he is a wealth of knowledge and was always willing to answer all my questions and give me advice on what I needed to do to get this book finished an online. THANK YOU DREW – you rock, bro.

The real bummer about the interview section came when musicians said they would do an interview but then they never responded again. Here is how the process went:

I contacted approximately 500 musicians. I sent messages to every band you could think of. From Def Leppard down to The Blonz. I sent messages to their management, official websites, their labels, and to all their social media pages. Of those 500 requests, approximately 150 responded that they would do an interview. The other 350 simply ignored the request – which is fine, I get it. I'm a "nobody" in the music world, with an unknown project. It's not like I'm representing Rolling Stone or the LA Times.

Only a handful of people flat out rejected our request. Sebastian Bach declined, saying it was an embarrassment to include him in the Hair Metal genre. That stung a little, as Bach is one of our favorite singers of all time. Zoltan Chaney told me "you've got the wrong guy"....even though he drums for Mark Slaughter and Vince Neil. And he is the guy who goes berserk with all the over-the-top crazy moves from the kit. Steven Adler's manager told us he wasn't currently doing interviews...and then I saw like 10 interviews by Adler over the following month. But I do respect those artists for having the decency to tell me they weren't interest. That was cool of them.

Ron Thal – aka: Bumblefoot – sent me the nicest rejection letter you could imagine. Thanked me for the request, said he was taking a break from interviews for a bit, and wished me the best of luck with my project and wished me a Happy Easter as well. Pure class act and a super nice guy.

The bummer aspect came when people said they'd do it…but then didn't. I tried to come up with interview questions that were interesting, funny and that they hadn't already been asked a million times – along with the obvious questions that had to be asked, of course. So when a musician agreed to an interview, I spent two hours doing research on his career and personal likes/beliefs; the history of any bands he has played with; and then I tried to read at least 10 interviews he had done in the past. I would try and read interviews spread out over his entire career (not just current ones promoting his latest project). From each of those things I'd usually be able to find random interesting facts. One funny or unusual comment a musician made in a 1984 interview was like finding a gold nugget.

I spent an average of two hours doing research for each and every interview. When approximately 100 guys say "yes, let's do it" and then they don't end up responding…that's literally more than 200 hours of wasted time. Two hundred hours I could have been doing something else, hanging with the family, etc. That's a lot of time down the drain. This paragraph isn't to send negative or discouraging vibes towards any of the musicians who did this. I 100% realize people get busy, things happen in life.

So if you are disappointed that nobody from your favorite band was included in this interview section, I do apologize. But it wasn't for lack of effort. I tried to get them!

Billy Sheehan
Mr. Big, Sons of Apollo, Winery Dogs…best rock bass player alive?

Photo courtesy of Mr. Sheehan.

__1. Is it safe to say that the Kozten/Martin era of Mr. Big decided to try and replace you because they were intimidated by your singing ability???__

Sheehan: I'd never heard that before. Not sure.

__2. Who do you kid the most? Gilbert for some of his one-piece suits he word, Vai for losing to Ralph Macchio in a guitar duel or Kotzen for playing in Poison?__

Sheehan: All equally, lol! No, actually none. Time marches on. There is no past.

__3. What do you do with Spooky when you go on tour? Does Spooky mind the tour bus life?__

Sheehan: There is always someone with her. She is never left alone. She doesn't travel ever. She's the Queen of the castle, and we are her servants!

__4. You've worked with some monster guitar players over the years, really the best musicians in the world. MacFarline, Vai, Gilbert, Kotzen, Glen Proudfoot, Kuni, Billy Gibbons, Michael Schenker amongst others. Is that a conscious effort and pairing on your part – if so, how come? (You like to be inspired, pushed by the best, etc)__

Sheehan: It kind of just happens. I like to play with great players, and nature takes its course. I'm mostly concerned with the drummer though, that's my main concern as a bass player.

__5. I know you are too classy of a guy to rank them. But is there one or__

*two of them that really standout in terms of amazing you with their
ability? Or how about one or two that you've really connected with on a
personal and professional level (IE: your string soul mate)?*

Sheehan: Hard to say. Everybody is different. The greatest musician I
know is a drummer Dennis Chambers.

*6. You are one of the most cordial rock stars in the world. Always
extremely friendly with your fans, you respond to fan's comments on
social media, etc. Why is it important for you – one of the biggest and
most famous musicians in the world – to take the time to engage with
your fans?*

Sheehan: Because they are everything to me. I'm supremely grateful to
them for listening to my music and attending shows and so much more. I
actually don't view them as fans---I consider them my friends. Plus, being
in direct contact and close contact is always enjoyable and enlightening.

*7. When did you first get involved with Scientology? What piqued your
interest and can you summarize what benefits it has had to your career?*

Sheehan: 1971. It's been a great help to me. I always want to improve in
life, in music, in every area I can. I read a lot---many subjects. I love
language and I'm a passionate self-educator. Especially scientific subjects.
It all goes together.

*8. From what I've read or watched on TV, it seems the leaders run a
pretty tight and regimented ship. They don't mind having a famous rock
star out touring the world? (Since rock music is often associated with
sex, drugs and craziness).*

Sheehan: I haven't had even an aspirin since 1971, I don't do any drugs
at all, and I've always been respectful to women, so that's not an issue
with me.

*9. Speaking of sex, drugs and rock n roll….Your FB page is full of
pictures of cats, trees, deer in your yard, meals you're cooking. I can tell
you as a fan, we love that kind of thing. It's refreshing to see guys we*

normally see as "larger than life" musicians are actually just normal people in real life.

Sheehan: We're all in this together. We are all equal. Your job is important too. And we all have to eat!

10. How come you haven't written a book about your life yet? You are a natural storyteller and have had a career that most musicians could only dream of. Have you thought about a book or a podcast?

Sheehan: I may write a book. An all-inclusive autobiography. I'm just a working musician trying to do my best to entertain and enlighten the best way I know how. Who knows how things might have been if circumstances were different---maybe even better, but either way, I'm supremely grateful to everyone who helped make things turn out the way they did.

11. What was the more fun, exciting and/or satisfying year for you: 1986 or 2012? Two amazing years for sure.

1986: DLR Band and Eat em' and Smile, plus albums with Kuni and Tony MacAlpine.
2012: Talas reunion, PSMS tour, formed Winery Dogs, and still fresh off the 2011 Mr. Big album and tour.

Sheehan: Pretty tough to beat 1986! But 1992 was amazing, and I was very fortunate at many other stages along the way. Again, I'm very grateful for it all.

12. How did you get involved with Japanese guitar player Kuni?

Sheehan: He contacted me to play on his record. Pretty simple story. We're still very good friends.

13. How come you choose to play with so many different artists and bands? There are some guys that just play for one band for 30 years – but you've played for so many different people that we can't even mention or ask you about them all or this interview would be 10 pages long.

Sheehan: I think it expands your musical vocabulary and broadens your range as a player, singer, songwriter, and performer. It's really not that many bands that I've been seriously involved with---especially when you consider I've been doing it for over 50 years.

14. Which solo album is your favorite? Is there one that you are most proud of or that showcases your skills the best?

Sheehan: *Holy Cow* was a pretty good one in my humble opinion. But each one was a snapshot of where I was at as a player, singer, songwriter, at a particular moment. It's all a learning process, and I'm pleased at how they all turned out.

15. Why put Winery Dogs on hiatus and start the Sons of Apollo band? Everybody seemed to love the Winery Dogs, both albums were Billboard hits, crowds loved you guys. It seemed like an odd time to shut that band down and start a new one?

Sheehan: The Winery Dogs are my favorite band. We did an album, a tour, another album, and another tour, and did not want to get caught in that never-ending cycle. There's a reason why the first record or so of a band are considered their best work(s). After that, the endless cycle of album/tour, album/tour begins to drain the creativity (not in all cases of course), and we didn't want that to happen. So we took a break. We'll continue with lots of fresh new ideas and life experiences to write about very soon. In the interim, Sons of Apollo has been a blast! We are enjoying it immensely, and plan to continue to do so.

16. You've played with the most incredible guitar players in the world. What interests you about Bumblefoot's skills? On a side note, he turned us down for an interview but gave us the most polite and friendly rejection letter that we've received.

Sheehan: He's a supreme talent with great ears and musical abilities. Very inspiring.

17. What can fans expect from a Sons of Apollo concert?

Sheehan: Extremely high energy execution of difficult musical pieces, interspersed with lots of fun. A non-serious approach to serious playing.

18. We read that the Sons of Apollo album took ten days to write and record. Axl Rose apparently took 13 million dollars and 13 years to write and release Chinese Democracy! Did you listen to that album and if so, did you enjoy it? What could you do with a 13 million dollar budget!!!

Sheehan: Never heard that record, no. With 13 million I could do 10 great records and open up a free hospital with what's left over.

19. You've played just about every genre of music, from jazz to rock to metal to pop. Is there one style that you enjoy playing the most?

Sheehan: Straight up rock is my thing. But there are lots of little pieces of other styles in rock. So doing other kinds of music adds to my musical "vocabulary" in many ways. But I do love many kinds of music in general.

20. If a label handed you a blank check for an album and tour in 2019 and gave you carte blanche to put together your own project…..what would you do? Any specific artists and style of music?

Sheehan: I'd get a great singing drummer and make sure everyone else in the band sings. I'd put together a supremely entertaining show with great songs and take it around the world. Oh wait---that was Mr. Big. And the Winery Dogs!

21. We read that you were an ACDC fan. What are your thoughts on Angus keeping the band together and doing an album/tour with Axl Rose?

Sheehan: I thought Axl sang it well! I only heard a snippet or two of a song or so, but it sounded good. Bon Scott was my favorite though. Though Brian Johnson is great too.

22. We know the proposed reunion with the DLR band a couple years ago got shut down by the fire marshal. Is there any chance that might happen again? Would you be into a one-off show or a mini-tour with those guys?

Sheehan: We all would love to, but it's up to Dave.

23. That band and DLR are so interesting. The first album was amazing, one of the best hard rock albums of the year. The second album had some great stuff on it.....but also clearly showed a bit of a change of style. How come you ended up leaving that band?

Sheehan: *Eat 'em & Smile* was a blast. Writing, recording, touring, hanging out--we had a great time. I loved the music and live shows. On *Skyscraper* everything changed. It was no longer fun. Not my thing. The record was put together a piece at a time, rather than the whole band actually playing together. *Unlike Eat em & Smile.* So I put together Mr. Big to do things together as a band again.

24. What do you think when you look at a guy like DLR's career? For a long time he was "THE" rock God singer out there. Lead singer of the best rock band alive. Every woman wanted him and every guy wanted to be him. Then his career went into the dumpster for awhile. Then he has some crazy stuff with a VH reunion, and reports are that his behavior ruined the VH reunion, and he hampered the dual-tour with Sammy Hagar. Finally, VH does reunite again…and the guy who used to be The Alpha Male of rock music comes out, his voice is shot and he's dancing around like he is in a Broadway play. There is nothing wrong with Broadway dancers and singers…but just not for the guy fronting Van Halen!!! Maybe I shouldn't even ask you that question. It's just a fascinating situation and I am curious what one of his peers thinks about it.

Sheehan: Dave was, is, and always will be a hero and an inspiration to me. His motivations are his own choice and I respect him for that. His legacy will endure.

25. You once said that To Be With You was one of the hardest songs for you to play. That was surprising to hear. You've played some of the most technically challenging music out there, you've personally invented bass playing techniques…but a rock power ballad is the toughest to play?

Sheehan: I don't believe I've ever said that. I know me and I remember very well. I would have never had any reason to say such a thing because it's simply not the case. I think someone misinterpreted something at the very least.

What may have been misinterpreted is that everyone was focusing on the flash and histrionics, a sweet little ballad came from behind and became number one. In the USA for 3 weeks, and in 14 other countries around the world. All of us loved that.

26. What's the story behind Shyboy? We've just listened to live versions from DLR and Eric Martin. And to be honest, that song kicks so much ass that both singers have trouble keeping up with it.

Sheehan: It's just a song I wrote in Talas. Dave liked it and put it on *Eat 'em & Smile*. Other bands have done it too. Usually somewhat against my will, as it's just been done too much.

27. Quick Thoughts on:

Paul Gilbert: Dear friend, brilliant player

Richie Kotzen: Dear friend, incredible vocal, genius guitar

Stevie Vai: Like a brother to me. A true artist

Niacin: I got to play with the KING! Dennis Chambers

Pat Torpey: Also like a brother to me, supreme grand master of drums, incredible singer, and dearly missed every single day.

Eric Martin: A voice as good as it gets, brilliant songwriter, very dear friend.

Glen Proudfoot: Enjoyed working w him very much

Explorer's Club: One of my favorite records ever. Criminally overlooked.

Jeff Pilson:
Dokken

Picture courtesy of Mr. Pilson's official Facebook page. See link below.

__1. Right off the bat, let's settle the question that you probably get asked a million times! Who is the better singer – you or Mick Brown?__

Pilson: Mick and I have completely different voices, that's part of what makes our chemistry so great. Mick has a wonderful natural rasp that immediately adds edge to a part- very important. We complement each other beautifully.

__2. I have you and Lynch in our Top 20 list of most under appreciated artists of the genre. Dokken is named after the singer, obviously, and he has the magic voice. But you and Lynch have writing credits on almost all the hits. Plus you are a great musician; Lynch is a guitar legend. And you are also a great singer. Do you feel that you (and maybe Lynch) don't get the recognition that you probably deserve?__

Pilson: I don't really think about that much. It's kind of baked in that, unless you're Nikki Sixx of course, as a bass player you're not going to get all the attention the singer (and guitar player) get- I can live with that.

I think George gets a lot of the credit he deserves. I don't think people give him the credit he deserves when it comes to songwriting- even melodies and occasionally lyrics. He's way more than just a brilliant guitarist.

3. Thinking about that question, is there another artist (or band) out there that you feel should be way more respected and talked about than they are?

Pilson: I've always felt that Winger got way too much unfair criticism and not NEAR the credit they deserved. What an amazing bunch of musicians, singers and songwriters. So Kip was a good dancer- that shouldn't take away from his recognition as a great musician!

4. You replaced Juan Croucier in Dokken back in the day. Did he have his killer theatrical stage moves back then? Do you remember the reasons why he left a band that appeared to be on the edge of stardom?

Pilson: Juan left because Ratt got their deal and he was more comfortable with them. And yes he was a great performer back then as well!!

5...You have toured with Judas Priest, ACDC, Aerosmith, Dio, Kiss, Scorpions, Van Halen, Metallica amongst many other superstars. As well as performing with numerous heavyweight musicians. Is there a band or musician that had the most impact on you? That you learned how to be a real professional by watching how they acted and behaved on tour and in the studio?

Pilson: Our biggest "wake up call" and learning experience was the Dio tour we did in 84 and 85. We learned so much from them about pretty much everything. George and I would watch every night. They were so tight, sounded so good and knew dynamics. Big learning experience.

6. How was the Monsters of Rock Tour? Who was the most professional band on the lineup and who was the craziest?

Pilson: Monsters of Rock was great- what I remember of it!!!!!! A lot of drink and drugs on that tour. Hard to say who was craziest, we all tried to outdo one another in that department! But Scorpions were definitely the most disciplined. They partied but they knew when to stop more than the rest of us!

7. War & Piece had a pretty legendary cast of musicians and your vocals were spot on. How come a label didn't get involved, put out a full length album and send you on tour opening for a major act?

Pilson: W&P was trying to get a record deal just as 80s metal was completely falling out of fashion with the labels. It was an impossible task in 92.

8. You collaborated with George Lynch on his first solo album – Sacred Groove. Do you remember the story behind Don not showing up to sing the song he co-wrote with George? And oddly enough the Nelson brothers and their long flowing blond hair were selected to fill in on vocals? Were the Milli Vanilli guys not available?

Pilson: I don't really remember much about that. I thought they sang it great!

9. I don't want to go into the behind the scenes drama with Dokken. That's all been covered to death. Two small questions though. Did John Norum tell you when he joined the band that he had prior commitments that would force him to drop out? It seems aggravating to try and replace a legend, spend time working with the new guy…and then for him to quickly bail? Then Beach comes, stays for a bit, and he bails.

Pilson: At the time I think we were all just playing it by ear. I don't exactly remember why John left, but I believe Reb left when I did.

10. Reb Beach is a monster on guitar. How was it working with him?

Pilson: I love Reb and I'd work with him anytime, anywhere for any reason! He's incredibly talented and amazing to collaborate with.

11. How fun and exciting was it when you and Lynch joined Dokken on stage at a 2009 show at the House of Blues. Reportedly it was the first time in 12 years the four classic guys had shared a stage. How did that all come about? Did you and Lynch just storm the stage or were you and Don talking before hand to set it up The audience must have lost their minds when you two walked out.

Pilson: It was very exciting and fun. As I recall it was kind of put to me (I think from George?) c'mon down, maybe we'll all play. I couldn't resist. It was a very special night. You could feel the chemistry.

12. How excited are you for the release of the 2017 live DVD? How were the Japanese fans on that mini-tour? What kind of crowd sizes were you playing to?

Pilson: I'm extremely excited for the release. The Japanese were amazing, the tour a lot of fun and the venues were anywhere from 2000 to Loudpark festival with 40,000 people.

13. Did you enjoy your acting career? Any chance of trying to become the next Tom Cruise after appearing in the movie Steel Dragon? How realistic was the movie in terms of what goes on in the studio, backstage and on tour? Did you and Marky Mark ever have a "best abs" competition? If so, who won?

Pilson: It was a great experience. I think it was more realistic than most music movies because the director made a point of consulting with us about many of the scenes. He wanted it close. There was a bit of "Hollywood" in there, but overall pretty damn good. Mark would win the abs competition hands down!!!!!

14. Can you share your experience at the Hear N' Aid shoot? That's probably the greatest assembly of rock talent at one place at one time in the history of rock music. Was it fun, were people having a good time, did everybody leave their egos at the door?

Pilson: That too was really fun. The session itself was only a few hours- but lots of laughs. I do remember the party extending until the next morning!

15. "Cum on Feel the Noize" gets the credit for being the song that started the Hair Metal genre. But in reality, "Breaking the Chains" might actually be the first song of the era to ever be recorded (overseas – but still, it was out there). I've read Don badmouth those who put Dokken in the hair metal or hair band genre. So he'd probably get mad

at this question! Thoughts on that? Dokken might have literally birthed the hair metal genre with Breaking the Chains!!!

Pilson: I look at it more as a movement that was gonna happen regardless. It only became "hair metal" at the end- after the glam stuff from Motley, Poison, us, etc. Before that it was just heavy metal and Dokken and The Boys (George and Mick's band) were right there with Van Halen as the big rock acts in Los Angeles. Van Halen were the first to break through, then the "new wave" happened, so Dokken went overseas. But really it was a continuation of what Van Halen was doing that brought rock and the metal scene back to LA.

16. Also, what are your thoughts on the label? In reality, it's just an easy way to describe a specific type of music that was mainly released in a specific time period. It's all rock and roll at the end of the day. But hair metal, sleaze metal, arena rock, hair band, glam – is there any label you'd prefer? Or do you get annoyed with the hair metal label like Don does? I wish I could come up with a better name to describe the genre. You have one?

Pilson: I just think saying hair metal minimizes a lot of the music that happened in that era. Are the Scorpions hair metal? The music is awfully similar to ours- just maybe not the amount of hair spray for about a two-year period! Labels are always limiting, but people use them anyways. When I hear hair metal, I associate it more with the end of the 80s and glam. Earlier in the 80s it was about being heavy, yet melodic.

17. Besides music, do you have any other hobbies that you really love doing? If you wouldn't have found success as a musician, what do you think you would have ended up doing as a career?

Pilson: Hard to say- music is too much a part of my life to even imagine anything else.

18. Do you remember the process of writing "Dream Warriors" with Lynch? That has to be the most successful Dokken song that doesn't feature Don on the song writing credits. Was he loosening the reigns a bit and letting you guys have more freedom?

Pilson: I remember the process well. We just got our new Akai 12 track recorder - very exciting. No it wasn't loosening the reins- there were no reins, we always had written a bit separately like that. It just came down to George and I wrote a Dream Warriors and so did Don, the movie picked George and mine. Pretty simple.

19. Shadowlife doesn't get a lot of love from Dokken fans. Thoughts on that album?

Pilson: Underrated for quality but not really a Dokken record at all. Good moments, but not overall cohesive. It fell apart. Tried to do something else and it didn't really work!

20. Have you ever gotten to play the Cello on an album? Do you regret switching over and going the bass route?

Pilson: No and no. But if Dokken ever does an acoustic remake of "Walk Away" I did write a cello part for that!

21. What kind of student were you back in the R.A. Long days? Popular, good kid, athlete, hoodlum, etc? Does a person of your stature go to class reunions? If so….how do your classmates treat you?

Pilson: I was a good student. I had to be for my parents to let me play clubs. I was also a joker but got along with pretty much everybody. I was always in bands and that helped. I haven't been to reunion yet but I'd love to. I keep in touch with a fair amount of high school mates, and social media helps with that.

22. In your younger days, you helped put on a rock opera called Rock Justice? How was that experience, what did you do, and was it a big hit? Did they rip off your production for Rock of Ages?

Pilson: I loved Rock Justice- big opportunity for me. Unfortunately the record turned out quite disappointing, the songs were better than what they got. Youth and inexperience. Oh well, huge learning experience and great lesson.

23…Do you remember your audition with Dokken? Did you go in and just jam or did you have to play specific songs? Was it Don or the entire band watching?

Pilson: I remember my audition well. We played (all four of us) for about 20 minutes. I don't remember what we played…then we blew the power. I remember right when the power went down they asked if I wanted the gig!!

24…What was it like working with Dio? He's basically a God in the rock music world – and you got to write with him, record songs, tour and just sit around and chat. How was he in real life (off the stage)?

Pilson: Ronnie was the greatest. So inspiring to work with. The feeling of playing with he and Vinny (and Tracy G) was awesome. We just knew we kicked ass - great feeling. Offstage Ron was completely down to earth and a great friend. I miss him every day.

25. Sebastian Bach sang on a T&N song for you guys. Is he as crazy as he seems?

Pilson: Sebastian was actually a joy in the studio. He was prepared, professional and did it until it was right. He kicked ass and sounded amazing. I hear stories about him, but have known him over 30 years - he's just a big kid. He's fun, a little wild, but very talented and perseverant.

26. You aren't writing as much as you normally have in the past with bands while you are working with Foreigner. But you are doing a lot of producing work for them. Was that by design or just the way things have worked out?

Pilson: Mostly just that for writing Mick is extremely comfortable working with Marti (Fredericksen) and why fix something that isn't broken? They have a great chemistry and the results speak for themselves.

27. If a major label – or crazy billionaire who loves rock music – called you up and offered a 10 million dollar check to work on whatever project you chose in 2019. What would you choose? To work as a

singer, writer, bass player or a producer. And which band members or band would you call up and offer the gig to?

Pilson: I would definitely produce, not sure what it would be. For that kind of $$$, I'd want to find the best for every position. That's not something you figure out quickly in an interview!!!!! But please, send the billionaire my way!!!

28. What was it like working with Steven Adler? Do you think the GnR semi-reunion crew should have brought Adler and Izzy along with them to share the glory and wealth?

Pilson: I'm biased because Steven is my best friend, but he's beyond amazing to work with. When he's "on" and in the groove, he brings something so magical to a recording. It's impossible to put in words. But there's no doubt in my mind that a lot of the raw energy in the tracks on *Appetite for Destruction* come from his reckless abandon and hellfire swing! I do really hope someday there's a full reunion with all five original GnR members. I think it'd be magic and such a shame if it were never to happen. I haven't given up hope because I believe deep down all five of those guys actually feel the same way.

29. Do you remember the infamous Axl-vs-Vince proposed fight? Vince Neil went on MTV and challenged Axl Rose to a fistfight.. Who would have won that one?

Pilson: Tough call- really don't know. Silly though, don't you think?

30. The online world has kind of ruined the good old days of when bands released albums every year or every other year. What are your thoughts on that? And was there something labels/bands could have did different to stop this from happening? And do you ever see it changing in the future. What everybody says now is that there isn't money in albums, the money comes from touring. Is that just what we have to live with now?

Pilson: I think the music business is in a huge slump right now, but no, I don't think it'll stay that way forever. We may be in a "singles" world for a while, where bands just do one or two songs at a time. But eventually someone will figure a way to monetize the Internet and serious musicians who want or need to do full records will find a way to make it work. Music isn't going away, it's just going through an awkward puberty!

31. Rock fans might be surprised that you wrote on and produced the album Loveless Fascination by Starship – Mickey Thomas. How was that experience. Is it hard to switch up your writing styles between different genres?

Pilson: What a joy that record was. Mickey is the real deal. You just don't find voices like that every day. And on top of it he's a wonderful guy and we had so much fun making that record. Rather, that record made us! It was as if we were just filling in the blanks for something that was destined to be there. I'm still very proud of that record and hope I get to work with Mickey again.

32. And in your free time – which you must have zero of – you occasionally find time to participate in rock 'n' roll fantasy camps! How is that experience? Are the musicians usually fairly decent or are they mainly interested in jamming with their rock heroes?

Pilson: It's real hit or miss cuz you have the full spectrum of levels of musicianship in there. Everyone has their own reason for going. But nearly without exception the campers have great attitudes and just want to play. You can't go wrong with that attitude.

33. You grew up in Washington and spent time in the Seattle area in the 80s. Is it safe to say that you started the Grunge movement?

Pilson: No but I was wearing flannel in the 70's!!!!!!!

34. We've read some of your interviews where you share some of your political opinions. Do you have any thoughts or suggestions on what we – the people – need to do to help combat and stop the wave of school shootings and mass shootings? What can we do?

Pilson: Go out and vote! Stay involved and pressure lawmakers to do the right thing - whatever you believe that to be. The students in Florida are such a great example of working together to make a statement and it got some results! A democracy (though we're really a republic) depends on the masses being informed. Stay informed and involved - whether you're right or left!

35. Who is your favorite bass player of all time?

Pilson: It would have to be Chris Squire of Yes. His playing and his tone affected me like no one else ever did. It changed my life. The Beatles changed my life musically. Chris changed my bass playing. He made me get very serious. I still get goose bumps from "Close to the Edge" and "Heart of the Sunrise!"

36. Finally. Can you tell us the handful of albums or songs that you are most proud of your work on? What ones really describe your career the way you want them to the most?

Pilson: Adler, Starship, TNN, Heavy Crown (Last in Line), Warrant, gosh the list goes on. Also, I love the Flame Still Burns track that was on the Foreigner 40 record. I've been lucky to work with so many great musicians and writers.

37. Final Quick Thoughts:

Don Dokken: Great lyricist and can be an extremely generous man

Mick Brown: Talented musician- very funny

George Lynch: Genius, fantastic sense of humor, dear friend for over half my life

GnR: Magical band when the chemistry is right

Dio: Greatest metal singer ever and one of the dearest friends ever- Miss him so much

Duff: Great bass player, great guy, frigging smart businessman

Jaimo Jamerson: Inventor of R&B funk electric bass playing. Genius

McCartney: inspired songwriter, inventive bass player, legend

John Paul Jones: Never given the real credit he is due. Phenomenal bass player, arranger and all around musician

Billy Sheehan: The best soloing bassist alive. And the reason is that he comes from deep roots that involve grooving and soul, which makes his soloing so special and musical

Welcome to the Jungle: Great song- started the whole ball rolling!

https://twitter.com/JeffPilson
https://jeffpilson.wordpress.com
https://www.facebook.com/OfficialJeffPilson

Mike Tramp
White Lion

Photo courtesy of Mr. Tramp's official webpage.

1. Does it bother you that a lot of fans have misidentified White Lion as a "melodic hair band"…mainly because of the When the Children Cry song/video? You guys were a straight up rock band, with a killer guitar sound, aggressive lyrics, arena anthem choruses. Heck, you guys opened for Ozzy, Aerosmith and ACDC for pete's sakes!!! And you guys were really heavy live. I always thought you guys got unfairly lumped in with bands that you were clearly a notch above.

Tramp: It's really just a lazy way of not identifying something the proper way. But it would be easier to say this. During the 80's no one called any band Hair bands, it was something that came later on, once the

80's were gone, and people had to identify bands of the 80's, when what they should have done is just name the bands for their music.

2. Speaking of ACDC, what do you think of Axl Rose touring with them? What do you think of the two super groups combining with Axl essentially joining ACDC?

Tramp: Here comes yet another mess of identifying or calling the beast by its proper name. We AC/DC fans know who AC/DC is, and there was no AC/DC once Malcolm Young, and later Brian Johnson and you can add Phil Rudd was gone. Now if you just went ahead and called it Angus Young & friends featuring Axl Rose, there would be very little crying or complaining. But this thing you mention makes no sense at all, especially because it sounds serious and not a side project done for fun. I like Axl and I like Angus, but I don't buy this, not at all.

3. What do you take more pride in – your songwriting skills or your vocal abilities and performances? Does it ever bother you that you don't always get the credit you deserve as a lyricist? You are kind of like the Neil Young of the rock world, your lyrics have always had more depth than the typical "hair metal" type song. It's crazy that Poison has sold more albums than White Lion.

Tramp: Again I appreciate that you see me for who I am. My fans see me for who I am, so it doesn't matter if a million metal fans or a selection of journalist around the world don't notice me for my song writing. I do put the creating of the songs before the singing and the performance, it is something that comes after the song is written.

4. Are you still an avid soccer player? When you were younger, do you think you were good enough to play in college or go pro?

Tramp: Ha, Ha, no not at all, I am 57 years old. But I love the sport like I always have, even though I think it's become a game of who has the most money. No I was not good enough to be a pro player back then, I simply just loved playing and never really had any goal to take it further.

5. We read that your band Lion shared a bill with Vito's band. And several people mentioned that you guys would sound good together.

Then you traveled back to Denmark after the tour was over. Is that accurate? What was it about his playing that made you want to travel almost 5,000 miles to form a band together? Did you just call him up and make an offer? And did you have an alternative plan if he said "no thanks."

Tramp: I think the words were more like - you guys would be great together, and there had to be a little bit of David Lee Roth & Eddie Van Halen vibe in that. This really was the beginning of what become an era of full blown visual rock 'n' roll and I wanted to be part of it. When I saw Vito play I knew he was light years ahead of the guys I was playing with, it was that simple. If you want to win the race, get a great car.

6. White Lion had a three album run that were off the charts. Three platinum albums, all were Billboard hits, several hit songs. What was the key to that tremendous success?

Tramp: It is really difficult to say. I know Vito and my song writing was up there with the best. But even so, there still had to be a big amount of hard work and also some luck involved. It was not just handed to us, and it also didn't go on and on, it stopped the second Grunge/Alternative took over, regardless if our songs were great. Maybe this is where the Hair Band issue became a factor and you were shown the door, you didn't fit in anymore, regardless that our rock 'n' roll was much more classic than the other bands we were associated with.

7. You guys were on top of the world, how come you decided to disband at that point?

Tramp: There comes a time when none of that matters anymore and something else takes over. You just want to get away, take control over your self and start fresh. Looking back, I wish the decision could have been made in a smarter way than just saying to Vito: The Band Is Over.

8. What's the story behind your band Freak of Nature? You guys were a lot heavier than White Lion. Was that a conscious choice to move away from the sound fans associated you with or did it just happen organically?

Tramp: It was all about getting back to being in a band that works together, all for one and one for all, writing the music together. The sound of the band came from the band. Each member being allowed to be himself and bring that into the writing of the song. It was the best years of my life.

9. How come you then decided to go solo? Just tired of band drama and wanted to run things on your own?

Tramp: Freak of nature was my third band and each of those three bands took a chunk of my heart. I needed the rest of my heart to live, so there was no way I was going to try again and it could never have topped Freak of nature anyway.

10. Which of your 10 solo albums is your favorite, or which one really captured the true Mike Tramp sound? Which is your favorite White Lion album?

Tramp: I simply can't pick one, cause they all are a part of my growth. But I would say that *Cobblestone Street* kind of rescued me as I was wandering around not knowing where to go. That album brought me back to the roots of my songwriting. And after that album was done and released I could once again build from there. And since then I have been on one path only, my path.
Pride is White Lion. It is where the band is the band.

11. I've read where you called it a mistake, but we actually really liked Return of the Pride. It's a really great album. Our favorite songs from it our "Dream", "Take Me Home" and "Never Let You Go." Any cool story behind those three tunes?

Tramp: How about just calling it a Mike Tramp project album. It was a mistake to call it White Lion for starters. Second, I took a lot of my solo songs and had the band make them sound harder and heavier than how they were written. They weren't written for this album.

12. I won't bother you with Vito Bratta questions, I'm sure you get tired of having to answer them in every interview. So we will just ask one......he was such a huge talent, it's a shame he has chosen to

disappear from the music world. Is there any comment you'd like to make about him?

Tramp: It's not a problem. I have never said it like this before. But as more and more time goes by I have more respect for the choice that he made of not being part of the music business, than I did early on when I didn't think before speaking. I also hate where everything has gone, but I am a man that never quits.

13. How do you feel about your U.S. career? In Denmark, you are one of the biggest rock stars in the country. And you can still sellout shows all across Europe. Is it a bummer to come to the U.S. and play to a couple hundred people?

Tramp: Not just was, but is. Both fun and rewarding, as there is nothing like taking everything down to the roots. Driving yourself, doing everything yourself and just being up there alone free to play any song you choose at any moment.

14. What brings you more enjoyment? Playing in a band setting to 10,000 fans. Or sitting in a club, just you and your guitar, and 100 die-hard Mike Tramp fans?

Tramp: They both have been rewarding. But now being much older and wiser, I get the rewards from the small intimate shows. At the same time, I can't remember last time there was 10,000 in front of the stage.

15. Same question about the touring side. Thirty years ago you traveled on a huge bus with first class accommodations and were treated like kings everywhere you went. We read an interview from a couple years ago that said you were driving yourself to shows in your own car. No roadies or crew members, no bus. Just you and your own car. The first one is awesome, but maybe the bells and whistles lead to God complexes and makes egos spiral?

Tramp: The times they are changing! There are no tour busses, crew or nice hotels anymore. But it is not what Mike Tramp is. What matters is how I feel. And I feel good being me today and not me trying to be me 30 years ago.

16. Maybe Tomorrow went to #1 on the Denmark album chart. How is it that a 50-year-old rocker is still putting out number one albums!!!! What's the secret magic trick for you to still be so successful today, when the majority of the musicians from the 80s/90s are struggling to stay relevant.

Tramp: Oh I could possibly stretch this one, but won't. What is a number one in Denmark for one week, compared to being No. 1 in the 80's (is a lot different). What it does is help the label promote the album and my booking agent having an opening line when he tries to sell me to a venue.

17. Did you enjoy playing on the Monsters of Rock Cruise? So many bands from "the day" all together, on a ship, it's a crazy concept. Do you enjoy hanging out with all the rock stars that you ruled the world with 20 years ago?

Tramp: It is great, especially because I like to talk to the fans and hear the stories. I haven't met any rock stars on the boat, but of course I meet my musician friends (which they should be called) and we enjoy shooting the shit and trading stories.

18. Do you enjoy the up close and personal aspect of being with the fans on the cruise? I can't imagine Axl Rose or Don Dokken enjoying having fans come chill with them while they are having a beer or eating a turkey sandwich. Do you enjoy that fan interaction?

Tramp: Ha, Ha, I guess you know who they are. I have always been who I am, which is why I don't have a problem dealing with people face-to-face and upfront. I think it's what have saved me and why I can deal easily with how it is today.

19. If a label gave you a blank check for a 2019 album and tour, what guys would you put in your band? And what band would you take to open for you (money is no object).

Tramp: I would take my Band of brothers who I play with now. And I would take my friend Conny Blooms band (Electric Boys), cause I like how they write interesting rock songs.

 20. "No more presidents, and all the wars will end" those lyrics were written when Ronald Reagan was the president. They seem even more relevant today. How can you explain the current government system in the U.S. How did Donald Trump get voted as president? What do the people of Denmark think about that?

Tramp: I heard the great Roger Waters say that it's more about the American blue collar worker being let down over the many years by their government, and it made an opening for someone like Trump to come through cause he didn't speak like the rest. The American dream is gone, it is non-existing. I loved my 20 years in the USA, it was always the only place I wanted to live and I loved the American way of life. But it isn't any more and I am not sure what will be next.

21. We were listening to "Coming Home" while coming up with these questions. And I got a vibe of Tom Petty's serious side. Were you a fan of his at all?

Tramp: Of course I am. I grew up with Bob Dylan and found a natural connection to folk music. It's where all my song writing is coming from. So when Springsteen, Petty, Mellencamp came around and even today Ryan Adams and Jason Isbell I am very much at home with all of that.

And interesting enough, my great love for Van Halen have been tarnished and shattered so many times by all the shit they are dishing out about each other. The band that gave me the spark to build White Lion, doesn't mean anything to me anymore.

22. That official video has gotten more than 150,000 listens. With 1,300 thumbs up and just 32 thumbs down. Those are pretty amazing numbers in 2017. Fans are still loving what you are doing!!!

Tramp: It is a Mike Tramp song, it is me100%.

24. How do you feel about the technical change in how the music world works. Twenty years ago, a label would sign a band, let them develop over a couple albums, take care of the publicity etc. But today every thing is pushed by the online presence. Labels rarely touch rock bands anymore. So the Internet/Soundcloud/YouTube/etc allows bands to basically use their own home studio/computer to record an album and then release it online. In one way it's easier for bands to get their music out. But the downfall is there are a million bands putting out music without any filter to keep out the crap. And they can release music that hasn't been edited/critiqued and nobody is telling them "these two songs are great, but these three songs need work." Do you like today's version or how the music industry worked when you first started out?

Tramp: Yeah you're right. Who am I to tell anyone what they should do, I can't win this it's just a fact. Everything has changed, we're powerless and in one way or another have to follow even against our will. I HATE HOW IT IS TODAY, I HATE IT.

25. Also, as a fan I have to thank you for releasing albums and sharing your music. A lot of the bands I grew up loving have stopped releasing new music and they just tour the old songs. GnR – one album since 1991. Van Halen? Ozzy? All these bands rarely release music. So thank you for sharing your music with the fans. We really appreciate it!!!

Tramp: I release albums because at this moment the songs are pouring out of me, they come easy and I have something to say. At the same time I am also keeping the flame burning that my heroes started 50-60 years ago. It's almost becoming a duty to stand your ground.

26. Do you think albums will ever make a mainstream comeback? When I was young, bands put out an album ever year or every other year. Now major bands are on 5-6 year cycles with albums.

Tramp: I don't think so, looks more like we're becoming a members only cigar club.

27. What are your feelings on bands that have a revolving door of members, but that one original member keeps touring and keeps the band name alive? You've got more albums with your solo career than you did with White Lion. But so many other guys just keep their popular name and continually change members. Do you think it's OK for a musician to do that or should he eventually stop, and start a new band?

Tramp: Holy shit it's almost like you're reading my mind or know almost all my secrets. I think it's a bloody joke, a friend of mine told me Whitesnake had 57 people go through their revolving door. At the same time, when you have been lucky enough and I call it lucky, to make a living from music. Why should you ever give it up? So of course many will do anything to stay alive. But even as my children need new shoes and I could definitely do better financially. I would never again be tempted to go back to the old band.

28. Lol, what is it with guitar players! You've had your troubles with Vito. Axl had his troubles with Slash. Ratt and LA Guns both just had big reunions, and within a few months, Michael Grant and Johnny Monaco left LA Guns and Warren DiMartini left Ratt. Richie Sambora left Bon Jovi. What is it about the relationship guitar players have with their bands!!!

Tramp: Guitar players are a different creature than singers that is for sure.

29. So many rock stars have their careers ruined – or nearly ruined – because of drugs and alcohol. How have you been able to restrain from that lifestyle. Is that a big reason as to why you still sound as good today as you did 30 years ago?

Tramp: Even though I grew up in a heavy drinking and drug infested neighborhood. I have never had any interest in heavy drinking or doing any drugs at all, it is easy for me to say no.

30. What do you think about the Ronny James Dio hologram tour?

Tramp: The Ronnie James Dio Hologram, give me a fucking break. Did anyone ask Ronnie, did Wendy Dio ask Ronnie before he left us if it was ok to go out and do this?

I don't give a rats ass about how technical they can get or what they're saying they doing it for. It is wrong in every way and only something they do to make money from. Don't tarnish the great memories of the greatest rock singer of all time. He made some of the best rock albums ever with, Rainbow, Sabbath and Dio.

31. Thoughts on Jani Lane? Did you spend much time with him?

Tramp: I met Jani once at a joint radio event, it was a pleasant meeting.

32. Lol, is Van Halen III still the worst album you've ever heard?

Tramp: Holy shit are you tapping my phone? Not just the worst VH album, but up there with Gene Simmons "Kiss my ass" album, as albums that should never have been made.

33. Who is your favorite hockey player and team? Or what sport do you enjoy watching the most?

Tramp: Mark Messier Oilers/Rangers and no one have replaced him. I am a Ranger supporter. But to be honest, I almost don't know the name of any player on the current team. It's hard when you're not living in the USA anymore.

34. I read an interview where you talked about what Bon Jovi has become as a band, and we couldn't agree more. It's like they sold out for the money….which is weird, because he has reported net worth of more than 400 million dollars. Jon can't enjoy the creative level of his last few albums and tours. He went from being a hard rock star….to an arena rock star…..to a pretty serious artist (These Days is a really great album) to what he does now, which is boring music with no soul or energy and playing some sort of country-rock-adult contemporary music. It just seems like it would be so boring and with no passion.

Tramp: If I had the money and wealth Jon has, and still had the passion to do music, I wouldn't do the albums he has done lately. He had two massive albums, he became one of the biggest in the world, everybody knows his name. So why go out and do this, it clearly doesn't come from the heart. But this is just how I see it and I paid $5,000 for my car and don't own a house.

35. We've put together a top 1,000 songs of all time compilation (1981-

2017). **Broken down to 650 rockers and 350 ballads. Can you give us your thoughts on the songs we have rated the highest:**

Wait: It is the perfect song for the decade it was written in, it can also stand the test of time as most other WL songs can.

Broken Heart: Vito and my first baby and a favorite of all fans.

Little Fighter: Tramp steps away from the rest of the pussy and tits lyric bands, even though it was a hard sell, the song is a personal life vest for many who have suffered in life

When the Children Cry: If you get down to the dissecting of 80's ballads. This one stands by itself.

**36. In our opinion, "You're All I Need" is one of the most underrated ballads of the genre. And your most underrated song is "Out With The Boys" – it's such a great, timeless classic song. Do you remember writing those two?**

Tramp: The _Mane Attraction_ album and songs. Came two years too late, they could not compete with Cobain and Vedder. Still in the long run these songs have a big place with fans

**37. What does 2018 and 2019 have in store for Mike Tramp?**

Tramp: More of the same, I am just one thing, Mike Tramp, and I kind of want to be like an item in a fridge, that when you feel like having that specific taste, you reach for it, and when you're not, you just leave it on the shelf.

**38. Is there anything else you'd like us to mention?**

Tramp: You know me by now, it's what I do, and say thank you for giving me a canvas to paint my thoughts and opinion on.

https://miketramp.dk
http://miketramp.rockpapermerch.com/

https://www.facebook.com/MikeTrampOfficial

John "Jay Jay" French
Twisted Sister, Motivational Speaker

Photo courtesy of Mr. French's official Facebook page. See links below.

1. Did you recognize the potential in Metallica when you toured with them in the early 80s?

French: No. Not really. They opened for us in 1982 at a huge concert hall in New Jersey called The Fountain Casino. Our fans were a little rough on them and I watched a couple of songs and went to the dressing room. A year later we toured Europe and played eight dates with them. We headlined all but one of them. It was at the Paradisio in Amsterdam. Metallica had reached a certain stride at that show and I could see at that point, that they found a niche where they could flourish.

2. You've been in the band longer than any of the other members. What do you want Twisted Sister to be known as down the road when future generations look back at your career?

French: I hear so many different opinions of how the band will be judged. We certainly are not a "hair band". We are a super heavy 70's rock 'n' roll bar band that made it in the 80's.

3. You received an award from the New Hampshire School titled "Efforts to Curb Substance Abuse Among Young People"....can you share facts behind that story?

French: I appeared at a school in New Hampshire at an anti drug and alcohol lecture at the request of a person who has, over the years, become one of my best friends. His name is Fred Bramante. Fred was the owner of a very successful music store chain in the Northeast called Daddy's Junkie Music. When we first met I told him my story, which included the fact that I hate drugs and alcohol in the workplace. He couldn't believe that I was in a world famous band and was totally straight!

I had no idea that that appearance would lead to that award!

4. TS has performed at several fund raisers, including a 911 show, a show benefiting victims of Hurricane Sandy....why is it so important to you to give back to the community or those struggling?

French: Ever since we "came back" in 2001 we have done at least one benefit every year. It just feels good to give back!

5. Do you remember the first time you heard Dee sing? What were your thoughts, did you think he would end up being a hall of fame level singer/writer?

French: We needed a singer that could sing Led Zep songs so that we could become more popular. The very first audition that Dee sang, I knew he could do the job. At that point that was enough. I wasn't thinking of original music when I hired him.

6. Whose idea was it to go with the comedic aspect for the hits "We're Not Gonna Take It" and "I Wanna Rock" videos?

French: That was Dee's concept.

7. What are your thoughts – or what were you thoughts on the time – with Leader of the Pack being released as a single? On rock message boards, that's the one thing that fans say killed the band's success.

French: We made very strategic errors of image. "Leader of the Pack" just crushed us but what was surprising was that we used to play it in the bars and people loved it. It was a very huge mistake.

8. *How did you and the rest of the band feel about Love is for Suckers being labeled as a Twisted Sister album? From what we read, it was initially a Dee Snider solo album. But the label said they would only finance it if was titled as a Twisted Sister album. So Dee went that route – even though none of the actual band played on it?*

French: The band was so fragmented by that time that I felt that we were just going through the motions.

9. *How would you rank the movie Strangeland. A ten being worthy of an Academy Award and a one being a romantic comedy featuring a love affair between Rosie O'Donnell and Pauly Shore.*

French: I give Dee credit for getting it made because he had a vision.

10. *How did you get involved with the band Lordi? That doesn't seem like a band that would be associated with Twisted Sister! Those guys are extremely heavy.*

French: We were headlining a very heavy black metal festival in Germany. We closed the festival over Slayer. At that show, Lordi was at the very bottom of a 50 band bill. They wanted to meet us. Tommy (Lordi) was the president of the KISS fan club in Finland and loves stage theatrics (obviously)! Anyway, they asked both me & Dee to be on the upcoming album. Who knew at the time that the band would appear on the (very pop) Eurovision song contest, win it and the album would go on to sell millions!

11. Was that 2016 tour really the last one for Twisted Sister? What if a promoter gave you a blank check for a one-day festival that Twisted would headline. With an unlimited amount of money (meaning you could get any band you wanted) what four other bands would you put on the bill?

French: I believe that the final show in Mexico in 2016 was the final show.

Having said that, I said we would never play again after 1988 and we did so take my comments for what they are worth.

As far as putting on a 'dream' show. Well....that's not how we roll. Our entire history is built on the premise that we destroy the competition. Why would any band want to be shown up? This predatory mentality started back in the bars where it was 'kill or be killed'. We had to wipe the floor with all the other bands in order to increase our popularity and, as an incentive, get paid more money.

There is no fraternity, no brotherhood. At least not on the stage, which is our "playing field." Yes, we have friends in other bands but when it comes to the show, look out because we are coming to get you.

We come to every show with the purpose of demolishing and demoralizing the competition. This is not a Kumbaya way to engender a 'family spirit' but it does lead to a night of great entertainment for the fans which, at the end of the day, is all that really matters. Seeing us live has been called a "religious experience" by too many journalists (and fans) who witness our power.

You may want to ask "What four bands would you care to destroy on a single night?" The answer to that is found in the heap of reviews that have followed us since we returned in 2003. Over the 150+ shows that we either headlined or co-headlined, we absolutely demolished the festivals.

Now I get that some people feel that this kind of hubris is just so much hyperbole and arrogance. I get that. What really shocks me is how uninteresting and predictable most of the headlining bands we played with are live.

How they don't get it.

When we played the Arrow festival in Holland in 2008, I went into the audience to watch the headliner. We, on this bill, were just a special guest and I was looking forward to seeing the headliner as I had not seen them since 1976.

There were two guys standing in front of me who had seen the headliner several times that summer. The conversation between them was eye opening. One of the guys says "Now the singer is going to look to the right and say blah, blah blah...and, like out of a script, the singer looked to the right and quoted what the guy says. After that song the guy says "Now the singer is going to looked to the left and say"....and that's exactly what the singer did. So, what does that tell us? It tells us that the band goes through its show verbatim with no spontaneity. No real connection, just going to script. This is what happens and why it's all so damn boring.

The entire bill was actually a great one-day lineup. Kansas, REO Speedwagon, Motorhead, Def Leppard, Journey Twisted Sister & KISS. The next day, in the national Dutch press, the show got great reviews but there was only 1 photo (in the center of the double page spread).

It was of us.

The caption read in part: The only band to provide a religious experience and, by far, the only universal response from the crowd was Twisted Sister. Case closed.

Occasionally I watch a song or two of the competition but only to see what they are doing wrong. Not one single band we have played with in the last 15 years have made me go ...whoa!

Trust me, I wish they did but blowing them way has just been way to easy. How, after all these years, they still don't understand how to actually make 100,000 people really go crazy. Are we really that good or are most of the bands we play with really the mediocre.

I say this because I just can't understand why other bands can't take us out.

Really.

It just makes the night better. Reach for the stars and give a great show. Blow us off the stage. Most just are not capable of it and we show them all up over and over.

The proof?

Bands don't want to go on after us. We suck up all the oxygen in the room and leave nothing. I can't tell you how many times when we are not the closer, we are asked to close by the promoter under the guise of some lame excuse as the original closer has to leave early for another show the next day....yawn...

So lame.

I don't need to name names. Just look at the bills we are on and you will see 100% "best live band" in the reviews.

This is what we are most proud of.

Being the absolute best and having said that, the suggestion you made would never happen!

12. Are you still running marathons? What's been your best run so far – any New York Marathon championships?

French: I ran the 1981 and 1986 NYC Marathons. I ran the' 81 in 3:50) on a bet that I could run under 4 hours). I stopped running 20 years ago and my knees, ankles and feet thank me for that everyday! I do walk a lot. Sometimes up to 10 miles a day, however.

13. What were you trying to accomplish – or what point were you trying to make – when you ran your underground newspaper in high school?

French: The times were very different then they are now. The newspaper that got me in trouble was a parody of the official school newspaper.

14. Were you relieved or happy when Snider came on board in Twisted and you didn't have to sing anymore?

French: I am not a singer. I was thrilled have a real singer.

15. You've run your own management company and your own producing company. You are an accomplished writer, and a well-known motivational speaker! Is there one of those things that excites you the most or that you feel like you are the best at?

French: Motivational speaking and keynote speaking really excite me these days.

16. How did the motivational speaking career get started? Has it been a successful ride for you?

French: I met a great speaker/author Steve Farber, who has become my mentor.

17. In an old interview you mentioned that Joe Perry wasn't always the guitar player who was doing it in studio. Joe Perry is a legend, fans would be surprised to hear somebody else was laying down Aerosmith guitar parts.

French: Most musicians learn that the producer the record label brings in has, on many occasions, a shortlist of musicians he (or she) can call, in a pinch, to get a desired part correctly played.

Any musician who gets replaced probably feels slighted but the "hired Gun" is never allowed to tell so that person rarely ever gets the credit. Everyone is pissed except the producer (if the record become a hit).

18. You are a huge ACDC fan What do you think of what they've done the last couple years. It's being reported that Axl Rose is going to record and tour with ACDC. Would you be more interested in a new GnR album or an ACDC album with Axl on vocals?

French: I stopped buying albums from my contemporaries 20 years ago so I'm not the one to ask.

19. What do you think about a guy like Vince Neil. At one point he

was fronting one of the most popular bands in the world. But now, he is still charging $100 a show to come see him perform – but he shows up out of shape, only sings half the lyrics, and actually just mumbles part of the lyrics as well. Isn't that a lack of respect for the fans that are paying good money to come see him perform?

French: We live in a society of free will and choice. If one pays for a terrible performance but keeps paying...well then that's your problem.

20. You don't have to share your finances with us. But just a general question. How much would it cost for a movie or commercial to use a hit song like "We're Not Going to Take It" - if The Rock wanted it for his next movie is the studio giving you guys $10,000 or closer to $100,000 or a million? (just asking as a fan, as we don't know what movies/TV/advertisers pay bands to use their tunes in movies).

French: Licensing music is complex. In movies it is based on how many seconds, in what space, in a movie or movie trailer. Is it a major studio or an indie film.

For TV, it's based on local or national use, length of time (4,6,8, or more week run) optional re-use, specific product, Internet use, free on air tv/radio, cable, pay cable premium, etc.

It really is like filling out a menu so the fees are very unpredictable.

21. Do you think albums will ever make a comeback? With the internet and how easy it is for people to download music without paying for it, bands stopped sharing new music with their fans. In the days I was a kid, bands put out an album every year or every other year. Now, major bands put out an album every 5-6 years. Which sucks for fans. Do you think albums will ever make a comeback or has that ship sailed.

French: Albums or album cycles. The two are very different issues.

People really don't buy albums so most rock artists waste time releasing a full (10 or more tracks) album. Better, if you are a working and touring band, to release a new track every couple of months, consistently.

22. What do you think about bands that carry on with just one original member and a revolving door of musicians? At some point, should that guy call it a day and start a new band? Or is it OK to use that band name to continue making money for his career?

The public will decide if they accept the substitutions or if they consider you nothing more then a cover band. The use of the name is also a legal one. Who owns it? What terms would be negotiated to use it etc.

23. Is there anything else you'd like us to mention or promote for you?

I can be hired for either keynote or motivational speaking engagements by sending an email to: Frenchmgmt@gmail.com

Read my series of articles for Copper (an online audio magazine) through the PS Audio website

The column is called "Twisted Systems"

Read my Beatles column in Goldmine called "Now We're 64"

Read my music business articles for Inc.com

Find them at jayjayfrench/inc.com

Support Uveitis research here **http://www.uveitis.org/**

www.inc.com/author/jay-jay-french
https://twitter.com/jayjayfrench

Steve Lynch
Autograph

Photo courtesy of Mr. Lynch's official Facebook page.

1. Let's get the question out of the way that you probably get tired of being asked! Will there ever be a Yellow Dog or Outlawed reunion?

Lynch: No, unfortunately there will never be a reunion with either of those bands. I've lost touch with them over the many years since then, which was the early 70's. The only ones I'm still in touch with are Rob Ricketts, the bass player from Yellow Dog and Billy Ray, the singer from Outlawed.

2. What do you enjoy more – playing on stage, creating in the studio, or teaching young inspiring musicians?

Lynch: I actually like all three pretty much equally but I'd have to say my favorite is creating in the studio.

3. We read that you decided to dedicate yourself to music after the death of the legendary Jimi Hendrix. Why did his passing inspire you so much?

Lynch: I used to listen to Jimi very consistently but was playing bass at the time with a guitar player that lived down the street from me. When Hendrix passed away I decided to dedicate myself to guitar only. I traded in my bass for a Fender Stratocaster that very day, September 18th 1970.

4. You are from the Seattle, WA area. Were you a fan of the Grunge movement of music?

Lynch: No, I wasn't a fan of the grunge music scene at all. I grew up with 60's and 70's music which was for the most part very positive and had a good message. Much of what the grunge scene focused on was negativity...like drug addiction, depression and suicide. That's not the message I want to hear in music.

5. *You are world wide famous for being the "The Two-Handed Guitarist"....is that technique still what draws in a large portion of your students?*

Lynch: Yes it does bring in some students for that reason alone, but most want to take lessons from me because of my technique in teaching music theory. I make it very easy to understand how theory works with guitar.

6. *Do you mind that label, as you were the innovator for the hard rock world or do you wish people wouldn't label you as one thing and would just appreciate your overall skills and ability?*

Lynch: I've never even thought of myself being viewed that way by others. I'm quite content with the respect I get for my innovation with guitar alone. Only my close friends know about my views on spirituality, philosophy, nature or my vast book collection of various topics which most don't concern themselves with.

7. Guitar Magazine gave you the "Guitar Solo of the Year" for your solo in Turn Up the Radio. Can you describe to fans how the solo experience works for you? When/how do you develop it, how long does it take to create, how do you make it fit into the concept of the overall song, etc.

Lynch: I sit down and configure my solos specifically for the song. Sometimes it can take as long as six eight-hour days as it did with Turn Up The Radio. I also listen to the solo section again and again that I'm going to be recording over without a guitar in my hands to create it in my head first, then figure out on guitar what I'm hearing. I look at the solo being an integral part of the overall song itself. I have always doubled my solos in the studio on a separate track, one being recorded at 99% tape speed on the Studer and one at 101%. This gives it a fuller and slightly out of pitch sound when you combine the two at regular speed. I would then pan one at 10 o'clock and the other at 2.

8. Why and how did you put Network 23 together? Your drummers on that album are out of this world.

Lynch: The Network 23 album was a labor of love. It was something that was more personal to me because it was my writing, arranging, production and performance, which of course gave me total freedom. The drummer Chris Frazier, who played with Steve Vai, Whitesnake, etc. and is now with Foreigner, really brought the tracks to life! He is incredibly creative and can spontaneously come up with the most innovative parts on the spot. Mike Mangini who has been with Dream Theater for years was a wild man in the studio! He is an extremely intense player that is an absolute perfectionist. I was just amazed watching him play...lol! Much love and respect to them both!

9. You probably get tired of being asked this, so we'll just briefly touch on it. Did Eddie Van Halen ever call you up and say "thank you for the inspiration." Or did the band members ever apologize to you guys for how they treated you on that first tour. In the "fan world" most rock guitar enthusiastic believe that Eddie has gotten a lot of the glory/credit that rightly should have been sent your way.

Lynch: I never received a phone call from Eddie, he and I were influenced by the same players growing up as we are the same age (almost anyway, I'm 10 days older...lol), so neither of us were inspired by the other. There were some things that I deemed inappropriate as far as our treatment when touring with them...but we got a record deal out of that tour so who's complaining!! Lol, I'm not concerned about who received more credit for that particular style of playing, I don't look at music as being competitive, it's emotional expression from the artist to the listener.

10. In the 80s, a lot of your music was featured on TV shows and movies – most famously Miami Vice, Fright Night and Secret Admirer. Do you still get checks for those types of collaborations or do they just pay you one time for the song and that's what the band splits? And even in today's era, you had a song on Hot Tub Time Machine!

Lynch: I still get paid and always will as long as they are replayed, rented or bought...fortunately that never goes away...until I'm dead anyway! Lol.

11. How did you get Ozzy and Vince Neil to participate in your video for "Loud and Clear" - were you friends with those two guys? Did they take the girls and leave after the video or did you all hang out afterwards? Both those dudes are known as hard core party animals – was that all true or just exaggerations to build up their rock image.

Lynch: We knew Ozzy from co-hosting Headbanger's Ball on MTV and hit if off with him right away. He was really into coming down to the shoot. He brought Sharon and the kids (they were quite young at the time) so there was no partying...lol. Vince was equally excited to partake in it as we had just finished touring with Motley Crue. It was a lot of fun having them there!

12. Who was the craziest band/musicians that you guys hung out with while touring? Conversely, who was the most professional that you were able to sit back and watch and learn "that's the way to handle our business."

Lynch: Motley Crue was the craziest by far!! I quit drinking after that tour because I didn't remember most of it...and neither did they!! Way too much fun!! When we toured with Aerosmith their team ran a very meticulous show, I was quite impressed with how every detail was maintained.

13. Why do you think Autograph never broke through to the true A-level rock band range? Before your first album, you guys were everybody's favorite unsigned band. Then once signed, you had a hit album, huge hit single that everybody knows, great singer, one of the best guitar players in the world, huge tours with A-level bands....why do you think you guys never reached that GnR, Def Leppard, Bon Jovi and Aerosmith level?

Lynch: This is very simple to answer: RCA Records. During the release of our first record *Sign In Please* we found that we had to tell them a lot about how it should be marketed. They didn't even want "Turn Up the Radio" to be on the album, it made it on after much debating between the band and them. Then when the second album was released the president of RCA unfortunately died and they brought in a newer guy to run the show. He hired young people fresh out of college to help promote the artists on RCA...big mistake!! It wasn't only us that took a hit from this, it was also Mister Mister, The Pointer Sisters, Kenny Rogers and the Eurythmics. No one was very happy to say the least.

14. How much fun has Lynchlicks.com been? Did you see early on that you had unique abilities and could make a living by teaching and sharing your knowledge with aspiring guitar players? So many musicians tie their career to their band, and then ride that boat for life – I saw a band that was pretty big in the 80s playing awhile back at a club with about 30 people in the audience. You, on the other hand, have created a job that probably has made you way more money than being in your popular band did.

Lynch: Lynch Licks was a great investment of time because it allowed players to get an inside look at my playing. But the best thing I EVER did for my career was attending the Guitar Institute of Technology, (now called MI or Musicians Institute). It opened up a whole new world to me as far as guitar and music in general is concerned. It gave me the ability to communicate to others my technique and theory ideas. It also inspired me to open a music school in Seattle, The Federal Way School of Music which I released over to a teacher when I moved to Florida two years ago.

15. Have you always been a savvy businessman or did you just love guitar, wanted to share your knowledge and then BAM it became huge?

Lynch: I just loved playing guitar, I never really considered myself a businessman until I opened the music school. Now I've become even more of a businessman because I am the tour, business and general manager of Autograph. Who would have known?? Lol.

16. We were snooping around the website and holy cow, you have a TON of content available. How much time do you dedicate to the site, and who helped you put it all together?

Lynch: It took many months to put the lynchlicks.com site together. I wrote all the content myself but had Shane Gillespie complete the site itself. The filming took two 12-hour days at my friend Chad McMurray's studio in Seattle.

17. How come Plunkett didn't want to be part of the 2013 reunion? And have fans been cool with a new singer touring?

Lynch: Steve Plunkett turned the reunion down saying he didn't think his voice could no longer handle it, which is very understandable. He is and has been writing music for TV and movies for quite some time now and is very successful at it. He gave us his blessing though and wished us well. Our new singer Simon absolutely loves playing in the band and all the fans have accepted him gracefully! He does a great job and we all love having him in the band!

18. 2017 was a huge year for classic rock bands. What do you think sparked that rejuvenation? LA Guns, Jack Russell, Slaughter, Vain, Stephen Pearcy, Babylon AD, Autograph. Do you think that classic rock music will continue that trend?

Lynch: I hope the trend continues...lol!!! I believe it will because the people who grew up in that genre of music get to relive their youth and reminisce about how fun it was. Most have kids or grandkids now and bring them to the shows which ushers in a newer generation of fans. I believe it's still popular because it continues to bring positive energy and messages to the listeners.

19. GnR is putting out a Box Set this year. One of the versions sells for $1,000! Does Autograph have a bunch of unpublished demos lying around you could spruce up and sell!!!!

Lynch: Most of the Autograph material from that era has already been released, especially on the album *Missing Pieces*, (released in 1997). We are now putting all our efforts into new material because we are a new band with a new sound and we have a lot to say.

20. Sign In Please reportedly only took 30 days of studio time to completion. Speaking of GnR again, Axl Rose spent 13 years and 14 million dollars of cash to create his last album Chinese Democracy. 1. Did you hear that album and what did you think?

2. What could you do/create if a label gave you 14 million dollars and gave you a decade to complete your work!

Lynch: I haven't heard Axl's new album. I listen to more eclectic obscure music that most people don't know about. But if a label gave me 14 million to do a record I'd invest 13 million and spend the remaining one million on the record and have it done within a year. Lol!!

21. What's it like being on the road today as opposed to when you guys were touring in the 80s?

Lynch: It's actually much easier to tour today then it was back then. In the 80's we were on a tour bus with our crew and equipment trucks for 11 months at a time. Now we fly out on the weekends and play a couple shows then fly back...that's right, we are now weekend warriors! It's much more professional as well, the partying has reduced itself to a livable level.

22. Do you enjoy playing the big festivals now, with 10-15 other bands? Or would you rather play a small club with die-hard Autograph fans?

Lynch: I love playing the festivals, arenas and casinos with other bands from the same era. It's like a family reunion with our old friends. We still enjoy playing some of the smaller venues because of the intimacy with the fans...but there's nothing like the excitement and energy that you feel playing to thousands!

23. "I literally would practice seven days a week anywhere from 10 to 16 hours a day!" – that's just incredible. What advice would you give to young musicians who want to become a professional guitar player? What specific things should they practice?

Lynch: I would say to the young aspiring players out there to learn theory! This is extremely important! The other advice I would give would be to stop trying to sound like someone else. There are millions of players throughout the world that can sweep and speed pick incredibly fast...but where is the emotion? Listen to a variety of players you like from a vast array of musical styles...then take from them what you like and create your own style from this. At one point you want to stop listening to other guitarists all together and concentrate on your own sound. This is what I did in 1978 while attending GIT. The last person I was influenced by was Alan Holdsworth from the album Enigmatic Ocean by Jean Luc Ponte and the album U.K. Both of which were classic albums!

24. You guys were given a huge break by a band member's friendship with David Lee Roth back in the day. And were friends with and toured with Motley Crue. As a professional musician, and somebody who actually knows these guys, do you have thoughts on or how do you explain what Neil/DLR have turned into today in terms of their live music performances?

Lynch: I really don't pay attention to what other musicians or bands are doing. I never have. I only paid attention to the bands I listened to back in the 60's and 70's because I was listening and watching from a fans perspective. I believe musicians have different reasons why they continue to play live...some do it because they love it, some do it because they feel lost without it...and some do it because they need the money! Lol.

25. You once said in an interview that you'd like to write movie scores. Plunkett has gone that route, have you gotten to do that yet? And if so, any particular genre interest you the most?

Lynch: I still want to write movie scores! I love creating something new while having it challenging. It's difficult to find the time nowadays to invest in it but I am writing some material now that would be perfect for movie scores. Most of my time and energy goes into Autograph though.

26. What was your favorite toy or thing to do as a child – that wasn't music related? And same thing today. If you aren't working on something music related, what do you enjoy doing for fun or relaxation?

Lynch: Hiking in the woods or anything that's nature related. I also love to travel to learn more about different cultures and the diversity of the land and people.

27. What does 2018 and 2019 have in store for you and for Autograph?

Lynch: The remainder of 2018 we are to continue touring and putting out new videos for songs from the Get Off Your Ass album. In 2019 we plan to release new material with a bit of a different spin on it. And of course we'll be releasing new videos and continue touring as well.

28. Is there anything at all you'd want us to mention or promote???

Lynch: The best way for fans, friends and family to see what we're up to is by going to the Autograph social media sites on Facebook, Twitter, Instagram, etc., or to go directly to: http://www.autographband.com

http://www.lynchlicks.com
https://www.facebook.com/stevenllynch

Alex Grossi

Picture courtesy of Mr. Grossi.

Grossi is a fascinating member of the hair metal genre. He started giving guitar lessons while just a teenager. Since those days, Grossi has worked with numerous A-level music talents. In some aspect of writing, recording, playing, touring or being a member of, Grossi has been associated with: Hookers & Blow, Quiet Riot, Bang Tango, Adler's Appetite, Jani Lane, Beautiful Creatures, Love/Hate, Skid Row, Ignite, Hotel Diablo and Aimee Allen. His songs have also been featured in multiple TV show and movies, including: Sons of Anarchy and The Proposal.

1. HOOKERS & BLOW is celebrating its 15 year anniversary this summer, that is quite the impressive run for a band that doesn't seem to

take itself too seriously! How is Dizzy Reed to work with?

Grossi: If you had told us in 2004 that we would still be doing HN'B, and at the level that it has gotten to, I would have said that you were higher than we probably were. But it's kinda become a "thing" - and we have a great time doing it.

How is Dizzy to work with? I don't really think we have actually ever "worked", so I'm not really sure...

2. How was it growing up in a small town in Connecticut? How in the world does a town of 25,000 people produce professional athletes like Marcus Camby, Chris Clark, Geoff Sanderson......as well as the Porcaro brothers, from the band TOTO!

Grossi: Everybody is originally from somewhere, the key is to know when to get out and go for it if you find that where you are has nothing left to offer. I am pretty sure everyone you just mentioned didn't sit around in CT waiting for it to happen. I liked growing up there, but there is big world out there, you need to go out and see it. We are all only here once.

3. If we walked the streets there this weekend, would more people recognize your name or Oliver Wolcott?

Grossi: Who the fuck is Oliver Wolcott?

4. You started teaching guitar lessons at age 17. That's amazing, you were already professional level as a teenager?

Grossi: Not really, but I was very fortunate to have been given the opportunity and encouragement to do so at a CT. music store that I used to hang out at. It really forced me to be the best I could be. Teaching 40 kids a week ultimately taught me just as much as I tried to teach them.

5. How did you get picked up by Quiet Riot and what was the experience like working with Kevin DuBrow? (Sorry, I know you've been asked that a million times).

Grossi: I met Kevin DuBrow through a former agent that I was working with in 2003, and was initially just hired to do a handful of shows. We really hit it off and it went from there. Him and Frankie really took me in and taught me a lot - I miss him every day.

6. How was your experience with Bang Tango? We recently interviewed Mark Knight and that guy is one of the nicest musicians we've talked to.

Grossi: Joe Leste was one of the first guys I met in Hollywood, he is a true rockstar and a great guy. We are still very close and I am really proud of the music we made, and still make. Bang Tango was a band that was far more talented and unique than they get credit for, much like Love/Hate. Learning those songs taught me a lot - Mark Knight is a seriously underrated guitarist, and has always been cool to me.

7. Jani Lane is one of our favorite artists of the hard rock genre. Was the Bad Boys of Metal tour the only time you worked with him? Did you ever write with him?

Grossi: I did several runs with Jani, mainly doing the Warrant set - but we also did write a few songs that sadly never will see the light of day. But he was hands down one of the best songwriters of the genre. It came so naturally to him, he was very gifted - and also funny as hell.

8. And another GN'R connection – Gilby Clarke produced your Hotel Diablo album! What was it like working with Gilby? (By the way - that band was great. I'm amazed you didn't blow up).

Grossi: Thank you. I am very proud of what we created and Gilby really got what we were trying to do and took it to the next level. He got me some of the best guitar tones I have ever recorded and had a really cool loose approach to recording, most of what we did on that record were 1 or 2 takes, not perfect - but had a great vibe. And he MAY have the best moustache in the 818 area code!

9. You have worked with Gilby Clarke, Steven Adler, Frank Ferrer and Dizzy Reed (and even replaced DJ Ashba in a band). You have played with Todd Kerns who has been with Slash for a while now) - You also

recorded a few tracks on Dizzy's solo record that Richard Fortus, Tommy Stinson and Del James were all a major part of..... Is that all just a bit of a coincidence or is there something about GN'R that draws you towards that band?

Grossi: I am a firm believer in the Laws Of Attraction (Google it) - It's not about any one band or player, but it's more where you fit in and what you put out there.

10. Would you rather have a Billboard number one album in 2019 or win on Oscar for best actor?

Grossi: That's a tough one, I'm still trying to figure out if I like Target better than Wal-Mart.. But I am pretty sure by next year both stores will have basically stopped selling records, so I guess I would take the Oscar.

11. How did you and James Durbin hook up? A lot of people downplay shows like Idol and The Voice as they say it sterilizes the music process. Are you a fan of or cool with those types of reality music competitions?

Grossi: I met Durbin in 2011 in LA when he was on "Idol" - He is probably one of the most talented people I have ever met, as well as one of the coolest. Talent is Talent, it really doesn't matter if you get noticed in a shitty garage band or on national TV - Either you have it, or you don't.

People can say whatever they want about singing shows, but do you really care about the opinion of some bitter failed musician posting a rant on a message board from the desk job he hates?

12. Any thoughts on Hardcore Superstar? For our money, they are best current hard rock band out there right now. Are there any bands you are really into right now?

Grossi: I really like what I have heard from them, I also really like the latest Shinedown record and that OffSet track that features Ric Flair. Fucking genius.

13. What does 2018 and 2019 hold for Alex Grossi?

Grossi: A lot of touring with QUIET RIOT and probably some more HOOKERS & BLOW shows if GN'R and QR's off dates line up. I have also been writing and recording out here in Vegas with some really talented guys - not sure what we are gonna do with it , but even a broken clock is right twice a day, so fuck it.....we'll see what happens....lol.

https://www.facebook.com/HNBMerch
https://www.facebook.com/ALEXGROSSI1976
www.alexgrossimusic.com

Anthony Corder
Tora Tora

Photo courtesy of Tora Tora's official Facebook page.

1. The one question you probably get tired of being asked - let's just get it out of the way. What happened with your MMA fighting career? It looks like you retired after going 0-2? Or is that a different Anthony Corder? (We like to start off with a lighthearted question!!!)

Corder: Must be a different guy haha.

2. Do you have a favorite city/venue to play?

Corder: So many good memories, each city/venue are special. I would really like to add favorite city/venue from Europe and Japan, we have never played overseas as a band.

3. We actually saw you guys back in 1989ish on the tour with LA Guns and Dangerous Toys. You've said that was one of the most enjoyable tours of your career. What made that one stick out?

Corder: LA Guns made us feel at home, they were already road dogs and established. We also had the southern vibe going with Dangerous Toys. We loved that tour because we were fans of the other bands and we got to spend time hanging with them.

4. It's interesting as we've also got Dangerous Toys listed in our most underrated bands. You guys, them and Junkyard – all such great bands that should have been huge. Did you guys ever hang out or play with Junkyard?

Corder: We have not done any shows together, but would like to in the future. I did hear a rumor that we shared a video set back in the day. I think the director/producer for our song "Guilty" shot our video one day and had the Junkyard guys on the same set in a warehouse in downtown LA the next day.

5. You opened for Alice Cooper. How was that tour? Seems like an odd pairing? Did you get to hang out with Alice at all, how was he in real life?

Corder: It was our first "real" show. A local radio station in Memphis got us the bill with Motorhead/Alice. Motorhead could not pass through customs so we were given open slot. Great memory in Cook Convention Center, Memphis TN.

6. We saw a video of you singing Aerosmith and ACDC...you are known for your bluesy southern rock vocals. Your voice is so amazing, we had no idea it was also so versatile. Have you ever played in a band where you sang the heavier/raspier type stuff?

Corder: I actually have sang in a few different projects over the years (definitely raspier) but I have always kept my blues influence integrated into those performances.

7. You've performed at the Monsters of Rock Cruise. How do you like that set up? Do you enjoy getting to hang out – up close and personal – with your fans?

Corder: WE LOVE MORC and the fans. Patrick our bass player had been diagnosed with cancer in 2016. He received a clean bill of health and had a new perspective on life. We were introduced to the MORC family by a friend April Lee. It was one of the best experiences for our band! Look forward to participating in many more cruises with that family.

8. Is there a private area where the musicians get to hang out and visit? How's that VIP area compare now to how it would have been in 1989!

Corder: We do hang out, we are fans of the bands on board. The music and performances are great, we would have loved this in '89.

9. Was there any band last year that you really wanted to see? You've been in the business so long and have seen so many things, on a cruise like this (or a festival) do you still sneak over and watch certain bands perform?

Corder: KIX is a must! Love Steve Whitman, that guy is incredible. We have had an opportunity to get to know some others through the years. John Corabi was awesome. The Answer was a killer as well as Tom Kiefer.

10. Did you like the Bill and Ted movie? How did you guys get involved with licensing one of your songs to be in the film?

Corder: We dug the film. A&M Records was licensing their content for the soundtrack and the timing lined up for us to put "Dancing With A Gypsy" on there.

11. Tora Tora really got signed because of how you guys grinded it out to get noticed. Playing high schools, playing local events, putting your own huge signs up and drawing crowds in (you did a great interview with the Decibel Geeks podcast describing it). To us, it seems like experiences like that really bring a band together. Do you think that's

why you guys have been able to keep the main lineup together all these years and have/had such great chemistry?

Corder: We are very close, shared some incredible experiences together. We have had some periods where we were focused away from each other, but we always pick up right where we left off. I do think we have some special chemistry when the four of us combine our influences and instruments. We have a sound.

12. How do you think the internet/social media/YouTube/etc has effected bands of this generation. Now young bands don't have to go grind it out for years, they can just slap a few songs together and put them on YouTube, Soundcloud, FB. Is it good because it's easier to get noticed – or bad because they don't have to put in years of legwork to fine-tune their skills?

Corder: Content has to be good, that part is subjective. Quality content and respecting your audience (finding your tribe) is key. It is a great tool to help you build relationships with each other, but I think you still have to work for it. Flip side it is not considered work when you are doing something you love.

13. Because of the internet/YouTube/file sharing, does it piss you off as an artist that people basically "steal or take" music for free as soon as it's released? When I was a teen and in college, I would save $35 from all of my paychecks so I could buy two CDs. But today, as soon as an album is released somebody will download it onto YouTube and then thousands of people just grab it for free.

Corder: One side, it is intellectual property, it is my lively hood to be paid. Other side, I want to share my voice, my vision, my platform with as many people as possible. Rock and a hard place, in the end I have to make income if this is my sole revenue stream. I need to convert listeners into supporting my art, technology makes that possible.

14. Do you think anything can be done to bring albums back to the forefront? Again, back in the day, bands put out albums every year or every other year. But today even popular bands are on a 5-6 year cycle instead of yearly. I have to tell you that it sucks as a fan. Do you think

Albums will ever be viable again?

Corder: We are always looking for trends and cycles in the music industry. Vinyl has gained traction but can it continue to grow and maintain traction yet proven. Streaming is growing (Singles mentality/Greatest Hits Personal On-Demand Playlist) but it depends on your specific audience and who you are servicing.

**15. Also, do you think it's OK for bands to still tour the band "name" even if they only have one original band member? Is it OK for that one original member to make a living off the band they helped create, or at some point, do you think the name should be retired and a new band created?**

Corder: Depends on band agreement, legal ownership, the brand and the individual situation, most of all how the fans react will answer the question for you. It's a chemistry thing.

**16. Any news or plans for a new album this year or in 2019?**

Corder: New album, tracking summer/fall 2018 on track for Frontiers SRL early 2019

**17. Did I read it correctly that after Tora Tora, you use to perform every Monday night at a club in Memphis? That must have been an amazing experience for fans. It's not often you can just go see a legendary singer at a club, I would have been there every week! As a musician, do you like that kind of intimate setting? Would you prefer to play in an arena to 5,000 people or at a seedy blues club with 200 diehard fans?**

Corder: I love playing period!

**18. Did you ever record music with Uprisin or Route 61?**

Corder: Yes, I did those sessions with guitarist Hal McCormack and a revolving group of musicians. Patrick played on these sessions as well. There are some studio outtakes floating around, very blues influenced tunes.

19. You were going to college to learn about the entertainment law industry. What drew you do that field and do you plan on going there as a profession after your singing days are over?

Corder: Yes I am focusing on up and coming industry professionals. I am invested in this industry and excited where it is headed. I am currently Entertainment Business Program Chair at SAE Institute in Nashville.

20. We've also got two little ones – age 6 and 5. Don't they just make life totally different and worthwhile compared to life before having kids?

Corder: Yes, they are a gift, gives you good perspective.

21. Do you blame Grunge for the hair metal / sleaze rock generation going to a huge halt? Honestly, we think that the oversaturation of "hair bands" had just as much to do with the downfall.

Corder: No, I agree. Many bands, singers and their productions were sounding similar. Very homogenous template was working for a long period. The industry and fans embraced the change in paradigm into raw as an option into new approach. The corporate entities were behind the strategic shift of presentation to audience.

22. What's the story with Revolution Day finally being after being shelved for so long? There is no doubt in our minds that ToraTora would have still been a viable band in the 90s. You guys weren't a hair band, but a rock band with a blues sound. We are amazed that the label dropped you guys.

Corder: Our A&R rep was offered another contract and when he left, we lost our voice in the corporate wheel. We always felt that it could end at any time, so we tried not to take our opportunities for granted. We had an incredible experience with A&M Records.

23. Revolution Day is a really quality album, we were quite impressed with it. Tora Tora was different from a lot of bands from that genre.

The typical run was a solid debut album with a few good songs. Then a second album that had a hit, but didn't hold up to the first. And by the third album, the band was changing their sound to fight the grunge craze. Then that band was done. But Tora Tora always stayed true to your roots. You can see a definition connection/progression between those first three albums.

Corder: We were going through a lot of changes, business and personal during Rev Day. We wanted to continue to grow, experiment but still maintain our sound and audience. We are proud of this recording.

24. Is there one album that you are most proud of or that you think captures the Tora Tora sound the best?

Corder: Loved them each for different reasons. Wild America was my fav. We had become better on our instruments and gained confidence in our abilities as writers. Loved the sessions and that project.

25. We think Shelter From the Rain is the album's masterpiece. We have it ranked as the best ballad of 2011. What's the story behind writing that song?

Corder: We wrote it with Taylor Rhodes in Nashville TN. One of my favorites, Keith and I also wrote Amnesia/Faith Healer with him.

26. We've also got Rescue Me, Candle in the Stone and Living a World Away ranked in the top 1,000 list. Do any of those songs have special meaning for you?

Corder: Each one had a special meaning, Rescue Me is one that I continue to play to this day, every time I play acoustic set.

27. Album wise, we love Revolution Day. How was the writing/recording process compared to your initial two albums?

Corder: It was darker time for us, much pressure from ourselves as the industry was changing, the second album had not performed as well as the first, so we were our own hardest critics and felt much pressure to deliver good project. Also, it was an incredibly fun time musically for us.

28. *Surprise Attack was one of the greatest debut albums in rock history!!! Were these songs you grew up crafting over time or were they all written new for the album?*

Corder:
We wrote it over a year...signed 1988, delivered and dropped 1989.

29. *Phantom Rider, imo, is the best Tora Tora song of all time. And one that really highlights your amazing voice. What's the story with that beautiful piece of music? Power ballads were obviously huge in the genre, but yours sounded nothing like anything that any other band was doing.*

Corder: I wrote that with my friend Thomas Howard. He was a very good lyricist and musician. We were neighbors in high school and collaborated on many TORA songs together.

30. *Obviously, Walkin' Shoes was the song that broke you guys into the mainstream. A classic blues rock song that still holds up today. Is there a cool story behind writing that one?*

Corder: It was one of the fastest tunes we put together, right near the end of project. Keith had the riff and idea for tune. It came together very quickly one afternoon in his apartment.

31. *Who is the girl from the video....and who is the African-American gentlemen in the video? They are both pretty great in their own way!!!*

Corder: Uncle Ben was a Beale Street musician, sweet soul and talented. Rhonda was cast in video, still bump into her from time to time in Memphis...she looks the same and is married to policeman. Great folks!

32. *A lot of your videos were black and white – why did you guys go that route?*

Corder: Directors picked production elements with our input., we liked the vibe.

**33. I couldn't find a video of you guys doing Being There live. Did you
ever play it live and how come it isn't part of your normal set? Such a
great song, we've got it as one of the 100 best ballads of the genre.**

Corder: We do, but depends on our set list...thanks!

**34. Wild America was a brilliant follow up, seemed a little heavier than
your debut.
For us, the key songs were the incredible Wild America, Amnesia,
Nowhere to Go, Time Goes By (all made our top 1,000). Any interesting
stories or thoughts about any of them?**

Corder: Nowhere is my absolute favorite. Keith, Stan Lynch (drummer
for Tom Petty) and I wrote it. I play this tune every time I play...love it,
and to me it represents TORA in a different setting.

35. What's the story with Miss B Haven?

Corder: Outtakes from Wild America, lots of fun memories and picture
of us at that period.

Quick Thoughts On:

Axl Rose album with ACDC or GnR?   GNR

Tom Keifer: ROCKS!

Def Leppard: IN THE ROUND

Junkyard: Want to do a gig together

Dangerous Toys: Anytime, still talk to Jason

Great White: Outdoor Festivals great times!

Warrant: We toured with them and Lynch Mob, they were tons of fun

Bonham: Toured with them and the CULT (First arena tour dates, made me realize I wanted to do music the rest of my life)

Bang Tango: JAM!

Vain: Fun Times!

https://www.facebook.com/ToraToraBand/
https://www.toratoramusic.com

Brian Forsythe
Kix

Picture courtesy of Brian Forsythe's official Facebook page.

__1. We saw that you are a Chuck Berry fan. Would you agree it's a sham that people list Satisfaction or Stairway to Heaven as the best rock song of all time…when it's clearly Johnny B Goode!__

Forsythe: There are lots of great songs and everyone has their own opinion on which one is the greatest. That doesn't make them wrong, it's just their opinion. Chuck Berry definitely influenced and inspired a lot of people along the way, including myself.

__2. You post a lot of pictures of your flights! Do you enjoy all flying on road trips? Do you guys board/check in like regular people or do you__

get special treatment so the fans don't mob you? And what kind of flier
are you? Do you talk the guy's ear off next to you or do you chill by
yourself? How often do you get a fan sitting next to you?

Forsythe: I do enjoy traveling most of the time. Occasionally something will come up to cause a little extra stress but I've pretty much gotten the routine down. I fly mostly Southwest and board just like everybody else, no real special treatment although I have had a few gate attendants offer to help me out with my boarding position. I fly so much that I have A-List status on Southwest which means I don't have to wait in the check-in line. I go through the Priority line. And I'm checked in automatically for my flights which gives me a decent number in the A boarding group. I also have the TSA Pre which saves time going through security.

3. The Rhythm Slaves sounded cool. What happened with that band?
How was it working with Pat Muzingo?

Forsythe: The Rhythm Slaves was a nice change of direction after I left Kix in the early '90s but short lived. I formed that band with Eric Stacy of Faster Pussycat but soon came to find out Eric wasn't the most trust worthy guy to work with and had a major drug problem. We ended up kicking him out and continuing on as Catfish but that didn't last long either. Pat was cool to work with, we've remained friends since then. In fact he's the guy who introduced me to my current girlfriend Janiss.

4. You opened for GnR in 1985 at the Troubadour. What memories do
you have of the guys back then? Today they are all larger than life
characters. What was an Axl rose or Slash like in 1985 before they
became rock stars. And watching them play, did you know they would

end up being as huge as they were?

Forsythe: I had already heard of them before we got out there and already knew they were going to be huge. They definitely had a cool vibe on stage and also had a nice following built up out here in LA. They all came back after the show to where we were staying and hug out all night. They were big Kix fans so we had mutual respect.

5. Thoughts on Axl joining ACDC? More interested in a new GnR album or an ACDC/Axl album?

Forsythe: I thought it was weird at first but he did a great job! I wasn't into that last Guns & Roses record Axl did. I think he completely lost focus so I don't know if Slash can keep him on track for another one without Izzy being involved. They'll never repeat that first record. An AC/DC record with Axl? …hmm, I don't know, maybe.

6. What are the main differences between playing with Rhino Bucket and Kix? Do you get a lot of the same fans or are the crowds a lot different?

Forsythe: Rhino Bucket fits my playing style a lot better than Kix. Rhino Bucket does well on the East coast because of all the Kix fans that show up. It's hard to get gigs in other places around the US though. We do well in Europe and even though those are primarily true Rhino Bucket fans I still sign the occasional Kix CD over there.

7. Do you remember the 2008 Rocklahoma show, in front of 20,000 fans? You guys apparently stole the show, according to most fans.

__What was that like? And which do you prefer – playing a festival in front of 20,000 people or playing an intimate club in front of 200 die-hard Kix or Rhino Bucket fans?__

Forsythe: Of course I remember! It was a magic night and I know it opened Steve's eye to the possibility of taking it on full time again. Of course I enjoy a huge crowd but there is something cool about a small sweaty club. I like doing both.

__8. After being broken up for so long, what prompted the return for Kix and the album Rock Your Face Off?__

Forsythe: Steve's band Funny Money and Ronnie's band The Blues Vulture's were doing shows together back east and at the end of the night Ronnie would jump up on stage with them and play a few Kix songs. It went over so well that the club owners were offering them a bonus to continue doing it. Steve then called me to see if I'd be interested in making a surprise appearance at one of these shows. That never came about but it got us talking about actually putting the band back together for a few "reunion shows". That went so well that we continued on and the rest is history.

The new record came about through the Live In Baltimore DVD. We signed with Frontiers Records in Europe to have them distribute it and as part of the contract we were supposed to deliver a new studio record. They messed up on the handling of the DVD which turned out to be a good thing. It allowed us to get out of the contract and sign with Loud & Proud Records instead.

__9. Rock Your Face Off was actually one of the biggest rock albums of__ *the year. While writing and recording, did you have any idea that it was going to be so huge?*

Forsythe: No! That record took a lot of hard work and didn't seem to come together until we mixed it. I think we were so caught up in writing, re-writing, recording and tweaking the songs that we didn't know what we had until we were finished and actually sat back and listened.

10. Donnie Purnell had been your guy's primary songwriter. How was it on RYFO without him, and with the album being an entire group effort writing project?

Forsythe: That's why it took us so long to finally decide to do a new record. We were worried about doing it without Donnie and weren't sure we could pull it off. Luckily Mark had written some good songs. Some were on the heavier "metal" sounding side but we worked them out and got them sounding like Kix songs.
My main concern was keeping it sounding like Kix so by bringing Taylor Rhodes in to it, it made it a lot easier to achieve that.

11. Are you ever going to release the stuff you've written that doesn't fit in with Kix or Rhino. Ron Keel did a country rock album, any thoughts of going that route?

Forsythe: I've got songs from over the years laying around, some rock songs, some country songs a few novelty songs too but I don't know, maybe some day. I'm not the most motivated guy in the world unless I'm working on someone else's stuff.

12. After an album that went platinum, some great tours, some songs that made billboard and all the rock charts, successful videos…..how in the world were you two million in debt to the label? Were the labels screwing all you young bands back then? (I've read other stories of bands have a platinum album and a couple hits – but still being in debt).

Forsythe: The record contract was a bad deal. It was totally in the record company's favor. They actually made money but all the losses were charged back to the band so there was no way for us to get ahead. This happens a lot. Unless a band has a really good manager looking out for them and they hit it big right out of the gate, most bands are doomed to financial failure.

13. How much time did you spend practicing as a youngster and how much time now do you practice to maintain your skills? Is it all by memory now or do you still have to practice and work things out?

Forsythe: I was obsessed with guitar at an early age and never put it down. In my Jr. high and high school years, I'd get home from school and go straight to my room until dinnertime, then return until bedtime sitting in front of my record player learning guitar licks. I would practice at least four hours a night back then. Then I would go out and sit in with any band that would let me.
Now I only practice if I have to. If there's a show coming up I'll go over the set once a night the week leading up to it.

14. As an instructor: should a kid learn on an acoustic or electric? Is it better to learn the fundamentals/scales/etc….learn how to play the classics…..or sit back and try and create your own licks?

Forsythe: It's important to know the fundamentals like the basic chords, the notes on the fretboard, how to hold a pick and picking techniques. I learned by ear myself, some people do better learning by reading tab. Whichever way keeps the student interested is best. If a kid wants to play rock, you don't want to teach him or her nursery rhymes. It's got to be fun for the student or what's the point?

15. Have to ask about the Donnie Purnell situation. Was it weird reforming Kix without him there? Was he offered a spot or was that not even an option? Have you guys talked since the old days?

Forsythe: I talked to Donnie about six months before Steve initially called me. I hadn't talked to him in 10 years, we talked about old times and it was cool. Then when Steve and everyone were talking about putting the band together, no one wanted Donnie involved so we went with Mark. Donnie hasn't spoken to any of us since except Taylor who he sent a scathing email to for his involvement in our new record.

16. How come you changed your name from The Shooze to Kix!!

Forsythe: There was already a band in the Midwest called The Shoes with songs on the radio. Kix was a spur of the moment decision.

17. Do you think it's easier or harder now to become successful? Anybody can release an album on ITunes or YouTube – but there is no quality control monitor. But label contracts and support are hard to come by. In your day, bands were allowed to find and develop their sound and build up their success over a couple albums – which never happens today.

Forsythe: It seems harder but all the rules have changed so on one hand everyone has a shot but on the other hand it's all self promotion. It's always been about luck & timing but in the old days a record company could make or break you.

18. You've always been a hardcore road dog. How come you like being on the road so much?

Forsythe: I adapt easily to most situations, that really helps! I just love playing and feel most at home traveling, preparing for a show and playing the show. I love everything about it even the hotels and rent-a-cars!

19. What's your favorite city, state and country you've played in? Favorite venue of all time?

Forsythe: It's hard to pick a favorite but with Rhino Bucket, Germany is on the top of the list for countries that rock! Back in the old days with Kix I would've said Japan. Hammerjack's was a great place to play but Rams Head Live is not too shabby.

20. In 1989 you did your first huge road major tour with Ratt. How was that experience?

Forsythe: That was our first major extended tour so it was a blast! We'd always been in a van driving ourselves up to that point so riding on a tour bus, playing arenas night after night was all new and exiting!

21. Ratt has been a bit dysfunctional, the Blotzer situation, two different Ratts touring, fighting over the name, and now the main guys are back – but apparently DiMartini and Cavazo are now out. What do you think - just egos, attitudes, different opinions on the band's sound, money, etc?

Forsythe: I can't speak for them specifically but a band is a family with interacting relationships. Being on the road can add stress to that situation. It all comes down to the different personalities and how well they can compromise with each other. The Ratt guys seem pretty stubborn in their ways.

22. Then you toured with Tesla and Great White. How was it touring and hanging out with those guys?

Forsythe: Another great tour! Both bands were easy to get along with and the audience seemed to dig us.

23. If Alan Niven had interceded and told your label to release Don't Close Your Eyes…would you guys have eventually released the ballad?

Forsthye: No, Atlantic Records had already informed us that the Tesla / Great White tour was the last one for the Blow My Fuse run and to start thinking about our next record. They were done spending money on that record.

24. Personally, we think Cold Blood is the ultimate Kix song and one of the best hard rock songs of the era. Memories on writing/recording and performing that song?

Forsythe: I always liked that song, especially playing it live. It's easy to play and always sounds good! As far as recording it, I do remember recording the overdubs and solos at Cherokee Studios in Hollywood. We had recently moved over to there from Conway Studios where we'd done the basic tracks. Cherokee had a better sound for guitars than Conway so that made it easier and a little more inspirational for playing the solos.

25. You worked a bit with The Vagabonds and Joe Leste. What happened with that project and how was it working with Joe.

Forsythe: That was primarily a live band. We wrote a bunch of originals together but never recorded any of them which was a shame. Joe was easy to work with but his business practices were a little shady and with me being at the height of my drug use at the time, wasn't financially beneficial. John Corabi was in that band as well for a while playing rhythm guitar.

26. You worked at a pet clinic and painted billboards while in-between bands? What did you do at the clinic? What's the oddest job you've ever had? And if not a guitar legend, what career do you think you would have ended up doing?

Forsythe: I worked for my older brother's sign company when I first moved out to LA. That was a huge change going from a semi-rockstar to that, and was very hard physical work. The pet clinic came a little later after I went through rehab and got sober. I was living at a sober recovery house at the time and one of the requirements was to go out and get a job to become self-supporting. I just stumbled onto the pet clinic thing by accident but ended up loving it and working there for the next 12 years. I had no experience except for my love of animals and having grown up with pets and they hired my anyway. I started out as the kennel guy / assistant and eventually expanded my duties over the years. I did the feeding, cleaning, grooming, flea baths & dips, ears, nails, vaccines, x-rays, assisted the doctors restraining the animals during procedures and I also did all the food and office supply ordering.

27. How did you find Steve Whiteman back in the day? You were the band's lead vocalist for a couple years in the 70s! How come you switched over to Whiteman?

Forsythe: I sang vocals early on in high school bands only because no one else wanted to do it. I never sang in this band. I don't consider myself a singer although I can handle the occasional back up part. We specifically hired Steve for his vocal abilities.

26. Chocolate, 10/10, Damage – how come the nicknames and why no name for Steve?

Forsythe: Ronnie was first with 10/10. We called him Ron 10 /10 like Rin Tin Tin because he always played his amp & guitars on 10. I got the nickname Damage from brain damage, I was always hungover. Jimmy jumped on the bandwagon with Chocolate because no one could ever pronounce Chalfant right. I don't know why Steve never got one, although I used to call him Bun Head (Ste-bun instead of Steven which was eventually shortened to just Bun with head tacked on the end).

29. What was the East Coast music scene like back in the early days? Were there any other bands from your era that broke out of it?

Forsythe: It was actually quite happening coming out of the '70s and heading into the '80s. Cover bands were big at the beginning and to get gigs you had to play cover songs. But there were so many music venues at that time, there was never a shortage of gigs.

The first band we came in contact with that had a record deal in our area was Face Dancer from Baltimore. They had a couple of albums out on Capital Records. We hooked up with their manager to eventually land our record deal with Atlantic Records.

After we got sign then there were several other bands from our area that ended up getting signed as well. None of those other bands seemed to go as far as we did.

30. What compelled you to join Rhino Bucket? To us, it sounds like RB is the sound that Kix appeared to headed towards after the first two albums. More of a pure hard rock band as opposed to the more pop-rock-friendly sound Kix ended up at?

Forsythe: I joined Rhino Bucket around 2000 - 2001 while Kix was on hiatus. I was a fan of the early Rhino Bucket stuff and then had played in several bands during the '90s with Reeve, their bass player so when they decided to put the band back together they asked me to join because their original guitar player Greg, wasn't interested.

31. Kix came back and toured together in 2003. Why and how come you just toured and didn't release an album?

Forsythe: We initially did it just to have some fun and make a little money. We had no idea it would take back off like it did. Then we just got caught up in doing shows and at the time we all had our individual projects going which were all recording new music. Part of the reason it took so long for us to finally put out a record was fear of the unknown. How many times have you seen a band reunite put out new music and it sucks? We weren't sure if we could still do it, especially without Donnie. We all wondered, will it still sound like Kix? So that really became our main focus while recording the new record, to keep it on the Kix track. I think it came out okay!

32. How was it writing the 2014 album without Purnell. Rock Your Face Off was extremely successful, a top 50 album, number one rock song. How in the world did that happen and did you except it? The entire album is a mishmash of you guys writing together, how did that happen. You had a couple credits on Cool Kids...then not much on the next couple, but then several on rock your face off.

Forsythe: It was a lot of work and thank God for Mark Schenker! Mark was a big asset not only for his home studio but also with his songwriting. Then there was Taylor Rhodes who co-wrote with Donnie in the past and had a good grasp on our sound. Mark and I did the initial sifting through a pile of songs and song ideas that everyone threw in and got them down to about 20 or so. Then we started sending them off to Taylor who finally got the list down to about 12 of the best ones.

33. Wiki says RB toured in 2006 with Kix. Did you play in both bands? What was that like, having both your bands playing the same show?

Forsythe: Yes we did several shows together and yes I was doing both! Physically it was no problem but it was mentally draining. I can only focus on one thing at a time so having to focus on two different shows in one night was rough. It has happened a few times since but I try to avoid it. When it happens, I ask for another band to play between Rhino Bucket and Kix just to give me an hour or so break between shows.

34. Now days, how do you decide which band you are playing/touring with if same dates come up?

Forsythe: Kix takes priority because there is more money involved... money talks! If Rhino Bucket is planning a European tour, I'll arrange it with Kix's booking agent to block out the dates.
Unfortunately, Georg has announced his retirement from Rhino Bucket so I won't have that to deal with that in the future.

35. Do you enjoy the Monster of Rock cruises? So many bands full of guys you must have grown up in the business with, and also being so up close and personal with the fans.

Forsythe: Yes I do... and they pay well! When we were initially asked to do the cruise in whatever year that was, back when they first started doing them, I was skeptical. I didn't know how it was going to work. I pictured this giant floating party hotel full of drunken fans and us being trapped with nowhere to hide. It isn't like that at all! For the most part the fans are really courteous and give you space. I've also learned which places to avoid to avoid the drunk people, like the pool deck during the day. I always take the stairs whenever possible so I don't get trapped in the elevator with a bunch of people. I can be very stealth when I want to be.

And to answer the other part of your question, it is cool to see all our old fellow musician friends, hang out and go to each other's shows.

36. From being booed off the stage opening for Triumph to sharing the stage with David Lee Roth, The Ramones and Aerosmith....What the hell was wrong with those Triumph fans!!!

Forsythe: That was a big mismatch! No one knew who we were at that time and anyone going to see Triumph wouldn't get where we were coming from. Seattle was about as far from Baltimore as you could get!

37. Wiki says you worked on music for the E Hollywood true story about Eminem?

Forsythe: Yes, an acquaintance of mine was the producer and was looking for someone to do the music. He asked me if I knew anything about rap music, I lied and said yes. That was a great learning experience but in the end I spent way too much time for very little money. I submitted around ten pieces of music out of which they used only two.

38. Playing with two major bands, plus working on side projects, how do you have time to also give guitar lessons through the Maryland Institute of Music?

Forsythe: I don't have a day job so I have plenty of time!

39. Rhino Bucket has been touring overseas – how's that going? Good size crowds?

Forsythe: We do clubs over there some bigger, some smaller but the crowds are always awesome! The European music scene is happening, especially in Germany! We can pretty much play seven days a week over there to packed crowds every night. We couldn't do that over here in the US. We tried booking a few runs here over the last couple of years but had to bail on them at the last second because it wasn't financially viable. We couldn't make enough to cover our expenses let alone make any money so it wasn't worth it.

__40. Did you guys play the Sunset Strip during the early years? What's it like playing there now compared to the 80s? Got any crazy stories you can share?__

Forsythe: We didn't really fit in with that whole scene but did do the Roxy (which was on Sunset) a couple of times back then. We also played other places not on the strip. There definitely was a scene going on back then not like now. There is no scene.
I don't really have any crazy stories but it seemed like anytime we'd play somewhere out there, it was a who's who of rockstars in the audience. We weren't famous to most of America but we had a reputation in the band circle.

__41. Do you remember playing the Hair Metal Holiday in Austin a couple years ago? After a lifetime of waiting, that was our first time being able to see you guys live. We've been to two of them now, and you guys clearly blew the other major acts off the stage.__

Forsythe: I remember being in Austin and thinking we hadn't been there since the '80s but have no recollection of that show.

42. *Your wife is a published author- Janiss Garza - who wrote for RIP – that's cool. Were you a big Lemmy fan?*

Forsythe: I was Motorhead fan, not obsessed but enjoyed them on occasion. In fact I was once in Motorhead for a day… actually it was for a scene in a movie (Frezno Smooth). They wanted to use Motorhead for the scene but Lemmy was the only one from the band who was in town at the time so they got me on guitar and Randy Castillo on drums for the scene. They didn't actually know who I was, the direct just happened to see me playing one night at the Coconut Teaser with Joe Lesté in the Vagabonds.
https://www.amazon.com/Frezno-Smooth/dp/B000SJAPA8

43. *ANYTHING at all else you want us to mention?????*

Forsythe: Thanks to all our dedicated fans! If it weren't for you we couldn't do this. And I can speak for the rest of the guys but I'm going to continue playing music until the wheels fall off!

42. *QUICK FIRST THOUGHT when seeing the name:*
Steve Whiteman - Crazy (on stage)
Donnie Purnell - Great songwriter
Ronnie Younkins - Him and I are like Keith & Ron Wood
Jimmy Chalfant - Punctual
George Dolivo - I used to think "beer" but he has since quit drinking.
Reeve Downes - Groovy
Slash - Top hat

George Lynch - Weedlie deedlie

Warren DiMartini - A born natural

Vito Bratta - How do you tune that thing?

Mark Kendall - Laid back

http://brianforsythe.com
https://www.facebook.com/Brian-Damage-Forsythe-115269085177368
https://twitter.com/RealBrianDamage
https://www.facebook.com/OfficialKIX

Brian Tichy
Guitar, drummer and speed-bag champion!!!

Photo courtesy of Mr. Tichy's personal webpage.

Tichy has been involved (played, written, toured, or been a part of the band) with: Steven Tyler, Lynch Mob, Ace Frehley, Slash's Snakepit, Foreigner, Richie Kotzen, Shameless, Ozzy Osbourne, Glenn Hughes, Velvet Revolver, Seeither, Geoff Take, Seether, Jack Blades, Sass Jordan, Stevie Salas, Vinnie Moore, Gilby Clarke, Kenny Wayne Shepherd, Billy Idol, Dead Daisies and numerous other bands.

__1. So how does a drummer end up forming the greatest Randy Rhoads tribute concert and album known to man!__

Tichy: I've also played guitar for a long time.
Randy / Blizzard / Diary / we're huge influences on me back then! Probably some of the biggest as far as inspiring me to practice and use my ear and learn things I knew nothing about. I was just starting out and not good at all but I tried hard to learn Randy's stuff as I loved it. It took starting the RRR events to realize the first LP that kick-started me getting

serious on guitar was Blizzard of Ozz!

2. *You played guitar, bass and drums on various songs for the album. You've got to be a pretty fantastic musician to be able to blend in with the heavyweights of the rock world. Any intimidation doing that – was it nerve-wracking or just fun to get to play with the greats?*

Tichy: It wasn't intimidating because the event and LP were my ideas. I was asking musicians from the events to get involved in it. Most of them, if not all, are my friends, and we all share a love of Randy. I just wanted it to be fun, classy and respectful.

3. *The additions you gave fans with the pre-orders to the album were pretty spectacular. How were the sales of the album….and how was the fan/critical response?*

Tichy: The sales could have been better. I didn't have a label's support or any type of proper deal. I didn't even have a publicist.
We were close to a couple deals but it didn't pan out.
The fan/ critic response was great though!
The album sounds loud and fresh and raw.
There is a cohesive spirit throughout which is obviously because everyone that played on it loves Randy. When you have no budget you know people are doing it for pure reasons!

4. *How did you pick which musicians would play what parts and in what songs?*

Tichy: I asked them, and as long as everyone is flexible it usually isn't too hard to get together.

5. *Did anybody real shine with their performance? As you were producing/mixing the album, you thought "Man, this guy really should be more well-known and famous, he is incredible."*

Tichy: I didn't think that as I was familiar with everyone's styles and playing prior to recording the RRR. I was just always excited to either have a musician come up to my place and record, or receive tracks back from them. I know all their abilities so I wasn't overly shocked by someone's performance. I simply enjoyed hearing the genuine excitement and fire in everyone's performances based on us all being lifelong Randy fans!

I knew everyone would throw down their best stuff and they did!

6. You also organized and ran "Bonzo, The Groove Remains the Same" – celebrating the career of John Bonham. How was that event? And you've honored Bonham and Rhoads, if you were given a blank check to do another show/album next year to honor a legend of your choice – who would you choose?

Tichy: Bonzo Bash (originally called The Groove Remains The Same) was the first idea of mine of this kind. It spawned RRR a few years later. I'm not sure who it would be if I did another event celebrating another musician that deeply affected me.

There's far too many but some that come to mind are Jimmy Page, Alex Van Halen, Peter Criss and Neil Peart.

7. You've toured with numerous big name artists and bands. Is there one or two tours that really stand out as being real standouts?

Tichy: I have had a great time on them all, but it was pretty heavy to be Ozzy's drummer and headline Ozzfest 2000. At the same playing on new LP's from Whitesnake and Foreigner and writing and releasing new music with Billy Idol was also super cool... there are lots of great memories and it's not just the actual gig, it's where I was at in my life and who I met then and what each gig did to affect my future mindset, decisions, happiness, and knowledge via experience.

8. Along the same lines, whether touring or in the studio, is there a couple musicians that you've observed and really learned from? Guys that you watched work and said "this guy knows how to run a band/career. I can learn from watching him."

Tichy: Yes, tons. Steven Tyler, David Coverdale, Zakk Wylde, Slash, Stevie Salas, Jeff Pilson, Kelly Hansen, Billy Idol, Mick Jones, and many more. There's always something to learn business-wise and professionally in all situations, for better or worse. The guys I mentioned all have great work ethics and are real talented and have kept their shit together! This biz ain't that easy and survival and longevity are not things that are easy to come by.

9. Now that Lonzo Ball and his crazy family are making his surname a viral name....any chance of putting the old band back together and using Lonzo on a couple songs?

Tichy: Sorry I don't follow news and am really bad with current events. But no, I'm
not putting Ball back together. It was fun for it's time, but it was a long time ago with minimal impact outside of me going for fronting my own band w my own tunes.

10. You've recorded with numerous artists of many different genres. Was that a conscious effort on your part? Rather than being the guy who is in the same band for 30 years, you enjoy playing different styles with multiple different bands?

Tichy: I didn't choose the path, the path was not pre-determined. Life happens and you try your best and you end up in situations you never thought you'd be in. And that is to be expected!
Randy Rhoads probably thought and wanted Quiet Riot to be his priority and to take over the rock world a la Van Halen.
But he auditioned for Ozzy and made two iconic LPs! Neil Peart went to England in the early 70's to become a successful Drummer only to move back home and join Rush!
Ultimately, I wanted to be the Drummer in my own band and write in that band. I tried, but it didn't pan out. So I also tried getting Drummer gigs if I heard of any or was recommended. Mind you this goes back to 1989, and being a Berklee music college kid not knowing anything about the biz; so you go for anything you can and try to make something happen.

11. How did you get hooked up with Billy Idol and how was the experience playing/writing with him?

Tichy: My bud, current Pink Drummer Mark Schulman called me about that. He was leaving Billy and asked if I wanted to try out.
This was 2001, and I did Ozzfest 2000, and even got the call from the Ozzy camp to start the new LP with them, but somehow they changed

their minds. I never got started on that. So I was home, did some gigs with Glenn Hughes, and the label my band Ball was on was falling apart. I auditioned for Billy, got it, and it lead to 8-9 years with him including writing new music.

12. We think Body Snatcher is actually his best song he's ever released. Do you remember writing/recording it?

Tichy: Cool. Thx! Yeah, I had the main riff and groove and Billy started humming over it.
He came up with all the lyrics and melodies.

13. You've been a member of Foreigner numerous different times. What keeps drawing you back to those guys? One time you filled in for Jason Bonham, how do you rank his drumming skills?

Tichy: I love Foreigner. Always have. I learned how to play drums as a ten-year old kid playing to their records.
I have filled in for them many times but have only left and rejoined once. I joined in 98-2000, and left to do the Ozzy Tour. Foreigner had yet to book more than a few shows that year and I heard about Ozzy needing a drummer. I knew too many people in that camp NOT to make some calls and try out.

I rejoined Foreigner in 2009 as they called and asked if I'd play on the new LP and do the tour. I was with Billy but he was unsure of his next move and we didn't have anything guaranteed on the plate.

I think Jason is great. I always have since owning his first Bonham LP.

14. You've played on two Sweet & Lynch albums, both that received very positive critical reviews How has the experience been working with that band?

Tichy: I had a good time recording those records.
It was myself, Michael Sweet, and James LoMenzo in the studio together tracking.
Michael knows what he wants but also allows a certain amount of freedom to be yourself. So I listen to him and mix that with how I play

and mix that with trying to play what makes sense for the song.
It's Michael's vision so I listen to him first.
He is very easy to work with and a solid, talented guy!

15. Lynch and Sweet both have "interesting" reputations as being somewhat difficult to work with at times. Has that been your experience or is that just silly internet fan gossip?

Tichy: I respect anyone that can be themselves and be true to themselves even if it may affect your reputation. We all want to be liked by everyone and we try to not offend anyone but at some point you have to accept that's never going to happen, so you might as well be happy being true to yourself.
George and Michael both speak their minds.
Maybe others don't as much. But they have both done real well in their careers so I guess their reputations haven't been affected too negatively by any Internet rumor gossip stuff.

16. Do you have a favorite song or two that you enjoy playing with them the most?

Tichy: I enjoyed playing some Dokken and Lynch Mob tunes with George. I grew up trying to learn all his rhythms and solos in Dokken.

17. Before S&L you worked with the legendary David Coverdale and Whitesnake. In our opinion that lineup was one of the best in Whitesnake history. And of course....thoughts on Coverdale?

Tichy: Thx. I thought we were a pretty good rock n roll outfit!
My thoughts on the guys are that they are all very talented and I had a blast touring
with them.
Re: DC; I have great respect for him.
He's a legendary singer who when I first heard on MTV singing Slow and Easy I was like "wtf"! What a badass voice! He's also a great guy who knows what he wants and genuinely wants everything positive and effervescent around him. If you give him
positivity and 100%, he'll give it back.
He has no problem telling you "great job" or whatever... he wants his

band feeling powerful and confident. He's very involved in all he does from top to bottom, and very aware of everything around him.

18. How was the experience of writing/recording/touring the Forevermore album? We ranked Forevermore as the BEST album released in 2011, sparked by the songs Steal Your Heart Away and One of These Days.

Tichy: It was cool. Doug Aldrich and I got together for pre production for a few days then we went in and tracked the Drums in a week. We'd send tracks up to David who couldn't be with us that week. That was it. Go in the studio, get good sounds and focus on solid takes!

19. How did you get involved in the speed bag world? We just watched one of your videos and it has over 100,000 views! Do you do it for fun or have you been able to monetize it somehow – maybe your own line of punching bags?

Tichy: I always loved the speed bag, and one day on tour I YouTube'd Speed Bag and saw these badasses doing amazing things. I was hooked and determined to learn it.
I got home and set up the one my wife got me years before but I left sitting in the box. That was it. I put hours a day into it and worked on it seriously like anything you enjoy.
There's not much money in speed bagging that I know of, ha!
And no, I haven't really thought about a line of speed bag products....

20. The Dead Daisies are a great rock band. John Corabi is such a great singer. How has your experience been playing with that band?

Tichy: I had a great time with the guys in the Daisies. They are all long time friends.

21. Is there a lot of difference for you in terms of a band like the Daisies, where you have free will to write/create and make major decisions as compared to some other bands you've been in where you weren't given as much freedom?

Tichy: The Daisies write their own music but are still hired to create and convey a certain style and atmosphere that founder David Lowy and management have as a vision.

There's some freedom but it's still a band we were all hired to be in. It's not the same as a band started from the ground up as equal partners. And rightfully so because the budget comes from the founder. Major decisions are made by management.

It's a unique situation on many fronts and I know of no other band started or existing like them.

22. You've played with Richard Fortus and Dizzy Reed, who are killing it right now with the GnR partial-reunion tour. Did that huge influx of cash change those two dude's attitudes or are they the same guys they've always been! Lol, we've been trying to interview Dizzy Reed for years, but he won't return our messages!!!

Tichy:_Haha... "huge influx of cash"... as if you or I know anything about that...! Dizzy and Richard were never NOT in GNR, they did the Daisies when they could. It just worked out for a couple years.
But no, their attitudes didn't change at all...they simply went back to GnR when they got called about the upcoming years of touring.
That's that.

23. You've got a huge GnR connection. Were you a fan of that group in your younger days? What did you think of the album Chinese Democracy?

Tichy: I loved Appetite and how it set them apart from all the safe, clean, boring 80's hair rock that was being regurgitated. All the sudden every band got a little dirtier and loved bandanas! Haha...
Re: Chinese Democracy. I have only listened to it a couple times... but I like a couple tunes on it.

24. You've played with Fortus/Dizzy.....and then three albums with Gilby Clarke, you toured with Slash's Snakepit and with Velvet Revolver!!! So you've basically played or toured with almost the entire band except for Axl!!!

Tichy: Yes , this is all true....

25. _Any fun or cool memories or experiences you can share about your time with Slash....or with VR (slash/duff)?_

Tichy: I had a great time with Slash. I love his playing and passion for guitar and music.
We toured the world and had a barrel of laughs. He was my boss but made me feel like we were simply mutual music fans and friends playing together. He's very funny and clever and I always had a great time hanging w him.
Yes there are lots of stories but it would take way to long to get into.
And playing with VR was also great.
It was in between Billy Idol tours so it was quite stressful to learn all their music while on tour w Billy, get off the plane straight to rehearsal and 3 days later do the shows.
But the guys were all real cool, helpful and supportive.

26. _If Axl called you in 2019 and said he needed a new drummer for GnR.....do you hop on a plane or politely decline?_

Tichy: It wouldn't be something I'd say no to.
I know everyone in the band outside of Axl and love the music. And it's the world's biggest rock tour going. But with that, and, in my "not as young as I used to be" age... haha... you still ask basic questions and consider the commitment verses all else you may have going on in your life. But yeah, that would certainly be fun, wouldn't it!?

27. _What do you have in store for 2018 and 2019?_

Tichy: I'm doing some Euro festivals with WASP in August and did some in June as well.
I have a new band my management is shopping right now. I'll leave it at that so as not to jinx something so new and unknown. And there's a few other twists and turns in the pipeline that I'm working on.

28. _Is there anything else you want me to mention?_

Tichy: Oh! I will say this.... I have this band .... "A Farewell To Kings"... it's a celebration to Rush.
Great players.... Francesco DiCosmo on Bass and vox, Walter Ino on Gtr,

Jonathan Sindelman on keys. I had a funny novelty sort of idea for an original song in the spirit of Rush. We wrote the music the other day and will finish next week. The novelty is in the title of the song.
We will probably hire a publicist and release it next month! I'm excited as I think Rush fans will really dig it!

http://www.briantichy.com/

Brian Young
Beau Nasty

Photo courtesy of Brian Young.

1. I see you live in Austin! Are you active in the Austin music scene? And do you ever hang out or work with Jason McMaster?

Young: I don't know Jason McMaster. I play in Dallas, San Antonio, Corpus Christi, Houston and all around Texas but we only play one public show in Austin and that is at a club called Cedar Street Courtyard. Any other show in Austin is a private event.

2. Toured with Love/Hate and Loverboy – two bands that weren't really staples of the "hair metal" genre. Whose decision was that and do you think it would have been better if you guys would have went out with Dokken, Winger and Ratt? How it is that you guys didn't tour with Winger?

Young: The tours we did with Loverboy and Love/Hate were decided by our record label. We had no say in who we toured with so there was not an option to tour with Dokken, Winger or Ratt.

3. Did you get to spend any time with Jizzy Pearl? He's a semi-legend of the genre, how was he back then and how did he treat you guys on tour?

Young: Yeah, we hung out with him once in a while on tour. He kept to himself a lot and I don't like to bother people so I didn't try too hard to converse with him. Hung out with Jon E. Love more often than Jizzy. Us guitar players seem to have more in common.

4. Did you guys do the whole "sunset strip" thing to get signed? If so, got any crazy stories? What bands were you competing with on a nightly basis on the strip? Any band stand out as being full of really cool/nice guys.....and any that were way too cocky and arrogant?

Young: We didn't do the "Strip" thing to get signed. Our singer (Mark Anthony Fretz) had label interest from CBS and that turned into demo recordings that got passed along to Jerry Greenberg and that is how we got signed. That's why we broke up so quickly. No roots.

5. What can you say about your time with Mike Terrana? He has – not exaggerating – played on 84 different albums – from German metal bands to female opera singers to Beau Nasty, and says he would love to put out a fusion jazz instrumental album. That's not the typical catalog of a hair metal drummer. How was he back in 1989, could you tell he was going to go on to greatness?

Young: LOVED working with Mike Terrana. One of the hardest working, ethical, and funny people I've ever known. He had already achieved greatness when I met him.... the public just didn't know it yet.

6.
Terrana went from you to working with Yngwie Malmsteen, Axel Rudi Pell and Tony MacApline. Do you think he jumped around with these A-list guitar players because he was searching for a guitar player of your immense skill level? Who are your guitar heroes?

Young: No. I don't think he "sought out" guitar heroes. He was just the right drummer at a time when there were many guitar heroes doing records. I don't know how he got the Tony MacAlpine gig or how he ended up with Yngwie but we were all running in those same circles at the time and it was a very natural progression for him to work with those guys.

7. You had Beau Hill on board, a semi-major tour, a well received album....how come the label didn't let you guys record a second album?

Young: We had a multi-record deal but after the first album and tours I was not happy with the direction, musically OR business wise and I quit. Then Mike quit and then George Bernhardt turned down the option to do a second record.

8. Was it just a coincidence: BEAU Hill and BEAU nasty, or was the band named after him? Was the story of you guys finding a dead vagrant with the name Beau Nasty tattooed on him actually true?

Young: Total coincidence. George Bernhardt stumbled upon the name in some dictionary or book and months later, after we met with a few different producers, Beau Hill ended up being the guy. Just a coincidence.

9. You played with Malmsteen in 1985. Did Yngwie ever "unleash the fuckin' fury" on you? It's rumored that he has a bit of an ego and is tough to work with. How was he back in the mid-80s?

Young: I jammed with Yngwie a bunch of times just hanging out with guitars and he actually asked me to play bass for him on a tour after Marcel Jacob left but we were never in a band together. We had some fun times together and a few uncomfortable times (because he dated my ex-girlfriend) but it was all good.

10. Jeff Scott Soto says you saved the 2007 Talisman tour after they had two guitar players drop out. How as that tour? And what are you feelings on Jeff Scott Soto – how's it been working with him?

Young: I've been working with Jeff Scott Soto off and on since late 1985 (almost 33 years!) We've been through a lot together. He is a top-notch vocalist. As good as it gets. The Talisman tour was a one month whirlwind through Europe. I had 8 days to learn their whole set. Very demanding stuff. It definitely put the one hair I have on my chest!!!

11. You played and toured with the legendary David Lee Roth. Again, another legend. Can you describe that experience to your fans?

Young: Uuuuuhhhh..... no. I can't possibly describe six years on the road with David Lee Roth without writing a small novel. I'll leave this to your imagination.

12. And like Malmsteen, DLR has quite a reputation for being large personality. Which one had the bigger ego? Who was easier to work with?

Young: I think Dave has a bigger ego than Yngwie and he'll be the first one to tell you. I never actually "worked" with Yngwie but since Dave pays more, he's probably "easier" to work with.

13. All the old 80s bands are coming back now and doing festivals, small tours, monsters of rock cruise – has Beau Nasty talked about that at all? Would you be up for it?

Young: Absofuckinglutely NOT! And I don't think there is very much interest for that band anyway.

14. Hypothetical question. You wake up tomorrow with four offers. A million dollars for two years of work, including an album and world tour. The four are offers from Malmsteen, DLR, Beau Nasty and Jeff Scott Soto. Which ones do you consider, which ones do you laugh and not call back and finally....which one do you choose?

Young: Beau Nasty? No. Yngwie? No. DLR... probably not. Jeff Scott Soto... a solid maybe (at least we'd have fun.) Happily, I'm in a position now that I could actually turn down that offer. A million dollars for a ONE year world tour I would consider.

15. Beau Nasty are a hard bunch to find a lot of information on. One story said you were billed as a California band, but in reality, the band members came from all over the place (even out of country) and were

put together to cash in the popularity of the hair metal scene. Can you elaborate on what was the reality of Beau Nasty's birth as a band?

Young: In a nutshell. Some guitar player in Hollywood that had an investor and interest from Wendy Dio found a demo tape of Mark Anthony in a box in an office in Hollywood. Mark came to Hollywood and did a demo with this guy. Things didn't work out and through a mutual friend, Mark found me (living in North Hollywood, I'm from Ventura county). Mark asked me if I would be willing to work with his old guitarist (from Toronto who was currently living in Milwaukee) George Bernhardt. I said sure and we flew him out and started writing songs. Meanwhile, Mike Varney (of Guitar Player magazine Spotlight Column) had been offering me a solo record deal and hooked me up with an awesome drummer (Mike Terrana). Mike had also worked with Mark Anthony in the past. He was playing with a bass player named Doug Baker (with Jeff Scott Soto and a Japanese guitar shredder named Kuni) and we all pulled together, wrote and recorded a demo and got signed to WTG (CBS) So like many other bands, we formed in LA but other than me and the bass player were not from Southern California.

16. *Besides the Sota and DLR gigs what have you been doing since Beau Nasty dissolved? Music industry or something else? Can you update your fans on your life/career over the past 30 years?*

Young: When I quit Beau Nasty I jumped into a band with my brother and some old friends that became Sykotik Sinfoney. Now THAT was a fun and crazy band. Kind of like Slipknot but a few years too soon. I did a lot of session work and had the opportunity to record with Paul Stanley, John Wetton, Johnny Van Zant, Jamie Jamison, Eddie Money, Sammy Hagar and many others. Then I had a tiny stint with Eddie Money in his band (didn't play any shows), I did some demos with him and played one song on one record but I left to play with The Boogie Knights and Perfect World Entertainment (Jeff Scott Soto got me into that). Then, in 1999, I was recruited by The Atomic Punks, the world class Van Halen tribute band. After three years with them

David Lee Roth "stole" me from them. I spent six years touring and recording with DLR until he went back to VH in '08. Since then, I've been living in Austin, Texas and playing about 240 shows a year with The Spazmatics.

17. We put three Beau Nasty songs in our top 1,000 songs of the era list. Shake It on the rock side, and Paradise and Make a Wish on the ballad side. What were your favorite songs off the album – or what songs were you most proud of?

Young: I loved my guitar solo in Make a Wish. I like the song Gemini and Goodbye Rosie but some of my favorite songs didn't make the record and all I have is the demos of them.

18. What guitar players or musicians were your main influences?

Young: Started out listening to The Beatles, Elvis, Little Richard, Chet Atkins, Simon and Garfunkel. Then KISS and Ace Frehley got me into PLAYING guitar. Then Hendrix, Nugent, Page, Beck, Blackmore, Foghat, Cheap Trick, Yes, Kansas, Edward Van Halen.
Then got into Al DiMeola, Bill Bruford, Allan Holdsworth, Mahavishnu, UK, Paganini. Then along came Yngwie, Vai, Satriani, Eric Johnson. And on and on.

19. If Beau Nasty had a reunion tour, who would your ideal tour mate be?

Young: Well, like I said before. No way. But Terrana, Bernhardt and Baker are all guys I would love to hang out with.

20. Do you stay in touch with any of your old band members?

Young: Yes, from MANY different bands. Still in touch with George Bernhardt, Doug Baker, Jeff Scott Soto, guys from Sykotik Sinfoney, Ray Luzier, Todd Jenson and Jimmy DeGrasso (DLR)

21. What advice would you give to young guitar players who want to make a living in the music business?

Young: Practice your ass off. Take EVERY possible paying gig you ever get (you never know which of these leads to MANY others). Learn as many styles as you can and learn cover songs that you like AND that you don't like. (Those are the ones I learned the most from).

Quick Reponse:

George Bernhardt: Meticulous genius
Doug Baker: Solid as a rock
Mike Terrana: Hilarious and serious
David Lee Rot: Demanding and complex
Van Halen: DLR or Sammy Hagar? DLR era for pure fucking metal and Hagar for when Eddie went to keyboards and strumming.
Guns n Roses: One great album and don't care much after that
Axl Rose: Great on that one album (see above)
Motley Crue: Cool fucking Hollywood rock-n-roll.
Def Leppard: Great songs. Great production.
Bon Jovi: Good pop hits.

And if you can remember….of the hair metal genre ……

Best:
Band: Whitesnake

Album: Motley Crue-Too Fast for Love

Singer: David Coverdale

Guitar player: Warren DiMartini

Bass player: Nikki Sixx

Finally…..do you have a favorite band or two that you feel were extremely underrated? You thought they should have been much bigger than they were? Are there any bands you feel didn't get the credit they deserved?

Young: KIX

Chriz Van Jaarsveld
Sleeze Beez

Photo courtesy of Jaarsveld's Official Facebook page.

1. When did you start playing guitar and when did you realize you were good enough to do it for a living?

Van Jaarsveld: I started playing guitar round '74, when I was 17 years old (or young, for that matter ;-)
I actually wanted to be a bass player but one day I could get a cheap guitar from a friend, and I thought: 'Let's get this guitar, and just put 4 strings on it, and there you have it: A BASS!" but that didn't work of course. While playing the guitar more and more I improved fairly quickly, and I formed my first band already after a few months of playing. We played (or tried to play) mainly Blues, and some Stones covers. Simple stuff.

Round '77 I joined my first real band, called Captain Coke. Round '79 we gained some fame over here in Holland and gigged quite frequently, like three times a week, and we did some big festivals and opening slots for Cheap Trick, Doctor Feelgood, and The Boomtown Rats. Round 1980 we called it quits, and I struggled for a few years.

I was totally dedicated to music and didn't have any money. I auditioned here and there and finally, in '83, I was asked to audition for a Dutch metal band called Picture, who were quite big at the time already. I got the job, and since Picture had a record deal with a major record label, it was the stepping stone for me to becoming a professional musician. I had quite a chunk in the writing of Picture's Eternal dark album, which sold quite well in the Netherlands, Belgium, Germany, Italy, Spain, and it climbed the charts in South America, where it is still considered a classic. I stayed with Picture 'till '87, and then I moved on.

I wanted to play more 'rock 'n roll based' music, more catchy, but raunchy stuff, with strong riffs, catchy sing-along choruses, and with that in mind I started Sleeze Beez, that same year, together with Jan Koster, who had gained some fame as well round that time.

2. How did you and Jan actually meet?

Van Jaarsveld: TRUE story! One night in '85, in my hometown Amsterdam, after a gig somewhere, I ended up at this bar, a nightclub, called The Rose. I was a bit toasted (read: plain drunk) and I was obnoxious, loud, offensive, and you name it, so, eventually, I got thrown out by two bouncers.

In the meantime there was a lot of tumultuous shouting going on in the back of the bar, with the sound of breaking glass. After I ended up on the pavement, while I crawled back up and shook the dirt of my clothes, the door swung open and a guy with long black hair was thrown out. He landed right in front of my feet. So I helped him up. Back on his feet, he said: "Hey, you are Chriz eh? The guitarist of Picture" and I replied with: "'Yeah, and you must be Jan, drummer of Highway Chile..."
We laughed.
Jan said: 'People keep on telling me that you and I are alike..."
"Yeah, I hear the same at times" I said.
We hugged and Jan said: 'One day you and me will start a band!"
I said: "Yeah, man, maybe we will!" and we parted ways....

3. You guys went through three singers in 1988. What happened? What was it about Andrew Elt that allowed him to fit what you guys were looking for?

Van Jaarsveld: The first singer, Tigo 'Tiger' Fawzi, was a good singer, soulful, powerful voice, a gentle soul, but in the long run it didn't work out. Musical differences, so to speak. So we moved on.

We knew a singer called Thijs Hameleers and offered him the spot, but he couldn't keep up with us, so in the meantime we kept on looking for another singer.

I remembered seeing Andrew Elt once, on TV. He and his band had won some contest over here in Holland, and I liked Andrew's attitude and performance. Accidentally, when we were looking for a singer, I got an invitation to be part of an 'All Star' Jam, organized by the Metal Hammer rock magazine and Andrew would be part of it as well.

Andrew and I shared the same bill. Although we both had a similar attitude towards each other (big ego's ;-) we unmistakably had some strong musical chemistry going on stage, with mutual respect. So I asked Andrew to come over to the studio. When he heard the stuff we recorded already (for what became the Screwed, Blued & Tattooed album) he was blown away. He sang Don't Talk about Roses as a sort of an 'audition' and he fit right in. From then on we were ready for take off.

4. Off the success of your debut album, SB got picked up to tour with Skid Row. How was that experience? Was Sebastian Bach as crazy as he seems?

Van Jaarsveld: Before we embarked on that tour, we were more than ready. We had the experience, the chops, the tunes, and we were utterly dedicated and determined. A force to be reckoned with ;-)
When we did the 1st gig with the Skids, in Detroit, it was obvious to everybody there that we WERE a force to be reckoned with, so the next night we got less space on stage, and the lights were dimmed a bit... We took it as a compliment ;-)

To be honest: the guys from Skid Row were really great: Snake, Scotti... we hung out and partied together. Sebastian Bach was a nice guy too. He wasn't that crazy really. He was young though, at the time, and he became a rock star almost overnight. It may have been hard for him to deal with the success at times. but overall he seemed like an okay guy really. During the last show of that tour there were pranks going on (like changing the water in the bottles on stage with vodka) and they joined us on stage, and we joined them to play ac/dc's Highway to hell together. It was a great experience to be gigging in the US for the first time. The crowd embraced us straight away, and we felt right at home. It was a blast!

5. You guys stayed popular in Japan for several years after your US fame declined. Why do you think the Japanese rock fans love you guys so much?

Van Jaarsveld: When grunge became popular in the US and Europe, hardrock/glamrock etc. was still popular in Japan, so things didn't change much over there.

6. I've read that the band was starting to not get along towards the end. Was it a bitter split or did everybody just decide to do their own thing? You guys had just recorded a strong album and had tour dates set up, seems like an odd time to break up the band. What was going on to make you guys call it a day?

Van Jaarsveld: Being in a band is like being in a marriage or relationship. When a band becomes popular the whole scene around you changes, and you have to stick together through thick and thin, so you have to get along (very) well.

We, the five of us, stuck through it and we became as close as brothers are. But after nine years we sort of grew apart. People evolve, and at a certain point we realized that we weren't on the same page anymore. So we called it quits. And yeah, we recorded Insanity beach and had a European tour planned, but Jan got a wrist injury round that time and couldn't play drums properly so we had to postpone the first shows of the tour. But at the same time most of us felt that we weren't the band we used to be anymore and actually disliked the idea of going on tour in that capacity. So we talked about it and agreed on splitting up. I think we were exhausted as well. It wasn't a bitter split up, but to some degree it felt like that for some of us, I'm sure.

7. You and Jan stayed together and formed Jetland, which was a lot heavier than SB. Why the change in sound to more of a punk rock band?

Van Jaarsveld: Round the time the Beez spilt up, I played Jan a new tune I wrote. It was called 'I don't Care' it had this punk vibe to it, it was playful, fresh. Jan liked it straight away and presented me a tune he wrote that same morning, called 'Dead With You' and it had the same vibe as the tune I wrote.

The songs fit together seamlessly. I think we needed a breath of fresh air, something completely different. We needed to blow off steam, have some fun, go crazy. Jan couldn't drum at the time, but he could pick up a guitar. So we started jamming a bit. We called Edd, the Beez bass player up to play some bass, Jan did the lead vocals as well, and before we knew it we were looking for a drummer.

We knocked out song after song and we had material ready for an album in no time. We went to the ICP Studio's in Brussels, recorded the album in a frenzy, got Chris Sheldon (Radiohead, Therapy and many others) to mix it, and Flowers for Wendy, and the first Jetland album was a fact.

Jetland did quite well, really. We had a song - And The Crowd Goes - in the charts over here and we gigged very frequently. Of course a lot of people didn't get Jetland; the new musical turn we took, and accused us of being 'opportunists' since upcoming bands like the Foo Fighters also had a former drummer play guitar and sing, but it actually just turned out the way it did. There was no plan, or whatever, we just felt like doing something totally different, something fresh, something we enjoyed to do. It was fun.

8. How come SB reformed in 2010? And how did you manage to secure a spot opening for Aerosmith, one of the most popular bands in the world? Did you get a chance to hang out with Tyler and the boys?

Van Jaarsveld: It was actually BECAUSE of Aerosmith that we decided to get back together again ;-)
We were asked by a well-known Dutch agency to open for Aerosmith. They thought it would be a great event that way, with the Beez reuniting on a bill like that. We actually liked the idea, so we got together just for that event. Afterwards, we liked it so much that we decided to do one more gig at the legendary Paradiso in our hometown of Amsterdam – a farewell show as a closure that never happened back in the day. For the fans and for us, it was great, really.

I actually had a brief encounter with Steven Tyler, backstage, just before Aerosmith was about to go on. We said hi, talked shortly. I told him that I was honored to meet him and he said he liked our stuff, and the show, and that he remembered us from Stranger than Paradise and always liked the Screwed, Blued & Tattooed album, things like that. And then I wished him a good show and moved on. That was it.

9. Of the four Sleeze Beez studio albums, do you have a favorite or does one really capture the real Chriz sound?

Van Jaarsveld: Ha, good question. The real Chriz-sound ;-)

I don't listen to albums I'm on very much, but I´m a bit of an audiophile and when I got this great vintage Sansui amp one day, I plowed through my CD collection (yes, I have a 'collection'- or piles of cd's stacked up in a corner, for that matter) and I came across a copy of *Screwed*.

For the first time in 20 years I sat down and listened to the whole album. Objective, as if I was hearing it for the first time. I always only kept on hearing the flaws or parts that I found disturbing and could have been better (in my opinion). I've never been able to listen to it without analyzing (same goes for other albums we did or I'm on) but now I could actually just sit down and enjoy the ride. I really enjoyed it, and I can imagine why it did for us what it did. There's a great energy about it. Uplifting. Spunky. Good tunes too. I actually played air guitar to it!

And speaking of the 'Chriz sound' (for as far as that exists) Screwed, Blued and tattooed was actually the album where I found my style, so to speak.
I'm definitely(!) not the best guitar player around, but I DID have a bit of a style of my own, in those days, I must admit. Recognizable even (so I have been told;-)
So, yes it did (capture the 'real Chriz sound' more or less;-)

10. We put together a top 1,000 songs list. Your three highest ranked songs were: I Don't Want to Live Without You, Stranger Than Paradise and This Time. Thoughts or memories on recording those great tunes?

Van Jaarsveld: I remember we couldn't capture the right vibe for Stranger than Paradise straight away. And also the arrangement needed work still. So we recorded a couple of versions of it, until we were convinced we had it.

Jan, as well as I, had the idea that an acoustic solo would be nice. The chord changes underneath the solo have a somewhat different timing, so I worked a solo out, before I came to the studio.

In the studio, when I sat down with the acoustic guitar, I asked producer John Sonneveld to press record and just let me play over the chords, to find out if it would fit. I played it and it worked straight away. It was THE take. Those are the better moments in a studio.

I have fond memories of that time anyway. Recording Screwed was a blast! We had incredible fun, and that oozes through the music as well, of course.

11. Do you think we missed songs that should be higher ranked than those three?

Van Jaarsveld: Yeah, they are all ballads! Put a tune like Rock in the Western World or Screwed, Blued and Tattooed up there! ;-)
(and When the brains go to the Balls, House is on Fire, Damned if we Do, Don't talk about Roses, Raise a little Hell, Save Myself... ;-P)

12. Who came up with the name and lyrics for 'When the Brains go to the Balls'?

Van Jaarsveld: Jan (Koster) did....

13. Picture was a pretty cool band. But it seemed like there was a bit of constant turmoil with them. How was the experience with that band?

Van Jaarsveld: I liked playing in Picture.

When I just joined them there was plenty of turmoil going on. But with the Eternal Dark line up we had loads a fun and we worked very hard to get Picture on the Rails again.

Eternal Dark is still considered a 'classic' here and there, and Picture is touring in the original line up again. They're doing pretty well. I wish them all the luck in the world. No hard feelings.
Later on things became more complicated with Picture, and I left.

14. Did grunge music take over the music scene in the Netherlands?

Van Jaarsveld: Yes, it did.

15. You guys covered Faithfull by Journey? What brought that about? Lots of casual fans don't realize that the real backbone of Journey wasn't Steve Perry's amazing vocals, but a potent 1-2 guitar attack.

Van Jaarsveld: Before we did the Paradiso-beez-reunion-show we thought it would be nice to record Journey's Faithfully and release it as a single to get some radio attention so everybody would know we were reuniting for one last gig. We recorded the track, but didn't do anything with it, because it was a bit short notice really.

16. What projects or bands are you working with now? What does 2018 and 2019 have in store for you?

Van Jaarsveld: I've got my own studio (not a big one) and I'm recording ideas, songs... I have plenty ideas for music, and my studio is my playground. I've always been a fan of the Fender Stratocaster (although I was endorsed by Gibson, in the past;-) and later on in my career I switched to the Strat completely. That change also implicates that my way of playing has changed (somehow, when I pick up a Strat, I approach it differently than a Les Paul or SG for instance, so I sound differently, and I come up with other stuff than I do on a Gibson) so I come up with more bluesy riffs, or more psychedelic stuff. It's not really 'heavy' what I'm doing, although it rocks too at times, of course. I write these 'Suites' from 20 minutes long, and stuff. I have no idea what I'm going to do with it yet.

17. The hair metal festival tours are pretty huge in America right now. You put 5-10 bands on a bill and they are drawing crowds of 5,000-to-10,000 fans. The Monsters of Rock Cruise quickly sells out every year. For the right amount of money, would SB ever reunite and come play a handful of these festivals? I think the American crowds would really enjoy seeing you guys again.

Van Jaarsveld: Good to hear that it is still alive! But people tend to underestimate that it must be worthwhile for a band to get back together and perform the way they used to. It takes a lot of preparation. But also dedication. We have lives of our own. Everybody's got different projects or obligations, and nobody really feels the urge to get back into that old groove, just like that. For the right amount of money, I can imagine that it's easier to put other things on hold for a while.

So yeah, for the right amount of money, we would consider it, I reckon.

18. What musicians inspired you as a youngster? And who do you enjoy listening to now?

Van Jaarsveld: Guitarists like Jimi Hendrix, Ritchie Blackmore, Rory Gallagher, David Gilmour inspired me to go and play the guitar myself, and I still enjoy listening to them to this day.

And although I played mostly in hard-rocking bands, I always listened to bands like Jethro Tull, Yes, Gentle Giant, The Who, Frank Zappa, Pink Floyd, Steve Hillage, David Bowie, Sex Pistols... also Deep Purple, Led Zeppelin, Black Sabbath (always loved Black Sabbath) of course, but not particularly hard rock. I liked some Def Leppard tunes, I liked Motley Crue. Motorhead was great!
But at the moment I'm more into Steve Hillage for instance (Fish Rising, Green). Mainly old stuff, but I find it interesting. And due to the Internet and YouTube, there is sooo much to discover. So right now I listen to everything I find interesting.

I also enjoy watching old stuff from Deep Purple with Blackmore in his heyday, or Yngwie Malmsteen, stuff like that. But...every now and again I'll put on Back in Black, or Back Ice... AC/DC is always good ;-)

19. What bands from the "hair metal" era did you enjoy listening to?

Van Jaarsveld: Def Leppard, Motley Crue, Ratt, some Cinderella... and (although not glam) Motorhead, Metallica's Black album and AC/DC. I've never been a metalhead per se, if you catch my drift, I just loved playing extremely loud(!) with hard rocking bands to match. The energy, the volume, the attitude. Strong, powerful riffs. The enthusiasm of the rock audiences (best crowd there is). The excessive lifestyle. Going crazy. I like punk too. But my musical taste always has been broader than that.

20. What do you like to do that isn't music related? Are you a talented painter too?

Van Jaarsveld: Yep, I'm a painter as well.
I went to art school before I became a musician.
Right now my art and music go hand in hand, so to speak.

21. Is there anything else you want us to mention or promote for you???

Van Jaarsveld: If people are interested in my art, or music, send a friend request via Facebook, or check my YouTube channel every now and again (although there is not much going on there) Just type Chriz van Jaarsveld, and you'll find me.

https://www.facebook.com/chriz.vanjaarsveld
http://www.sleezebeez.com
https://www.facebook.com/SleezeBeez

Conny Bloom
Electric Boys

Photo courtesy of Conny Bloom Official Facebook page.

1. Let's get right to it with the question you probably get tired of being asked! Ted Poley of Danger Danger was a big tennis player growing up. Who would win if you guys battled it out on the court?

Bloom: Ted! I haven't played for maaaany many years. In fact, Lars Ulrich and I were gonna play at one time. He's a fan of our stuff and I challenged him, as a joke. He really wanted to find a court but drinks were pouring, and well, first things first - this was at the last gig of their Black Album tour.

2. What compliment gives you the greatest sense of satisfaction – being praised for your songwriting skills, guitar skills or vocal ability?

Bloom: Probably the singing, cuz I don't consider myself that great of a singer.

3. How did you end up doing an acoustic show with the amazing John Corabi? You guys fit together very well, same styles, same great voices, great guitar players.

Bloom: We met at Sweden Rock and it turned out he'd been to one of our shows with Tommy Lee in LA. We thought it would be fun to do something so when he came to town doing an acoustic show I sat in for a few songs. Amazing singer and great guy.

4. Electric Boys were such a great rock band, why do you think the label lost faith in you after the third album? You guys seemed heavy enough to endure the grunge era and you had a unique sound. Ready To Believe is such a great song.

Bloom: They put up the cash to record the *Freewheelin* album. Then when it was done they said they didn't have any money left to promote it. Not very smart planning eh?

5. Wiki page says you were a "local guitar hero at 14"....can you expand on what that means?

Bloom: We'll I was playing behind my head and stuff already at 14, at the youth clubs. I wasn't into wine and women back then, just wanted to play guitar all the time.

6. Is there one solo that you are most proud of or that really captured your sound the best?

Bloom: I like melodic solos, that means something to the song and "Lips" is definitely like that. 'Mary In The Mystery World' has got some fun whammy bar licks in it. 'The Day The Gypsies Came To Town' is one of my favorites.

7. We really love 'I'll Be Fine' – is there a cool story behind that song?

Bloom: The main inspiration was from my grandmother (RIP), who was a big part of my upbringing. (Maybe I sung it so it could be about a girlfriend as well, I can't remember.)

8. If a label gave you a blank check, what band would you put together? And who would you pick to tour with you (money is no object).

Bloom: I actually have a very cool band name that should be used sometime, so I might put something interesting together at around that. Something heavy.

9. We've put together a list of the top 1,000 songs of the 1981-2017 sleaze rock era. All Lips N' Hips, Ready to Believe and She's Into Something Heavy are the songs we have rated the highest. Any thoughts on that?

Bloom: Wow that's a compliment. I was never that "at ease with the sleaze" thing though since I was a Doors, Hendrix, T-Rex, Deep Purple, etc fan. I was listening to funk and soul and 50-60-70s rock. When we were around I always felt we were a little outside of things and kind of belonged to another era. Glam and big curly hair for me was always Marc Bolan and Ian Hunter.

10. "All Lips N' Hips" is obviously the signature Electric Boys song. Do you remember writing it and at the time, could you tell it was going to be a huge hit?

Bloom: I was trying to find an identity music wise. Then one day, when I stopped looking, that riff came up. I thought, hang on a minute, THIS is cool. Then followed a few more, "Psychedelic Eyes" being one of them.

11. How did you first meet up with Andy Christell?

Bloom: At school. He looked like an outsider and we started talking. Turned out he was a big Alice Cooper fan like me, and we started hanging.

12. What spurred the comeback in 2011?

Bloom: After 4 1/2 years in Hanoi Rocks it just felt good to play that kind of music again. I never though they all would agree, but here we are. We've actually been together longer now than our first run.

13. Any plans for an American tour in the future?

Bloom: We'd LOVE to!! Need somebody over there to help co-ordinate it though.

14. What was it like playing with Hanoi Rocks, a very legendary band. Did you mind playing guitar for a band and not being the singer?

Bloom: I consider myself a guitar player first and foremost, so not singing felt like luxury to me. I could focus on the playing and hang out in rowdy "will kill your voice" bars with the other boys.
Andy was very cool with me playing solos. It was kind of Stonesy like that. We're both just "guitar players", not divided into just lead or just rhythm.

15. How was it writing with McCoy and Monroe? A lot of people thought it was the most "rock" album Hanoi ever did.

Bloom: It was great fun! Came up with about five song ideas I think, that we then worked on together. It was very much a "band album" and we had a great time in the studio.

16. I've read that Michael Monroe is supposed to be one of the nicest men in the music world. You've worked with him, is that a true statement?

Bloom: He's great. I thought it would last a year or something but ended up being almost 5 years. That says it all. The whole band was great.

17. Did you enjoy your time with Silver Ginger 5? Did you get to write with Ginger on the second album? Is that ever going to be released?

Bloom: I love Silver Ginger 5! When G contacted me I thought if this is just "ok" I'll do it (cuz I wanted to get out of Sweden) but it turned out that the songs were great! One of the best things Ginger has done I think.

18. Did you ever get to play with or meet Betty Davis? I have to give you a special Thank You for that. I'd never heard of her until reading that you liked her, so I looked her up and holy crap - that lady could sing.

Bloom: Never met her. Mind-blowing stuff!

19. Basic advice for a youngster who wants to play guitar for a living? Learn on an acoustic or electric? Master anything particular? More important to create your own sounds or learn the classic riffs. How many hours a day practice?

Bloom: You gotta love it. If you love it, you will play a lot. If you play a lot, you get good. Copy lots of different licks to learn. Eventually you might find that all that mixed, played by you, will have a unique sound. Probably good to start on acoustic guitar.

20. You have traveled the world. Any city/area or country that you enjoy playing the most?

Bloom: UK, Sweden and America were our main territories with Electric Boys but I also love Japan. And Spain. And I'd like to get something going in Germany.

21. Where is your favorite place to play in America?

Bloom: Don't think I have a favorite town. Wanna go to New Orleans though! There's a line in "Dying To Be Loved" about Bourbon Street. I thought if I sing about it I might get there, but haven't been so far.

22. You said in an interview that you loved the Hellacopters. They seem way heavier than anything you've done or been associated with – what's it about their sound you like? And would you like to do something that heavy?

Bloom: Heavier doesn't seem like the right word to me. Punkier, more rocking maybe. I think stuff like "Ready to Believe" is heavier. I love the attitude. They really inspired lots of bands in Sweden. Great guys and "I'm With the Band" is a great song.

23. Hardcore Superstar seems to be really making a name for themselves internationally. Just a really strong rock n roll band. Thoughts on those guys?

Bloom: Longevity rocks! They've stuck with their thing and it pays off. Nice guys too.

Is there anything you'd like us to mention or promote?
Yes, I'd like to mention that we're doing a Pledge Music campaign for our next album, so go there, and find all sorts of fun stuff!

https://www.facebook.com/ConnyBloomOfficial/
https://www.facebook.com/pg/electricboys
https://twitter.com/ConnyBloom2015

Darrell Millar
Killer Dwarfs

Photo courtesy of Millar's official webpage.

1. Are you fans of Slik Toxik? Personally, I think they were one of the most underrated bands of all time from that era. They beat you guys out for the 1992 Much Music Best Metal Video. Was there a rivalry or were you all buddies back then?

Millar: Dwarfs came out 10 years before them and already had five records out when their debut hit. There was no rivalry. The Juno Awards is not a competition and you get the same amount of press just being nominated as you do winning. I don't look at it like we lost to Slik Toxic. But when we were nominated for Best Metal Record category years earlier, I was happy to lose that one to the mighty Rush. Just being in that category with Rush was good enough for me.

2. Sorry, we have to ask. Nickleback…..yes or no?

Millar: YES. Great rock act of talented songwriters and musicians. Saw them live twice. Great both times.

3. How is the Canadian rock scene compared to America?

Millar: When it comes to #DwarfNation, both countries are just as passionate for the band. America just has a larger population of Rock Fans and we can play more markets.

4. What's the main difference between touring in Canada and the U.S.? And do you have a favorite city and venue in both places?

Millar: As I said in the last question. USA has more population of Rockers and more markets to rock in. M3 Fest, Monsters Of Rock Cruise and anything in Texas, Los Angeles, NYC, Chicago, Vegas. Hell, all the cities kick ASSSS!!!

5. Better singer….Russ Graham or Graham Russell?

Millar: Russ Graham hands down. Head Stands Up!!

6. We are doing a top 1,000 songs and 300 albums list. You've got six songs in our list, led by "Doesn't Matter", "Driftin' Back" and "Last Laugh". Thoughts or memories on those songs?

Millar: They remind me of Andy Johns, the late great producer who helped make us who we are today.

7. We've also got "Lonely Road" from Start @ One on the list. Is there a cool story behind the writing/recording of that one?

Millar: No. Except we were desperate recording that record riding the Grunge Wave and dropped from our label Epic Records at the time.

8. What album do you consider to be the best Killer Dwarf's disc?

Millar: The new *Live No Guff* record. *Weapons, Big Deal, Method to the Madness* next.

9. What do you think of the current state of the music industry. Because of Napster/YouTube and the Internet, releasing albums have became a thing of the past. One person buys it and then downloads it on the net for thousands of people to grab it for free. As an artist, what are you thoughts on people getting your music for free without having to pay for it?

Millar: Well it doesn't make me feel great about how things have turned out. Russ and I have been around this business for 40 years and have seen many phases of it. This is just another one and the biz will always reinvent itself and musicians will get paid other ways. The live show is back like the days of old paying out. Fans buy merch and physical discs to meet us and get them signed. It's a fair trade off.

10. Do you think the Internet is a good or bad thing for bands today. Any band can record an album's worth of songs and release them online – so no label is needed. Bu there is also no quality control method, so any band can release an album's worth of songs online.

Millar: It has made it watered down and one must search for the real songwriters and players now. It has helped in a great way that we can actually talk and be friends with our fan base and reach out to them easily with Info on releases and tours. I like that part.

11. Do you think there is anything that musicians can ever do to bring back albums and make it financially feasible to release them? We grew up when our favorite bands released an album every year or every other year. But now, it's every five or six years at most, which sucks as a fan.

Millar: Vinyl is on a come back now and more and more bands are doing limited runs. We will ourselves at some point.

12. You are fans of ACDC. What do you think about Angus recording a new album (and touring) with Axl Rose handling vocals?

Millar: Don't like it as great as Axl is. Let ACDC go with Bon, Malcolm and George Young passed away. Cliff Williams retired. Save the legacy.

13. I've seen you guys mention John Corabi a few times in interviews. What's your connection with him? (Great singer and guitar player, we loved his album with Motley Crue).

Millar: I first met John when I was in Laidlaw in the late 90s and he was in Union with Bruce Kulick and Brent Fitz. Now on MORC we are good friends. He's a talented musician and just a nice guy all around.

14. What's in store for the rest of 2018 and 2019 for you and the band?

Millar: Tour and record a new Studio record.

15. If you could put on a music festival this year, besides Killer Dwarfs, what five other bands would you put on the bill?

Millar: Aerosmith, Alice Cooper, Van Halen, Judas Priest and Iron Maiden.

16. Automan.ca is a great band. How much fun was it to front a band on vocals?

Millar: It is too much fun but that band was a lot of work building it from the ground up and was also a big deal for me to have all the singer/song writer duties to share with Carleton Lockhart. And I produced the records that are released. A bucket list for me for sure. More will come from that act.

17. *Laidlaw was also great. Any chance to ever revive that? You guys had great album, great songs and support from Nikki Sixx and even Michael Anthony helping out. How much fun was that band?*

Millar: I recorded two records with that band over seven years and have nothing but fond memories of it. Don't see a reunion for it though.

18. *What do you like to do for fun outside of music?*

Millar: Party. Watch hockey and football. Sit by pools basking in the sun or on a cruise ship. Patio or beach with a cold one in my hand with good company. Keep the stress low as much a possible. I am also raising an eight-year-old, which is a full time job.

19. *Who are your favorite drummers of all time?*

Millar: Toss up. Ian Paice, Neil Peart, John Bonham.

20. *What advice would you give to a young kid starting off who wants to become a great drummer?*

Millar: Learn your rudiments on a practice pad or snare drum before you even sit on a kit. It's the foundation of what you will do on a drum kit. Once your comfortable with Para Diddles and such and get them up to speed, then take a crash course on reading drum music to understand how the Hi Hat Snare and Bass Drum sync up to play your first groove.

21. *Is there anything else you'd like us to mention?*

Millar: Drop by our social media pages. Visit my Pirate Shop. I am a Rock n Roll Pirate. #Savvy
www.killerdwarfsband.com
www.dunkpirateshop.com
http://darrellmillar.com/

David Glen Eisley
Giuffria

Photo courtesy of Mr. Eisley

1. What brings you the most joy and satisfaction: singing a great song, writing a great song, throwing a no-hitter or acting in a great role?

Eisley: First off, the acting thing was really a fluke as my wife's agent quite awhile ago said he thought he could send me out looking the way I did and thought I'd book some acting gigs if I was interested. I didn't give it much thought but said "yea, sure."

He sent me out and managed to book a few! That was really all that was about. My dad was a actor in the 50's, 60's & 70's so I grew up with all that oddness!

Writing a really good song as definitely on a par with a no-hitter or a decent vocal performance. They only come "now & then" but it's really the same kind of feeling. For a few moments your happy with yourself. Then you go back searching again. Just how it works.

2. Would you rather have an Oscar or a Cy Young trophy in your trophy case?

Eisley: Never really thought of Awards but if I had to choose and the ones you mentioned were available "I wouldn't be able too!" All totally different but say the same thing. Guess I'd have to have one of each! LOL...

3. What ended your baseball career, how come it stopped at the double-A level?

Eisley: My real passion being young was baseball straight away as well as music. I started drum lessons at 12 and was playing ball simultaneously all throughout my life. Being groomed as a pitcher and throwing a no-hitter would have been a thrill and I did in High School, Legion ball which is where I was scouted by the Giants. I lasted 18 months with them until I attempted to decapitate my pitching coach who hated me with my unorthodox attitude and I didn't care for him as well. It was an abrupt end to my pro career as we mutually told each other to "shove it!"

Music was now "IT." And has been ever since.

4. Were there a lot of differences between baseball and Giuffria road trips?

Eisley: Being on the road with a relatively big band is definitely more rewarding and fun than slogging around with a baseball team unless you ARE playing in "the big show." The Majors would be quite different. But that wasn't in the cards for me.

5. You grew up with famous parents. How was your childhood? Did you grow up hanging in mansions with famous actors or was it a more normal environment?

Eisley: As I said my dad was an actor and quite recognizable at the time but not many actors at that time, especially TV actors, made a whole lot of dough. We did ok but there were no mansions, real fancy cars, etc. I was raised pretty normal.

6. You come from an acting family. Your parents were both well-known actors, you, your brother, your daughter – what's it about the art of

acting that fascinates the Eisley bloodline? Even your wife is a pretty famous actor. Who is the best actor in the family?

Eisley: My mom never went into the profession full blow. Before she met my dad she was being groomed at FOX to be the next Judy Holiday. She then met Dad and stopped pursuing the acting. None of us even knew that until she passed away and some of her old friends told my dad and us. Bit surprised we all were.

My wife is basically an "icon" coming from Romeo & Juliet, Jesus of Nazareth, etc. She has millions of fans around the world and new young ones come aboard everyday as both those two productions alone are timeless. Our daughter India, pound for pound is probably the most varied and multi dimensional actor of the bunch. I think your going to find that out very soon this year. She is a rare bird and is the "full package!"

7. Do you remember the story behind Love You Forever? It's our favorite Giuffria song.

Eisley: "Love You Forever" I wrote with Gregg in two different periods. We had the verse you hear now written in another song long before. That song was "Say it Ain't True" on the *Gotcha* sound track. Few years later I then wrote the Chorus that you hear and we put the original verse to the "Love You Forever" chorus! Then wrote a new verse for "Say it Ain't True!" Sorta crazy but that's what happens sometimes. I wrote the lyrics about a friend and in 3rd person as it was from their possible point of view. I do that a lot when I see people going through stuff.

8. How did you get involved with the band? Did you have to audition or did Gregg just call you up and offer you the gig?

Eisley: I met Gregg indirectly through a bass player that he was working with that knew me. They couldn't find a singer and I was recommended. Thus, I was called to come down and meet with he and Punky (Angel) We immediately hit it off and wrote "My Heartache" the day we met. We knew we had some strange connection and from that point on we could write a song together drunk in a snowstorm, tied to a tree in the dark! Might not be a great song but it would BE a song!

9. Did you guys have to battle the Sunset Strip crowd or were you too big for that?

Eisley: As far as Sunset Blvd scene we were spared that whole thing as we got immediately signed to our label on the strength of the three songs that were on it. Gregg had already had moderate success with Angel so he'd sorta "been there" already. BUT it took songs to make them bite. Two of the three were "Do Me Right" & "Lonely in Love."

10. What's the story behind Sweet Victory and SpongeBob? How did that collaboration come about?

Eisley: "Sweet Victory" came about with guitarist Bob Kulick coming to me during a weekly softball game we played saying he had this publishing company that was looking for a sporting song "of sorts" and he just kinda said "whadda you think?"

We monkeyed around a little and I took what we fiddled about with and developed some melody and lyrics. Then Bob embellished some guitar stuff and we did a recording of it. They flipped out. Then all went quiet. Nothing happened at all or at least WE didn't think anything was happening until one morning my young daughter at the time came running into my room saying "Dad Sponge Bob has your voice!!! I went "Huh, What?" She pulled me into her room and there was Bob, in all his yellow sponge like glory singing my song with my voice! Needless to say MTV nor Nickelodeon ever told us of this "behind the scene" deal so we commenced to call our attorneys and find out what was up. Welcome to "show biz", "writers biz", whatever biz!" Uggh!!

11. How was the experiences of working on TV shows like Beverly Hills 90210 and 7ᵗʰ Heaven? Were you treated special or different on the set since you were a big rock star? Was the 90210 cast (Shannon, Tori, etc) friendly and easy to work with?

Eisley: 90210 & 7th Heaven were fun. I didn't really take them too serious as that whole thing was really not my deal. The casting director who casted for both shows at different times was aware of me and called me in. Actually she called in 90210 which I did the reading route and I booked it. Few years later she just called for me "sight unseen" for "7th Heaven."

The folks on 90210 were a little bit wrapped up in themselves really as they were all young and sorta commanded their space. LOL! I didn't have much to say to them nor them to me. The 7th Heaven folks were happy to have us there as it was a fun concept that this preacher's former rock band showed up on his porch!! It was a fun shoot actually.

We weren't really treated super special just respectfully. Peter was from the Monkees, Keith Allison from Paul Revere & the Raiders and "yours truly." They knew we knew what we were doing in our world so the respect feelings rubbed off all through the cast & set.

12. Action Jackson was a fun movie back in the day. Did you get to hang out with Vanity and Sharon Stone on the set?

Eisley: Action Jackson was a oddity as I had just finished the "Silk & Steel" album and my ex brother-in-law's cousin was going to be directing the film and he was aware of my Martial Arts training and thought I'd be an odd addition to the group of baddies. He arranged a meeting with myself and the producer Joel Silver. I showed up, was asked into his office, was introduced and Joel asked if I would be willing to cut my hair. I immediately answered "FUCK NO!" His eyes widened and he smiled and said " I want this guy!" That was it.

I knew Vanity indirectly from Nikki Six who was seeing her at the time. He'd show up on occasion to visit her but not much more than that. I saw Sharon in passing but none of our scenes brought us together for any amount of time. She seemed very "one pointed" & excited to be there as I think it was really one of her first larger gigs. Anyways, terrible film but I had a great time short of splitting my head open by a piece of falling glass! But that's another story! LOL!!

13. The Eisley/Goldy album has been getting great reviews. What's the story behind this band?

Eisley: Thank you to ALL for the kind reviews for the most part on the Eisley/Goldy *Blood, Guts & Games* album. Beyond the title there is not much more to say on the subject! Let's just say it was another "moment in time." We do what we can with what is given to us.

14. You managed India's acting career for several years. Did you enjoy that experience? Hollywood is supposed to be such a cutthroat world, it must have been nice for India to have you in her corner (as opposed to just a normal manager/agent).

Eisley: Our daughter India has been working since she was 14. Starting with the hit series for ABC "Secret Life of The American Teenager" along with Molly Ringwald playing her mom. As she was still a minor I was with her on set for a majority of the time. As far as managing I basically kind of managed the reps as I had been around this stuff with my dad, many years with my wife and now it's my 14-year-old daughters head and career were talking about so I was and still am to a point very protective. She is a total pro at the age of 24 and knows this business inside & out. So I backed off a while ago. She does her thing and does it quite well with no help from anyone!

15. How disappointing was the Dirty White Boy process? Beau Hill sounds like he screwed up the entire process when you guys had a band that seemed to have the talent to be a pretty big group.

Eisley: DWB was a mix of very bad timing, totally the wrong producer being shoved down our throats and the rumblings of "Grunge" taking over the airwaves at both MTV & radio. Long story short, Earl Slick and I met with Neil Geraldo (Pat Benatar) and he was our pick to produce or co-produce the record with us. He'd been out to rehearsal, we talked bout stuff, he and Slick admired each other's guitar stuff and it WAS a musical fit. Management & Label saw "numbers" with Beau and he really lobbied them for the gig. He won out in the end. Not such a good fit! Lastly we released in Europe first and by a day missed out on jumping on board the AC/DC tour at the same time as their special guest. Instead we were out with a Euro band called Magnum. Ok...but NOT ACDC!!

16. Who are your favorite singers? Favorite bands?

Eisley: Favorite singers? People I am nothing remotely like! LOL!
Lennon (RIP) incredible soulful voice, Steve Winwood, Steve Stills in his

day, the Great Paul Rodgers of course, Bowie was ridiculously good, McCartney could sing his ass off, some old Rod Stewart was great and Nat King Cole always could bring it!! Just a few for ya.

Bands? Beatles, CS&N as well as CSN&Y. Joni Mitchell (although not a band), Dylan, some of Springsteen's stuff, Metallica, Pearl Jam. And might sound weird coming from me but I (as a favor) went to see Journey to keep someone company in 1983 (their year) I wasn't a fan at all, never ever gave them a single thought. Thought they were a bit on the light side. BUT that night they were on ALL cylinders and I was a bit blown away and surprised.

Six degrees of separation. Giuffria comes out, I get compared to Steve Perry - big compliment! Twenty years later my daughter is shooting this huge mini-series with Patty Jenkins (Monster, Wonder Woman) and who is on set and becomes friends with my daughter??? Yup – Steve Perry who happens to be one of Ms. Jenkin's best friends! "Say hi to your Dad for me!" "Oh cool India, tell him Hi back!"

Anyways, all that being said Ol Steve has shredded some GREAT vocal performances in his time as well so Id have to throw him in the pile of greats as well!

17. What advice would you give to young singers who want to make it in the music industry?

Eisley: I really couldn't give ANY advice to a young cat today other than do it because you have to do it because it's who you are. It HAS to be because IT is what calls to you from the inside. Any other reason for starters, you're bullshitting yourself. Most likely be sorely disappointed and it won't really mean anything down your road of life.

18. Is there anything you'd like us to mention or promote?

Eisley: Yea. My wife's autobiography is coming out on July 31rst: "The Girl on the Balcony" The Life of Olivia Hussey. And look out for our daughter's upcoming mini series called "One Day She'll Darken" co-starring Chris Pine (Star Trek, Wonder Woman) on TNT Network. True incredible story and India apparently was insanely great!! There are my two plugs!!

Thank you all & better days ahead for ALL!! Keep the Rock Rollin!

https://twitter.com/DavidGlenEisley
http://www.davidgleneisley.com

Dennis Ogle
Blonz

1. What were your thoughts on seeing Nathan Utz possibly getting the vocalist job for Lynch Mob?

Ogle: I love Nathan singing with Lynch Mob!

2. How was the experience in writing/recording Clean Again, your solo album from 2010? Did you do all the writing, play all the instruments and do all the vocals?

Ogle: Clean again was a collection of songs I wrote that needed to get off the shelf. I recorded it on my home studio, and it sounds like it. I really wish I had put more time into it, but it wasn't my intention to release it.

3. Can you describe your experience with Blonz? The band came and went in a couple years, what kept the band from putting out more albums? Your debut album was solid enough and had a nice variety of song types, it seems odd the label didn't let you guys do a quick follow up.

Ogle: Blonz was a blast, and I still trip on people that remember us. Good times. We started as Dirty Blonz. We had to change it due to a "Dirty Blonde" In LA. We lost our deal with Imagine/Epic when we were touring with Don Dokken. I was bustin' my balls trying to figure out why, and later found that there was a battle going on between Epic and Imagine/epic. Sony Music was buying CBS records, and also Grunge was just getting started. Bands like mine began getting the ax.

Firehouse won the Battle of the Epics. Not sure how long they stayed signed. Danger Danger did a Japanese deal, and we kept playing until Nathan left for anther band, Torn Lace. Nathan soon returned to front Chaingang.

I'm pretty sure our demise was a matter of timing, technology, and the arrival of grunge

4. We've got "What's On Your Mind" as one of the best songs of the hair metal era. When writing the album, could you guys tell that you had something special and what the top songs were going to be? What songs from the album are you most proud of?

Ogle: You know, hindsight is 20/20, but I'm proud of the album. A lot of people told us that the album wasn't as good as our live show. It was produced by Steve Walsh and Phil Eheart of Kansas, and I think that contributed to the loss of our live edge.

5. Quick Thoughts:

Blonz: My most cherished music project.

Steve Taylor: Steve Taylor is my friend from freshman year at high school. He heard me humming to myself in art class. He asked me if I sang, and it was on. We made a goal to get a record deal, and kept going until it happened.

Aaron Tate: Aaron was Nate's high school friend. Love the guy.

Nathan Utz: Nathan and Steve are brothers. Written many songs together. Played many stages together. Nathan just started a tour as the new singer for Lynch Mob.

Guns N' Roses: Legends

GnR reunion tour – without Izzy and Adler: Axl and Slash. It'll work

Van Halen – Dave or Sammy? (Or Cherone):   Dave or Sammy: YES!

Def Leppard: The only connection I have to Def Leppard is Retro. Jammed with Vivian Campbell at foundations forum in the Epic room.

Bon Jovi: Bon Jovi played a big part in getting us signed. After attending a show in Augusta GA. And hanging out we got the call a couple of days later from Jason Flomax at Atlantic records. We eventually ended up signing with Imagine/Epic.

Warrant: Our second gig at Atlanta's Cotton Club was opening for Warrant. When we walked in the club for sound check, they were all hanging our in front of the TV cause "Down Boys" was #6 on the MTV video countdown. A few of us went to Tampa a few years later while they were recording "Dog Eat Dog".

Jani Lane: Jani Lane is the only human being on the planet to ever drink me under the table. Bitter sweet. He's gone and I've been sober 17 years.

Cinderella: Never crossed paths with Cinderella. "Last mile" is my favorite song by them.

6. While researching the band, we found two blogs of yours. You are a great and very creative writer. Have you always loved writing? Have you ever thought about writing a book? Or selling your original songs to other artists?

Ogle:

I love writing. I would love to be successful writing songs for other artists. Blogging was a way to get use to the changing political landscape.

7. Did you learn anything from the punching game you played with Fred Saunders….hopefully that was the last time!!!

Ogle: Fred Saunders put me on my ass for SIX weeks! To say I learned something is an understatement.

8. Danger Danger's Ted Poley called you guys a "cool band" back in the day. Did you guys get to work with any of the bigger name genre bands? If so, any great stories – or horror – stories about your experiences with them?

Ogle: Blonz opened for lots of great artists. Meatloaf, Quiet Riot….we actually toured with Don Dokken on his solo tour. Then Nate went on to rock with George Lynch! Full Circle!!!

Brad Divens
Kix, THE Mixing Engineer, Souls at Zero

Picture courtesy of Mr. Diven's business page.

1. So the sound engineer really controls how good the band sounds in a live setting. I think fans know this…but maybe they don't know just how much work goes into it. We saw a video where you talked about how your goal is to make sure the energy level is at the right height and you want the audience to feel like they are just as much a part of the show as the band is. In terms of quality, how much responsibility goes towards the sound engineer? (If a band put on the exact same performance at two places, and one sound guy was mediocre and one was awesome – would it be really obvious to the fans?)

Divens: I feel that next to the band the engineer is also an important part of the performance and adds to the quality of the show. I think the audience knows the difference between a great show and a mediocre one. There are so many elements that make up a great show. The band, the crowd, the mix, lighting and sound all working together as one big spectacle.

2. This is a dumb fan question! But we see the mixing board and it has literally 500 knobs and levers on it. Are they all really necessary or useful? It seems humanly impossible to know the meanings and perfect exact location of all 500 knobs!

Divens: Yes I know what every knob on the mixing console does and they are all necessary. It's really not a complicated as it looks.

3. Does a band tour with its own engineer/equipment or does the concert venue provide either or both? One thing we've never understood is how much technical difficulty the band Guns N Roses has. Axl seems to always be having difficulty with his mic, or earplug or the sound. You can see tons of videos on YouTube where he is pissed off, complaining and yelling at the sound guys. As one of the richest bands in the world, you would think they would have the highest quality equipment and staff.

Divens: The band almost always travels with it's own engineer. The budget will dictate whether the artist carries his own gear or the venue provides it. Some times the person that's having the most difficult time performing will try to blame it on the gear or the engineer. Maybe it' the gear, maybe it's the performer.

4. (Sorry for all the fan questions). Are there instruments that are harder/easier to produce? Like the bass sound is straight forward…but the guitar sound is much more difficult with many layers, etc.

Divens: I don't find one instrument more difficult than the other. It is important to me that everyone on stage is heard in the mix. Mixing a show inside of a giant arena is the most challenging. Making the show sound good for the audience is the priority.

5. Same question about musicians. Are there some musicians that make your job a piece of cake? They put their full trust in you and it's a pleasure to work with them. And conversely, guys that just moan and complain about everything and you know it's going to be a long night – no matter how great of a job you do.

Divens: I've had the pleasure of working with some very talented musicians. Coming from a musical background and the fact that I am a musician helped me to earn their trust right away. Everyone has a bad night every now and then. We all just persevere and get through it.

6. Do you get more enjoyment running the board, making sure the band sounds on point as opposed to be the guy standing ON stage making the fans go crazy? One guy has 20,000 fans cheering for them and thinking he is awesome. The other guy doesn't get the fan love – but is highly appreciated/loved by the 4-5 band members.

Divens: It's hard to compare being onstage performing for the audience, to the person responsible for the crowd's enjoyment of the show. I feel very fortunate that I've been able to experience both. They are both rewarding for me.

7. You have been the sound engineer for so many great – and diverse – acts. Are there a couple that have been the most fun for you? Or one that was the most challenging or made you work the hardest?

Divens: I've enjoyed every act that I've worked for. I love music and I always find the enjoyment in what I do. They've all been fun to mix!

8. Or is there a style/genre that is harder/easier than the rest? It has to be different to do a metal show like Linkin Park to a pop singer like Cyndi Lauper to a dad band like Bob Seger and then a hair metal band like Motley Crue.

Divens: All bands are different but the end result is the same. To create a great mix representing the act I'm working for and give the audience the best show possible. I like mixing all types of music.

9. Of all the bands you've worked with, who has the best and craziest fans?

Divens: I'd have to say Enrique Iglesias. Everywhere we go in the world the fans are there and they love him.

10. You recently built your own mega studio at your house! So how does that work? A band sends you some raw cuts of music, and then you work your magic and make it sound better. Do you just work on other band's material or do you create your own music too?

Divens: I built the studio in my home so that I would always have a place to be creative. Whether it's a band sending me tracks to mix, or something I've recorded live with a band I'm working for, I have my own place to mix in.

11. How did you get hired for Kix….how was the experience with them…..and how come you left after just one album?

Divens:
I received a call from one of the members telling me they wanted me to play with the band. The experience was great and I learned a lot about the business in a short amount of time. Going to Miami and recording at Criteria studios in 1982 was definitely a high point for me. I was 20 years old and making a record. I was on top of the world!

12. Are you still in contact with any of the Kix guys?

Divens: Yes, I recently mixed their live record. *Can't Stop The Show.*

13. We personally never fret about the past. Because our past is what made us who we are today. But….do you ever look back and get a little annoyed or think "what if" about your time with Kix? After you left, they exploded in the music world and became a huge band. One more year with them and you might have been the next Eddie Van Halen!

Divens: I feel that everything happens for a reason. I never look back and think, what if? I am exactly where I'm supposed to be at this moment.

14. *You played bass, guitar and are a great singer. Is there one aspect that you preferred or loved doing more than the others? Which one would you say was your greatest musical skill?*

Divens: My greatest musical skill was being able to play an instrument and sing at the same time. I never thought about either one, I just did it.

15. *Whose idea was it to film a music video in the freezer of an ice cream shop!!! (Souls at Zero – Never).*

Divens: I can't remember where the idea came from. I do remember it being around four degrees at one point during the shoot.

16. *Lol, it's amazing to watch/listen to the Souls at Zero and then watch your video on sound engineering! Are you sure you don't have a twin brother? One is the heavy metal rocker dude and the other is the conservative academic computer nerd type! When the venue is empty, the band has already left, do you ever jump on stage, grab a guitar and just go crazy and tear things up for a bit?*

Divens: There is some down time during the day when we're waiting on Enrique to show up for sound check. It's during this time that I will get up onstage and jam with the other crew members. It's a good time and sometimes I'll reminisce back to the days when the stage was mine.

17. *Are Souls at Zero still active? Any chance of another album or tour dates?*

Divens: We are planning on doing a show at some point in the near future. It's a matter of everyone being able to get together and also finding the proper venue for the show.

www.fixintogetmixin.com
https://www.facebook.com/fixintogetmixin
https://www.instagram.com/fixintogetmixin
https://www.linkedin.com/in/brad-divens-10909647

Pat Fontaine
XYZ

Pictures courtesy of Mr. Fontaine and the band's official Facebook pages.

__1. The question everybody wants an answer to.....walk us through your date with Demi Moore!!!! And you dated Susanna Hoffs and Tori Wells? You were The Man!!!__

Fontaine: Far from being the man! I have to credit Rock 'n' Roll 100%! It was not really a formal date with Demi, but more of "hang" at some release party for St Elmo's Fire. XYZ was in a development deal with Atlantic records at that time, probably 1985, maybe 1986, and as an up-and-coming band we were invited to most of the movie wrap-up parties they were involved with.

Anyway it was a time before fame and notoriety for Demi Moore. She was sitting with a drink, alone, at a coffee table, in a dark corner of this fancy club in Hollywood. I thought she was attractive, no idea who she was, so I just invited myself to sit across from her. She reacted with good energy and we just had small chit-chat for the rest of the evening. I don't remember much about it as I trust we were BOTH high on something ...lol...something white and powdery...lol.

The rest of the cast were shaking hands and working the room with the director, but Demi seemed detached from that apparently and opted for a more secluded stance. We talked about Rock 'n' Roll and what was happening on the Sunset Strip, that type of thing. She never mentioned St Elmo's fire at all strangely. We were both 20 something and didn't have the necessary distance to reflect on the moment, of course. A few times during the evening a photographer came by to snap a pic of both of us. Where are those pictures now?...lol... I didn't ask to stay in touch when my manager dragged me away, 'cos back then it was complicated, lol, no Facebook. I gave her a hug when the party was over...she smelled good...never saw her again, so really, not much of a date is it?

A few years later XYZ got signed to Enigma and we had a wonderful PR lady, Lisa Gladfelter, who wanted us to be seen around town with hot girls and celebrities, and we had no problem with that...lol. The Bangles had a big song on the air at that time, and my record label arranged for a "date" with Susanna at some industry party of some kind or another.

Susanna and I actually got along just fine. I had a bit of a cocaine problem back then, lol, so strangely blow took priority over women...lol. I've changed my ways since. What I mean is I didn't pursue dating as intensely as I should have, as I just saw Susanna a few times at events here and there, and little by little I decided that strippers were a little more open minded and a little less high maintenance...lol...around that time I met Tory Welles at the Seventh Veil, a strip joint on Sunset where she worked, as I was going there with Terry, my singer, to pick up HIS then girl-friend after work. The four of us went back to my pad, a few blocks away, to get high and share a few bottles. Man, we hit it off big time and Tory moved in with us the next day...lol...she was NOT a porn star quite yet, but would become full fledge a few months later. I must admit it was interesting to have a romantic relation ship with a porn star, as she would come home after "work" to run straight to the shower and then lay in my arms exhausted and shaking. Very odd as I now reflect. We are still good friends and we chat once in a while. She was a treasure.

2. But what's up – no Samantha Fox or Belinda Carlisle?

Fontaine: Sorry, lol, I failed on those two!....lol

3. Your wiki page says XYZ was the unofficial house band of the Whisky A Go Go. What does that exactly mean? How crazy was that scene?

Fontaine: The Whisky never really had a true house band, but Louie the Lip, manager of the place, took us under his wing and booked us in there every other weekend. He was nice enough to let us paint a giant XYZ logo on the windows outside, and it is that logo that got people to refer to the club as the XYZ club...lol...it only holds 350 people but we manage to pack it pretty solid month after month.

Up the street Warrant had Gazzaris, XYZ had the Whisky and we all lived in peace! Sunset Boulevard was a complete zoo late 80's and it got so crowded the sheriff would shut it down to vehicular traffic on Saturday nights. Tens of thousands of big-haired kids would descend on the boulevard, cowboy boots and leather jackets, mini skirts and ripped fishnets. It was an awesome sight, Aquanet, I bet, still lingers in the air!

4. You must have experienced all the big bands that came through. Is there a band that just killed it and you could instantly tell they were going to be absolutely huge? Conversely, a band that you thought would be huge – but they never made it? And finally….a band that you thought was mediocre and then a year later they were charting on Billboard and killing it on MTV?

Fontaine: Shark Island was destined to greatness in my book, as Richard Black, frontman, was Axl Rose before Axl Rose...lol....and of course I saw GnR a few times at the troubadour and thought they were terrible. I got it all wrong apparently...never trust me and my poor judgment...lol.

5. Poison was big when you guys were grinding it out. Could you tell they were going to be huge? No offense if they are your friends, but I don't know if MTV hadn't been so popular then how big Poison would have got? Average singer, CC DeVille had a crazy style but he isn't known as one of the "Guitar Gods" of the era, they had catchy songs – but really cheesy lyrics. GnR on the other hand. From the videos we've watched of them from the day, they seemed destined to become huge.

Fontaine: I believe the answer lies in how hard your work at it, and not really in your level of talent.
Poison worked and worked and worked every day and every night, promoting themselves like mad. They were an inspiration to all Sunset bands. Brett was on the strip 24/7 it seems, chit-chatting everybody about Poison. CC is a excellent bluesy player in my book, as I caught him in coffee shops and dive bars in Hollywood quite a few times in the 90's. And Brett is so fucking good looking, does it matter that he doesn't really sing like Ronnie James Dio ?

As for GnR I was completely wrong. Dead wrong. I never got it. I do get it now as they have the quintessential "who gives a fuck" attitude, but at the time I though they were just a bunch of junkies and boozers...which they were...lol. Somehow Axl became a fantastic singer with a strong voice, but early in the days, it wasn't the case...lol.

6. Were you there when Warrant made there way through? If so, how was Jani Lane back in the early days?

Fontaine: Jani was a treasure of a man and always a gentleman. Talented guy with a penchant for anything in a bottle. I always got along fine with him, spent numerous nights at the Rainbow, shared a few groupies of course, and gallons of booze. Warrant was a self promotional machine. They worked as hard as Poison and had a fantastic sense of humor. They got signed a few months before we did, and we instantly lost a few girl friends to them! Years later we all played M3 and Jani was at the hotel bar, after the show, alone, and we talked about Hollywood and its ugly descent into mainstream. He looked terrible by then, like a shadow of the past. I bought him a few beers, he had no cash ...no wallet...he had lost his room key card...he was a mess.
But what a sweet and gentle soul! I miss him and his strange eyes.

7. How did you and Terry Ilous first hook up?

Fontaine: Terry was in a cover band in our hometown and we had a common friend. One night both of them came to a recording session we were having, just to hang out and smoke a little pot really, and I asked Terry to step behind the mike for the sheer fuck of it. He obliged and his voice blew me away. He was smooth and strong and confident. But obviously had no desire to join XYZ at all as we were messy and punkish a bit really, but we had attitude and a following that eventually got to him. He saw me as a mediocre bass player BUT with strong determination, and that is probably what decided him to join. Determination trumps talent I always say...lol.

8. Did you guys really have to sleep in your car while living in New York? What finally broke or happened that allowed you guys to get an apartment and move out of the vehicle!

Fontaine: We landed in NYC with nothing but guitars…but guitars don't keep you warm at night do they! So after a few nights of sleeping at JFK airport, we opted to buy a station wagon and turn it into a bedroom, lol. I had to sell my beloved Rickenbacker 4001 to do so but we found a junker for 300 bucks from some seedy private party in a back alley in Bridgeport CT. It just had a for sale sign written in chalk on the windshield. One wheel was angled funny and the car wobbled painfully as it went. It reeked of cigarettes and who knows what else!!! Was it stolen? No idea! We never bothered to register it, nor to insure it or anything of that sort. It was an AMC Ambassador, yellow in color, with a huge cargo space, perfect for a few sleeping bags. We lived in it throughout the summer of 1982, mostly parking at rest areas and truck stops up and down I-95, in NY, NJ, CT. But didn't drive it much because we couldn't afford much gas.

We got pulled over once by highway patrol and were given all kinds of citations for this and that, and all that paper work went in the glove compartment never to be seen again, lol. We only had our French drivers licenses and no physical residence, what are they gonna do ?

When winter came, California seemed like a much better idea. I sold the Ambassador for $200 cash to a junkyard, as I was told they rarely ask for proof of ownership. With that money we somehow managed our way to LA and some needed sunshine. We slept on Venice beach for weeks because the sand is softer than concrete and they had cold showers on the boardwalk. Then we squatted for a year or so in a condemned house in Hollywood, all boarded up, until the wrecking ball came one morning. For power we had borrowed a long extension cord from the rock n roll neighbors. And water? What water, lol!

Eventually I scored a part time job delivering flowers and managed to save enough tips to afford first and last on a two-bedroom apartment on Fountain Ave, two blocks from Guitar Center. It was spring of 1984 and that's where I would live for the next 30 years. I moved to Las Vegas in 2014.

9. One of your first tours was with Enuff Z'Nuff and Alice Cooper? How was that experience and how did those bands treat you?

Fontaine: First tour was Ted Nugent, Cooper was a few months later. Enuff was a club tour in between, and Chip Enuff was the most charismatic and funny motherfucker I have ever met. Ted Nugent was and still is a true character with a big mouth and a pistol, but we got along great. He would come backstage to trade guitar licks with Marc, our guitarist. To watch them both playing over each other was surreal. It was our fist time playing arenas, and what a rush that was, damn, to step onto that massive stage, night after night, man oh man!

I remember one of our first nights on the bus, Ted came to say hi. I told him how lucky he was to have a long line of young and pretty girls waiting for him after the show. He tapped me on the shoulder like I was his 15-year-old son, and said: Kid, those girls are here for YOU, not me! Turns out he was right, lol!

Alice Copper was a much shorter tour, but it was a big deal for me because I had a huge poster of him with his snake in my bedroom back in Europe. What a kick!

We also met Eric Singer (Kiss) at that time, as he was Alice's drummer. Great guy! What a life back then, on the road, we all met for dinner at truck stops in the middle of nowhere. Buses parked neatly next to one another. We were pirates and our ships had wheels.

10. You probably have been asked this a million times. But how did you hook up with Don Dokken, who was a huge star back then?

Fontaine: Don was brought into our rehearsal basement, at Musician Institute, one night accompanied by our record label A&R guy, Curtis Beck, just as a visitor really. We were a bit nervous, but Don was so casual, even grabbing a microphone to join us on a song or two. After rehearsal I insisted he come over to our pad in Hollywood where I made him spaghetti. We had a few beers, a few lines, and a few laughs. He didn't care for my cooking much but he really liked the cute strippers living with us, lol.

We talked about working together on a couple of songs and eventually decided to have him as a producer for our first release. It was not always a smooth relation ship and we hit a few bumps here and there. We were a bit more bluesy than he was. Don is very quick at writing a very decent song, melody and lyrics. He also had great road stories with crazy videos to back it up...LOL.

11. Don has a reputation for being a bit cranky now days.....does he still take your phone calls?

Fontaine: Haha, I run into Don here and there at festivals and I must say we still get along fine. We always take time for a sit down beer or something. He is has a very caustic sense of humor and yes he can be cranky, but so can I, lol!
Phone calls? What's that? I never call anyone, it s all about Facebook today, isn't it ?

12. What prompted the 2002 reunion?

Fontaine: 2002? I want to say Rocklahoma 2007. First time Terry and I reunited after taking a break in the mid 90's. It seemed that the winds of Rock 'n' roll were blowing again, Seattle was long gone, rap was getting old, and it felt right to put it all back together. Supply and demand I guess. We all are just pawns on the great ocean of fashion it seems.

13. Does Ilous side job with Great White ever cause you guys scheduling issues? I think Great White made a great choice with him to replace Jack Russell. Instead of going with a Russell sound-alike singer, they grabbed a guy with a very unique voice.

Fontaine: Who is this Great White you mentioned...is Terry a fisher-man nowadays?

14. You guys have done all the big festivals – from Rocklahoma to M3 Rock Festival and I think even the Monsters of Rock Cruise. As a performer, which avenue gives you more pleasure in a live setting. Playing to 10,000 at a festival (with 10 other bands involved) or playing to 100 die-hard XYZ fans at a seedy rock club.

Fontaine: Security makes it hard to mingle at arenas and I like to mingle with the fans after the show. So in a way, I favor the seedy clubs. Now on

Monster cruises it is the best of both worlds as we get to play on large pro stages AND still maintain the close up and personal contact with the fans after the gig. I love being on the ship every year for that very reason.

15. Do you consider yourself a better songwriter/lyricist or better bass player?

Fontaine: I am a mediocre bass player and think of myself as an acceptable lyricist.

16. Ilous also said in an interview that XYZ sold two million albums, but because of all the expenses, he didn't make a dime from it. That seems crazy. How many albums would a band have to sell before they overcame the label greed and the band members started making bank?

Fontaine: We owed quite a bit of money to some good folks when we finally got signed as a generous porn producer had kept us alive for years prior, and we felt it was the right thing to do to reimburse them for every dime. So we did.

When all debts were settled, we walked away with enough cash for sporty convertibles and a few playboy models for long weekends. But yes, I would say that selling twice more than we did could have bought us an actual garage for the convertibles and maybe more permanent playboy models, lol. We never had enough to buy ourselves houses, but who the fuck would complain? We had a good run!!!
PS: The cars and playboy models are long gone, lol!

17. Fans have always been told that it's basically $1 per album goes to the band. How many albums need to be sold for a band to make a million bucks each.

Fontaine: One dollar per CD sold is almost correct. CD retail for $10. Half of that is for the retailer and the other half for the record company. Then 10% of that goes to band's management and 10% of that goes to attorney/agent, the rest goes to band.
So if you sell a million record as an example, 1 million X $10 = 10 $ million. Half for record company is 5 million. 10 % of 5M is 500K...50K to management, 50K to attorney/agent...that 's about 400 K left. Four

band members, $100,000 each…and a hundred grand doesn't last very long in Hollywood!

NOW, never mind the royalties from your label, publishing is where it's at! Publishing royalties are completely separated from your greedy record people and end up being a slow and steady stream of cash, going on for years, and that's what pro level musicians rely on! And, of course, all the T-shirts you sell on the road are crucial!

Nowadays with "downloading" being the norm, it's very hard to audit the label to find out just how many songs an artist has sold. How the hell can you double check and prove anything? It's impossible on low budget, difficult at best if you throw big money at it and who wants to do that? Publishing is much more regulated and consistent than record sales.

18. How in the world did you get Michael Bay to direct on your music videos? Was he fun to work with?

Fontaine: Michael Bay was SOOOO fucking brilliant on a Slaughter video, that I begged our record company to hire him. He was damn expensive though!

He was and is the most energized and talented motherfucker in Hollywood. Very directive, firm and passionate and we had zero desire to argue with him, even though we argue with everybody, lol.
P.S.: his wife was so HOT she ended up in the video...no charge...lol.

10. How did you guys end up touring with Soundgarden…..one of the bands that helped kill the hair metal era!

Fontaine: We only were paired with SG on few shows, starting in Cabo Wabo Mexico, and followed by a few gigs w Ozzy on the west coast. Soundgarden was a new comer to Hollywood and we didn't really know what to make of their views on things. They seem depressed and on low grade heroin, and we were just the opposite, happy party people on speed. We never really communicated with them as they had complete disregard for us. They looked at Hollywood as the problem, I think, and we looked at Hollywood as the great hope!

Having said that, it is undeniable that Cornell was a magical singer loaded with raw talent. I never enjoyed grunge, but it must be said they brought needed darkness into our party scene, and possibly injected some realism into our very basic equation. We lived by a simple motto of Sex, Drugs and Rock 'n' Roll. And those pale face strangers came down from the great North with army boots and lumber jacks shirts to convince our women to dress up, self-reflect and go to church. Were they fucking crazy or what, lol!

11. We put together a list of the top 1,000 songs of all time. These songs are the highest we rated from XYZ: Inside Out, United, Souvenirs, What Keeps Me Loving You, After The Rain, and Rainy Days. Thoughts/memories on any of those songs?

Fontaine: My favorite would be "Souvenirs". Written when we left Europe with great hope and dreams. "After the Rain" also has a warm spot in my heart because it is so naked and so basic. The others you mention went through several versions and may have lost a bit of truth in favor of mass appeal...such is the music biz!

12. And do you think we missed one or two that should be up there with those?

Fontaine: "Take What You Can" I favor. It was written about our experience in Hollywood and still remains a great way for me to drift back in time to a place of comfortable madness.

13. Quick Thoughts on these guys, just the first thing that pops in your head:

Jani Lane: Gentle and genuine
Guns N Roses: Raw
Don Dokken: Prolific
Duff McKagan: Tall
Billy Sheehan: Fast
Jeff Pilson: Hot wife
Dana Strum: Business man in leather jacket

14. What does the rest of 2018 and 2019 have in store for you?

Fontaine: I have started my own private world tour...lol...I want to see the world...the good and the bad...the rich and the poor...the highs and the lows...I will insert a few XYZ shows here and there though!

15. Is there any thing else you would want us to mention or promote?

Fontaine: Well, as you asked, I wish to say that I am sincerely flattered and touched that 30 years later, our little stint in Hollywood is still remembered by younger folks.

We were just lucky to arrive in LA early 80's, and to dwell deep into what would become the party of the century. Debauchery at that time was not a word we used often, cos it was our every day/night norm. Women were sexy and liberated, men were funny and sly, all of us wore black eyeliner, and political correctness was not yet invented.

I hope that when the last of us gets buried, someone young and smart will say: "Fuck, did they have a good time or what?"

http://www.officialxyz.com
https://www.facebook.com/xyz.band

Drew Fortier
Zen From Mars, Bang Tango, Stephen Shareaux, documentary maker, actor, guitar player

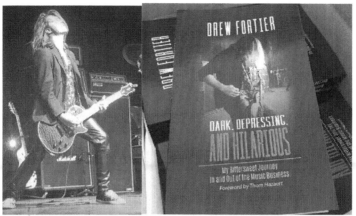

First photo courtesy of Tharasa DiMeo. Second photo is front cover of Mr. Fortier's new book. Both pictures courtesy of Mr. Fortier's official Facebook page.

1. Mark Knight offered to donate money to my project! Is he one of the nicest guys you've had the pleasure of working with?

Fortier: Mark is definitely one of the nicest guys in the world! He helped out so much with The Bang Tango Movie and has become a very good friend of mine. I actually shot and edited a few music videos for him too for the songs "Lies" and "Sink Your Teeth Into".

I remember in 2012 I was on tour with him for an acoustic run in the south and he had Mark Tremalgia performing with him. Mark T. actually was Kyle Stevens replacement in Bang Tango. During that tour I was shooting footage for The Bang Tango Movie as well as footage for his music video for the song "Lies". During a day off, I twisted Mark Knight's arm into the three of us doing an acoustic version of Bang Tango's "Someone Like You". I actually shot it and it's up on YouTube and it came out really cool!

It's been so amazing watching Mark Knight's solo career progress since I've known him and everyone should check out his new record *Don't Kill The Cat*!

2. What are your favorite Bang Tango songs to play live?

Fortier: Aside from the typical answer of "all of them!" I would have to say without a doubt my favorite would have to by "My Favorite 9" (no pun intended). But that has always been my favorite Bang Tango song. It's from the *Love After Death* record that was recorded in 92/93 and is the final album by the original line up of the band and has yet to be released in America.

But I remember when I first started the Bang Tango Movie in 2011, every time I would see the band I would persist that they add the song to their setlist. I ended up annoying them with that question for years. It was almost gonna be a subplot to the movie haha. They finally added the song to their shows in 2014 and it was such a glorious victory. Then when I joined the band, I was in absolute bliss being able to play that song every night. Recently we have been opening with it and it works so perfect as a set opener. Such a great heavy mean funky piece of music.

Other than that song, I would have to say being able to trade off solos with Rowan Robertson in most of the songs has been an absolute honor. "Untied and True", "Soul to Soul", "Attack of Life", etc. Pretty much all the songs he and I have been trading the leads back and forth like how they were recorded on the records and that has been an incredible experience.

3. In our opinion, Someone Like You is one of the greatest hard rock songs of the last 30 years. Thoughts on that great tune, is it fun to play live?

Fortier: I absolutely love the song and still do to this day. The song is so incredibly fun to play live. Rowan and I, when we're feeling froggy and up for it, we actually start off the intro in a way to where a delay pedal isn't needed. So I would come in first with the intro lick then Rowan would come in at the precise time acting as the delay part of it and it sounds absolutely killer! It's been such an honor to be apart of this band and to keep the legacy of the original members alive by doing everything in our heart to do the songs and shows justice.

4. Have you guys thought about recording a new album?

Fortier: Absofreakinglutely! That's been in the cards for a while now. But it's one of those things that cannot be forced. When the time is right and the planets align for the right reasons, we will most certainly put together a great and memorable Bang Tango record. For me personally, I would love to make it a follow up to *Love After Death* rather than *Pistol Whipped in the Bible Belt*. I love *Pistol Whipped* to death, but it would be so cool to pick up musically where the original band left off and bring back that unapologetic heaviness, thoughtfulness, and funkiness that they showcased on *Love After Death* and progress it just a little bit more.

5. You've had a weird relationship with the band. They hired you to make a documentary about the band – which is amazing, by the way – but, lead singer Joe Leste didn't like how you featured him in the doc. In spite of that, the rest of the band liked hanging with you so much and were impressed with your guitar skills so much that they hired you to be in the band! But the relationship with Joe led to you leaving for a year. But then you came back and are again a full time family member. Does that all sound about right?

Fortier: Haha, the truth of the matter is actually back in June 2011, they had been booked to play the club I was bartending for at the time in Chicago. The day of the show was on my day off so I decided to bring a video camera with me to get some footage of them playing. The band shows up for sound check and we all hit it off famously.

Joe then turned to me and was like "what's that in your hand?" and I explained that it was a camera, and he was like "Oh cool! We're recording an album in Chicago in two weeks, you should come out and do a studio documentary on it or something." I then eagerly agreed even though I had no clue how to shoot or edit a studio documentary…which ended up turning into a full on feature.

So then I took four years to learn how to make a movie and finished The Bang Tango Movie. We had one screening in Chicago, for which the band was in attendance for, and as a thank you the band let me sit in on guitar for their whole set at their Chicago show. A few days later, I was at work and Joe called me on my lunch break and said "Hey man... question... how would you feel about playing in front of 20,000 people tomorrow at the M3 festival in Maryland?" I then replied with "I'm renting a car right now...I'm on my way!!"

I then drove 12 hours straight from Chicago to Maryland to do M3 with them and it was absolutely incredible. From there they kind of adopted me in as the second guitar player of the band. The band was originally a two guitar player band so it made sense to get another guy to do the other half of the parts. Rowan and I have such an absolute blast with the songs. I truly love being in the band.

But then in late 2016, I ended up hooking up with Thom Hazaert and David Ellefson from the EMP Label Group. I decided to take some time off from Tango to learn more about the record business and was so glad I did. Thom and Dave had become good friends of mine and it's been an absolute pleasure working with them and helping out anyway I can. So many amazing road trips with Thom Hazaert. The laughter never ended. During the year that I began working with Dave and Thom, I actually only missed maybe four or five Bang Tango shows.

But to set the record straight, Joe and I have always been the best of buds and his opinion on the movie had nothing to do with me taking time off from the band. I remember Joe actually really enjoying the movie at the screening. Though he played a great prank on me during the screen. It was his first time ever seeing the movie and toward the end he got this angry look on his face while watching and stormed out of the venue. I then chased after him and he turns around and goes "gotcha!"

But fast forward to August of 2017, Joe and I start talking about bringing me back into the band for shows, and I made my return at a festival in Des Moines, IA. Then we did the Rainbow Bash in Hollywood and Rocktember Music Fest in Minnesota with Styx. It felt amazing to be back, it feels amazing to be back, and absolutely cannot way for more shows!

6. Speaking of the documentary, how has the public response been? Can you give us a quick run down on how that experience was. And why release it for free on YouTube instead of selling it? We thought it was fantastic.

Fortier: The overall response has been absolutely amazing. My whole goal with the movie was to be able to appeal not only to Bang Tango fans, but to people who have never even heard of the band. And I'm so proud to have achieved that.

I spent four years shooting and editing the movie. A lot of help came from Anu Gunn who had shot many of the L.A. interviews for me and I have been super thankful to have him involved. Without Anu, I honestly don't think the movie would have been finished.

But overall I ended up with over 400 hours of footage to go through. Interviews, live footage, backstage footage, on the road footage, you name it. I definitely lost my mind going through all the footage and piecing the movie together, but in the end it was so worth it.

At the end of the whole thing, I ran into trouble trying to clear the songs for the movie via Universal Music. I ended up getting passed around from representative to representative for months and ended up waking up one day and decided to put the movie out on YouTube for free, seeing that this would probably be the only way people will ever be able to see it. At the end of the day I was absolutely at peace with the whole situation, but was and am just so happy it's out there and people are still discovering it and getting something out of it to this day.

7.How did you get hooked up with Stephen Shareaux – and how is playing with him different than touring with Bang Tango?

Fortier: After finishing and releasing The Bang Tango Movie I was in the headspace of "Okay. What's my next project?" I had fallen down the rabbit hole on YouTube one night and saw that YouTube had suggested Kik Tracee's video for their song "Don't Need Rules". I had remembered hearing them from my brother when I was younger, I clicked the link and was just absolutely blown away and told myself "I NEED to be in a band with that singer!!!"

I also thought "I bet they have a great story too... maybe this could be my next movie?" I then reached out to the guys which lead to a phone call with their frontman Stephen Shareaux and we just absolutely hit it off and decided we wanted to work together on music, which quickly lead to Zen From Mars forming.

But Stephen and I mainly do acoustic shows, ironically one of which was opening for Bang Tango at the Buffalo Rose in Colorado for which I pulled double duty that evening. Playing with Stephen is amazing. We just feed off of each other's energies and just totally vibe out live. He is without a doubt my musical soul mate. The words to my music. He is also one of my best friends and I love him dearly.

Comparing playing with him to Bang Tango, I absolutely love both situations but they are both incredibly different situations. With Bang Tango it's more of putting on a great show and keeping the Bang Tango music alive. With Stephen, it's more so about musical exploration. For instance "Hey, let's take "In Trance" (Kik Tracee song) and go into Kashmir by Led Zeppelin during the bridge and see what happens from there." We love going different places with the songs in a live setting. I love it. There's really no rules with Stephen, and I wouldn't have it any other way.

8. Were you involved in the writing of his Golden album? Kamikaze is a really, really good rock song. One of the best songs of 2013.

Fortier: I wasn't involved with Golden, that was before we met, but I absolutely love the album and we do play a lot of those songs live at our acoustic gigs. Kamikaze is indeed a great song and a super fun one to play live!!

9. After the Bang Tango doc, I read somewhere online where you said you were done doing them. What changed your mind....and do you have a third one on deck?

Fortier: After the whole stress inspiring experience of putting four years of my heart and soul into The Bang Tango Movie, and with how positive the public's response was to it, I just wanted to leave it alone at that and move on and not have to go through that experience again. But when I had met Chuck and gotten to know him and his life experiences, I felt that it would be absolutely worth the time and effort to get his story out there in the form of a documentary film. I didn't know him long before he passed, but he will always have an everlasting impression on me and I am proud to be the one, with Doug, to help keep his legacy alive by doing this film for him.

As for another film, I had actually pursued doing a Fear Factory documentary shortly after I completed The Bang Tango Movie. Fear Factory are one of my favorite bands and I actually wrote up a treatment and met up with their frontman, Burton C. Bell, in Chicago a few years back, and ended up having one of the best two hour conversations I've ever had. He and Dino really liked the treatment for the film, but I believe due to the ongoing litigation involving ex band members, it was decided that it wasn't a good time to do a movie on the band. Hopefully one day though. I'd be all over that one! Ironically my drummer in Zen From Mars is Fear Factory's drummer Mike Heller.

10. How did you get involved with playing with Chuck Mosley and doing his documentary? Did that get finished before he unfortunately passed away – did he get to see it?

Fortier: That all happened because of Thom Hazaert actually. I'm an incredibly huge Faith No More fan and Chuck was on the EMP label run by Dave Ellefson and Thom. And since I met Thom, he always felt I'd make a great fit playing guitar for Chuck.

Thom and Chuck's manager/percussionist/babysitter Douglas Esper really put that whole situation in motion. It just so happened Chuck was playing in Indianapolis (where I live) one night, and my now fiancé Tharasa and I went to go see him. The show was incredible. I met Chuck and Doug after the show and absolutely fell in love with the guys. Chuck and I hit it off and just meshed so well together. That's how he was with almost everyone he met, which is a testament to who he was as a person. He was such an open, warm, and loving person that was so incredibly easy to talk to and have a great time with.

So after I had met him, he and Doug decided to make me part of the band and we had an absolute blast on the road together. Non-stop laughter. We also talked about possibly doing a documentary on his life. He was all for it. We talked on the phone all the time and a week before he passed, left me a voicemail saying how he 100% wants to do this film. Doug and his family still felt I should go on with Chuck's wishes and make the film, which I am currently doing with Doug as Producer. We have a few interviews so far including Faith No More Producer Matt Wallace and Anne D'Agnillo, for whom the Faith No More song "Anne's Song" was written about. But I am looking forward to putting the film together and it's been a very bittersweet ordeal. I love and miss Chuck with all my heart and think about him every day. It's still so hard to hear his voice. It's instant waterworks for me.

11. What was the big difference between putting the two docs together?

Fortier: The Chuck Movie will most certainly be a breeze compared to the Bang Tango Movie. With The Bang Tango Movie I literally learned how to make a movie by learning how NOT to make a movie. So with that knowledge and applying it to Chuck's film, it will be able to come together incredibly smooth.

12. You've turned into the go-to guy now for putting together promotional videos/material for rock bands. From Vince Neil to Mark Slaughter and numerous artists in between. Do you get to hang out with the artists or do you just do all the work from home on your computer?

Fortier: I actually got to hang out with Mark Slaughter a few times! He's definitely one of my favorites. It's always a great time with Mark. His impressions and voices are absolutely amazing and hysterical. His Rodney Dangerfield is on point!

Stephen and I put a solo band together with Dallas Sheppard on bass (also from Chuck Mosley's band) and Mike Heller on drums (Zen From Mars/Fear Factory/Raven). We did a one-off show opening for Mark Slaughter in New Jersey and Mark was kind enough to let me use his Kemper amp and pedal board. That was a surreal show. Bumblefoot actually showed up to give his support. He's another one of those incredibly kind people that's just amazing.

But as far as the other acts I've done work for, it's about half and half as far as if I've spent time with them in person or not.

13. So you are in three different bands, directing documentaries, acting in movies, playing one-off shows for other bands, putting together promotional videos for numerous bands.....but because you had a few minutes of spare time, then you decided to start your own brand new band – Zen From Mars?

Fortier: Haha yep!! I have to feed my creative monster at all times otherwise I get bored and depressed in that regard! So that's why I love having so many things to keep my creative attention fed. All this as well as my day job and planning a wedding for next year. A lot on my plate, but all well worth it!

14. You were already playing with Shareaux, why didn't you just bring your songs to that band (instead of starting a brand new band)? (We read where you were writing for Bang Tango but the songs didn't fit their style, so that's why you went with bringing them to the Zen From Mars band).

Fortier: I consider myself a member of Stephen Shareaux's band in regards to the acoustic shows we do for which we perform his solo material, Kik Tracee songs as well as Zen From Mars songs. But when I first met Stephen I had actually composed five songs that were intended for the proposed next Bang Tango album. I personally felt the songs didn't fit the style of what Bang Tango were all about and decided to send them to Stephen to see what he thought. The next thing I know he starts sending them all back with these amazing lyrics and melodies and really turning them into songs.

Those songs are now "Downtown", "New Leaf", Aflame", "Cry", and "Celestial"; all of which will be on the Zen From Mars record we have been working on the past three years. We have 12 songs for the album now. But to answer your question, when Stephen and I do the acoustic shows, it's billed as Stephen Shareaux, but when we do songs with the full band it will be Zen From Mars and who knows, with ZFM we just might throw in a Kik Tracee song or two.

15. How did you put Zen From Mars together? You've got quite the eclectic group of musicians. How did you get Chip Z'Nuff to join?

Fortier: I absolutely love the dynamic in the band. Technical Death Metal drummer, Power Pop bass player, Alternative Rock singer, etc. It's almost as if it was a mad scientist experiment.

As far as Chip, he had been a good friend of mine from when I was doing

The Bang Tango Movie and lived right down the street from me in Chicago, so I was always by his house hanging out and getting a contact high from the copious amounts of pot he would smoke. So Chip was the first person I had in my mind as far as a bass player and he was all for being apart of the band. Then came his incredibly talented wife Kate Catalina who we have on Keyboards.

Mike Heller, our drummer, I got to know him through pursuing that Fear Factory documentary I had mentioned. It turns out he really likes Bang Tango and we just completely hit it off. Early on I sent Mike some of the demos Stephen and I were doing to get his opinion, and he pretty much said "I don't care who you have in mind for drums right now, I am your drummer for this." Mike has been one of the most fascinating and loveable characters I have ever met before in my life. He is just a wound up ball of energy that just wants to create constantly. It's been amazing working with him on the ZFM record. I've learned so much from him about making an album production wise, not to mention he has the absolute best sense of humor in the world.

So from there we then recruited one of Stephen's old friends Brynn Arens on guitar. Brynn is the frontman for the band Flipp, whom are ridiculously awesome. We then started recording the album around Halloween of 2015. Mike recorded his drums in New York, Stephen recorded his vocals at his home studio in California, Brynn recorded in his studio in Minnesota, I recorded my parts at my home studio in Chicago, and Chip & Kate recorded at Chip Z'Nuff studios in Chicago. With that said, it's been tough rounding everything up from everybody since we're all scattered all around the country, but we're finally in the mixing stage of the record and we have Richard Easterling doing that for us. He's also our producer and will be mastering the record as well. He is doing such an incredible job and we are aiming to shop the record around very soon and hopefully have it out by summer/fall of this year.

16. In 2017, you also worked as the Operations Coordinator for Megadeth's David Ellefson's EMP Label Group. How does a rock star and budding Steven Spielberg end up taking an OC job?

Fortier: I absolutely loved working for Dave Ellefson and Thom Hazaert. I still do small things for them here and there. But with how much Thom and I hit it off when we first met, there was a point to where he wanted me to get involved in the label and I absolutely couldn't say no. It's been an honor and immense pleasure working with and getting to know Thom and Dave. They do some incredible stuff together and I loved being apart of some of it.

I actually ended up helping get Autograph, Kik Tracee, and American Bombshell signed to their label too. More than anything it was amazing to learn more about the business side of music through Thom and Dave. I've gotten so much out of listening to them and have been applying what I've learned to all of my endeavors since. When Dave had the Grand Opening for his first brick and motor coffee shop for his coffee company Ellefson Coffee Co., he had Stephen and I come out and performed at it acoustically. It was such an incredible experience to be apart of.

Also, at the Grand Opening that same weekend Thom, Dave and I performed a mini-set of Megadeth songs acoustically and it was absolutely nerve racking but so much fun at the same time. I remember we did a medley with "Peace Sells", "Symphony of Destruction", "Tornado of Souls", and wrapped it up with more of "Symphony of Destruction". But we all still keep in touch and I'm sure we'll all be working together on something again in the future.

17. We've got an interesting "relationship" with you and your boys! We complimented your Bang Tango video on the FB page and you gave us a really friendly "thanks for the compliment" message. And when we asked you for an interview – you responded very kindly. BUT…..Chip Z'Nuff – didn't respond. Mark Slaughter – didn't respond. Joe Leste – no response. Steve Shareaux – no response. Lol, are you just a really nice guy or are those other guy's just ……don't care, only do interviews with major publications, too big of egos, too busy, get too many interview requests, etc, etc. Obviously you can't speak for other people, but as somebody in the business, what do you think? Are there some guys that just don't want to do interviews?

Fortier: Haha. Well Chip is always incredibly busy and never really gets online that much from what I understand, so I know it's nothing personally with him. Same goes for Mark Slaughter, who is one of the nicest guys in the world. Stephen hardly ever uses Facebook, I know that, and Joe's Facebook profile actually isn't him! Haha. I guess when Facebook came out somebody claimed the page pretending to be him and it just never got corrected. Plus I know Joe isn't very computer savvy anyhow.

18. What is your story in the music world! How does a young dude like yourself end up being friends with everybody from the guys in Bang Tango to Chip Z'Nuff to members of Megadeth!!!

Fortier: Oh wow. The best I way can describe my story is just one happy accident after another. One big random snowball effect that has been gaining more and more momentum ever since it started. I have been trying to keep up with it ever since. But I genuinely love people and the friends I have made in this business mean the world to me.

19. When is The Ultra Head Frequency coming out, and what can fans expect it to sound like?

Fortier: We are hoping to shop the record around very soon and wish to have it out for late summer/early fall of this year. As for how it sounds, that's a really tough question to answer! The first track on the album, "Inner Mission", sounds like Black Sabbath and by the outro gets very heavy but Beatles-y at the same time.

"Aflame", sounds like if the music for "Wicked Game" by Chris Isaak made love to the music of "Waterfalls" by TLC while Type O Negative watched haha.

"Downtown" sounds like James Brown meets Metallica. We actually have Jesse Camp from MTV doing backing vocals on that one. "Poppy" reminds me of the band Hum from the 90's. It's a really cool power pop tune. "Mother Evolution" is almost a heavy progressive piece; structurally none of the riffs repeat itself. It just keeps on changing and morphing. The only thing that stays the same is the chorus which technically only happens once but shows up again as the outro.

"Hand in a Fist" reminds me of Corrosion of Conformity and Marilyn Manson. That's a super heavy one. "Turnstile" is kind of like almost folky 60's rock with some Alice in Chains mixed in there. "Like a Vampire" feels like it could be in a heavy metal musical, it's a very cool theatrical song. "New Leaf" is sort of our big heavy pop rock song.

"Celestial", which will probably be closing out the album, is literally one big build up. It's a very cinematic tune. It's hard to classify it as a song but it just keeps on building and building and building, climaxes, then ends. "Cry" is something that feels like it could be on Led Zeppelin III, It's a very cool acoustic piece. "Alien to Me" is an extremely ethereal song with a ton of layers and its very Bowie-ish. It's a super sexy sounding song too! Wow. I think I literally just described all of the songs on the record here haha. Oops! Well you heard it here first!! Needless to say, I probably should have just answered with "Alternative Rock" in regards to what it sounds like haha.

20. OK. So we know you are a rock star. And an accomplished director/documentary maker. Songwriter. And.....you also somehow find time to act? How did your movie roles come about?

Fortier: Haha. Well I had been a big fan of this actor James L. Edwards since I was a kid. He was in this amazing movie called Bloodletting that has always stuck with me. It's about this girl who blackmails this serial killer into teaching her how to kill and they fall in love along the way. It's awesome. So I had found him on Facebook and friended him to keep up with what he has been up to since.

He then made a casting call post about his then upcoming directorial debut for which he was also starring in called "Her Name Was Christa". On a whim I decided to reach out and audition for a part that turned out to be one of the leads of the film. Also it turned out that James remembered Bang Tango from back then and really enjoyed the documentary.

It just so happened, now this is super surreal as I type this, I was in Cleveland at Chuck Mosley's house with Douglas Esper, Stephen Shareaux and Thom Hazaert. We were about to go to the Rock and Roll Hall of Fame together, which is an incredible and surreal story but won't bore you with it haha. After Chuck's movie and the ZFM album I'm actually going to write a full on book about all of these crazy experiences. You heard it here first!

So I told James I was in town, he lives in Cleveland, and I invited James to come over to Chuck's house to say hey. He mentioned he had something he wanted to tell me too. So in Chuck's living room James tells me I had gotten the part in the film. It was an amazing day. And it was so crazy to think back at that day in Chuck's house because every project I'm working on now was present in that living room. The Chuck Mosley Movie, Zen From Mars, Her Name Was Christa, and working for EMP Label Group.

We shot my parts in September of last year and to say I had an incredible time is such an understatement. Definitely some of the most fun and most memorable moments happened during the shoot. The whole cast and crew were absolutely amazing. Absolutely amazing. Also I had orchestrated a top-secret plan to propose to my now fiancé' Tharasa on the set of the movie. I had James and the crew in on it and James let me cast Tharasa as a small role of someone who interacts with my character. My only line to her in the film is "Hey...mind your business."

So it's 4:30 in the morning and the last take of the night, and James gives me the nod to go for it, and during the take I go "Hey! ... will you marry me?" and she said yes! It was amazing. The footage is actually on my YouTube channel if you want to see it. Tharasa is the most amazing human being I have ever met in my life and I love and adore her and her kids more than anything and I couldn't be happier to have such an incredible domesticated life. Who'da thunk it? Haha. So now we are planning our wedding for September, 2019.

21. When is Her Name Was Christa coming out and what can you tell us about it?

Fortier: They are wrapping up shooting in June/July I believe and I am hoping to see it out before the end of the year, The movie is going to be so cool! It's a straight up horror comedy and the hardcore horror movie fans are absolutely going to love it. I can't wait!

22. And you are also starring in a horror anthology too?

Fortier: Yep! That one begins shooting later in the year I believe, also directed by James L. Edwards. I can't say too much about that one but I will be the lead character throughout the wraparound stories for the anthology. His plan is to put me in at least two movies a year and I absolutely cannot wait!!!

23. So if I hit the lotto and gave you a blank check to use on any project you wanted in 2019.....what would you choose? New album by one of your bands, documentary of your choosing, a starring role in a movie that you get to write, something else?

Fortier: Haha, great question! I would actually humbly put it towards mine and Tharasa's wedding/honeymoon!!!

24. Would you rather win: an Oscar for Best Actor, write a song for another artist that goes to #1 (IE: earns you a check for $1,000,000), or win a Grammy for album of the year?

Fortier: Now this is an incredibly tough choice! I would honestly say the Oscar. I know the music world a little bit too well by now and would be fun to jump into the acting world a bit more and learn everything I can about it!

25. Is there anything at all you would want us to mention or promote?

Fortier:
*Zen From Mars album The Ultra Head Frequency, due out later this year.
*Thanks. And Sorry: The Chuck Mosley Movie, hopefully finished by the end of the year.
*Her Name Was Christa, which is hopefully due out by the end of the year.
Aside from that, next up for me would be to write a book about all of this fun nonsense!
Thank you SO much for dealing with all of my long-winded answers and crazy tangents! It's been an honored to be interviewed by you guys!

http://drewfortier.net
https://www.facebook.com/drew.fortier
https://twitter.com/drewfortier
https://www.facebook.com/BangTangoOfficial

Frankie Muriel
KINGOFTHEHILL, Dr. Zhivegas

Photos courtesy of Mr. Muriel's official Facebook page. See links below.

__1. What was the Warhol print you discovered at an estate sale awhile back? Some of his works sell for millions! Do you guys still have it?__

Muriel: Found in Vegas in hotel ballroom wandering by when they were packing up! Was a great find has COA from the estate.

__2. We also read that you have a Mick Jagger portrait by artist Sebastian Kruger. Kruger has a really distinct style of paining. Is he one of your favorites?__

Muriel: Another Vegas find when we had a residency out there love his work.

__3. Are you a big art collector? And if so, who are some of your favorite artists? Do you paint?__

Muriel: I don't paint. I'm a fan of pop art and have few pieces and some commissions, no big deal.

__4. What is the longest you've ever went without doing something music related? And what do you enjoy doing that isn't music related?__

Muriel: I've been playing professionally since I was 16 so here's never been a time when I wasn't doing something musically. Love traveling, great places, great meals - cooking and eating them!

5. Do you still go to Paris every year? What intrigues you about the city? Where is your favorite place to travel to? Where would you love to go to but haven't yet?

Muriel: Love it! I try to go every year, sometimes our schedule does not permit. First time I stepped off the KOTH tour bus in 1991 I was hooked with the City of Light, the vibe and the history just clicked as I walked the streets

Capri is my favorite place in the world. Love to get there when I can but the food, the wine, people, the art fashion and history of Florence and Tuscany can't be beat!!

6. The spelling of KINGOFTHEHILL is different depending on what website/story you read. Can you give me the definite spelling?

Muriel: KINGOFTHEHILL – all one word, all caps. I don't know why, ha!

7. What made you decide to start Dr. Zhivegas? And did you ever imagine it would blow up and become your career band?

Muriel: Had NO idea I was gonna do it for a month and hear we are 23 years in and people still come and fly us around to perform!

I was between albums and some friends and Doug were doing his disco thing. I said I should come sit in and I never left!

8. You do it all for the band – sing, produce, compose, records, etc – is there one thing that you enjoy doing the most? Are you a singer at heart, or do you love doing all the other musical stuff that is involved?

Muriel: I love the creative process in the studio. I'm a student of tone and how records got their sounds, so I enjoy that very much. Funny thing, being in a cover band you really get an understanding of how all these amazing pop songs are constructed and recorded.

But I also love working a crowd it's what I do :)

9. You guys kill it in Vegas. Is there a city/state/venue that you enjoy playing the most or where the crowds really love you guys the most?

Muriel: I mean nothing like home, but Vegas is always fun. We just picked up the brand new Hard Rock in Atlantic City, so that'll be fun. We love going down south. Biloxi, Memphis - the people and food are amazing!! It's a theme with the people and food...ha makes the road life better!!

10. "Do You Want It" feels like a Prince song. How big of a Prince fan are you and how big of an influence was he on your career?

Muriel: Prince was a huge influence on me as a young musician. I grew up listening to all kinds of music had a very musical family. But when you're hitting your teens that music is really what shapes you. For me it was Prince and Van Halen which pretty much sums up what I do and the approach I take !

11. Your band did a Prince tribute show. Would you ever think about releasing a Prince tribute album?

Muriel: Good question! We thought about putting out a prince cover. We'll see. You don't wanna dip your toe in that water unless you kill it.

12. How was the process of writing the Dr. Zhivegas album Get Down compared to writing the KINGOFTHEHILL albums?

Muriel: That album was different in the fact that it was a long time coming. We hadn't done an album before, only a song or two. There was some acrimony with certain members and new collaborations kind of dragging that one across the finish line! But we captured a couple of good ones I think, despite all that.

13. How many shows are you guys doing a year? And how in the world have you guys managed to stay together for more than 20 years now?

Muriel: We still do about 200! We have an amazing line up of guys and a girl! And the fans are great, we wouldn't be able to do anything if people didn't show up!!

14. What is the story of the Unreleased album? We actually like it better than the first one. How come the label didn't release it – it's really, really good!

Muriel: Thank you! We turned the album in and it was accepted. Then our A&R man got fired. The new guy cleaned out his desk and our album was caught in that! And the whole genre got blown out. We had a few offers from labels to release the album but our label wanted to recoup too much on it so they wouldn't accept the offers and shelved it. We revisited it when we got together for a reunion in 2006 and thought "let's just remix and put it out"…so we did!

15. Was Lisa written about anybody specific?

Muriel: It was a news story of a little girl on the East Coast that suffered tremendous abuse. We had saw - or Jimmy saw - the story and we wrote the song.

16. Is it true that there is a third album of unreleased songs? What are the odds those songs will see the light of day?

Muriel: At this point it's songs that were cut or demos that didn't make the first or second album. You never know…

17. Is there any chance that KINGOFTHEHILL would ever do a reunion tour and album? Would you be interested in that – there is a lot of interest right now on the festival tour for the popular hair metal bands?

Muriel: Well we did a reunion show last November and had a blast! Going to do one in St. Louis on November 9, 2018.

18. *What do you think about those old bands that are keeping the band name alive and touring – but they have a revolving door of members, and some even still with not only ONE original member – but they are on their 3rd or 4th guitar player since the classic line-up. Are you cool with that concept or do you think at some point guys should retire the band name and start a new band?*

Muriel: Well in some cases – like Foreigner - it's not even the same band. But the songs stay alive and whoever is in it is bringing those songs to new audiences like a great cover band does.
It's harder, I think, without the singer. Unless the new guy makes you forget about the original guy!

19. *Who were some of your favorite hair metal / sleaze rock bands from back in the day?*

Muriel: Always loved the Scream album. And of course Motley Crüe and GnR. We wore out the first Ratt album.

20. *Are there any bands from back then that you look at and go "how in the world did they become so popular?"*

Muriel: Ha ha a few! Funny thing is we toured with all of them! many of them Our album and MTV videos did better than some of the fringe guys (like we were) but they are on Hair Nation and KOTH isn't !!

21. *Jimmy Griffin fronts a Pink Floyd cover band. What's up with KOTH guys fronting cover acts!!! What are your thoughts on Jimmy as a guitar player and musician?*

Muriel: Great guitarist, always mindful to melody which is important. He does what's best for the song. A lot of great players don't think of the big picture.

22. *Thoughts on George Postos?*

Muriel: Energizer Jimmy man! He's always hyped up, biggest cheerleader you can have and minder inbuilt face bass player!

23. Vito Bono?

Muriel: Funniest, most sarcastic dark humored guy you'll ever meet! Ha ha he's been cracking me up for 30 years!! But behind all that clowning he has great instincts.

24. We couldn't find any information about your alum Big Fat Love. What's the story behind that? Was it similar in style to KINGOFTHEHILL?

Muriel: It was a more funkier personal album, like a Lenny Kravitz type solo album. I played a lot of instruments myself on it.

25. Were you the main songwriter for KOTH?

Muriel: Yes Jimmy and I wrote all the songs. *Unreleased* had a couple co-writers.

26. Who were the biggest bands you toured with back in the day? Did any stand out in terms of being friendly and helping you guys?

Muriel: We were with Extreme all through Europe when "More Than Words" shot up the chart. That was eye opening to see what a song will do when it goes to number one. Fun tour!

27. What did you think about the pairing of Gary Cherone with Van Halen?

Muriel: Gary is a great guy, one of nicest in the business that I've met or toured with. But Van Halen is the original to me, I'm a purist!! Van Halen is Van Halen! Van Hagar is Van Hagar.

28. If KINGOFTHEHILL reunited for an album and tour in 2018, which bands would you want to tour with?

Muriel: Some from the same era would be fun to see and catch up with. Some of the guys we toured with back then.

29. Can you comment on Like an Army and how that project started and went? We LOVE the video and song for Taste of It and the song Home. How did the band get started, who did the writing and sadly....how come it seems to have disbanded?

Muriel: LOVED that project. I was reflecting on changes in my life, what I have done what I haven't. And playing dance music for so long I felt like I wanted to rock again. I called the guys in not knowing what we were gonna do. Wrote "Down" the first night. Then once a week we popped out another one. Then the project started taking off. My old buddy Rich Fortus from Guns N' Roses came and played guitar and killed it. It was fun doing a swag rock album again!!

Home is absolutely one of my favorite songs I've ever been a part of. My drummer Paul Chickey and I wrote it about our moms, who have both passed on and a lot of the lines were literally my last moments with her. It's amazing to have that in a song for myself and my family.

30. Can you comment on these songs?

I Do You

Muriel:
Fun video to make.

Dream Segue

Muriel:
Ha Segue gets rated!

If I Say

Muriel:
That song took us around the world and made our career happen.

Place in my Heart

Muriel:
Always reminds me of that magical era before we got signed and we were on our way up, packing clubs playing our music!

__31. So we've got nine of your songs rated in our top 1,000 songs of all time. And your two albums are both in the top 150 albums list. What do you think about that – does it sound about right to you?__

Muriel:
I just appreciate being included and that people are finding the old songs!

https://www.facebook.com/drzhivegas
https://www.facebook.com/kingofthehillstl

Tim Gaines
Faithsedge, Stryper

Photo courtesy of Mr. Gaines' official Facebook page.

__1. Stryper is one of the very few bands that started during the Hair Metal era that still has their albums chart on Billboard in the 2000s. What do you think it was about your guys that resonated so hard with rock fans?__

Gaines: It was a combination of our look, sounds, and message. Different people liked different things about us.
Some hated our message but loved the songs, while others loved the message, and finally found a band they could listen to with a positive message and good music.

__2. Restoration is a pretty great rock album. How did you get involved with Faithsedge? You guys have an all-star group of musicians, are keeping their egos in check and putting the band's success as the top of__ *the list? And what are your upcoming plans for the group?*

Gaines: I've known Giancarlo Floridia for many years.
I became involved in 2015 when he asked me to play bass on the album.
It did well in the Japanese and European markets. The other guys are all
top-notch players but there is a humbleness about us and nobody really
has an ego problem. It's great to play in a band with great people.

We are in the middle of recording a follow-up album that we hope to
release later in 2018.

**3. In an earlier interview, you mentioned you might be putting together
a supergroup of 80s rockers. It feels like THIS interview would be the
perfect time to spill the beans on who that band is gonna be!**

Gaines: Funny, I am in several "Supergroups" at the moment besides
Faithsedge. Locally, where I live in Phoenix I am playing with a bunch of
great musicians in a band called Sons Of Metal. Features Bret Kaiser
(Madam X) vocals, John Aquilino (Icon) Guitar, Steve Conelly
(Flotsam& Jetsam) Guitar, Dwayne Miller (Keel) Drums. We are doing
80's Metal covers and writing songs. Stay tuned for that one.

I am also part of a new supergroup in the studio right now called Of Gods
& Monsters, featuring Kevin Goocher (Omen) vocals, Joey Tafolla
Guitars, & Deen Castronovo on drums. We also hope to have an album
out later in 2018.

**4. What do you think about bands still touring under their famous
name even though they might only have one original member and
they've had a revolving door of musicians? Keep it going or start a
brand new band?**

Gaines: Some bands should call it a day. Others, I don't think really
matter who's in the band because the music is so great and it's bigger than
the band itself. Journey comes to mind.

**5. When you guys were Roxx Regime, what type/style of music was the
band playing?**

Gaines: Same style as we did on the *Yellow & Black Attack* EP. Those were Roxx Regime songs with reworked lyrics.

6. How come Stryper decided to go the Christian music route? Was it daunting knowing that a lot of rock fans wouldn't give you a chance because of it?

Gaines: I think at the time we were just going with positive lyrics, but then it became a big deal, so we just went with it.

7. How was it playing with Bon Jovi back in the day? There must have been a ton of trim at that show. Was it hard to stay straight and narrow on the road, where there are sooo many temptations thrown your way?

Gaines: We did play one show with Bon Jovi in 1984 at a little club called The Country Club in Reseda CA.
But touring with bands regardless of who they were or for their reputations weren't any different than not. Just another night on the road.

8. Sin Dizzy was essentially a heavy metal band. What was the process of starting that band? Was the metal sound a move towards distinguishing yourself from the mellower Stryper sound or was that just organically what you were into at the time?

Gaines: Oz and I started Sin Dizzy as a "jam band." Something to do on Saturday afternoons after Stryper had broken up.

The music was influenced by bands like Rush, Alice N Chains, and Stone Temple Pilots… sort of grunge meets progressive. It was just stuff we were into at that time.

9. What bands did you most enjoy listening to back in the 80s/90s glory days? Who do you listen to now?

Gaines: I listened to just about everything at that time. 90's I found myself listening to more of the women in rock type of artists like Alanis, Sheryl Crow, Joan Osborne, etc and then bands like Toy Matinee and Kevin Gilbert

10. When did you start playing bass? And when did you realize you had

the talent to do it at the professional level?

Gaines: I started at 13, and was already playing in bands at 14. I just knew that it was the thing I wanted to do with my life. I felt like I was a natural talent. By the time I was 15 I was playing with bands with the members 5-8 years older than I was. I had played every club there was to play at that time in Hollywood by the time I was 17. I just never looked backwards. Always forward.

11. What advice would you give to a young kid who wants to make a living in a band? How many hours a day should they be practicing?

Gaines: Practice as much as you can. I practiced about eight hours a day when I first started off. As far as making a living at music? That's a tough one because today's music business is nothing like it was back in the 80's. Not so much money to be made these days. But writing songs, touring, and selling merchandise should be part of your goals if you want to make it. And leave the drugs and partying out.

12. How was it playing with Richard Marx?

Gaines: Touring with Richard was great. He is a great talent. Treated his band with class and paid us well.

13. You released the instrumental album Breakfast @ Timothy's – what sparked that album and any plans to release another one? Who all played on Breakfast?

Gaines: That album was with my best friend Chris Eddy. He wrote and produced it in the same approach as something his father Duane Eddy would have done, but instead of twangy guitar doing the lead we used the bass guitar. I am in the middle of writing for another album at this time.

14. What was the favorite – and least favorite – tour that you've been on?

Gaines: Favorite was probably the first half of In God We Trust with White Lion opening. The worst was 2003 "Seven" tour.

15. Favorite city or venue to play?

Gaines: Always love playing in San Juan Puerto Rico or Tokyo Japan.

16. We were sad to see that you have left Stryper and how it turned into a battle of words on social media. Do you want to comment on that?

Gaines: My Ex got the band in the divorce.

https://www.facebook.com/TimothyGainesOfficial
http://www.timothygaines.com

Adam Hamilton
L.A. Guns, producer for many bands: Vanilla Ice, Johnny Thunders, Leif Garrett, George Lynch, William Shatner, Vains of Jenna.

Photo courtesy of Mr. Hamilton's official Facebook page.

1. Let's get the one question out of the way that you probably get tired of being asked! From 1971-2002, your high school – Captain Shreve – won 15 state championships in Tennis. That's a crazy number for any sport. How come you guys were so good on the court....and did you play at all?

Hamilton: I had no idea! Shreve had a few really good sports programs. Played a bit of tennis as a kid but that is it.

2. Were you friends with LaMark Carter? He graduated in 1989 and went on to make the Olympic team as a triple-jumper.

Hamilton: Didn't know him. Lot of successful sports peeps from there too.

3. What was it like working with William Shatner for his album Seeking Major Tom? That must have been an odd phone call to receive?

Hamilton: It was an amazing call! It was from a label that I know the head of. He thought it would be a good fit. Shatner had never heard of me so he was a bit skeptical at first. It ended up working out great. He was here yesterday and we are finishing up on a Christmas album for him. We go over to the Shatner's and watch MNF in the fall!

4. We've chatted a bunch with Joey C. Jones while writing this project. Nicest guy in the world. When we told him we were listening to his songs on YouTube, he said that we needed better recordings and mailed us a couple CDs (out of his own pocket). Do you remember your time with him and CC DeVille? How was it playing with those guys?

Hamilton: That was a magical time in life. One of the greatest moments in my life that I used to dream about happening actually came true. I met CC in a club in Austin around 1992 and we became friends. Joey was a Texas star, I knew him and was honored to be apart of CC's first post Poison band. Joey and I still make music together albeit long distance. We both lived in CC's house in the Hollywood Hills for months that year. What a book I could write!

5. Were you involved in Summer Song at all? We think it's one of the hidden gems of the entire "hair metal" era. One of those songs that really had the potential to be huge.

Hamilton: Agreed! Summer Song is one of the best. I always enjoyed playing it live and wished we had put it on the JCJ and the Glory Hounds album. I didn't have anything to do with the writing.

6. How did you move from the hair metal scene into playing with the much heavier bands like Gods Child, Joe 90 and The Brian Jonestown Massacre?

Hamilton: Well, this bands you mentioned are actually not heavier than the hair metal scene, those are more mellow! I always loved many styles of music. I grew up around Blues and Country, my cousin is Mose

Allison, plus I loved all music so as I got older my tastes evolved and changed. When I was young I hated classical and jazz, now I love it.

7. This question you do probably get tired of being asked. But can you share with us how you became involved with LA Guns? Was it surreal getting that phone call and job offer?

Hamilton: My friend Muddy had produced the Brian Jonestown Massacre and brought me in to play drums on an album that the drummer got fired from. Muddy then went on to play bass for LA Guns. After a while, he decided to join a band called Colonel Parker and called me and asked if I might be interested in playing bass for them. The timing was perfect, I was between gigs and had been playing with a local Hollywood band on bass. I went on the audition and they liked me but they were kind of mad a Muddy for quitting so they told him they were going to keep looking for other people. After they audition more people they ended up calling me back after all and I got the gig. It was surreal for sure. They welcomed me like family and we were off and running and never looked back.

8. How was it working with Tracii and Phil?

Hamilton: It was a blast working with the two of them. They immediately invited me to bring in ideas and start writing with them and were like big brothers to me. Still friends with them today.

9. Not kissing your ass, but your time in LA Guns was – in our opinion – some of the best time periods for the band.

Hamilton: Awe thanks! I thought we made some good music too. As a fan I will always be fondest of the first album line up. So amazing and cool. I tried to stay true to what I thought as a fan was the essence of the LA Guns sound.

10. We put together a summary of every year of rock music between 1981-2017. Including a list of the top songs and albums of the year.

Hamilton: Awe thanks! I thought we made some good music too. As a fan I will always be fondest of the first album line up. So amazing and cool. I tried to stay true to what I thought as a fan was the essence of the LA Guns sound.

11. Believe it or not, we have Waking the Dead as the best rock album of 2002 and Hollywood Forever as the best rock album of 2012. Tales from the Strip came in as the 5th best album of 2005.

Hamilton: That's fantastic!

12. Can you share your memories/thoughts on the writing/recording of Waking the Dead? We've also got Don't You Cry as the best song of the year, Lost in a City of Angeles as the fourth best song and Revolution as the 8th best. Anything cool to remember about those songs?

Hamilton: That album was magic to make on so many levels. I was a member of LA Guns and every day was like a dream. I would go out in Hollywood at night and jam with Steel Panther and party on the Sunset Strip and then wake up late the next day and work on demos for a new La Guns album.

Life was so good and I was living the dream x10. Those three songs were three of mine that I demoed and brought in for *Waking The Dead*.

Revolution, the music was all but finished and we worked it up as a band and Phil wrote the lyrics. Done.

On the other two the music was close and we as a band finished them up and Phil again did such great lyrics. "Don't You Cry" and "City of Angels" were kind of similar in sound because that is where my head was at during that album. Driving, dark yet melodic sounds. Riffs that get stuck in your head. I am not a great lead guitarist so what I write ends up being simple but simple is best for rock and roll. They all added their touch and they became magic. I think the stand the test of time. I like hearing them today. What was so cool about the guys was that they all are so confident and secure in who they are and their talents, they never felt the need to change things just so they could add or take away things. If it was good and almost finished, great! Less for us to have to do! I only wrote lyrics for one song on that album. "The Ballad." Phil took what I had and expounded on them and made them something special. That song was written about Bianca Hallsted from Betty Blowtorch. She died during the making of our album and it is a bit of a tribute to her. Kinda like "The Ballad Of Jayne" is about Jayne Mansfield. We worked with Andy Johns on that album. You can imagine how cool that was. He was amazing and I will never forget those sessions.

13. 2012 was another stellar year for L A Guns. How did the vibe of the band change without Tracii Guns being there? How come you co-wrote the album but didn't tour with the band anymore?

Hamilton: Tracii leaving was huge. It was very complicated at the time. I decided to stick around when he went off to put together the Brides Of Destruction because the Brides was supposed to be a temporary thing and then Tracii would come back when Nikki eventually went back to Motley Crue. I thought *Tales* was a pretty good album despite Tracii's absence. It has some amazing moments.

14. Underneath the Sun came in as the 2ⁿᵈ best ballad of the year and Hollywood Forever (#4) and You Better Not Love Me (#9) were the winners on the rock side. How was the recording process for that album and were you involved in writing any of those three great songs?

Hamilton: *Hollywood Forever* was the album just after I had quit the band. They asked me if I had any songs that they could use for the album, I gave them "Underneath The Sun" which was written by myself and my dear friend Gary Wolf. We were trying to write our version of "Dream On." The band liked the song and cut it just like the demo sounds.

I also gave them the music for the song "Burn." Phil wrote lyrics. I also put together the albums intro sound collage. I visited the studio one afternoon but that was it. I didn't play on the album. To be honest, it was kinda weird being there and not being in the band anymore. No one was weird it was just my feeling.

15. This is kind of an odd question, but since you were in the band for almost a decade, fans would love to hear your thoughts. How come the core group hasn't been able to maintain one constant band? LA Guns has had two separate versions touring, more than 40 musicians have played in something like 35 different lineups of the band. Even this

year, with the big reunion with Tracii and Phil…..within months, they start changing out players again. As somebody who knows all the main guys, was in the band for a long time, and has been in the music industry for 30 years….how do you explain that?

Hamilton: One of the reasons the band has had so many members is simply because of the band's finances. L.A. Guns level of success can only afford to pay members so much. If the band had had more hits, sold more records and reached the next level it would probably be different.

I always had a second source of income with doing music for TV and film which preceded my time in the band. Also, times change, tastes change. Some guys out grow the band and want to do other things. Most people are not lifers. I always thought I was a lifer but as I got older I started to dislike leaving home for months at a time.

Playing for the fans is such a thrill but it is the other 23 hours a day away from home that weeds people out of the game. It seems like a glamorous life but I can assure you doing it at the level the band has been at, it is not at all. Cheap motels, bad food, long miles for not great money will get to you after a while. I had done it for so long that I just wasn't enjoying it like I once had. Plus I got sober and found it really difficult to maintain sobriety in the belly of the beast.

I love the guys like family and will always cherish my time in the band but I am more of a studio rat-home body these days. We live 20-30 minutes away from Hollywood. Even trekking there seems like a chore!

16. You played one show with Dokken, filling in for the legendary Mick Brown. How was that show?

Hamilton: Another magic moment that is captured on YouTube! We pulled into Tucson, AZ for one of the last shows of the Metal Edge summer tour and Mick got sick and couldn't play. The Dokken guys were going to have to cancel but I jumped on their bus and said I could fill in. I was a drummer first and foremost. Knew the whole set since we had been on tour with them for three months. I could have played it in my sleep!

We had a little make shift rehearsal so they could be confident that I could pull it off. It turned out really cool and it was a great way to end the tour. My dear friend Gary Wolf mentioned above had been wanted to fly out and ride the bus with me on tour for years. That turned out to be the day he was in town and he got to hang with me for that show. Amazing!

17. You got to work with another hard rock legend in the early days of Brides of Destruction. How was Nikki Sixx to work with?

Hamilton: After we got home from that Metal Edge tour, Tracii made it clear to all of us that he was staring a side band with Nikki. I helped him find a singer, London my hair stylist.

We recorded a demo in Tracii's living room for London to sing on so we could show Nikki that he can sing. It was a Sweet cover and it sounded really cool. We mixed it and Nikki came by to hear it. He was super cool and we planned to get them a rehearsal room at my pal Stevo's studios.

They moved in and proceeded jamming every day working on what became The Brides. I was there for the first few weeks. We jammed Motley songs, LAG songs and other covers. Then LAG booked a European tour using Brent Muscat from Faster Pussycat and Kerri Kelli on guitar. I had never been to Europe and was not going to miss the tour so off we went. It turned out to be life changing. I fell in love with Europe and loved it every time we went back.

18. You've worked with some of the biggest names of the hair metal / sleaze rock/ hard rock era. Are there one or two guys that really stick out to you in terms of them helping your career? Whether it was them teaching or guiding you or with you just watching how they handled themselves and their careers.

Hamilton: CC DeVille, for one, is probably the biggest since he discovered me and gave me my first big break. I have learned much from many, how to treat others and how not to treat others. I try to try people like I want to be treated. There are some kind people out there and so not so nice but you just try and remember the we are all just humans doing the best we can. No one is perfect.

19. What prompted your decision to move from the rock n' roll hero roll

Hamilton: I have always loved that side of things. As a kid I would spend much time recording on my little 4-track cassette machine and learning as much as I could. There have always been two sides to making music, writing. recording and playing live. Just the latter for me these days but both very important. I always loved both equally but as I got older touring got harder and harder. It is a young mans game!

The transition to just being behind the scenes was easy. I loved producing and recording other artists and bands. Just as much as making records being the main artist. It is fun to help teach and coach others and share with them what so many taught and shared with me. I love passing on the gifts and blessing that I have been given. Since I have always done all of the above I just knew that at some point I would segue into just the studio.

When I was about to be married, I had a moment where something happened and I knew that I had to get sober and try a new way of living. I made some huge changes and it was then that I realized that I didn't want to tour. I have been off the road for over ten years. There are parts that I miss - the brotherhood, seeing different places, but I got to see everywhere I ever dreamed of going, so I don't really miss it.

20. Is there one music artist that you've had the most fun working with? You've worked with a crazy variety – from Shatner to George Lynch to Vanilla Ice!!! Any of those jobs standout as being a favorite?

Hamilton: There have been so many! Shatner is a blast to work with. Pretty cool getting to produce Sheryl Crow and hear that incredible voice right there in the same room. Pretty funny getting to record Leif Garrett. He is so much fun and so smart and talented. He has had his share of trouble but is so cool. I had a cool conversation with Ringo one night about when I produced Jackie Lomax. Jackie was signed by the Beatles to Apple back in the day. Wow, too many to name.

21. Same question about your TV work. You've been featured on so many great shows. Family Guy, The Simpsons, SNL, The

Osbournes....any of those standout for you or that you are most proud of your creativity with them?

Hamilton: Having a song in The Bourne Identity is probably one of the highlights. I also had two songs in two different Simpson's episodes. Then ended up having two songs in two different Woody Allen movies. How is that for crazy!

22. Finances are personal, so we aren't asking for private info! But just in general terms, can you tell us which pays more? Writing a couple songs for a fairly popular rock band or writing a song for a popular TV show? If you wrote three songs for the next LA Guns album and it sold 50,000 copies....and you wrote a song for an episode of Family Guy.....which one would score you the bigger paycheck?

Hamilton: That is a tough question to figure out with all of the variables. Writing songs doesn't pay really anymore since streaming is the way most people listen to music. Back in the day a hit song would make you rich, now having a hit probably won't make you that much money…sad. You make royalties if your song airs on TV. So you want it to air on network TV and during prime time. Then your chances of making good money will be better.

23. We heard about how you got started in the music licensing business. Do you remember that first song you submitted that got picked up for a show? You had songs featured in a Jason Bourne movie and a Sex in the City movie. Do you get a check every time those movies are played on TV?

Hamilton: I was at a wedding reception in 1995 and met Marc Ferrari. We hit it off. I obviously knew who he was and he told me he was starting a company to place music in TV and film. I told him that was one of the things that I wanted to get into. We kept in touch and I sent him some songs.

Two weeks later he had it placed in a TV show. Can't remember what the first was. I have had songs in over fifty different shows and over a dozen movies and a handful of commercials. And one video game! Yes, you get quarterly royalty statements that track and pay every time your music airs on TV.

24. You produced a Vains of Jenna album. How was it working with Stevie Rachelle and what do you think of his website Metal Sludge?

Hamilton: Love Stevie! He and I have known each other over twenty years. He used to come up to the house when I played with CC. I then did a tour as drummer for Tuff around 1996. I have always liked him and love the site!

Cleopatra Records recommended me for the album. We had a great time. I loved the Vains Of Jenna guys. A shame the broke up and moved back to Sweden.

25. You basically play every instrument! Which one is your favorite to play and which one would you consider to be your best?

Hamilton: Drums will always be my first and best instrument. I love bass and guitars but I am realistic and know my limits and what my strengths and weaknesses are. If there is a part I know is too tough for me on guitar, I may call my pal Patrick Kenninson from Lita Ford's band to come knock it out. Part of being a producer is knowing when to bring in the right person for the job.

26. Who are your favorite current musicians? Regardless of position/success level/etc. Who are the guys you'd pay money to go see live?

Hamilton: I like Greta Van Fleet. Thank God at least some kids are rocking these days.

27. What do you have in store for the rest of 2018 and 2019? If CC or Joey or Phil/Tracii called you up for a new album and tour....do you take that phone call or are you pretty set and comfortable with your current work now?

Hamilton: Not sure what's in store for the future. I just get up and put it all in God's hands and let Him show me what's next. Anything is possible if you believe!

Joel Hoekstra
Whitesnake

Picture courtesy of Mr. Hoekstra's official Twitter page.

__1. We just listened to Joel Hoekstra's 13. And wow – what a fascinating album. It's definitely not an AC/DC album where every song sounds a little bit like the one before it. With multiple vocalists and a range of styles/sounds, the album definitely takes listeners on a musical journey. How did you choose the artists for the album – you've got some legends on it!!!__

Hoekstra: It started with Tony Franklin who I had just worked with on the VHF ep. He recommended Vinny Appice as a drummer. Then Russell Allen was hired for TSO and upon hearing him, I realized that he was the perfect singer for it. Jeff Scott Soto was nice enough to sing some backing vocals to Russ's tracks and once it became clear that it was more of a project album, I had Jeff do some lead singing as well. Derek Sherinian was also kind enough to do all the keyboards for me.

__2. You might be the most diverse musician in rock music right now!! How hard is it –mentally and physically – to not only play in three different bands, but three with such different sounds/vibe? (Whitesnake, Cher, TSO)__

Hoekstra: The only challenge is overlapping schedules. I often wish cloning was an option!

3. Is one band/style harder to play than the other? In terms of the difficulty level of the songs?

Hoekstra: Not really. My mindset is always to play everything to the best of my ability. So the challenge is constant.

4. Whitesnake's much anticipated new album was recently delayed. Do you know when fans can expect that to come out?

Hoekstra: As I understand it, early 2019 and will be followed by a world tour.

5. How was the experience of writing/recording the album? Can you share any thoughts on the sound? Is it pure old school "Still of the Night" or more modern, harder edged, ballad heavy, etc?

Hoekstra: We had 18 songs and there was a little something that was reminiscent of each era of Whitesnake and some new territory as well. It really depends on which songs David chooses for the album.

6. David Coverdale is amazing. Truly one of the living legends of rock music. So many singers of the 70s/80s have lost their voices, but Coverdale still sounds amazing. How has the experience been working with him? And how is he able to keep himself looking and sounding like he is still in his 30s!

Hoekstra: David is great. He is very funny and enjoys being one of the guys. Of course, he's also had an amazing career full of tremendous experiences and it's great when he shares those as well. I really don't know the secrets to his looks. I've never asked him. Haha!

7. How does a rock n roll guitar god end up playing with pop icon Cher? How do her crowds compare to Whitesnake fanatics? Cher and Coverdale are both legends, who have been around in music for 40-plus years. How similar/different are their preparations/practices/etc?

Hoekstra: When I learned that Whitesnake wasn't going to tour in 2017, I sent out texts to peers colleagues and Justin Derrico (Pink/The Voice) recommended me to Dave Barry who needed a sub at the time. The crowds are VERY different, as you could imagine. I really don't know the in's and out's of how David and Cher get ready for shows. I'm always prepping myself.

8. Wait a minute. Coverdale looks/sounds 30 years younger than he is. Same with Cher. Hmmm….are you the physical version of the Fountain of Youth? If you come jam with me, will I transport back to my 20s!!!

Hoekstra: Haha! I wish.

9. Have you checked out David's Twitter? It's so funny. A rock legend, made tens of millions of dollars, banged thousands of groupies, rocked a million faces in the crowd, toured the world with the biggest bands in history…..and on Twitter he posts Kermit the Frog pictures, photos of cute kittens, wild life scenery.

Hoekstra: Yes, David is very much about the laughs..

10. How is it playing side-by-side with Reb Beach? That dude is a legend in the hard rock guitar world. On stage he is a Guitar God…..is he a cool dude off the stage too? He didn't respond to our interview request, so this is a free opportunity to share something funny or embarrassing about him!!!

Hoekstra: Reb is really great guy. Very funny, talented. He's got some stories about himself that you can't un-hear. Haha!

11. Was it fun to perform in Rock of Ages – the musical and the movie? How different was doing a musical compared to performing a rock concert with 20,000 fans going crazy!!!

Hoekstra: The musical was a blessing. I could take off whenever I wanted, so it allowed me to continue to tour and basically have a gig every day for about six years. I just had a small cameo in the movie, but that was a fun life experience as well. It wasn't as cool as playing big rock shows, but it was still really fun.

12. Did you and the movie band ever talk about doing anything together? Bach, Bettencourt, Cronin and you....that would be a pretty interesting rock project!

Hoekstra: Not really, no. Sebastian asked me to do some shows shortly after, but they didn't line-up in terms of schedules. We all did an impromptu acoustic show for everyone in catering on the set. That was interesting.

13. How did you end up in Night Ranger and how was that gig?

Hoekstra: I used to play with Kelly Keagy at Jim Peterik's World Stage gigs. I expressed interest once I heard Jeff was no longer with the band. Eventually I got to fill in for a show and that led to being the full-time guitarist for about seven years or so. I learned a lot from those guys. A fantastic experience.

14. How do you explain their success? Their last real hit was in the early 80s. But they've managed to stick around more than 30 years after that, with a revolving door of outstanding musicians, but they still put out great albums and they still draw good crowds today.

Hoekstra: Lots of hard work.

15. It's impossible to interview you about your entire music career. It would be a 200-question interview!!!! But you've had such a fascinating run of performances, I hate to leave anything out. I'm just going to list some of your rock projects and maybe you could just give your quick thought on them?

Michael Sweet: I mimed in two videos for him, sat in on his acoustic sets and played on thee songs on his last solo album. He's a great guy, a friend and eventually we're going to write/release an album together.

Brandon Gibbs: Brandon and I do acoustic shows together. Great guy. Sings great, plays great. A good friend.

**Dee Snider:** I worked with Dee in Rock of Ages and also mimed in a video of his and played a couple of show with him as well.

17. Is there one of your solo albums that you are most proud of or that you feel captured your sound the best? Any plans in the future for a fourth one?

Hoekstra: I put out three instrumental solo albums and then one from Joel Hoekstra's 13 which I consider to be a rock side project. They all are pictures of what I was playing like at those specific times.

18. You've done a lot of TV gigs – from Jay Leno to The Metal Show to Duck Dynasty to Conan O'Brien!!! Again, how did you get involved in that circuit? And which ones did you have the most fun on?

Hoekstra: Rock of Ages did Leno, Conan, America's Got Talent, etc. TSO has done Fallon. Duck Dynasty used some of my music beds. The credits come from different places.

19. You performed for the Celebrity Apprentice. Did Donald Trump ask you for any political advice? How did you and Debbie Gibson become friends?

Hoekstra: Debbie was a part of the cameo scene in the Rock of Ages movie and she came to the Broadway show as well. I never met Donald Trump.

20. You are a big Angus Young fan. What did you think of the Axl/ACDC shows last year? Which would you be more interested in hearing – a new GnR album with Slash/Duff back in the band. Or a new ACDC album with Axl on vocals?

Hoekstra: I only saw clips, but he sounded good from what I heard. I'm a horrible listener these days, so neither one of the albums would mean much to me, sadly. I'm usually just prepping for the set of music that I have to play.

21. What do you have in store for 2018 and 2019?
Is there anything at all you'd want us to mention or promote???

Hoekstra: I'm wrapping up a run with Cher in Vegas right now, then Whitesnake hits the road with Foreigner and Jason Bonham for the Summer. The rest of the year looks like a mix of Cher, Whitesnake and TSO. Hopefully 2019 will be more of the same.

http://www.joelhoekstra.com
https://www.facebook.com/JoelHoekstra13
https://twitter.com/JoelHoekstra13

Kim Hooker
Bare Knuckle Messiahs, Tigertailz

Photo courtesy of Bare Knuckle Messiahs official webpage.

1. Holy cow. We just listened to the two Bare Knuckle Messiahs songs and just about had our face melted off. Are Tigertailz fans going to be able to handle this much ass-kicking from your new band?

Hooker: I hope Tailz fans will like the BKM sound. I honestly didn't think it was that heavy but general reaction seems to be it is so I guess that's the case. Tailz were always a heavy band though. Pepsi loved Megadeth and thought Dave was God.

2. Have you always been a true Metal guy? We know you from Tigertailz and as being a huge Kiss fan....I didn't know deep down you were a thrash metal guy.

Hooker: I've always leant towards the heavier stuff myself but I can't deny the buzz I get when I play "Love Bomb Baby" live (for the fan reaction) although I prefer to play "Dirty Needles."

I'm a huge fan of great drums, bass, and guitar though so for me it's always been great riffs, great bass sound (Gene Simmons). But most of all great drummers : Eric singer and Michael Jackson/ Madonna drummer Jonathan Moffett. Check him out...he's a machine !!!

3. Is the entire upcoming BKM as heavy as the first two songs?

Hooker:
I put the two songs "Spit in Your Eye" and "If Your Face is Your Fortune" on the website first because I thought they are a fair representation of the Bare Knuckle Messiahs album although there is a more commercial song called "We Know it's Cool" and a heavier song called "That Which Preys on the Dead" on there. But overall I'd say the two songs you've heard give a good indication of the overall flavor of the album.

4. If you could choose any band for BMK to tour with to support the album, what two bands would you pick?

Hooker: I'd have to say I'd love to tour with Kiss obviously and also Iron Maiden. Bruce has a big connection with my home city because he's based his Cardiff Aviation business here. I've been there and it's a great facility. I really wish him well with it and thank him for bringing so many skilled jobs to Wales. I guess he's done ok with the music so I can't help him on that one!

5. How many guitars do you own and do you have one that you are most proud of?

Hooker: I own over 12 guitars. I say over 12 because that's about the number I always have. I'm always buying and selling them. I love guitars! My most expensive is my 1979 Ibanez PS10. I have all the usual Gibson Les Paul's and Flying V's but the best is my Epiphone Ace Frehley. Every time I play it I can't believe how good it is.

Lately I've been playing Telecasters a lot which is something I thought

I'd never do. I also have two basses, my red BC rich Ironbird from my Rankelson days (Pepsi used it in the "Love Bomb Baby" video) and a fender precision I use for recording. I've been told I should do a Vlog about my guitar collection…someday I will!!

6. What prompted the 2005 Tigertailz reunion?

Hooker: For my part I'd have to say Tailz reformed because of the success of the Darkness. None of us had spoken for over 10 years. Not because of any bad blood. We just moved in different circles outside of the band. First Jay and myself got in touch when a mutual friend exchanged our numbers. Then we roped Pepsi in. It was weird, but great times though...we laughed a hell of a lot .

7. How different is touring in Wales compared to the United States? Travel, venues, band rooms, groupies, etc?

Hooker: I can't really compare touring in Wales to anywhere else ..I'm not really sure a band could do a tour of Wales. I have toured Wales many times on my motorcycle, it's such a beautiful place. I can tour the whole country in a day though.

In other countries I find the fans pretty much the same. Always lovely people and I love meeting them because they're fellow metalheads. I wish I could get to look around the places I play more though but that rarely happens.

8. What were you doing in the year prior to Tigertailz guys calling you to replace Steevi Jaimz? And was it an automatic "yes" or did you have to debate it?

Hooker: This is complicated. I was in a band called Rankelson. Pepsi was a close friend of guitarist Fox and myself. We used to go to Pepsi's house and sit up all night drinking coffee and talking about our bands. At the time Tailz had a singer called Jim Dovey. Rankelson split and Pepsi asked us to jam with them with a view to joining.

Rankelson then had an offer from Ebony records to make some albums ("Hungry For Blood" and the "Bastards of Rock and Roll") so we got

back together and Pepsi got Steevi in. Then after some time had passed
we were in a club one night together and Pepsi said he'd been listening to
the tapes we'd made and asked would I be interested in joining. It was a
no-brainier for me. Tailz were going places and I loved Ace Finchum's
playing. Steevi was great and he always hung out with me and my
Rankelson buddies when he lived in Wales but he was too much for Pepsi
and Jay to deal with day-to-day. We loved him. He was fucking nuts.
Such a great laugh, but they just couldn't deal with it. I remember he
covered Pepsi in sauce one night. I love Steevi but he doesn't have an off
switch. He is the epitome of a rock 'n' roll legend. We had great times
together back then.

9. For a metal band, you guys had a lot of great ballads. Where did that soft side come from?

Hooker: Everybody did ballads back then. It was just the done thing.
The demo of "Heaven" was good but it only really took shape when Don
Airey rocked it up, he really pulled the whole thing together. Before his
input it was a bit disjointed with no really idea of where it was going.

Jay wrote the chorus. I believe which was originally called Carrie Ann
(get it) and I wrote the verse which was a "homage" to Angels telephone
exchange. I hated singing it though. Back then we never experimented
with keys and I always struggled with it.

10. On that first reunion tour, you played with Whitesnake and Twisted Sister, two of the most famous metal bands of all time. How was it playing with those two bands, how did they treat you guys?

Hooker: We never really dealt with twisted sister because they just
turned up and played then left. But fuck they were loud. I know most
bands say they're loud but other than Motörhead, Sister was the only
band I've ever seen that I really noticed how loud they actually were. I
loved them though!

Played with Whitesnake a few times and they're great. All lovely guys
and really professional musicians. We'd heard stories that support acts
shouldn't walk about the backstage area when Coverdale's around
because he won't have it. I was standing there when someone thrust this

hand towards me and said: "hi, I'm David Coverdale." I nearly fell through the fucking floor. He was great, just a great down to earth guy as were all his band. We had a blast with those guys, a really great experience. Another diamond is Marco Mendoza!

11. We really loved that Bezerk 2.0 album in 2006. "I Believe" is our favorite. Any memories or thoughts on that album and writing/recording "I Believe"?

Hooker: As I said before "I Believe" doesn't hold great memories for me. When we got back together I had the original masters and I went back into the studio to sing it again. It was the strangest thing putting the headphones on and hearing me from 20 years ago like it was yesterday. In a way sad how life is so short...one minute you're here then you're gone ...

12. "Milez Away" was our favorite song off of Thrill Pistol. Were you guys happy with how that album came out? And lol – that album cover would draw huge controversy today from the whiny PC crowd.

Hooker: I'm glad you liked "Milez Away" because I wrote it and played a lot of it. The song was one of many I wrote when the band first split. I wrote it for the Rankelson singer Colin Sargent to sing because I thought it suited his voice. But when Pepsi became unwell we were desperate for songs for Thrill Pistol so we used it. It was a rush to finish that album because we knew Pepsi had no chance. It was the worst time in my life so I wouldn't say I have any good memories of Thrill Pistol ..sadly Rankelson singer Colin died the same week as Pepsi. All in all a very sad and painful period.

13. You guys toured with Ace Frehley in 2008. How was that tour? Frehley is a legend, did he treat you guys with respect?

Hooker: Ace Frehley...oh man that was a story!

I was at the venue when I heard security saying Ace is two minutes away. With that the door opened and Ace walks in. He looks straight at me and does a double take (people have remarked I look like him). I introduce myself and he says "hey man where's my dressing room?"

So I ask him if he's had a good journey and show him to it. Then I walk into ours where bassist Nailz is sitting and collapse on the floor saying "fucking hell I've just met Ace Frehley, I've just met Ace Frehley fucking hell!"

There was a toilet opposite out dressing room and later Nailz was banging on the door saying come on hurry up. The door opened and it was Ace. Nailz nearly fainted. He walks in and says "I should've seen if he'd left any floaters, I could've sold them on eBay!!!"

Nailz and I always had a laugh when they played. I stood at the side of the stage with a bottle of Jack and as the Jack went down I went more nuts. By the end I was virtually onstage with the band and they were laughing their heads off because I knew every word and every lick. When I turned up the next night in London they jumped on me expecting me to go nuts but I just couldn't do it as I was as so hung over! Still it was my own fault, I ruined the experience for myself ..when I was a kid Ace was and always will be my God and I blew it!

14. You guys seemed to go through a lot of members over the years. Why was there so much difficulty keeping one steady lineup?

Hooker: The line changes I think were mainly due, I think, to not wanting to be seen to be replacing Pepsi or indeed knowing how to replace him as far as bassist go. All I know is I hated it. I hate lineup changes ..always have and always will.

15. What led to your split with Tigertailz?

Hooker: What led to the split was that I just couldn't see a way forward after Pepsi died and I was always left feeling like we were short changing fans as a band. I asked myself would I want to see Motley without Sixx or Motörhead without Lemmy and the answer was obvious. Pepsi was that important in Tigertailz. He was 90% of the band, it was a huge loss.

I remember playing in Spain and that morning I'd been told that Stuart Cable from the Stereophonics had died. He was also a friend of Pepsi's (in fact he sent us an audition tape when Ace went, I can still see the pic) and I'd arranged to meet Stuart at Download where he was playing with his new band - Killing For Company - the next weekend. I dedicated "Heaven" to him and when I sang it I remember looking at the fan's faces and thinking you're being conned, I can't do this anymore.

Also two very close friends of the band, both in the industry from back in the day said: "you should have done one or two tours in Pepsi's memory then called it a day." The only solution I could see was to get Ace back then at least there would be three from the Bezerk line up and that made sense to me. Jay could see my point but wasn't having any of it. Neither was Tailz producer Tim Lewis.

Myself, Sarah, and the Tailz manager at the time pressured Jay into getting Ace back and I feel bad about that now because generally he makes good decisions and always does what's best for the band. At only the second date (Northern Ireland) it became obvious to me that the miracle cure I'd hoped for wasn't to be. I'd told myself that this was going to be the last lineup change I'd put up with so that was it. I was done. I knew then it was over for me.

To me the answer was obvious. If I put my own band together fans won't expect to get the Bezerk Tailz experience and be left wanting...so that's what I did.

16. Pepsi Tate was such a great musician, and apparently a real fantastic guy as well. How devastating was it to lose him – or is there anything you'd like to say about Mr. Tate?

Hooker: Losing Pepsi Tate was a massive blow both personally and professionally. He was a friend years before I joined the band and it's fair to say if it were not for him I would have never been in it. He was a funny and very intelligent guy and was without a doubt the band's driving force. He really was a powerhouse and it was his death that ultimately lead me to leave the band. I really couldn't see the point in carrying on without him. We used to call him the captain and he was.

17. At what age did you start singing? How old were you when you realized you were good enough to be a professional musician?

Hooker: I started playing guitar when I was 12 maybe 13 and it was totally because of Kiss. Before Kiss I was into Queen and Status Quo but Kiss was the first band I truly loved to the point that when I first saw them on TV I burst into tears. I never really got to the point where I considered myself good enough to turn pro, it just kind of happened.

I'm still learning to this day and still find learning exciting. My guitar playing is the best it's ever been simply because I've been practicing more. I put that down solely to the fact I've discovered Telecasters. For some reason I can't put them down. I don't know if there's ever a point that you're good enough to turn pro because there are many pro musicians who've made millions who are actually shit at playing their instrument but very good at selling themselves and their band.

18. When you aren't doing something music related, what do you enjoy doing for fun?

Hooker: For fun I ride my motorcycle and play guitar.

19. Do you have a Tigertailz album that you are most proud of or that you think captures your sound the best?

Hooker: I'd have to say my best Tailz album is *Bezerk*. It's an album that couldn't be made today and captures that time and the vibe that was happening back then so well. Like when I listen to Hendrix it takes me right back to that place. And then there's Pepsi's artwork on the cover - such an iconic image. It's definitely the most complete Tailz package and the epitome of what Pepsi's Tailz vision was...it's the one I'd take to a party.

20. What's on the plate for you in 2018 and 2019?

Hooker: 2018/19 will be making a video which is a ball ache for me. I've never liked doing it. I'd much prefer people to come to shows and film their own then put that on YouTube. Then releasing the debut Bare Knuckle Messiahs album, then going out to play wherever we can!!!

21. Have you ever gotten the chance to jam/sing with any of the Kiss

members? Or have Singer play drums with you?

Hooker: Never jammed with Kiss (although in my mind I have many times) but obviously that would be my greatest moment if it ever happened.

22. In an interview you said you'd love to be part of the band Velvet Revolver. They held an audition process before signing Scott, did you ever call Slash or Duff up and tell them you'd be interested?

Hooker: No I never called about the VR job but I love that band so much. I'm a believer in fate so I figure if being the singer in VR is my destiny Slash will call me. I would love to do it though. I love Scott's STP stuff too.

23. What album would you be more curious in hearing. A 2017 GnR album with Slash/Duff in the band. Or an ACDC album with Axl Rose on vocals?

Hooker: Axl with GnR. I know DC are great but I've never really been into them in a big way (yeah I know I'm a dick).

https://m.facebook.com/bkmessiahsofficial
http://www.bareknucklemessiahs.com
https://twitter.com/KimHookeromg

Ian Hatton
Bonham, writer, producer, music engineer and numerous other amazing things! Has worked with Cheap Trick, Paul Rodgers, Robert Plant amongst many others.

Photo courtesy of Mr. Hatton's official website.

1. Bonham hasn't reunited like all the other 80s and early 90s genre bands have over the last decade. If Jason called you up and wanted to do a Bonham (or Motherland) album and tour in 2019, would you be up for it? What are the odds of that actually happening? Bonham would be a cool addition to the guys touring now that are doing all the festivals, monsters of rock cruise, etc.

Hatton: Sadly, Daniel passed away in 2008 so a true Bonham reunion couldn't be done. But I'd love to do something like that. I still see Jason regularly but he's busy with Sammy Hagar and JBLZE, so unlikely at the moment.

2. Motherland was a real change of pace. It still had the Bonham vibe, but definitely seemed to be going down the grunge road. Was the name change related to a new band with a grunge sound, or was it more to try and separate the band from the Bonham name?

Hatton: A bit of both really.

3. Looking back now, do you think having Jason in the band was a blessing or a curse? Or maybe a combination of both? His name definitely helped you guys some publicity, but then also stereotyped the band as a Led Zeppelin clone.

Hatton: The band wouldn't really have been created without Jason and the interest after the Atlantic 40th celebration. We were already working together and Jason had worked with John before so this gave us the opportunity to form the band.
But then, yes, of course by using the name we were stereotyped. But the pros of all the interest that instantly got us very much outweighed the cons.

4. With a legendary name in the band, a debut album that went Gold and had a pretty big rock hit on it, and Sharon Osbourne on board – how in the world did your label not put forth full effort into the second CD? Was the Grunge revolution that strong where labels were abandoning even money making "hair metal" groups?

Hatton: Don't get me started on that! Oh how I love record companies!!!!! The second album was done and ready as far as we were concerned but the record company in their infinite wisdom decided we needed a few more "radio friendly" tracks. It took so long that between writing them and working with different people, by the time the album hit Nirvana were happening and everything was changing.

So in a nutshell if the f***ing record company had done their job and let us do ours the album would have come out at least a year earlier and had a chance at really establishing the band's career. Instead they ruined it, trying to have us chase the radio.

__5. Your resume is off the charts, easily one of the most impressive of all musicians from the genre. Nominated for a Grammy, nominated for an Emmy, earned a Gold Record, produced albums, scored TV shows and movies, and was a consultant for some cutting-edge Bose systems. Is there anything that you can't do? Of all those things, which was/is your favorite and which are you most proud of?__

Hatton: I'm very proud of everything!!! I've been lucky. The Bonham years were probably some of the best years of my life, we had so much fun. Since then it's been a roller coaster ride between bands and then trying to establish myself in film and TV, which I really enjoy being able to create with more freedom.

__6. You've partnered or worked with some of the biggest names in the music industry. Paul Rodgers, Robert Plant, Sarah Brightman, Cheap Trick. How does a guy who isn't usually listed in the "guitar god" category (Slash, Eddie, etc) end up collaborating with the biggest names in the music industry?__

Hatton: I just do my thing, bit of luck, bit of timing, keep working and hopefully things happen. I've never had a plan.

__7. Of all those acts, which one was the most interesting/exciting project for you? Which one are you most proud of?__

Hatton: Bonham.

8. What is your biggest love – or, what aspect of your career do you enjoy the most? Playing guitar, writing, producing, etc?

Hatton: That's tough. I'm a guitar player but I love to write and lost interest in touring because it seemed so much wasted time just to play a show. And that's fine if it's your band, but if you're more of a hired gun it's not the same. That being said, the last couple of years I've really been missing playing and touring and I guess be careful what you wish for, as I'm going on tour this summer with Debbie Bonham for 6 weeks in the summer. So that'll be interesting!

9. You played with Robert Plant, then joined a band with Jason Bonham. Were you a big Led Zeppelin fan growing up or was the connection to Plant/Bonham just a coincidence?

Hatton: I was a big Zep fan, who wasn't? But it was coincidence too. I was playing in a rock 'n' roll band called "Melvin's Mauraders" and Robert used to come out and do a few Elvis songs if he was around so that's how that started. Jason was probably 15 then maybe. We knew each other but didn't start hanging out until a few years later, so yes, coincidence.

10. If offered these jobs in 2019, which one would be your first choice? New Bonham album, new Katrina Chester album, produce a biography on Sister Rosetta Tharpe, tour with Robert Plant or score a movie directed by David Fincher about Led Zeppelin?

Hatton: That's a lot of choices!! I have to be loyal and say new Bonham album although the opportunity to tour with Robert would be pretty nice!!

11. Or a better question, if an investor handed you a check for $5 million dollars and gave you free reign to put together any project you wanted – what would you do? What would your dream project be?

Hatton: The time and freedom to create something unique would be fantastic. I would love to work on a record recorded the old way, where people actually sit in the same room together and have fun doing what they're doing. So I guess that would give the freedom to fuse the old technology with the new and really get the best of both worlds. I do love techy shit so that side would be fun, and then having the time and money to collaborate and work with great musicians would be the icing.

12. What guitar players inspired you….and what advice would you give to young musicians trying to make it in the business today?

Hatton: Jeff Beck, David Gilmore, Allen Holdsworth to name a few favorites, plus early on I was lucky to be turned on to all the old blues players. I'm big Freddie King fan.
As for advice, dream and keep dreaming and stick to it, be true to yourself. It's the only way you have a chance at being happy in my mind.

13. When writing Wait For You, did you instantly know it was going to be a rock hit? In our opinion, it's one of the select few songs from the era that still holds up today. We have it ranked as the 77th best song of the era – does that seem about right to you?

Hatton: Thought it would do way better than 77, come on!! Ha.. Ironically, when we first wrote it we thought it should be an instrumental!!

14. 1989 is considered one of – if the not best – year of music for the genre. How do you feel you guys stacked up - musician-wise – against those bands? Were you fans of any of the big guys from that year? (Skid Row, Motley, Warrant, Tora Tora, Enuff Z' Nuff, L.A. Guns, Great White, Tesla, etc).

Hatton: To be honest I wasn't really a fan of most of those bands even though there were some good ones. I guess we were trying to be a bit more muso and I didn't really listen to that much current music if that makes sense. When I first started working with Jason he was alarmed because I'd never heard any Van Halen!! I know Daniel was a big Tesla fan we played with them a few times back in the day.

15. Two bands that we always thought had a Bonham feel were Salty Dog and of course, Kingdom Come. Did you dig those guys or care about them at all?

Hatton: They had a couple good songs but didn't really pay to much attention.

16. *What's your opinion on all the bands from the 80s that have turned into a revolving door of musicians and tour today, sometimes with just one original member? Do you think it's OK for band members to keep their band's name alive or do you think at some point a band name should be retired, and the one lone remaining member should start a new band?*

Hatton: That's an interesting question, I guess you have to weigh up the question of fans wanting to see the band and then a fine line of whether its basically a tribute band although some wouldn't like to admit that I'm sure.

17. *What band from back in your rock days did you feel should have been much bigger than they ended up being?*

Hatton: Bonham!!!!! Ha!

18. *Do you mind being referred to as being in a hair metal band? Are you one of the guys who get offended by that specific genre title?*

Hatton: I realize that was the era so I get it, but don't really like being lumped in with the Poison and Warrants of the world. To me that was the hair band stuff. We had the image but I think a little more music too.

19. *Are there any bands you would pay money to go see today?*

Hatton: Not if I can help it. :-)

20. *Are you a fan of David Coverdale and Whitesnake?*

Hatton: Not really. That had become a little ridiculous, but we had fun listening to "In the Still of the Night" Still do. Ha!

21. *What upcoming projects do you have? And is there anything you'd like us to promote?*

Hatton: Working on a film called "Apple Seed" right now and then on tour with Debbie Bonham in the summer. We're opening up for Jeff Beck, Paul Rodgers and Nancy Wilson!!! So look out for both.

https://www.ianhatton.com

Jay Pepper
Tigertailz

Photo courtesy of Tigertailz official Facebook page.

1. How different is touring in Wales compared to the United States? Travel, venues, band rooms, groupies, etc.

Pepper: Apart from the weather (it always rains in Wales :)) a gig is a gig no matter where it is. But the obvious difference is the distance you need to travel to play in the US. But as for the venues, they're all much the same. And groupies…I'm way too old for all that now!

2. How did you guys find Kim Hooker after getting rid of Steevi Jaimz?

Pepper: Kim was a friend of ours from the local music scene in Cardiff. He played Bass in a band called Rankelson. But we knew he had a voice too. So when we were looking for a singer he seemed the obvious choice as he looked great and was into the same kind of vibe as us.

3. For a metal band, you guys had a lot of great ballads. Where did that soft side come from?

Pepper: I guess that's mostly down to me. I've always been a bit of a softy and feeling of melancholy. So I tend to find it easy to write those kind of tunes. And no hair metal album is complete with the obligatory ballad :)

4. What prompted the 2005 reunion?

Pepper: There had been a big resurgence of Rock in the UK. And the success of the Darkness made it ok to be an image band in Rock again. Kim contacted me to see if I wanted to do something. I can't say I was keen - and Pepsi was even less keen. But we talked, had a laugh and agreed to do it - as long as it didn't take over our lives again. Demolition and Sanctuary Records wanted to reissue our albums. So we gave it a go.

5. On that first reunion tour, you played with Whitesnake and Twisted Sister, two of the most famous metal bands of all time. How was it playing with those two bands, how did they treat you guys?

Pepper: Yes, those shows were great. As I said, we weren't looking for Tigertailz to take over our lives again. And just wanted to keep it all low key. But playing those shows meant it was all up and running like it had never stopped in the 90's. And all of those guys were great. Particularly Mr. Coverdale. He's a gent!

6. We really loved that Bezerk 2.0 album in 2006. "I Believe" is our favorite song. Any memories or thoughts on that album and writing/recording I Believe?

Pepper: Thank you. "I Believe" came about from a verse / bridge that Kim had wrote. We didn't really have a chorus. So I came up with the chorus, but called in Carianne. Thankfully Pepsi suggested changing the lyrics to two words, rather than a two syllable single word. And that's how it came to be. Although we've re-recorded it about five times in different forms.

7. "Milez Away" was our favorite song off of Thrill Pistol. Were you guys happy with how that album came out? And lol – that album cover would draw huge controversy today from the whiny PC crowd.

Pepper: *Thrill Pistol* will always be an album that brings back dark memories. For the obvious reason that Pepsi was very ill at the time. It took all he had to make that record. And we lost him just after it was released. So everything about making that record was fraught with difficulty, problems and friction between everyone involved. So am I happy with it? No, not from a musical point of view. I think it could have been way better. It has its moments. The intro and "Brain The Sucker" and "Long Live The New Flesh" are great. Real Punk Metal, which I love! But it falls away after that due to the issues we were faced with. Having said all that, and given the circumstances, it's a miracle it ever got made at all.

8. You guys toured with Ace Frehley in 2008. How was that tour? Frehley is a legend, did he treat you guys with respect? Is he a guitar player that you admired?

Pepper: We did two shows with Ace. The first one from his point of view was a disaster. He turned up late. His merch wasn't there. He complained about his gear etc. But we had a great show. The second night at the Astoria he had the doctor there for some reason or another. That show went much better for both bands. I can't say he was great to us. His band refused to move any of their gear when there was no room for us (usual crap). And Ace himself was aloof and not interested in anyone. Kim is a massive Kiss / Ace fan and loved the shows. To me he was unrecognizable from the guitar player I knew in Kiss.

9. You guys seemed to go through a lot of members over the years. Why was there so much difficulty keeping one steady lineup? Why are you the guy who has managed to stay the course and lead the team?

Pepper: Regardless of what level your band is at it's extremely difficult to keep the same unit together over 30+ years. People become difficult to work with which means you can't function as a band, so you need to change. People leave for whatever reason, so you need to change. And worst of all people die. And at that point you either give up or you need to change again. So you can appreciate it's a constant battle. I don't know why I'm the guy who keeps it together. It's just the way I am, I get shit done. And I refuse to let people destroy something Pepsi and I created and believed in. When Tigertailz ends that will be a decision for both him and me.

Pepper:

- Bad decisions from me. I should have known better
- Bad decisions from people working for the band
- Recruiting the wrong personnel
- People being unreasonable
- People being ungrateful
- People forgetting who their friends are
- People holding a gun to your head
- People stabbing you in the back

I'd say that about sums it up!

11. In support of the solid Knives EP, you guys once again toured with some of the biggest bands in the world: Kiss and Cheap Trick on the Kiss Kruize. That's a different environment than the typical land tour, how was it being out on the ocean?

Pepper: Those experiences are the very reason Pepsi and I agreed to get back together. So we could dip in and out and do shows like that – but without the band taking over our lives again. So yes, those shows were amazing. And being on a cruise ship with Kiss is about as bizarre as Rock n Roll gets!

12. Pepsi Tate was such a great musician, and apparently a real fantastic guy as well. How devastating was it to lose him – or is there anything you'd like to say about Mr. Tate?

Pepper: When you lose your friend at such a young age there are no words really. It was devastating. And as I've said many times. Pepsi was Tigertailz. He contributed more to this band than anyone else. It's been my job to continue that legacy since he passed away. But he was also a great guy and massively creative in anything he did. He was and still is a huge loss.

13. You got to see Mick Mars at the Godz of Metal tour. Did you grow up listening to Mars? In our opinion he is extremely underrated. Not a "shredder" but a guy who can play anything and has his own unique style.

Pepper:_Yes, and I think Mick Mars is a legend in his own right. He has his own vibe that isn't a copy of the usual suspects. He's more old school like Hendrix. Watching him from the side of the stage you see him and think wow! I couldn't do that. He was awesome!

14. How's it been with Rob as the lead singer?

Pepper: Rob's great. A real pro who make sure he's got his act together when he sings the songs. He knows what he's doing and leaves nothing to chance – i.e. he doesn't try and just wing something on the night. He sings the songs how they should be sung. I love working with this line-up. Rob, Berty, Matt. All the guys are great!

15. At what age did you start playing guitar? How old were you when you realized you were good enough to be a professional musician?

Pepper: I was about 14 when I had my first guitar. It was an Eros Les Paul. But when I realized how difficult it was to play I gave up instantly. Then rediscovered it at 16 when a guy showed me how to play some Status Quo riffs. I'm not really a confident person. So it gradually came about over many years. I used to see many incredible guitar players and think, woh I could never play like that. But then you realize those guys fell apart in other ways. They couldn't get their act together to get to a gig. Had crap equipment, or couldn't play live because they were drunk or on drugs. Don't get me wrong, I have my demons too! But it was a gradual realization that being good enough to be in a professional band meant having your shit together in all ways. I might not be the best player in the world. But I get to where I need to be. My equipment is top draw. I will know how to play the songs. I'm polite and considerate to everyone I work with. And I look good and smell nice! :)

16. When you aren't doing something music related, what do you enjoy doing for fun?

Pepper: Driving my car and watching football. And being with my family.

17. Do you have a Tigertailz album that you are most proud of or that you think captures your sound the best?

Pepper: Yes, in my view our last album *BLAST* was as good a record as the band has ever made. It contains everything that defines Tigertailz. Great riffs, great hooks, massive choruses, rip your face off metal tunes. They're all beautifully constructed songs on that record. It has everything. And it took everything I had to make it.

18. Quick thoughts on:

Eddie Van Halen = Legend
CC DeVille = Glam Legend
Paul Gilbert = Shredder Legend
Ace Frehley = Spaceman Legend
Slash = Coolest Legend
George Lynch = Melodic Legend
Warren DiMartini = Riff and Melodic 2 Legend
Vito Bratta = Melodic 3 Legend
But you forgot to include the greatest guitar player ever! So I've added him: Rick Parfitt = the BIGGEST LEDG for me. My hero and the reason I started playing guitar. Completely underrated and a fantastic guitar virtuoso!

19. What's on the plate for you guys in 2018 and 2019?

Pepper: We have the HRH festivals coming up. We're also working on our first animated video for the "Bloodsuckers" track off the *BLAST* album. We're also editing the Live show that was filed to remember 10 years of Pepsi's passing. That should get released later this year or early 2019.

20. Is there anything you want us to mention or promote?

Pepper:

Only peace, love, good health and happiness to everyone reading this.

https://twitter.com/jaypepper007
http://www.tigertailz.co.uk/
https://www.facebook.com/OfficialTigertailz

Jizzy Pearl
Love/Hate, LA Guns, Quiet Riot

Photo courtesy of Mr. Pearl's official Facebook page.

1. For people who don't know you are a published author, what book would you recommend they check out first?

Pearl: I've written three so I guess the most logical thing would be to read the first one first—I GOT MORE CRICKETS THAN FRIENDS—all my books are available on Amazon.com

2. Have you ever thought about writing a book about your life and career? We've ranked the to 30 hard rock books of all time. And even several of the ones that made the top 10 clearly didn't spend any extra money to hire an editor. It's actually kind of shocking.

Pearl: No not really. My career as a musician is probably the same as most, ups and downs, good times and lean times. However I will say my books were written wholly by myself. Most of these 'autobiographies' you see are really just a Rocker reminiscing into a tape recorder and someone transcribing it or trying to make sense of it all.

3. What would you rather score in 2019 - a book that hit number on the

NY times list....or a song hit number one on Billboard?

Pearl: BOTH!

4. Can you share any crazy Sunset Strip stories? Was it as crazy as people say?

Pearl: I could but it seems a little silly these days to rehash debauchery, lets just say everyone got laid but not everyone got paid.

5. What venues were your favorite to play?

Pearl: Arenas with AC/DC, the UK when we were sorta famous back in the day, that sort of thing.

6. What was Val Kilmer like in high school? We're you guys buddies? Was he a cool humble guy?

Pearl: I knew him when he was 16 and I was 17. Drama club alumni. Nice guy, his parents had $ so his house was the party house. After high school he went on to Juilliard and became a famous actor and I discovered weed.

7. We really love Dreamtime by LA Guns. It's one of our favorite songs by LA Guns and our favorite overall Jizzy Pearl song. Do you remember the process writing/creating/recording it?

Pearl: Tracii came in with a song, sort of a 50's vibe—I made up a story about lost love and that's how it came about. Best song on that record for sure.

8. Who were your favorite singers and bands growing up?

Pearl: If you took Robert Plant, Roger Daltrey and Ronnie James Dio and put them in a blender that would be me.

9. You played and recorded with Steven Adler. How was that process? He seems like a really funny, sincere and honest guy....but might be a little crazy to work with!

Pearl: He's better now, he was sort of hit and miss when I played with him. He seems to have his shit together these days so I'm happy for him.

10. What are your thoughts on GnR having a reunion but not including Izzy and Adler?

Pearl: My thought is the newest incarnation of GnR is just fine. Those guys are Gold in my opinion.

11. What would you be more interested in hearing, a new GnR album (with Slash/Duff) or the reported Axl/ACDC album?

Pearl: Some people didn't dig it but I thought Axl did a great job singing the AC/DC songs—very hard material and he came in like a pro and delivered.

12. How was your time with Ratt? Again, another band in turmoil. They get a ton of great press for the reunion, but now Warren DiMartini has apparently bailed. And Blotzer still wants control of the name. Hell, even the LA Guns reunion is now going crazy with Michael Grant leaving and Johnny Monaco coming on board and then leaving.

Pearl: I dug certain aspects of the RATT experience, I thought DeMartini was a guitar hero and still do. It was fun for a few years but then 'someone' fucked it up.

13. As a professional musician, and also as a guy who actually knows ALL these people we're talking about can you explain how all these fractured reunions happen? For a fan it's hard to wrap our fandom/brains around. We wanted GnR to reunite – but why leave out Adler/Izzy? We loved that LA Guns got back together – but a couple months later they are already rotating members? We loved that Ratt got back together, but then DiMartini leaves? Warren is a lot of people's favorite "Ratt" member.
The fan thinks "why can't these guys just get together as professionals, record an album, do a tour, rake in the money….why the fuck is there

always drama!!! Can you shed light on that?

Pearl: Being in a band is like being in a marriage and sometimes people just get sick of each other. I know the fans always want the original line-up but as the Stones say "you can't always get what you want" When you get to a certain age you just don't want to deal with the Drama anymore.

14. Have you ever thought about forming a band with Keri Kelly, Billy Sheehan and Mike Terrana? Between you all, you've literally played with every single rock musician that was been born between 1960-1980. Kelly/Terrana have both played on albums for more than 30 different bands. Sheehan is at 16 different bands/artists, but has played with dozens more. What would you call that band?

Pearl: I guess I would call that band The Formerly Ofs.

15. What do you like to do for fun and entertainment that is non-music related?

Pearl: I read, I work out—I try to defy gravity and stay relevant.

16. Did you ever get to spend time with Jani Lane? Can you share your thoughts on him?

Pearl: Nice guy but troubled. Great songwriter. I was touring with LA Guns when he died.

17. Was there any band from back in the day that you thought were going to be huge stars, but for whatever reason, they never made it?

Pearl: The Zeros were very good, and original. I always thought they deserved a shot but maybe they were a little too weird for mainstream America.

18. Of all the projects and bands you've been a part of, which one has been the most fun? And the most satisfying?

Pearl: Doing my own music is always best. How could it not be?

19. What are you plans for the second half of 2018? Is there anything you want us to promote?

Pearl: New record, touring, festivals, travelling---its all good.

http://jizzypearl.com
https://www.facebook.com/jizzy.pearl.7
https://www.facebook.com/Jizzy-Pearls-LoveHate-227540804471525https://twitter.com/jizzypearl13

Joey Allen
Warrant

Picture courtesy of Mr. Allen's official Facebook page.

1. How many of Erik Turner's paintings grace the walls of your house?

Allen: He quit painting long before I could get one, so 0.

2. You, Axl Rose and Izzy Stradlin were all born in Indiana….did you and the GnR boys ever tour together or hang out at all back in the glory days?

Allen: I hung out with Steven a bit. I know Erik used to jam with Izzy prior to GnR and Warrant. We never toured together. Most of those guys, minus Steven Adler who is one of the nicest guys in the world, talk shit on Warrant…so FUCK 'em! :o)

3. What do you think of them having a reunion tour, but not including Izzy and Adler?

Allen: I'm sure they all have their reasons. Too bad for the fans.

4. Louder Harder Faster received pretty positive reviews. Are you surprised that after 30 years in the business, fans are still loving your work?

Allen: We are blessed to be able to continue to work and we work hard to do our best for our fan base.

5. We saw on an "income" website that your reported net income was approximately 54 million dollars…..with that much cash, how come you are still out there grinding it out on the road?

Allen: $54M…LOL…not even close. I do what I do because I enjoy it, not for the money. Anything I have ever done for monetary gain only has always ended in disappointment.

6. Will we ever see a Knightmare II reunion, album and tour?

Allen: Interesting. It would be fun to do a song or two with Rotten Rod and Erik…maybe some day.

7. A lot of people don't know that you graduated from college with a degree in electronic engineering. How come you decided to put that on the back burner and went the music route?

Allen: I was always on the music route, the degree was so that if/when music ever didn't work out I would have a career and could generate income and contribute. It served me well.

8. Speaking of being an intellectual, while on leave from Warrant in the middle 90s you also became a Microsoft Certified Professional and worked for a software company. How was that experience? That must have been a crazy experience for your coworkers and customers – to be working with a bonafide rock star.

Allen: I'm not an intellectual, anyone can go to school. I'm not a rock star, I'm a normal guy. Everything I have ever done with education has served me well in many ways. The MCP+I was fun and a bunch of work. My co-workers had fun with it but the customers were never aware. I have never worn my music career like a badge, I just do what I do and keep a low profile. That is why I don't post personal shit online…for the most part.

9. We couldn't find much information on the Joey Allen Project. But we did find two videos on YouTube. "Holy Mother" is actually a pretty fantastic song. Were you doing the vocals for that group? Can you give us a brief run down on the band and how everything went for you guys?

Allen: That song was written and recorded in Dallas during the "dark years". Ron Oberman, the gentlemen that signed Warrant to Columbia, gave me some money to produce a demo for MCA. I found a singer in Dallas named Stanley Rose and he and I had some fun. I don't remember the bass player but Chopper played drums and owned the studio. Again…those were dark, dark times. The Joey Allen Project was more of a OC Punk vibe. That project will never see the light of day, but it served its purpose.

10. The 1991 tour with Poison apparently came to an end because of backstage conflict between the two bands. Is there a crazy story there? How was your experience with Bret Michaels – we've read extreme opposites about him. Some say he is the friendliest guy ever, while others paint him as an extreme egomaniac.

Allen: No crazy story, just nine large egos on tour. Add some alcohol, no sleep and shit is going to happen sooner or later. Bret has always treated me fairly. He treats Warrant very well when we tour with him. Have you ever been in a band or owned a business with three to four other people? It isn't easy. Not to put words into Bret's mouth but it is a lot easier to tour without any drama.

It took Warrant a long time to get to that point and it is very cool when 4 or 5 guys can all get along and have fun playing some killer music. I wish Bret all the success in the world, he works his ass off for sure. I also love CC, he is one of my closest friends as we live close to one another.

My advise to any fan is to listen to the music and leave the Internet troll(ing) bullshit behind.

11. You guys were actually my first ever concert. I saw you and Danger Danger at The Paramount in Seattle, WA back in......boy, must have been 1988 or 1989. You remember me from the audience – front row, long blond hair, rocking out hard?

Allen: I don't even remember that gig. I love the guys in Danger Danger. Andy is a badass player!

12. Great show, by the way. One thing Warrant has NEVER gotten the credit you guys deserve is for your live performances. Obviously the white outfits and Heaven video sort of clouded the vision of casual or non-fans and got you guys lumped in with the "hair band" craze. But live, I always thought you guys were more Van Halen and Aerosmith than a mere hair band.

Allen: Thank you. We just do what we do.

13. You guys toured with everybody from Motley Crue to Poison to Iron Maiden to David Lee Roth. Which band was the craziest group off the stage? One that you guys couldn't keep up with!

Allen: Crue was sober, for the most part, so they took themselves out of the game. Everyone was mostly cool, Maiden was EPIC...I'm a huge fan. I ran into Nicko a few months ago...great guy. We could keep up with most of them but today we are pretty mellow.

14. In 2008 you guys shared a bill with Great White. You played your set, then Great White played.....with Jani Lane handling vocals. Was that weird, awkward, totally cool, etc?

Allen: It was fine. Jani did a great job for them.

15. After several years full of a bit of turmoil – changing band members, canceled tours – how did you guys manage to get past all that to end up releasing what was a really great album: Rockaholic? A lot of bands would have just called it quits, but you guys managed to put out one of the best rock albums of the year.

Allen: Never say die, that is how.

16. We put together a list of the top 1,000 songs and 350 albums of the hair metal / sleaze rock era of 1981-2017. We've got Rockaholic coming in as one of the 150 best albums released over that 26 year period. Our favorite songs: "Snake", "Home" and "Tears in the City". Memories of recording those songs and that great album?

Allen: Working with Keith Olsen was great. The band was coming out of a dark period and it was refreshing to work in a clean environment.

17. On our top 1,000 list, we've got 31 Warrant songs. Besides the obvious ones (Cherry Pie, Down Boys, Heaven) some of the more interesting or underrated songs – in our opinion – are listed below. Can you give us your quick thought or memory on them:

Mr. Rainmaker
Allen: Fun song to play live. I remember cutting the solo with Jimmy Hoyson, the engineer on CP, and Beau Hill not being involved much on that one. We ran into Jimmy last year in Pittsburgh, maybe we will work with him in the future because he really produced CP in my opinion.

Hole In My Wall
Allen: Michael Wagener…DUDESKI! The best time EVER making a record. We did some bizarre shit with talk box on that one. Vocal tracks back through it, guitar through it…just fun. Fun to play live. It is in our current set.

Sad Theresa
Allen: Old school Warrant form the club days. The first solo recorded on DED. Some people really like that song.

Those are the three Warrant songs we felt should have been huge hits!

Allen: Coulda, shoulda…woulda!

18: Can you share your memories or thoughts on the writing/recording/touring process of Dog Eat Dog? We are like a lot of fans/critics in thinking that DED is Warrant's masterpiece. "Machine Gun", "Inside Out", "Hole in My Wall", "Sad Theresa." It's an amazing album.

Allen: Thank you. We had a great time making that one. Everyone stepped up in a big way. That CD and the tour after had that version of the band in top form. It was short lived.

19. How was the experience of hanging with David Coverdale, who is kind of the Godfather of the genre?

Allen: We have played with Whitesnake and Cinderella since I got back in 2004. David is a true gentlemen and the guys in WS have always been cool, especially Reb. I'm closest to Fred Coury from the Cinderella camp. He is the nicest, happiest guy I have ever met. It is fun to hang with him. All the guys in that camp are cool and Tom is a very talented singer/writer.

20: QUICK FIRST THOUGHT:

Jani Lane – talented motherfucker. Truly sad that he is no longer with us.
Erik Turner – Brother from another mother.
Steven Sweet – Brother from another mother.
Jerry Dixon – Brother from another mother.
Robert Mason – Brother from another mother.
Dokken or Ratt? – Shit…making me choose? I'll take Ratten or DATT. Love both bands.
LA Guns or Cinderella? - Cinderella
GnR or Def Leppard? – Def Leppard

Motley Crue or Bon Jovi? - Crue

Skid Row without Sebastian Bach – They sound fucking killer today, and no fucking drama in their camp! Love Scotti, Dave, Rachel and Rob. Their new singer is a bad ass.

New GnR album with Slash/Duff or new ACDC album with Axl on vocals? – If I have to take one I'll go with Angus.

Warren DeMartini – I opened for him when he was in Enforcer, I was 15. He's one of the best in the business and the nicest guy you could meet.

George Lynch – Love to listen to George. I remember painting fences while listening to Under Lock and Key…his phrasing is killer and totally original.

CC Deville – Brother from another mother. Very under-rated as a player and writer.

Vita Bratta – Da…Vito…great player.

Keri Kelly – We grew up in the same housing tract. Love Keri, he's a shredder!

Brent Woods – great player!

http://www.warrantrocks.com/
https://www.facebook.com/warrantrocks/
https://twitter.com/warrantrocks

Joey C. Jones

Pictures courtesy of Mr. Jones official Facebook page.

1. What's your favorite venue in Texas to play? And do you have any scheduled upcoming dates?

Jones: Houston has always been my favorite city in Texas to play, but right now my favorite venue is Gas Monkey Live in Dallas. I just did a show there with Lita Ford and it went quite well. No Texas dates at the moment - I am working in a new band member and am going to be recording in May and June.

2. You've lived this amazing life in the rock and roll world. Smoked out Ronnie Dio, best buddies with Jani Lane, lived with CC DeVille and partied with Sam Kinison. Toured and shared the stage with all the greats. Have you ever thought about writing a book? We should collaborate – we'd make millions!

Jones: A lot of friends have told me I have enough stories for a good book. I'm not sure if I've moved enough units to attract a major publisher, but I'm not done yet. I definitely have a good 500 pages of stories!

3. With all those crazy and amazing experiences, what pushes you to keep grinding it out now? Are you still hoping to write that hit song and album or are you doing this to pay the bills or is it just the love of being on stage and rocking out?

Jones: What makes me keep going is, my voice and songwriting continues to get better, my live performances get better every year, and I think I'm still doing a great job of displaying my influences.

4. Jason McMasters (Dangerous Toys) lives in Austin – do you ever hang out or jam with him?

Jones: I've done a couple shows with Dangerous Toys and Broken Teeth, Jason's other band. Jason is a super nice guy and I'm glad to see him still doing it. He is a lifer.

5. We are absolutely obsessed with Summer Song. Can you tell us everything about that tune please. Who wrote it, when, why, thoughts on it, etc.

Jones: In 1987, I was living in Laurel Canyon. I wasn't happy with my songwriting at all. I would spend countless hours listening to K-Earth 101 FM, and they kept saying, "K-Earth 101, playing your favorite summer songs." That song came together in about 10 minutes. There are three recorded versions of that song; I hope that you heard the best version, which was the version I recorded with Rick Nielsen and Robin Zander. It's the version that's on my Best Of Vol. 1, available at demondollrecords.com, along with 20 other gems.

I have played that song at every show I have done since 1987. Thank you for liking it!

6. We've got Summer Song coming in as 5ᵗʰ best song of the 2000s.

Jones: I am very flattered - thank you! You are obviously someone who loves great melodies. I wanted that song to reflect my love of the super hits of the 1970's.

7. We know you released an EP back in the 80s. It seems weird to list these songs like Summer Song as a 2004 release, since they were originally from the 80s. But was that EP an official label release or something you guys put together on your own and sold? Trying to figure out if I should leave it (and Picture Yourself) as a 2004 release from the album Archives???

Jones: You must be talking about the Sweet Savage Archives CD. That was my former bandmate Chris Sheridan who put that out. He didn't ask me about the songs. Summer Song was not a Sweet Savage song. The version he released was basically done live in the studio with zero overdubs. It was simply live. I hate that version. I will gladly send you the real version, featuring myself, Rick Nielsen, and Robin Zander.

8. Not to bring up a sad subject, but Warrant/Jani Lane were our second favorite artist growing up. We were GnR fans, but Warrant was a close second. How did you meet Jani and the band? I read that you and Jani were great friends and spent a lot of time together? Got any fun and cool stories about him?

Jones: Jani and I are both from Ohio, and he used to show up at all the Sweet Savage shows in Hollywood. He would always sing "Fox on the Run" by Sweet with us for the encore.

Jani spent a lot of time at the Pal Joey House in Laurel Canyon. Him and I would jam on the acoustic, drunk as fuck. We came up with brilliant stuff, but it was just in the fun of the moment. A lot of people don't know that Jani was more than a singer-songwriter. He was an excellent guitar player, bass player, drummer, piano player, and he recorded some songs with producer Dito Godwin, who did the Joey C. Jones and the Gloryhounds album, and I feel that those songs were Jani's best work. I don't know why that stuff has not been released - I guess Dito Godwin is holding onto it - but this stuff is just fantastic.

 A lot of people look at Jani as an '80s hair metal guy, but he was so much deeper than that. I did a lot of shows with Jani and Warrant, and there is no doubt in my mind that he loved this business more than anyone I've ever met, and nobody ever worked as hard onstage as Jani. Maybe James Brown, but I can think of no one else. Yes, we double-teamed several girls in the '80s, but we were nice to them and they were into it, because Jani and I have good hearts.

I'm glad to see Warrant out there. Robert is doing a great job filling Jani's shoes.

9. Lots of hair metal fans list Lane as the best songwriter from the genre. Do you think that's an accurate statement?

Jones: He was better than Poison, Bon Jovi, Def Leppard, and Crue and

I'll leave it at that.

10. Could you tell he was going to be a star when watching him perform (before they broke?). Same with Michaels/Poison? Watching them as young bands, was it obvious they were going to be huge?

Jones: Yes - Jani worked the Sunset Strip better than anyone. He was there six nights a week, handing out Warrant flyers, hugging all the girls, shaking all the guys' hands. Poison and Warrant got over because they simply outworked every Sunset Strip band of that era. I never handed out a flyer in my life!

11. Warrant had a lot of hits. Did you have a favorite song or two from them? Our favorite was the underrated "Sad Theresa." Did you like it? Also, we thought Dog Eat Dog was one of the best albums from the genre. Thoughts?

Jones: My favorite stuff I ever heard was the stuff Jani and Dito Godwin recorded. I don't know what is up with it, but it should be made available. I liked everything those guys did, because it goes back to how hard they worked, six nights a week on the Strip. I am more of a British Invasion guy, so none of that '80s stuff impresses me, but I like Warrant.

12. There is a great picture of you, Brett Michaels and Jani Lane just offstage at the Whisky. Do you remember what song they sang with you guys onstage?

Jones: We did "Fox on the Run" by Sweet and "Rock n Roll" by Zeppelin.

13. Was Brett Michaels already wearing a wig back then? What was he like back in the day?

Jones: Bret has always been a nice guy. I've always been friends with all four Poison guys. They have always been very kind to me, so I'm always going to say nice things about them.

14. Why do you think a band like Poison made it and you guys didn't? I only ask as you and Brett were friends. You were 10 times better of a

singer! You guys were friends with all the current bands, had support
from people like Dana Strum and Riki Rachtman. And you had some
great songs. What was the main reason – in your view – that Sweet
Savage didn't break out huge?

Jones: Because those guys kissed everyone's ass, hung out on the Strip
seven nights a week, handed out flyers at every show at the Forum. Sweet
Savage was offered a deal on Enigma Records a few months before
Poison signed it. We didn't take it because it wasn't a good deal; Poison
signed it, and the rest was history.

15. Honest question….who got more trim back then? You, Jani or
Brett!!!

Jones: Everybody was a rock star back in those days. It's hard to tell
who got the most women. I never counted, but I made sure I was nice to
every one of them and never did anything they were not up for. I would
say I had more in those days than the other two, though!

16. So what's it like playing now with all the same bands you used to
share the stage with back in the 80s? Just last year you played with
Faster Pussycat, Lita Ford, LA Guns, Pretty Boy Floyd, Y&T, Enuff
Z'Nuff. Is back stage and the after-party show a lot different now with
those bands than it was in 1986? What's the biggest difference?

Jones: The biggest difference is, the rooms are a hell of a lot smaller!
But every band from that era is simply thrilled to still be working and
getting attention.

17. How cool was the New Year's Eve show at the Whisky last year? I
suspect it was sold out. Did it feel like 1985 all over again? How did it
feel to play the Strip again to a sold out crowd?

Jones: It's always wonderful to play the Strip. Yes, the show was sold
out six months prior to the event. My bandmates and I did a really good
job, and I will be there again New Year's Eve 2018-19 - it's already
booked. This time, I may wear a dress.

18. I have to ask about your time with C.C. DeVille. Is it true you lived with him? How crazy were those nights? What was a typical evening like? You guys hung out, ate Pizza and rented Blockbuster Video movies?
You also mentioned that Sam Kinison would often come by. Onstage, both those guys seem to be dudes that went 150 miles per hour at all times. What were they like out of the spotlight?

Jones: After the MTV Video Awards in 1991, when Poison train wrecked "Unskinny Bop" CC called me at 2:00 AM and said he'd leave Poison if I did a band with him. I told him I'd show up at his house to write songs.

Our original lineup was legendary drummer Carmine Appice, Deep Purple/Dio bassist Jimmy Bain, CC, and myself. CC didn't have any songs written, so those guys learned some of my stuff. Unfortunately, CC and I were not at our best in those days, so Carmine and Jimmy left. CC grabbed Adam Hamilton and Chris Torok.

It was hard to concentrate on songwriting and rehearsing, because it was a nonstop party at that house. People passed out everywhere, and every sex, drug, and rock 'n' roll cliché imaginable. Sam Kinison was going through a divorce at that time. Sam lived close to CC, so to avoid going to jail, he just stayed at CC's for weeks on end.

Sam was always in character. His energy was amazing. Of course, it was aided by all the drugs that was going on. I used to have Sam call my friends all over the country at 3 or four AM and just tear them apart. My friends are still bragging about being shredded by Sam. Sam was a misunderstood guy. He was caught up in his own glory. He actually cried on my shoulder a couple times when everyone had passed out but him and I. I love him and miss him very much, and was lucky to know him. My comedy actually cracked him up constantly! God bless you, Sam.

19. How come the C.C. DeVille Experience didn't take off? It seems like that would have been a pretty cool band.

Jones: I think drugs and chicks are why me and CC didn't blow up. But I got very lucky, because his drummer Adam Hamilton, bass player

Chris Torok, and I formed Joey C. Jones and the Gloryhounds along with the brilliant Les Farrington and Craig Bradford.

The Gloryhounds' CD did well enough that our single, "I Can Wait All Night," was in heavy rotation around the free world, and our video made it to MTV at the height of grunge in 1994. I'm proud to say that the Gloryounds' CD is being reissued with two new tracks.

Check out what Adam Hamilton and Les Farrington have done since 1994. It's fabulous stuff.

20. Is the story about you guys turning down a label offer and them quickly moving to Poison a true one? Even with that, how come no label picked you guys up? Great singer, great look, great songs, great live band, friends with all the right music celebs. It seems crazy nobody took a chance with you guys.

Jones: Yes, that's true. We were not the first band that fell through the cracks. Egos, difference in music influences took a toll on that band. But the most fun I've ever had in my life will always be the Sweet Savage days. I think I can still get to heaven, with a little work.

21: What was Riki Rachtman like back in the day? Do you guys ever talk now?

Jones: Riki's enthusiasm in the mid-'80s was amazing. We had a lot of fun together. I ran into him at the Green Room in Dallas a couple years ago, and he didn't want to reminisce at all. He acted bitter, and I don't understand why. He did a great job co-managing Sweet Savage.

22. Riki told us to ask you about Sin City!

Jones: When I first moved to L.A., I immediately made friends with some high rollers, like I was supposed to. We went to Vegas. My friends were rich, I had $4,000 cash in my pocket. I put it all on one roll of the dice, and lost. But I'm glad that I did it. I still got raging drunk and left with the prettiest girls in the casino, but they had to buy my breakfast!

23. Dana Strum was a pretty big deal in the 80s/90s. We've heard a

couple rumors about him not being the nicest guy in the world. How was your experience with him?

Jones: I've always gotten along with him great, but he is definitely a prick. But I will always be glad to call him a friend.

24. True that Poison opened up for you guys back in the day on the Strip?

Jones: There was a show booked with Jetboy and Poison as our opening acts, but the booker backed out because of the price of the show. Savage was definitely hotter than Poison in those days, and we were better.

25. Besides Warrant and Poison, what other Strip bands were you battling it out against? Is there one band that you are still amazed that they never made it?

Jones: I thought Angora was really good - that was John Corabi's band from Philly. They were having problems getting booked, so I was able to help them out with shows at the Whisky and the Roxy. I love Corabi a lot and to me, the only time Crue ever sounded good was with John.

26. Along with "Summer Song" and "Picture Yourself", we've got I Can Wait All Night" from Joey C. Jones and the Glory Hounds in our top 1,000 songs. What's the story with that one, and what's your favorite song off the album?

Jones:
I recorded "I Can Wait All Night" with Rick Nielsen and Robin Zander. The song is on the Best of JCJ Volume 1. My favorite song off the Glory Hound's album is "The Role You Know So Well."

27. Any chance you are going to get to release the Shock Tu songs that were produced by Rick Nielsen and Robin Zander?
Jones: I have some labels asking about those songs. I will need to do some Pro Tools work - or should I say, a real engineer will need to do

some Pro Tools work before those songs are ready to release. But yes, they are coming soon.

28. _You went to school with Chris and Laine Sheridan – how did you initially meet them? What kind of student were you – popular, jock, loner, troublemaker, etc?_

Jones: Chris and I were skateboard buddies. We used to shred ramps together. Laine and Chris were good students. Their parents were professors, and I was a showoff troublemaker who was a good athlete and was the cockiest punk in the county. And I still am!

29. _So which was a cooler experience? Rob Halford jumping on stage with you and singing a few songs....or smoking out Ronnie James Dio at a house party?_

Jones: They were both equally great because they are the two greatest hard rock singers ever. They were both very, very kind to me and my bandmates. Lucky us! I also went to Halford's house in the Camelback Mountains in Phoenix.

30. _Did you actually try out for the Vinnie Vincent Invasion? If so, did you get to meet Vinnie?_

Jones: I didn't try out. I talked to Vinnie and that was all I needed to know I had absolutely zero interest.

31. _How were the Guns N' Roses guys back then? Axl turned into a bit of an egomaniac in the later days, how was he back in the Strip days?_

Jones: He's always been a terrible live singer. Before GnR, he was in Hollywood Rose. I caught a few shows, and left early, like most of the crowd. It was the A&R guy at Geffen that loved those guys so much. They were not as big on the Strip as Poison and Warrant. They got signed pretty quick, so they didn't have to hand out flyers or crap like that.

Axl tried to get into the dressing room at the Whisky after a Sweet Savage show and I told my brother (our security guy) not to let him in.

32. What do you think of Axl joining ACDC for an album and full tour?

Jones: I haven't been an AC/DC fan since "Highway to Hell," and I have never been a GnR or Axl fan, but if Angus is involved I'm sure it will be good.

33. If a label sent you a multi-million dollar check for an album and tour, which guys would you put in your band? And in your dream world, what band would you go on tour with?

Jones: My favorite bandmates have always been the Glory Hounds guys. I'd give them a call, but Adam Hamilton is way too busy with the likes of Joe Walsh and Brad Paisley. I would buy my way onto the ELO tour. I am known as an '80s guy, but I can't stand '80s music.

34: What's your opinion on bands that continue to tour and put out albums even though they only have one original member left? Is that OK or at some point should they retire the name and start a new band?

Jones: A lot of '80s bands are tarnishing their image by over-touring.

QUICK WORD ASSOCIATION:

Chris Sheridan: Love, class, kindness.
Laine Sheridan: Intelligent.
CC Deville: The most talented guy in Poison.
Jani Lane: One of the most well-rounded musicians from a very non-musical era.
Bret Michaels: Lucky, and a hard worker.
Great White: Major mileage out of boring blues riffs.
Guns N Roses: David Geffen's money.
Kix: Those guys were workers. Regional stars before national stars.

35. Finally.....the songs that top our list; Jungle as the best rock song, Love Song by Tesla as the best power ballad, and Appetite as the best album. Agree, disagree, thoughts?

Jones: I don't like '80s music, so I'm the wrong person to ask! I am a Beatles/ELO/Raspberries/Sweet/Slade/Cheap Trick guy. I don't need anything else.

https://www.facebook.com/joeycrabtreejones

Kristy Majors
Pretty Boy Floyd

Photo courtesy of Mr. Major's official webpage.

__1. Public Enemies has been getting great reviews. I know you put your heart and soul into the record, but were you a little surprised that in 2017 you would win over the critics?__

Majors: Yes. We are the band that people either love or hate. There's no in-betweens and I like it that way.

__2. What was the process behind the album as we hadn't heard anything new from the band for so long. You guys just thought it was time to rock the world with some new PFB?__

Majors: We started working on it about 6-7 years ago. Then we signed with Frontiers Records and that ignited us to make a great record for the fans. It was also time to put out some new music if we were to continue to perform live.

__3. Was it hard or easy – like riding a bike – to jump back in the studio__ *and write and record with Steve Summers again?*

Majors: Oh yeah. Lol. Recording, producing engineering and playing on a album is a battle. After listening to the same songs a hundred times you want to rip your hair out.

4. I saw you guys two winters ago at the Hair Metal Holiday show in Dallas. The band sounded great, vocals were all on point and you guys were easily one of the top bands on the bill. Do you remember that show?

Majors: Thank you. Yes I do. That was a good time. I like playing festivals like that. I think people underestimate PBF live . We are much heavier live !

5. Do ya'll like playing those types of festivals in front of 5,000 fans – but on a bill with numerous other bands. Or do you prefer the up close and personal shows at a seedy club in front of 250 die-hard PFB fans?

Majors: I like both. I'm grateful that we still get to perform in front of people after all these years. It's a blessing.

6. How did the band initially get put together? And how long did it go before you got signed by a label?

Majors: Really? Haven't we covered this question a million times? I think it was 10 shows until we landed our record deal.

7. You've been recognized as one of the most popular bands on the Sunset Strip during the time period you guys played. What bands were your main competition back then? And can you share a crazy story that will blow fan's minds!!!

Majors: I can't say anyone was our competition but we admired Poison, Warrant, LA Guns, Faster Pussycat, etc. We actually broke the attendance record at Gazzarri's set by Van Halen and Warrant .

8. *What bands/musicians inspired you back in the day?*

Majors: Kiss, Alice Cooper, The Sweet, Motley Crue, Gary Glitter and much more.

9. *How come the band initially broke up? You guys had a couple popular videos, a great album, and were a good touring draw. Were you and Steve fighting about who had the better voice!!!*

Majors: No. Haha, that's funny. Steve definitely has the better voice.

10. *How was it playing with Keri Kelli? That guy has literally played with every band in existence.*

Majors: Keri is a great musician and great guy. He's definitely a professional, easy to get along with and drama free. I love working with him.

11. *Sex, Drugs 'N' Rock N Roll is a pretty great album. Heavier than the normal PBF sound and you have a fantastic voice. What's the story behind the album?*

Majors: Thanks again. It's just me having some fun during PBF down time. It's a stress relief to go into the studio and forgot the world for a while.

12. *Same comment and question about Kristy Majors and the Thrill Kills. Great vocals and album. A bit heavier than the solo album and PBF. Kind of a punk-glam vibe.*

Majors: Same answer haha!

13. *What was your favorite Sunset Strip club to play?*

Majors: The whisky! It's legendary.

14. *What band has treated you guys the best over the decades. Any band*

a real nightmare band or musician to work with?

Majors: I never really had a problem with any bands or musicians. We are all in this together and I support music period.

15. You guys toured with Bulletboys, Enuff Z'Nuff and Bang Tango. How was that experience, a lot of different sounds and egos on that tour.

Majors: Never had a problem with anyone despite what people might make up on line. Maybe some minor disagreements that get resolved quickly. I try to always focus on the positive nowadays.

16. Thoughts on Axl joining ACDC and putting out an album and touring together? Would you rather hear a new GnR album or Axl/ACDC album?

Majors: I hope they both put out great albums.

17. On our top 1,000 songs of all time we've got Wild Angeles clocking in as the 17th best ballad of All Time, and Momma Won't Know as the 144nd best rocker of all time (we like it better than I Wanna Be With You). Memories of writing/recording those two songs?

Majors: Awesome. I love "Wild Angels." It's one of my favs off *Leather Boyz.* Your Momma is a great double bass basher. Much heavier live. Both staples in the PBF set.

18. Can you explain the story behind "I Wanna Be With You" to us? In the first part of the song it goes "Don't think I've ever seen you 'round here before, you must be new." But then after the chorus, it's "you really mean a lot to me" and "I've found the girl I've been looking for." How can she mean a lot to you if you literally just met? This is the first time you've talked. Anyway – that's why I always liked Your Momma Won't Know better! Classic lyrical content!!!

Majors: Hmmm. That's analyzing a song way too much lol. I personally hate the lyrics to that song so I'm just gonna pass here.

19. _Back before the debut album was officially released, did you guys have idea it was going to be so huge?_

Majors: I wish it was huge haha but I'm happy being the cult classic we have become.

20. _Frontiers is giving a lot of classic bands a chance to release music, how has your experience been with them? Are they treating you well?_

Majors: Yes. They are amazing. Hopefully we will record any album with them in the near future. Such a great label and people.

21. _And Jani Lane stories?_

Majors: He truly was such a great talent. His lyrics, voice and music is timeless. Especially the ballads.

22. _"Steve is an ungrateful asshole, Period." That's a pretty bold statement! Do you guys just fight like brothers or are you strictly just business partners in real life?_

Majors: Oh that's nothing lol. Steve and I always fight but now we just keep it private. We realized it's a big mistake to involve social media in such nonsense.

23. _If a label gave you a blank check for a 2019 album and tour – what project would you work with (PBF, solo, etc,) and what band would you take on the road with you?_

Majors: Pretty Boy Floyd. I would love to tour with Michael Monroe or Hardcore Superstar.

http://kristymajors.com
http://prettyboyfloydband.com
https://www.facebook.com/kristykmajors

Lanny Cordola
Giuffria, House of Lords, Magdallan

Photo courtesy of Mr. Cordola's official Facebook page.

__1. Let's start out by getting the obviously questions out of the way. You probably get tired of answering this one! Who is a better guitar player – you or Jesse Katsopolis? Any crazy stories you can share from the Full House set?__

Cordola: Jesse is a fine bluegrass picker and has mastered many advanced Greco/Tasmanian finger summersaults-and quite a photogenic chap as well-so edge to Jesse:)

__2. The Peace Through Music project is just an amazing thing. So many rock stars are obsessed with money, mansions, drugs, chasing trim…and you are going to Pakistan to teach underprivileged children how to play guitar/music. What Initially drew you to Peace Through Music?__

Cordola: I went to Pakistan after I met Mark Levine a professor/musician in LA who wrote a book about his travels through such Muslim countries as Lebanon-Egypt-Israel/Palestine and Pakistan. He, in turn, introduced me to the American humanitarian/musician Todd Shea who is based in Pakistan and learned of my interest in cross cultural music collaborations to benefit traumatized and vulnerable kids. In 2010 I began this journey and have been at it ever since.

__3. And then how did Lanny & The Miraculous Love Kids get started and how has the process been? How are you funding this absolutely amazing project?__

Cordola: I began The Miraculous Love Kids in Kabul 2014 after meeting a family who lost two sisters to a suicide bomb attack in Kabul- the intended target was western forces including US troops-one of their sisters showed an interest in the guitar. She is now our top girl with a guitar and is now teaching others how to play. Incredible rewarding most assuredly!

4. Have you encountered any resistance from the foreign government or police agencies? Do the communities support you guys 100% or is there backlash because your Americans coming into their domain? Do you ever fear for your life on your trips?
Has it been easy getting funding for the group? It seems like other musicians would be all over this, are you getting a lot of assistance/interest from other artists? I see contributions from Slash, Bono, Nancy Wilson of Heart and Brian Wilson of the beach boys. That's pretty good star power.

Cordola: We have had incredible support from the kid's families as they are very poor and we help support them and it also keeps them off the dangerous streets and gives them a voice through the music. Support wise a bit…but certainly we could use more.

5. One of the girls you've worked with said she wants to "become the best guitar teacher in the world and instruct other girls." That has to be such an incredible thing for you to hear. You are literally changing young kid's lives and changing the world!

Cordola: It is an immense privilege to witness the girls flourish and discover the deep layers of musical joy and truth.

6. What's next for the project?

Cordola: Next is to maintain and grow steadily our group and expand wherever and however we can.

7. What was Ken Tamplin like in a band setting? A lot of us only know him from his Vocal Academy. How does a guy who can mimic literally all the star vocalists not become a star singer himself?

Cordola: Ken Tamplin is an extremely creative and energetic force. Very open-minded and always up for a challenge.

8. How did a So Cal guitar payer end up with a Bulgarian rock group D 2?

Cordola: For me music has been a glorious journey into many cultures, styles and spirits. Bulgaria just popped up and off I went.

9. Favorite solo album and song? Which represents your talents the most? How would you describe the sounds of your solo albums? Are the male vocals you singing?

Cordola: Difficult to pick one. However *Your Quick Demise* stands out.

10. What is your favorite style of music to play? You've played so many different styles: Christian metal, Jazz, country, blues, rock, Bulgarian rock, melodic rock…..what is your favorite, is there any style you haven't done yet that you hope to do in the future?

Cordola: The style for me now is to continue to go deeper and deeper into the heart of things. The essence - the truth - artists who I glean much from are Leonard Cohen, David Sylvian, Peter Gabriel, Roger Waters, Daniel Lanois, Gene Clark, Mark Knopfler, Lenny Breau, Father John Misty, Steven Wilson, John Prine, Bob Dylan, Bill Frisell, Victor Jara, Talk Talk, John Coltrane.

11. You and Chuck Wright work together a lot. How come the two of you have such a strong connections?

Cordola: Chuck and I share the pursuit of musical excellence- progressive rock and are always up for something new, unique and off the beaten path.

12. I read that you recorded some songs at the studio of former Guns N' Roses guitarist Gilby Clarke. How did you like working with Clarke?

Cordola: Gilby is a very dear friend and musical brother. I really enjoy playing Lost Children by Tom Petty with him. We also played with Nancy Sinatra circa 2003 together.

13. Did you hang out with Brian Tochi in high school?

Cordola: Yes, I spent some time with Brian Tochi in high school. He is a lovely guy.

https://www.facebook.com/lanny.cordola
http://themiraculouslovekids.org

Mark Kendall
Great White

Photo courtesy of Mr. Kendall's official Facebook page.

1. Let's jump in with the question you probably get tired of being asked! How mad were you when George Lynch stole Lisa Baker away from your band?

Kendall: Not very, ha. Actually we weren't looking for a girl singer. It happened quite by accident when our bass player met her at a party and we auditioned her and liked her voice.

2. Sex, drugs and rock N' Roll has been a famous cliché for decades. But so many of these musicians go from being on top of the world, having millions in the bank, unlimited amounts of trim and millions of fans worshiping them to being broke and having a lifetime battling addictions. Is there something that can be done to help combat that?

Kendall: I believe an addict is an addict whether they're musicians or not. You can only hope they get help and start a path of recovery, before it's too late!!

3. Or is there some advice you can give to young up-and-coming musicians?

Kendall: I usually ask them, what are you celebrating, you haven't made it yet? Apart from that I might say I've never seen a heroin addict or a using alcoholic be successful and live happy ever after.

4. Pro sports teams/leagues have people set up to mentor the young draft picks about life once fame hits them. Is that an impossible thing to do for young 21-year-old musicians breaking into the scene?

Kendall: It's hard if you don't believe. When I say that though your stars do have to line up and you do have to receive some luck. It's usually the bands that work the hardest that are the luckiest!

5. You seem to be in a great place in life – what helped you get to this position?

Kendall: My sobriety, and learning what is most important.

6. Have you always been a Christian and how big of a role does that play in your life?

Kendall: I've been going to church since I was 12 years old.
I turned my life over to God completely November 2, 2008.
My way wasn't working, so I decided to start living how HE would like me to live. My life changed in an instant!!

7. What would give you more joy in life over the next twenty years?

Kendall: Spending time with my family and grandson and write the best music of my career!

8. Great White going multi-platinum again and producing a number

one song and album...or watching your grandson hit a home run in a Major League baseball game?

Kendall: That's easy, I'll take the home run!!

9. Alan Niven said you were one of the best blues-based rock guitarists around and how underrated you were as a player. Do you base your success on your parents being accomplished musicians or more so on the drinking water from Loma Linda, which was contaminated by rocket fuel chemicals that were leaked in the area?

Kendall: I got my ear from my mom, dad, and my grandpa.
You have to do something with your ear though. I chose to listen and play music. I was blessed to be able to hear things the way I do. It can be annoying though when I hear notes slightly off the mark...

10. Jani lane ended up filling in for you guys. How did you guys set that up and how cool was it?

Kendall: Same management at the time and he had suggested we give him a go. He came prepared and did well.

11. What's your greatest baseball memory? Any state championships, etc? Were you a fastball guy, a junkball pitcher, control guru? Could you hit?

Kendall: First grand slam at 10 year old. Fastball, curve and change up is what I used.

12. And what do you think of the "travel ball" culture now. When I was a kid, we went to the sandlot and played for hours – every day. But now, parents are putting their kids in travel ball and on elite teams as young as four and five years old. Parents are paying $100 an hour for a hitting coach, strength coach and fielding coach......for their SIX year old......who is playing 100 games a year. OK or too much?

Kendall: I'm glad they're able to play and get off their phones but the money they pay is over the top. I just went to our local girl softball championships because my cousin's daughter is on the team. They were playing total assembled ringers from all over the place. They were like an All Star team. They pay the coaches $400 a month, are forced to train, take batting lessons and drills paying additional money for that. Our girls are just locals, pay $60 a month expenses and our coaches volunteer. We just beat the Southern California Athletics in the Championship finals last Sunday and beat the ringers Saturday too!!

13. How did you and Jack Russell meet? You are this guitar virtuosos, star athlete….and Russell is a great singer, but just about to go to jail for drugs, robbery and shooting somebody. Seems like an odd match-up.

Kendall: It was but we hit it off and both had the same goals. To make it in a rock and roll band making the best music we could...

14. Was Russell just so talented that after he got out of jail you still wanted to form a band with him? His talent outrode his potential red flags?

Kendall: He made mistakes like we all do. He went through rehab in jail and came out ready to rock!! We accepted him with open arms!!

15. Do you still remember the first time you met Alan Niven? What was it about him that ended up being a lifetime friendship and like he was a member of the band?

Kendall: We met him at a gig in Hollywood California. He helped extract our influences, was a great lyricist and we just became close like a family.

16. It's been reported that Axl Rose fired Niven from GnR because he was mad that he was associated with you guys. Any idea why he had a problem with Great White? You guys were clearly more talented than 99% of the other band of the genre. Slash/Duff performed with you guys at the Children of the Night Benefit helping to raise money for abused homeless children. Why did Axl have such a big problem with Great White??? Was he mad that you guys did Wasted Rock Ranger?

Kendall: I've never heard anything about Axl having any problems with

Great White. We got along great with GnR. They were our friends and Axl's brother Stuart worked for us. They had some kind of falling out but it had nothing to do with us!

17. After Russell left, you guys must have had your choice of 1,000s of singers. How come you selected Terry Ilous, who really has a voice that is nothing like Russell. What that a conscious choice (moving away from the Russell style vocals?)

Kendall: Terry was an awesome singer with an incredible range. We weren't looking for another Jack. We were looking for a great singer and Terry fit perfectly. Michael Wagener said it's one of the best singers he's ever recorded. The guy never hits a bad note!

18. What was the most fun tour you've been on? Horrible tour, guys treated you badly, etc? Any that you look back on and say "man, that was horrible. That band treated us so poorly."

Kendall: When we supported big bands most of them wanted us to do well. Like Scorpions encouraged us to play hard and kick maximum ass every night.

Judas Priest again total encouragement. We learned how to treat people with respect from them. There were a couple bands that turned the whole PA down, so we weren't as loud but that was their crew, not the band gating the PA.

19. Memories of the 1999 tour with Ratt, Poison and L.A. Guns? In 1989-1991 that would have been the biggest tour in the United States. How were the crowds, the bands and attitudes, etc. Was it a more humble tour or did guys still have their hair metal god egos?

Kendall: Humble tour, fun and most amphitheaters were sold out.

20. How do you feel about the revolving band members and bands touring with one original member? At some point should a band hang it up and start a new band? Or is it OK for that one last remaining original guy to make a living off the name?

Kendall: As long as there are people in front of the stage, let them enjoy the music! Let the music live. I know some songs get so big people don't even know what band did it. People are at concerts to hear good music. Live and let live.

21. We loved your solo album 2.0 (Two Point Zero). Can you tell us the process behind it? What brought it on, how come that type of music, etc. It's really calm and mellow and relaxing. How was the fan reception?

Kendall: I'm straight ahead rock blues guy. When I write and jam with other people it doesn't sound much like great white, except the guitar. Fans were great and loved the record. It was more for fun because I had never sang on a record before, so I wanted to challenge myself.

22. "Lift Me Up" sounds like a Prince song? Were you a fan?

Kendall: I remember "Party Like It's 1999" but never owned any Prince. He was an excellent guitar player in which he wasn't given much credit for that. That dude could play!!

23. You've got a great voice. Did you ever think about being the singer for Great White?

Kendall: Never!!

24. In 2010, Russell was out and Lane, Ilous and Paul Shortino all filled in. What was the experience like?

Kendall: It was fun! Great guys, all three of them! We were happy when Ilous came on board when Jack couldn't return.

25. How was the experience record Elation compared to the older Great White albums?

Kendall: It was a new chapter in our book which actually gave us a lot of good positive energy and made us very creative!

26. From a non-musician, how does the Monsters of Rock tour work?

Kendall: You get a cabin and come on the cruise and watch maybe 40 or so bands and rock out for 5 days or so!

27. Bands flock to it. But in terms of a regular concert/festival, how is the pay?

Kendall: They pay excellent and run the cruise like experienced pro's!!

28. Do you like being up close and personal with the fans (stuck on a ship)?

Kendall: We mingle with the fans the entire time except when we're on stage. These cruises give us a chance to meet and speak to our fans and we take advantage of it!

29. Do the bands get a special section for themselves, where you can hang out without fans coming. What is like for veterans like you, do you get to hang out with old friends? Even something as silly as eating – do you just go to one of the restaurants like a normal person and sit with fans?

Kendall: We hang out, eat, watch bands play and do everything with the fans!! That's the whole point of the cruise, it's for the fans! We don't hide on the cruises. We hang out with friends and fans the whole time!!

30. Bluez Tone Records – how's it been running your own label?

Kendall: Great, we control everything. It makes it fun!

31. You guys sounded a little more metal on the first albums, then slowly have transitioned to more of a more Led Zeppelin-melodic-rock band....and now are more of a straight forward rock n roll group. Was that by choice, label pressure, etc?

Kendall: We were young and trying to be Priest and Scorpions. When Niven came on board he was able to bring out my influences and just become natural. He helped shape the band in what it became by bringing out our strengths.

32. What caused the split-up with Niven?

Kendall: It wasn't because he wasn't a great manager, we just felt it was time to explore things on our own.

33. It was after the Sail Away album – which we absolutely loved. Were you guys not happy with the sound of it?

Kendall: I loved it!!

34. Afterglow is our favorite GW song, even though it's a cover. Who chose that song, how come, Small Faces fans?

Kendall: Alan Niven. I was a huge Steve Marriot fan and loved the idea!!

35. Don Dokken shares some writing credits on a couple of your albums. How did that take place?

Kendall: Don helped us in our beginnings and introduced us to Niven... Are you guys lifetime buddies? It's odd for a singer to give up songs to another band. On a business side (for those of us not in the business) how does that work?

We're definitely still friends... A lot of bands do an occasional cover song, it's not uncommon to take a song and put your spin on it.

36. Your buddy just calls you up and says "Bro, I've got a song that seems like it would fit with your band".....do you guys have dinner together and then sit down and write together for fun......or is it a business transaction, where you pay a guy X amount of dollars and he gives you a song?

Kendall: Probably dinner or just an idea in passing.

37. You guys did a lot of covers. What was the thought process behind that?

Kendall: They keep the records from getting scratched!

38. And who picked "Once Bitten, Twice Shy"?

Kendall: Izzy Stradlin brought it to Niven and we liked it!

39. What's your favorite Great White album?

Kendall: I liked *Psycho City* and our latest *Full Circle* is real strong. For the time our very first record is good.

40. Which one encompasses the "band" the best?
You saw Van Halen at a house party when you were just in 8th grade. Could you tell that EVH was going to be one of the greatest ever, how was Roth, were the guys cool and hanging with people or had egos set in? I know you are a rock legend, but it still must be a cool feeling to have seen one of the biggest bands in the world playing at that age in a setting like that.

Kendall: I knew it would be Van Halen or Stormer that would get signed if it was gonna happen to anyone. EVH and Jimmy Bates were the two best guitar players in Southern California without a doubt and everyone knew it.

41. You guys toured with Tesla back in the day and also saw them when they were a Dokken cover band!!!.
They weren't one of the Big Guns back in the day, but they are one of the few bands that today can still tour arenas and not just festivals or clubs. How do you explain their sustained success?

Kendall: Tesla cannot headline arenas on their own. I always loved Tesla! They're great guys and work hard, that usually breeds success.

42. When did you become a Christian?

Kendall: Since 12 years old.

43. And how important is your faith in your life?

Kendall: My faith allows me to have a life, so it's very important to me.

44. I saw an interview where you mentioned hanging out with Ron Keel at the Monsters of Rock Tour. How much respect do you have for that guy?

Kendall: Ron has worked very hard his whole career. I have total respect for anyone that dedicates themselves as he has. When I heard his wife had cancer I couldn't start help fast enough!

45. High school students are protesting and holding rallies to guns/etc. What do you think is the solution? We hear a lot of complaining and demands – but not a lot of "real" solutions.

Kendall: Whether you're on the left or right I'm a fan of people that are logical and sensible. To me it would make sense to secure all schools with one entrance with multiple metal detectors and a couple armed security guards. It wouldn't be a huge cost and would keep all guns & knives out of the schools and everyone would be safe. You could open up additional exits at the end of the school day.

Taking certain weapons from responsible people isn't going to stop an unstable person from shooting up a school. You have a kid who's constantly bullied at school and made fun of, then he goes home to a dad that beats him that's an alcoholic, something could snap in that kid's head and then he goes off! You think banning a certain type of gun is gonna stop that kid from getting a gun into a school or somewhere else? I certainly don't.
I say make the schools safe for everyone.

The kids marching should be saying secure our schools and make us safe. Not ban a certain rifle! That would be sensible.

46. Any crazy sunset strip stories you can share from your early days? Was it as crazy as people say?

Kendall: Yes, we were once paid $6 from the Troubadour in Hollywood to a packed house! I remember saying to Jack, "Dude this is going to be a hard way to make a living"....
Then we said fuck it and split a Heineken!

47. Do you remember what band won the Battle Of The Bands contest you were in back in your younger days? Your band came in 4th, Vince Neil's band rock candy came in third. Who was good enough to beat Vince Neil and Mark Kendall?

Kendall: I'm not sure, but they had a badass black singer and did "Tie Your Mother Down" like Satan!! It was worthy of the win. I just remember that singer being spot on!!

48. Final words:

Kendall: Thank you to all the fans around the world. It has been a total blessing to have the opportunity to share our music with you!

We are grateful for your loyalty as fans!

https://www.facebook.com/MarkSKendall
https://twitter.com/MarkKendall_GW
http://officialgreatwhite.com

Mark Knight
Bang Tango

Photo courtesy of Mr. Knight's official webpage.

1. If a label called tomorrow and offered you a million dollars for an album and tour, and you got to choose whatever band you wanted......who gets your first phone call? Gravy, Worry Beads, Bang Tango, Solo band, Bang Tango Redux, Rhino Bucket?

KNIGHT: I'd definitely call the current lineup of Mark Knight & The Unsung Heroes. Wayne Lothian played bass on our latest record. Edward Shemansky played drums on the record. Kyle Stevens and I have played and toured together on and off for over 25 years. These guys are all professional players who I love playing with and would be able to handle going out on the road.

2. What do you prefer – singing/fronting a rock-blues-country-rock band at a seedy club in front of 200 people or playing guitar rocking Someone Like You in front of 25,000 people?

KNIGHT: I loved the music I made with Bang Tango at the time and playing to those crowds. That was an amazing experience. At this point in my life and career, I really prefer the seedy club with 200 people playing the songs that I've written throughout my solo career and really connecting on a more intimate level with the listeners.

3. Did you guys mind getting lumped into the hair metal or hair band genre when Bang Tango seemed like a much heavier band than 99% of the groups from that era? Some musicians embrace the label while others seem to hate the term.

KNIGHT: There was a lot of hair metal and glam happening around us at the time and because of the way we looked, we got slapped with that label, too, but I wasn't a huge fan of that. We honestly tried to distance ourselves from those bands and that label, and I think we did that with our sound, but we got lumped in anyway.

4. How would you rate Love After Death compared to your earlier albums? We actually have it rated higher than the first two albums on our top 300 albums of all time list.

KNIGHT: I personally think Love After Death was our best record and better than the first two studio albums. We were really fine tuning our sound and getting it where we wanted to be with Love After Death.

5. How did the European crowds on tour react to the songs from the album?

KNIGHT: The band was in turmoil during the "Love After Death" tour in Europe so I feel like the audiences didn't really get their money's worth. Joe Leste decided that we should play a bunch of covers and we didn't play much from the record. I recall a crowd in Scotland being very disappointed with us. It sucked because we loved *Love After Death* and wanted to work it, but the band was already starting to fall apart and we just had to get through the tour.

6. It makes no sense to us, can you explain the label's reason for not releasing it and then for the band to break up? You just recorded what was your best album, the band had a signature song on its resume, and you guys were heavy enough to not die along with the Poisons/Firehouses of the world and seemed to be one of the few bands (Guns n Roses, Skid Row) that could move right into the grunge era. How in the hell does the label bail and then you guys end it? To us, it seems like 1994 should have sent you guys to the A-list category – not to being dropped and broken up.

KNIGHT: I think we could have crossed over into the grunge era. We really liked what was happening in Seattle, musically, at the time and our sound was moving in that same direction with *Love After Death*. You know, as far as the label, things were changing at MCA at the time. We spent a good amount of money and time making *Love After Death*. I think maybe MCA thought they invested more money in us then they could get recoup, and it would have cost more money to promote. I think they should have just released it since it was already done, but they did let us have the record to shop to other labels. We spent two years doing that. Music for Nations picked it up in Europe finally. We toured Europe for a couple of weeks and then when we got back, we just kind of disbanded. It was gradual, not just an abrupt break up.

7. How did Mark Knight and the Unsung Heroes come about? Your sound is a big change from the Bang Tango vibe, even though two ex-BT members are in the band.

KNIGHT: I was always interested in venturing into the singer/songwriter direction and singing my own lyrics in addition to composing it. After Bang Tango broke up, I felt I needed to go for it. My style and taste in music was changing and I was not as interested in banging out loud music where no one even hears each other or even cares what the other guy is playing. In fact, I was so over it that in the last couple shows with Bang Tango, I intentionally played a guitar solo out of key to see if my band mates even noticed. No one said anything. That kind of said it all for me. I felt I had outgrown the music and wanted to move on.

I just started writing songs on an acoustic guitar then formed a band around these songs which became Worry Beads. It was a huge learning curve for me in singing and fronting a band and I knew I had a lot of work to do, so I went through a lot of musicians and played out as much as possible. Eventually I realized I was doing the lion's share of the work in Worry Beads from writing all the songs to booking and managing the band. After the making of the Worry Beads record *Iron Spittin' Horse*, I decided to make a solo record which became *Bone Rail Tight*. Throughout those incarnations of different bands, I built up a group of musicians that I liked working with. Kyle Stevens from Bang Tango played guitar with me in Worry Beads. Matt Abts from Gov't Mule played drums on some of *Bone Rail Tight*. From that ever- revolving group of musicians, I built The Unsung Heroes and here we are now.

8. How often do you get calls for Mark Knight from Toolroom Live, who is a DJ and music producer?

KNIGHT: Once in a while on social media I get a few followers who think I'm Mark Knight the DJ. I usually just throw up a post once in a while explaining that I'm not him. If people actually read and followed my posts, they would realize that real quickly on their own, lol.

9. Your old band covered "Only The Young" by Journey for a Hair Metal Covers album. Did you choose that song – were you a big Journey fan growing up?

KNIGHT: I wasn't a huge Journey fan, but I got a call asking me to cover the song for a tribute compilation and I thought, why not? It was just a group of studio musicians that backed me. I didn't play guitar on that and it wasn't my band.

10. What happened with Worry Beads? How come you moved onto the

Mark Knight and The Unsung Heroes? How would you describe your sound?

KNIGHT: As I said, I was doing all the work and it prompted me to move into a more solo or bandleader direction. I touch on a lot of different styles from blues to folk to reggae at times, and even country. I write what I feel and try not to let myself get stuck in a genre box. I would describe my sound as a classic singer/songwriter soulful rock based sound.

11. You seem like kind of an odd fit for a "hair metal" 80s band. A great vocalist, with a blues-country rock- Lynyrd Skynyrd feel…how does he end up in Bang Tango?

KNIGHT: Lol, I didn't end up in Bang Tango…I actually put the band together. I was a hard rock guitarist growing up and I came up on the Sunset Strip scene.

I wanted to be Jimmy Page or Randy Rhodes. I loved Aerosmith and Led Zeppelin so that's what I was after with Bang Tango. I had been in a band called City Slick with Kyle Kyle and we decided to form a new band together. I had grown up with Kyle Stevens and knew he'd be a great fit as a second guitar player. I had a friend in another band who had just auditioned a hundred singers. I asked him for the top two that they didn't pick for their band and that's how we found Joe. Joe knew Tigg Ketler from down in San Diego and he became our drummer. We didn't know when we set out that what we were doing was going to be labeled as hair-metal.

12. We loved the recent Bang Tango documentary. What was the thought process behind doing a band documentary? And were you satisfied with how it turned out?

KNIGHT: I was approached by a fan, Drew Fortier, about being interviewed for the documentary. The band really didn't have anything to do with the development of the project. We just agreed, individually, to participate. I thought the documentary got a lot of information out on the band and I actually liked the way some of it turned out, but I think there were a lot of unnecessary people in it that had nothing to do with the band who were throwing their two cents in, and kind of diluted the message. In the end, I don't believe that the truth about the breakup of the band was told in that story.

13. Bang Tango signed to a label six months after forming. Were those six months spent playing the Sunset Strip? If so, was it really the mountain of decadence that we've heard? Can you share any crazy stories you experienced?

KNIGHT: We actually spent nine months playing any gig and any shithole we could. We didn't pay-to-play and did a lot of jam nights where we would only play three songs. The scene was thriving beyond belief. We were out every night pushing our band and rolling in the streets literally with other bands. We were a gang of dogs with our logo on the back of our leather jackets bar-hopping every night. It was a part of rock and roll history that was so huge and I sometimes can't believe I was a part of it. It just doesn't happen like that anymore. The really crazy stuff happened after we got signed and went to Austin, Texas to make *Psycho Café*!

14. What bands were your main competitors during your few months on the Strip?

KNIGHT: At the time in '88 and '89 there was kind of a new scene developing with a club called the Cat House which was off the strip. There were the bands like Poison and Warrant that owned the Sunset Strip, but this new scene was starting to come on strong with bands like Jetboy, Faster Pussy Cat and Guns N' Roses. We felt we weren't one of those hair bands from the Strip, but we would often get into with bands that would say we weren't "Hollywood" band because some of us were from the San Fernando Valley. I'd get into it with guys that would give us shit for being from the Valley even though they came off a bus from Indiana or somewhere and tried to claim Hollywood as their own. I'm born and raised in Los Angeles, so I had issues with some of these poser band guys straight of the bus. Back then, we weren't just competing for gigs and fans, it was for credibility, too.

15. Read an interview that said you started playing live gigs in Los Angeles when you were just 16 years old. Were you playing guitar

and/or singing? And what style of music were you performing?

KNIGHT: I was in a metal band called Krude Witch when I was 16 and in high school. We opened clubs for Ratt and Wasp. I wasn't singing, just playing guitar. Shortly after that, I formed my own band, Mickey Knight that was named after my dad, and played with them until I quit. That's when I formed City Slick with Kyle Kyle which led into Bang Tango.

16. You guys Toured with LA Guns, Ratt and the BulletBoys. Who was the nicest group of guys you toured with –any bands really help you out – any not so nice or that treated you poorly?

KNIGHT: Most of the bands we toured with were really cool. We got along with all of them. We toured with Bad English which was a super group with members from Journey and the Babys. We were out clubbing after a gig in Canada on night and I bumped into Neal Schon (from Journey.) I told him I really liked the guitars he put out and he goes, "You really like them? Tomorrow at sound check I'll give you one." I was all giddy that night going back to the hotel like, wow. Neal's giving me a guitar tomorrow at sound check. Next day I'm like, "Hey Neal," and he didn't mention a thing about the guitar and completely forget he had mentioned it at all the night before. I guess it's the thought that counts lol.

17. Why do you think Dancin' On Coals didn't do as well as Psycho Café? Wasn't as raw and gritty as Psycho – true, but was that the plan, progression, etc?

KNIGHT: I think at the time we did "Dancin' On Coals," some of us wanted to bring in additional musicians to broaden the sound of the band. We brought strings in, a horn section, background singers and more piano and keys. I think we had the opportunity to do whatever we wanted with the label so we took advantage of it and went big. We changed our producer at the time, so maybe his glossy, more conservative way of mixing kind of lost some of rawness the fans that liked on "Psycho Cafe." I personally love "Dancin' On Coals."

18. The band split up in 1995, but then reformed in 1996. In the

documentary you said Joe called and offered it to you. Did the entire
original band turn it down or did he just offer the gig to you? And did
he ever apologize for missing the wedding?

KNIGHT: In 1996, Joe had formed a whole new incarnation of Bang
Tango without any of the other original members. I'm not sure, but I
think I'm the only one he called up to join that version of the band. I was
already excited about doing my own thing, musically, by then though.
Yes, Joe apologized for not attending my first wedding. I didn't invite
him to my second wedding, but he did send me a gift!

19. Joe did another regroup in 2003 – did they call you?

KNIGHT: I didn't get a call in 2003, but Joe always told me that it was
my band and I could come back any time I wanted. He still says that!

20. BT did the thing a lot of current bands are doing – revolving door of
musicians. Do u thin it cheapens the legacy? There are bands touring
with just one original member. Is it OK to make a living off the name or
at some point should a band call it quits and start with a new band
name?

KNIGHT: The name Bang Tango was pretty well branded, so I guess
Joe continuing to use it isn't the dumbest thing he could have done. I
suppose I could have formed my own Bang Tango as well, but I felt the
integrity of the music the original five of us made would have been
severely tainted.

These bands basically become tribute bands and just cover what the
original band has created. For the fans, I guess it's better than no band at
all. Some of these guys can play the stuff pretty damn well and some not
so well. No one has been able to get the intro to "Someone Like You"
quite right in the last 25 years. I think my answer for this question has
changed throughout the years, but this is how I feel now. Years back, I
would have said that I thought it was ridiculous to go on without the
original band members that made those records.

21. You guys did a one-off reunion show in 2006. How did that come about? How did it go? And was there any talk of reforming and touring/album? There is a lot of misinformation about that show on the Net – can you confirm that it was 2006 and where it was?

KNIGHT: We actually did three reunion shows. One was a tribute to Phil Lyant from Thin Lizzy. We played like three Thin Lizzy songs in like, '96. After that, I'm not sure what year it was, but we did a show in Long Beach opening for Dokken. In 2006, we did the Cat House 20 year reunion show at the Key Club in Hollywood. The crowds were good sized and we were stoked to see that people were still into it.

22. How come only two shows with Bang Tango Redux?

KNIGHT: We only did two Bang Tango Redux shows because the singer was unprepared and didn't have the material down. It was painful.

23. How did you end up collaborating with Vocalist Oni Logan (Lynch Mob) on "Hey Mama? How was he to work with?

KNIGHT: Oni and I have been friends for years and always wanted to collaborate on some music. My wife and I were out having a drink at our local pub and Oni walked in. I had just demoed all the songs for my new record, "Don't Kill the Cat," so I sent them to him. Some time went by and we didn't really get it together and then I wrote one more song that I felt was more suitable for him to sing on with me. I sent "Hey Mama" to him and a couple days later he showed up at the studio ready to sing. We had a blast. He is great dude and a good friend.

24. What 3-4 songs are you most proud of from your illustrious career?

KNIGHT t: I can't pick just a few. Songs are like kids. You don't love one more than another. They all mean so much to me.

25. We read that you enjoy woodwork and painting? Are those your main hobbies outside of your music world career?

KNIGHT: My hobbies are surfing and running. I enjoy the creativity that woodwork and painting afford me, but that's what I do to pay the bills along with music.

26. Who has been your biggest influence for your music career? And what advice would you give to young musicians hoping to make a living as a rocker?

KNIGHT: I have so many influences and musicians that I admire. I'm a big Keith Richards and Tom Petty fan. I love a lot of 70s classic rock. I listen to a lot of newer cats like Jason Isbell, Ryan Adams, John Morley, Hayes Carll and Elliot Smith.

For younger up and coming musicians, I would say continue to write songs. You can only get better. Find the best musicians you can to collaborate with. Practice every day and stay focused on small goals and don't get discouraged. Keep jumping hurdles. Fulfilling small goals will lead you to fulfilling big goals.

27. Final Quick comments:

Guns N Roses: Great first record. The original band had amazing chemistry and captured the raw essence of a real rock and roll band.
Motley Crue: They were a very entertaining band.
Def Leppard: I love the early stuff. Great song writing. Those guys are survivors.
Bon Jovi: Solid, hardworking band with great songs that still stand up today.
Joe Leste: Joe's a brother. We went into battle together.
Someone Like You: It was a great song that could have been bigger, but the promotion team pulled out on it.
Tigg Ketler: Tigg's a soul brother and an awesome, supportive friend. Love the guy.
Kyle Stevens: Kyle's another soul brother. We grow up together and I look at him as a chip off the old block. I've been like his big brother since we were in high school.
The current state of the rock music industry: Respectfully decline to answer!

28. Is there anything you want us to mention….and anything you want us to promote (albums, websites, etc).

KNIGHT: I just released a new record in March with Mark Knight & The Unsung Heroes called "Don't Kill the Cat." It's available for download as well as compact disc on iTunes, Amazon, Bandcamp, CD Baby, Spotify, Pandora. Basically every platform there is. And also on our newly re-launched website www.markknightandtheunsungheroes.com.

I'm also on Facebook as Mark Knight & The Unsung Heroes and on Instagram as @markknightmusic.

https://www.youtube.com/channel/UCPF0SBPBTFOSARvWHl0P8UQ
https://www.facebook.com/MarkKnightMusic

Nicholas Walsh
Slik Toxik, Famous Underground

Picture courtesy of Famous Underground's official Facebook page. Photographer is credited to: Lee-Ann Wylie.

__1. I love that you are a Megadeth fan. Train of Consequences is one of the best metal albums of all time.__

Walsh: I have been a fan of Megadeth ever since the Peace Sells album came out. My friends and I were into many types of metal and didn't care about the Metallica rivalry.

__2. I also love that they released a killer guitar song called Hangar 18. Then a decade later released Return To Hangar – and nobody complained! If Def Leppard released Pour Some More Sugar on Me, fans/critics would tear them apart.__

Walsh: Totally true

3. How did you hook up with Laurie-Anne Green?

Walsh: Actually, with one of my post Slik Toxik bands 'Raised On Mars' we had her old band Jane Doe open up for us. And when I was forming Revolver I had asked her to join as I had dug her playing, personality and work ethic.

4. Revolver played with Motley Crue, Def Leppard and Kid Rock. Crue and Leppard are hall of fame level rock bands. How was it playing with them? How did they treat you guys? I honestly thought you guys were going to be the next Motley Crue.

Walsh: We did some major festival stages with them. I had seen Kid Rock multiple times and partied with him before. Vivian Campbell was a cool guy he actually came side stage to watch us and the Crue, well, they just kept to themselves, even away from each other. LOL

5. Are you a closet Dokken fan? There are a couple Dokken posters on the wall for the Bullet Train video!

Walsh: Closet...NO...Fan...YES.
Always have been. George Lynch is one of my all time favorite lead guitarists. I've always wanted to play with him, he makes his guitar cry.

6. Famous Underground's self-titled debut album was produced with a German label – how did that happen? Favorite songs from the album? We were surprised by how heavy it was. Got great reviews and Bullet Train was a pretty big hit.

Walsh: Our management at the time was based out of Germany and given that metal and rock is still alive and kicking we decided to try our hand with that market. It was great because we received critical acclaim with some of the big publications over there. My roots were always a little heavier then what the music of Slik Toxik may have suggested. I was a fan of some of the earlier progressive and or thrash metal bands back in the day like Mercyful Fate, Queensryche, Fates Warning and of course the likes of Metallica, Priest and Maiden. As for my favorite songs go, it's a tough one. As the writer I like them all for different qualities that they all possess.

7. In 2017, you released a two song Digital 45 online – explain that process. Seems to be the future of music, as albums are not supported that much.

Walsh: Yes you're correct, the idea of buying music is pretty near extinct. That's why the subscription-based model is doing so well. We decided to do the Digital 45 as a way to get something out while we were working on the latest recordings. We are nearly finished recording and mixing our next batch. We have 15 new ones in the bag. As to how we are going to release them, we are not sure yet.

8. "Corrupted" is a great song. But that's what we expect from you! What's the story with the Peace Sells / Get Up, Stand Up mashup…very interesting tune.

Walsh: Well, we did a cover of "Peace Sells" and I just wanted to do something interesting and fresh with it and that idea popped into my head. When I orchestrated it with the band it seemed to work great! Even the lyrical content seemed to fit well. Both Dave Mustaine and Bob Marley are/were very politically driven and that is right up my alley too. I don't like to spread a personal agenda but feel the need to open people's eyes and ears to their surroundings.

9. How did you hook up with Japanese cartoon Beywarriors? How does a Canadian metal singer get hooked up with a Japanese cartoon?

Walsh: I do some work with a couple of writers that do film and television and it just so happened that that version of the theme with me on it was the one that the company picked. I even have a signature scream at the end of the track.

10. What was the big difference between touring in America compared to Canada?

Walsh: Well Canada is a big country with a small population, therefore we had a much longer haul in between shows. The fans are equally as into it but in the U.S. we would be at our next gig in a few hours not a day.

11. Were you fans of Harem Scarem, Killer Dwarfs, Kick Axe and Rush? Thoughts on Nickelback? They've reportedly sold 30 million albums world wide...but everybody claims to hate them!

Walsh: Oh yeah, although I am Canadian I was never a Rush guy. Don't get me wrong I totally respect the hell out of them it just wasn't my thing. The others you asked about were bands I liked and got to be friends with. As for Nickelback...once again I respect them and do like some of their songs. If it is in fact 30 million albums sold (I tend to think it's more but...) obviously they are doing something right.

12. This pay-to-play and buy-ons thing really sucks. I don't know how young bands can afford to go that route. It should be about talent and drawing power – not if your band can cough over hundreds of dollars.

Walsh: I agree, but once again with the fact that nobody buys music anymore bands are forced to create new revenue streams and that seems to be one of them.

13. Have you guys ever thought about doing the US festival circuit, where they get 8-20 bands on a weekend bill, or something like the Monsters of Rock Cruise where they have about 30 bands on a week long cruise? Do they do things like that in Canada?

Walsh: There isn't that type of show in Canada. As for would we do it? Probably if asked.

14. You've done a lot of cool projects, but the Metal On Ice is one of the more interesting ones. How was that experience?

Walsh: It was great! Sean Kelly and I go way back to the early Revolver days. When I was asked to be a part of it I was flattered that he revered me as an influence as much as some of the others on the project that I grew up a fan of. We ended up writing a theme song for the book and I did a Kick Axe song on the CD instead of re-doing a SLIK TOXIK tune. When and if time permits, I would work with Sean any day.

15. *How much fun was the celebration honoring Moxy? Were you a big fan of them growing up?*

Walsh: I always knew of them but didn't know the material. When I was asked to do it and heard the stuff I immediately fell in love with the songs.

16. *Slik Toxik actually toured with Yngwie Malmsteen….did Yngwie ever unleash the fuckin' fury on you? How did he treat you guys on tour?*

Walsh: After a couple of shows in I approached him at sound check to sing a song with him. He accepted and we did his song "You Don't Remember I'll Never Forget", as soon as I started singing he was all smiles, prancing around throwing out picks and swinging his guitar around. After that he was cool with us. We ended up touring with him for almost 2 months.

17. *You guested on Helix's 'Bastard of the Blues' – how did that come about? Are you a big fan of the band?*

Walsh: Yes I was a huge fan when I was a kid. After working with Brian on the Metal On Ice project, he and Sean were working on a new Helix record. They had a song that they felt they could use my range on and Brian Vollmer personally called me up and asked if I would be interested in which I responded 'FUCK YEAH!'

18. *You've covered David Bowie and Led Zeppelin for the Classic Albums Live event. Zepp seems obvious, but how did the Bowie cover arise? Your voice fits his sound and style?*

Walsh: I was asked to do the show by the producer of the series Craig Martin in which I was trying to get someone else the gig and he insisted I was the guy. After I started listening to the Ziggy Stardust album; again, I fell in love with it and was quite surprised as to how well my voice could go there. It was a great show which I would gladly do again.

19. *If you got to do the show again and could pick any band's album to*

cover….who are you choosing?

Walsh: I am going to be doing QUEEN: A Night at the Opera for CAL starting in June. Freddie was one of my all time favs growing up. It will be an honor to sing this one.

20. If you aren't doing something music related what do you enjoy doing for fun and/or relaxation?

Walsh: My family and I are die-hard baseball fans. We go to lots of games here at home to support the Toronto Blue Jays but also when I am on the road and have a day off, I like to catch a game in a different city.

21. Irrelevant had a totally different sound/vibe than Doin' The Nasty. It seemed more serious and not as much fun. Was that a conscious thing or just something that happened organically?

Walsh: A bit of both. We were very pissed off at the turn the industry had taken and were lashing back. We actually had a very 'Doin' The Nastyesque' album that nobody has ever heard.

22. What album captures the true essence or soul of Nick Walsh?

Walsh: Nick at 16 to 20 years old was definitely *Doin' The Nasty*, (some of those songs I had written when I was 18) and the latest unreleased material and Digital 45 from Famous Underground are most definitely the Nick of today.

23. There seems like a divide between the debut ST album and all the rest of your career. Is that just a difference of growing up and maturing?

Walsh: 100%. I have had opportunities to sing with the likes of some 'Hair metal' type bands and just can't get past singing juvenile lyrics. Imagine Gene Simmons singing 'Christine Sixteen' now? HAHA

24. No ass-kissing here for this interview, but I have to tell you that I think we are actually your biggest fans in America! And without a doubt, the biggest Doin' the Nasty supporters in the world. To us, it's

one of the few damn near perfect albums released in the entire "hair metal" era. As you look back to an album you wrote 25 years ago, what are you thoughts on it?

Walsh: First off, Thank You. I would have to say that if it had come out when it was finished which was a year before the release things might have been different for the band. In a bigger sense.

25. For this project, we've compiled a list of the top 1,000 songs and 350 albums of the hair metal / sleaze rock era between 1981-2017. The songs have been broken down to the top 650 rock songs and the top 350 ballads. For reference, we've got Welcome to the Jungle as the top rock song, Love Song by Tesla as the best ballad and Appetite For Destruction as the best overall album.

We've got Doin' The Nasty as the 28th best hair metal album ever released. Ahead of classics like Use Your Illusion from GnR and Cherry Pie from Warrant! Thoughts on that?

Walsh: Appreciate it tons. I absolutely love GnR, Appetite changed my life. But if Use your Illusions was put out as a single album with the best songs it would have been right up there too.

26. Stories behind the songs:

Helluva Time:
Walsh:
When we came up with that one, it was a few riffs started by Rob Bruce and myself, Dave Mercel's lyric was originally called "Killing Time." We then wanted it to be more uplifting and anthem like so we changed it to "Helluva Time." The band then worked as a group hanging around outside of our rehearsal space for a break to transform the lyrical content. That was a group effort.

Sweet Asylum:
Walsh: I remember when that one was conceived musically very well. Myself, Pat and Rob were hanging out and playing our guitars in my parent's basement. That's where a lot of the songs were conceived

By The Fireside:
Walsh: I remember that Kevin Gale had originally came up with the chorus riff first and I felt it sounded a little to much like Madonna's "Live to Tell" riff, so we changed a couple of notes to transform it.
We kicked it around for a while and it was EMI / Capital that wanted us to finish it as they felt we needed a power ballad to the album.

27. Quick Thoughts on:

Axl Rose: Big influence at the time.
Don Dokken: Big Influence at the time.
Tom Keifer: Very talented.
Sebastian Bach – do you get tired of the comparisons? Old friend and foe...LOL...as we both realized, same school and influences will always yield similarities.
James Hetfield: Love Metallica, one of my all time faves
Dave Mustaine: Love Megadeth too
Joe Elliott: Saw them on the Pyromania tour....Awesome!
Vince Neil: Crue was a big part of my youth.
Jani Lane: Very talented. Shame what happened to him.
Brett Michaels: Not much of a Poison fan but can respect what they did for the hair metal genre years later, by exposing bands of that genre of music on their tours IE:. Winger, Slaughter, Dokken, Cinderella.
Russ Graham: Old friend and talent. I used to crank "Dirty Weapons" when it came out. Before SLIK TOXIK were signed, we had the opportunity to support the Dwarfs on multiple occasions.

28. What is in store for you in 2018 and 2019?

Walsh: I am in the process of mixing the new Famous Underground recordings. We have 15 new songs ready to go but are still not sure how we are going to release them.
We haven't decided yet if we are gonna do a digital 45 again, and E.P., full length or shop for a label to support it.
Only time will tell.

https://www.facebook.com/OfficialNicholasWalsh
http://www.famousunderground.tv
https://twitter.com/nicktoxik

Paul Taylor
Winger, Alice Cooper, Steve Perry

Picture courtesy of Mr. Taylor's official Facebook page.

__1.   Let's kick it off with the question you probably get tired of asking, as you must have been asked it a million times: Will we ever get a Stark Raving Mad reunion!!! I would pay money to see that band play live in 2018.__

Taylor: Ha I am still great friends with Jay and Donovan and Eric, but we never have had any talks about doing one of those. But hey, you never know. Would be a total blast!!!

__2. Did Eric Martin have that magical voice then, and could you tell that he was going to end up as being a guy some say had one of the best voices in rock music?__

Taylor: Oh yeah, Eric always sounded amazing and I jumped through big hoops to get him to play with us back then. But it was cool. We had a lot of great times and wrote some cool tunes together.

__3. What is the real Kip Winger like? I've read/saw interviews where he seems like a really nice, humble and cool guy. Then others where he badmouths Metallica or a comment about he'll meet Joe Elliott any day for an acoustic-guitar battle. Without knowing him, some of the comments he makes about other bands make him seem a bit egotistical. So what's the real scoop on him?__

Taylor: You have to get to know Kip, He is very deep and sometimes his social skills aren't the best but he is never trying to be unfriendly, he just

is sometimes really in his own head composing stuff while someone else is trying to get a conversation
out of him LOL. He is like my brother theses days… we have been through a lot together.

4. You've played and toured with some of the best voices in rock music history. Steve Perry, Eric Martin and superstars like Alice Cooper, Sammy Hagar and Aldo Nova…along with Kip! Is there one singer that really crushed it the most in a live setting? Where you just sat back playing your instrument and thought to yourself "holy moly, I'm a part of something really amazing right now."

Taylor: I would have to say working with Steve Perry was the time that I was in awe.. I grew up in S.F. so Journey was a hometown band and I grew up listening and watching them. So to look over on stage and see Steve singing next to me really was a dream
come true.

5. How was it touring and writing with Steve Perry? You share a lot of writing credits on his 1994 album, including the albums biggest hit "You Better Wait."

Taylor: The time I spent with Steve Perry was amazing. It was about three years total. It took us quite awhile to put together the band and write the record. Then we hit the road for about two months. It was amazing and the band was incredible. We spent four months in Vocal Lessons before the tour and this vocal coach got us sounding like we had sampled vocals or tracks running and we didn't, it was all us singing.

6. You were the sole writer on one of Winger's biggest hits: Miles Away, which we have ranked one of best ballads of the hard rock era 1981-2017.

Taylor: I wrote "Miles Away" for my at the time girlfriend Emi Cannon who was one of the Nasty Habits, the singers with Motley.
One time when I was on the road she wanted to break up because I was going to be gone so long …so I wrote it about that.

7. If a promoter/label sent you a blank check and said "pick any singer

*of your choice and we'll finance a 10-city acoustic show"…..which
singer would be your first call and why! (money is no object so you can
literally take anybody you want).*

Taylor: I would love to do a 10-city our with PINK. I just saw her sing
in Chicago and she was incredible!!

8. Keyboards or guitar – which do you like playing better?

Taylor: I probably would pick guitar if I had to make a choice. But one
of the things I have liked about most the bands that I have played in is the
fact that I get to play both.

*9. You and Kip had a great deal touring with the Alice Cooper. What
made you decide to leave a legend and take the chance to start a new
band?*

Taylor: Me and Kip just hit it off writing. During the first year on the
road with Alice, and by the time we were in the second year, we had a
bunch of songs and so Kip said 'I'm gonna quit and go get us a record
deal.' I thought he was nuts quitting, but he
ended up getting us signed. Alice was happy for us and told us to go sell
a lot of records. I ended up going back out with Alice in later years along
with Reb on guitar.

*10. You've had an amazing career. You recorded or played/toured with
some of the biggest bands in the world. Why do you think you aren't
thought of as one of the "gods" of the hard rock world? Aldo Nova
ruled the rock world when you toured with him, that album was golden.
Then the Steve Perry solo album and tour – again, Perry is a legend.
Alice Cooper is a Hall of Fame legend in rock history. You were in a
band with Eric Friggin Martin.
You toured with Tom Keifer, who is amazing. And Winger is one of the
most popular hard rock bands of all time. One of the reasons we are
doing this project is to spotlight guys like yourself. Everybody knows
every second of Nikki Sixx or Sebastian Bach's life. But it's musicians
like you that deserve more of the spotlight and credit for their careers.*

Taylor: Well, being a utility guy like me doesn't put you in the spotlight,

but fortunately has always kept me working with some of the best in the business. And lucky for me I'm quite happy being in the background just getting to write and record and tour with
all the people I grew up idolizing.

11. Now you are a well-known composer for television series. Can you tell us what shows you've written for and what projects you have in the future?

Taylor: I don't usually write songs for a specific TV show. I write for Production Music Companies that just ask me to write a bunch of songs in a bunch of styles. Then they put them in collections that all the music supervisors know to go look through and so they can find what they are looking for with a specific scene or whatever. I did however write the Main Title for Sabrina The Teenage Witch. That I was given instructions on what they wanted and I wrote it and they took it, fortunately, because that song made me a lot of money over the years.

12. And is the writing/creative process a lot different writing for a show as opposed to an album?

Taylor: Yeah the songs I write for TV I just kind of pump out. I don't spend nearly as much time struggling with the lyrics. But I always try to make them good songs.

But I have learned that some of the songs I handed in for TV that I wasn't really wild about have still placed a lot.

13. You also have a passion for photography. What line or genre do you enjoy photographing the most?

Taylor: I haven't done the photography thing in a long time now but every year I tell myself this is the year I'm going to get the cameras back out. But I have been so busy it just hasn't happened yet.

14. Is there any tour that stands out to you as being the most fun or where you had the most creative time? It's amazing to see the acts you've been on the road with. From the ultimate cool guys in ZZ Top to hair metal Slaughter to glam/hard rock legends Kiss.

Taylor: I think my best tour was the first tour with Winger opening for Scorpions. It was just an amazing time in rock and we had singles going up the charts and MTV was playing the crap out of our videos. I was always a huge Scorpions fan so was an amazing time.

15. Did you ever play with or hang out with Warrant and Jani Lane?

Taylor: Yeah, I was at Jani's house warming at the first house he bought. It was a fun party. It was sad losing him. We have played a lot of shows with Warrant. They are good guys and a great band.

http://www.wingertheband.com
https://www.facebook.com/Officialwinger

Paul Laine
The Defiants, Darkhorse, Danger Danger

Photo courtesy of Mr. Laine's official Twitter page.

1. Did you know or spend any time with the boys from Slik Toxik or Killer Dwarfs? Opinions on those two bands?

Laine: The very first show I ever played as solo artist was with Joan Jett in Toronto, at the famed Molson Park, an outdoor festival. Killer Dwarfs were on the bill that day - amazing show!! The lead singer was half acrobat, half animal, full rock star!! Great band.

I never had the fortune to play with Slik Toxik, but they were another great band from the day.

2. Shugaazer – Shift – what's the story with that band and album? "When Ya Gonna Break My Heart" was our favorite song, was it written about somebody specific?

Laine: That song was a co-write with my guitar player, Chris Matheson. It was more personal for him, than it was for me…it was his story. He is a great writer, and would love to hear of your love of what was mainly his song!

Brilliant! Shugaazer was a band that I always wanted to do. Being in Danger Danger was a bit tough for me as I came from being a solo artist into a group. And when that happens, there's a pecking order and a group dynamic. Shugaazer was a way for me to spread my creative desires as a writer again. Our former label boss, Magnus Soderkvist from my D2 era, saw the songs and encouraged me to do the record under his new label at the time. I am eternally grateful to him for recognizing that in me, and getting me back on my own again.

3. How did you get involved with the Anderson-Laine-Readman project?

Laine: I just sang on that as a favor to my then manager, Micheal Raitzen. He managed Andre Anderson's band. In hindsight, I probably should have said no.

4. Darkhorse is a bit of a country-rock mix. Do you think you'll ever record with that band again?

Laine: I have another album completely recorded in the can. I am waiting for some business details to be worked out so I can finish and release.

5. The country rock thing is so different than the hair metal style of Danger Danger. And your solo albums and the Shugaazer/ALR projects fall more into the melodic rock genre. What's the real Paul Laine sound? How would you describe yourself as a singer?

Laine: It's funny…I don't think of myself as a singer really. I think more of myself as an artist. I do what I need to do when I feel the inspiration. If you follow my work, you know that everything comes from the heart…in that moment.

For better or worse, I have never cared about what anybody "wants" me to do…only what I NEED to do. I don't have the choice of what comes out of me. I just hear the music in my head, and it must come out. I must follow this muse until it has completely finished with me. That is to say, I never try… I just do.

As far as singing goes, ever since I can remember, I have sang. It's like breathing to me. I don't know how to describe it, except that its the only thing that I can use to communicate the way I feel, better than anything else I have been given as a human.

6. The Defiants, with two other members of Danger Danger - did you guys just want a break from the DD sound and explore some other styles that wouldn't fit in the DD sound?

Laine: Bruno and I wrote the record truly believing nobody would really care about it. We just wrote for ourselves and had fun with the process. With no expectations, there are no limits. I feel that it is so important to approach every record that you make with your absolute best that you can do in that moment.

The Defiants was a chance for Bruno and I to work together on our own, without having anybody look over our shoulder, and with no preconceived idea of what the record would be. I'm so tired of all of these bands now, that used to have great records, accepting a new record deal and then letting other writers write the record for them because a) they're too lazy, b) too frightened that they can't come up with the goods anymore (in my opinion you should just hang up your career then…) and c) most importantly…you are ripping off your fans when you do this. And you fuck with their own great legacy, by leaving that last thing you did in your career, the worst thing. Please stop doing this.

7. The debut album received great reviews. Favorite song from the album and do you plan to record more music and tour?

Laine: We are currently writing the second Defiants record and already booking shows for 2019. Favorite song from the record….hmmm…

that's a tough one. They're like kids to me...

8. _How's the rock scene in Canada right now? Any great young and up-and-coming bands we should watch out for?_

Laine: Rock in North America is not dead, it's just gone underground...that's how I feel. Isn't it crazy how the one biggest music scene is now the smallest scene? And yet there are still million and millions of fans. It's just not popular in the mainstream media. People still wanna rock though...one day it'll all be back, just in a different form.

9. _From your DD time, any cool stories or memories about the writing/creating/recording during that era of your career?_

Laine: Every time I made a Danger Danger album, I always felt like it was going to be my last. You have to remember, we existed during that whole grunge era and boy band era. Weird times for all of us. The songs I wrote during those years were always meant to be for a new band that I was going to start. And then D2 would get another record deal and I would hand over my songs like "Six Million Dollar Man"... and then start all over writing another album project for myself. Rinse Lather Repeat. My studio memories with D2 were always good...time always ages things into a better story , doesn't it?

10. _What is it like taking over for a popular singer in a successful band? Harder than starting a new band, because you already have a built in fan base and structure. Or more stressful as fans/critics will always compare you to the old singer? Was there a moment where you felt like you won the fans over or that you just immersed yourself and felt like it was your band?_

Laine: Kind of "all of the above." It was hard on me, as people either loved me or hated me, and I understood it. It was a good lesson in humility.

Look..Steve and Bruno and myself are musicians and songwriters first. When we set out to make an album or rehearse for a tour, we knew we had to gel, and we did. I thought we were a good band because we really did care. Whether that mattered to the listening audience, I'll never know.

But we had some EPIC moments on tour!

11. Cockroach is such a fascinating situation. Having the same albums released by both singers. For fans it was a really cool experience. But I imagine as a participant it probably wasn't as fun?

Laine: I never gave it a second thought actually. I try to lead with my heart first. It never bothered my ego at all, and I understood that it was fair to the fans. I'm a fan of lots of bands too… I would want both.

12. You were able to get label interest when you were just a teen. How do you feel about the state of the music industry today? Labels aren't signing bands left and right and giving them 2-3 album deals. Now bands are out there utilizing the internet to release music. Which is cool….but the downside (as a fan) is there isn't a filter to weed out stuff or to "push" a band to release its best work.

Laine: You said it exactly right. Now there is no money to develop bands, which is sad. There is also so much out there at once, on YouTube, ect, that how do you rise above? It's not just about being good anymore. People with their social media skills down, can create quite a following from a different fact than just the music. A good song is a good song, obviously, but if you sing your song, while lighting yourself on fire and doing naked cartwheels down the freeway, chances are you are going to get more attention, for all the wrong reasons. And that, kids, is the state of the music industry.

13. As a songwriter, how do you start a new song? I'm a fiction writer, and I'll just see something a little odd and think "hhmm, wouldn't it be crazy if this happened and then this happened….." and the story almost writes itself. But for a song, how do you start it?

Laine: It's just a feeling I have. Like feeling like there's a storm on the horizon…off in the distance… I know all of that sounds kind of flaky, but It's true. I feel it coming on, and then I just get myself ready to receive it. Writing music is the only truly sacred experience that I have in life.

14. Frontiers is really giving a lot of bands an avenue to release albums. How has it been working with them?

Laine: I hope it's working well for them!!! It's incredible in this day and age to have an old school style label to be able to release your music through. I hope they stick around for a long time.

15. So many bands from that genre are just a revolving door of members. Some tour with only one original member and four completely new dudes. Thoughts on that? At some point should a band just start over with a new name? As a musician, are you cool with that or do you think at some point a band should rename themselves and start over?

Laine: It's more about simple math than anything else. Name = Ticket sales. Plus…look…It's SO hard to keep a band together in this day and age. There's not enough money for most to hang on.

16. Dokken recently reunited for a mini-tour in Japan. GnR reunited. If the money was over-the-top, would you ever think about a small run again with Danger Danger or has that shipped sailed?

Laine: I love the guys, and would happily play any show with them…more for sentimental reasons than financial.

17. Do you and Ted ever run into each other out and about on the music scene? If so, how does that go?

Laine: We do, occasionally. And despite all the Paul versus Ted things that happened out there over the years in social media land, it's always been nice between us two. Ted is a great singer. I have always said that and always will. Is there really anything to talk about besides that? I never focus on the negative. Life is beautiful and short. I only believe in kindness and leaving something behind that was the best I could do in this life.

18. You guys wrote and recorded The Defiants album in separate places. In the old days, a band would get together and spend months in the studio writing and recording. Was it weird or comfortable doing it all on your own and transferring parts back and forth?

Laine: It was sheer bliss. And easy!!

19. Did you ever work with or spend any time with Jani Lane?

Laine: Sadly, I did not. Jani was a great writer. I wish he had gotten more credit for that.

20. What do you have planned for the rest of 2018?

Laine: Writing the new Defiants all summer and hopefully getting Darkhorse 2.0 out as well.

https://www.facebook.com/TheDefiantsRockBand
https://www.facebook.com/paullaineofficial
https://twitter.com/mrpaullaine

P.J. Farley
Trixter

Picture courtesy of Mr. Farley's official Facebook page.

1. Let's get the obvious question out of the way right off the bat. I'm sure you get tired of answering it!!!! In a battle of eye brows, who wins – you or Jerry Dixon?

Farley: Lolol. Jerry and I have actually had this discussion and it's a battle that still goes on. It's like watching two bad pool players play a game, ain't nobody winning anytime soon!

2. Your solo album – Boutique Sound Frames - is off the charts good. Doing research for this project we listened to EVERY album that we could find that fit into the hair metal genre (1981-2017). Thousands of

albums. Which included a lot of side projects from musicians away
from their normal bands. In all honesty – not just kissing your ass –
yours is one of the best. Can you share with us the process of how that
album came about?
Are there any songs from it that you are the most proud of or that you
think captured your essence or vibe the best?

Farley: Wow, that's awesome. Thank you for that!

I Think "You'd Stick Out", "Things We Hold Onto", "Keepin' It All
Together" and "Suckerpunch" are some of my favorites.

The record was a work in progress for many years. I was honestly just
writing and recording for the love of it, had no real focus or intent. I knew
the songs would be heard at some point but wasn't putting any timeframe
or plan along with it. Was very organic.

3. We just listened to some 40Ft Ringo songs on Youtube and again –
holy cow. I don't mean this as an insult, as Trixter obviously carved our
their status in the genre for good reason. But if we are being honest, I
think your work solo album and the 40Ft band far exceeds anything
Trixter did. Hair metal fans might boo me for saying that, but your
hard rock roots and singing…. Bro, you should be a star.

Farley: Again, thank you! I think I (Steve as well) evolved and grew as
songwriters by the time we got to putting 40ft together. Remember we
were literally kids in Trixter. That record has a nice Lil cult following
I've noticed over the years, it's nice to see.

4. While researching info for these interviews, I've seen several guys
with negative comments about Dana Strum. Have you interacted much
with him over your career?

Farley: I've toured with Dana and spent some time with him. He is
interesting to be around. When I first met him I was very young and he
was very seasoned and came off a a lil like a know it all, was somewhat
off putting but he's a strong personality thats all. Lots of great stories for
sure and I do enjoy hanging with him. If you are ever around him, pull up
a chair.

5. _You toured with Warrant early in your career. What was Jani Lane like back then before his addictions took over._

Farley: Speaking of strong personalities lol. Jani was literally a Quiet Riot. Fun to be around but I could always tell he was inside his own head a lot and struggled. He was a brother though and we had some epic times together. Very competitive, very talented and underrated in a big way! One of the best front men in that era as well.

6. _How come you and Steve Brown have remained so close after your Trixter days? And when did the two of you first hook up?_

Farley: Steve and I met when I was playing in another band early on(I was 14yrs old) and I guess he just knew I was the right fit for Trixter. We've always shared the same drive,ambition and humor so I thinks thats been the glue to our brotherhood and bond. You dont come across many friendships like that in a lifetime and I cherish it.

7. _Rank these singers/voices in order: Pete Loran, Steve Brown, Eric Martin, Lita Ford, P.J. Farley?_

Farley: Seriously??   Whats next? Which one of my kids is my favorite?? lolol. Not to puss out or anything but thats too hard, the only thing I DO know is that Sir E Martin is in the #1 position and would probably sit comfortably there regardless of who else is on the list.

8. _What prompted the Trixter comeback in 2007 and then another return with New Audio Machine in 2012?_

Farley: Steve was the motivating factor behind the "comeback". He started talking to our now booking agent and really wanted to get out and have some fun. Frontiers Records provoked the records. They asked us to do it at a good time, we'd been touring for about two years and felt we were in a good place so we agreed. Although I never would have thought of doing a record I'm glad we did, let alone two.

9. _We really loved "The Coolest Thing." Brown co-wrote it with Bobby August….who is that?_

Farley: I love that song too! Bobby is the guy that took over for me in Stereo Fallout (mine and Steve's band after 40ft Ringo) when I had to leave the band to tour with RA. That song was written for the Fallout.

10. Human Era was also a pretty strong album. How was the process of writing/recording that one? Our favorite song from it is "Rock to the Edge of the Night" (which we also think is the fifth best Trixter song of all time!)
The music world is a fascinating beast. Those two albums are just as good, if not better, than your first two. But those first two sold a million copies and made you guys superstars. While the last two probably didn't go Gold. As an artist, how does that make you feel?

Farley: Steve had a handful of songs, some finished, some half finished. We started with those and then continued writing from there. I would put some finishing touches to some of those tunes and also would send him ideas that I had, etc - a typical process for us. Then we tracked everything at his house except for vocals which Pete did at his house. As far as the business and success of the records...eh, we went into those records fully knowing that they would not bring us new levels of financial freedom or stardom lol. We just had fun writing and recording and producing something for anyone paying attention.

11. Do you think rock albums will ever become a "thing" again? I might be in the minority, but I miss the days when we fans PAID artists for their creative work. I liked buying an album and supporting my favorite bands – as opposed to what the internet did to the music world, where people just take band's music for free.

Fans love getting all this music for free. But they don't connect the dots and realize that their "free" music has virtually killed them getting new music from their favorite bands. Bands use to release albums every year or every other year. Now, major bands go on a 5-6 year cycle between albums. Hell, the Rolling Stones released more than 50 albums. Some years they would put out TWO albums the same year. I would much rather pay for albums and get new music from my favorite bands every year.

Farley: The system is broke and needs to be fixed for sure. I understand that music is more accessible and we need to adapt but we need to find a way to be paid for it haha. Music is just as powerful and meaningful to the listener and the listener wants his or her favorite artist to keep producing music but these days it means we have to take our time, our MONEY, and effort to put product out there. Essentially working full time for free. Oh, and then we have to sell it ourselves too AND promote it ourselves. I think it will get fixed but it's a real struggle to remain productive. In the meantime go support your favorite bands when they come to town!!!

12. We did a top 1,000 songs of all time list – broken down to 650 rockers and 350 ballads. The three highest ranked songs are: One in a Million…..Give it to Me Good…..As the Candle Burns.

Thoughts/memories/etc on those three brilliant tunes?

Farley: Awesome!!

One in a Million: One of the last songs written before we got signed.

Give it to Me Good: Knew it was gonna change our lives the minute it was finished. Was just different from anything out at that time, as was the video.

Candle: Bought my first fretless bass just for that song and had a blast writing that bass line.

13. How great was 1991 for you? Number one song on MTV, album goes gold and makes the Billboard top 40, toured with Poison, Scorpions, Warrant, FireHouse. All at just 19 years old. You must have been on top of the world.

Farley: Yeah I think you nailed it on the head, it ain't hard to imagine how I felt. I was 19 and (somewhat) on top of the world for a hot minute with my best friends. I had nothing to do or pay for...just living on a bus playing for thousands of people a night hanging with my heroes.

14. At that point, did you realize how fleeting fame was going to be?

Along came grunge and MCA just started dropping every band they represented.

Farley: We were pretty realistic from the jump, we always knew there was trap door on cloud nine! our saying was "we're just happy to be here."

15. Between Trixter, Poison, Warrant and FireHouse.....which band got the most trim?

Farley: Poison of course had the chicks, no contest.

16. Touring with Kiss must have been a blast. Those guys are legends. *But in retrospect, maybe it was showcasing you guys to the wrong audience. A Bon Jovi or Def Leppard tour probably would have been better for your career.*

Farley: We didnt care, we weren't gonna say no to our heros and Bon Jovi and Lep were on opposite touring cycles with us otherwise we would have toured with both. Also, we could say the same for touring with the Scorpions but it was a challenge that we gladly accepted. Nothing more gratifying than coming out to people sitting and leaving them standing!

17. VH1 ranked you guys as the 29th best hair band...does that seem about the right spot to you? That's a pretty good ranking considering you really only had two full length albums during The Day.

Farley: Oh hell yeah, just glad to be acknowledged.

18. You shared a stage with Dokken in 2009. How much different was the vibe, the backstage scene, the chicks different in 2009 than your 1991 shows?

Farley: Everything was/is exactly the same. Don goes right into telling us stories and there are no chicks there for Dokken lol. Uncle Don is the best, he's another one that gets a bad rap and deserves it a lot of the time but he's always been great to us and I love playing and hangin with him!

19. You guys are one of the very select few bands from that hair metal era to have stuck with your core group lineup. What made your foursome so special and able to do that?

Farley: I think because we grew up together, Trixter wasn't a band that got members from an ad in the music paper or anything, it started with legit friendships first. Nowadays life gets in the way and we have other obligations but I think we have something rare and I'm proud of it.

20. What do you think of bands like LA Guns, Ratt, GnR, etc that have stayed touring and putting out albums, but with a revolving door of musicians. Some of those bands have had two versions touring at once and have had 40 different band members. Do you think that's OK – guys just making a living. Or do you think once it's down to one original member and four brand new guys, maybe it would be better to just start a new band?

Farley: Ya know it's a tough question, guys gotta make a living and depending on how some bands formed there could be a lack of brotherhood so I can see how bands want to carry on. I for one am a fan of seeing the guys I vision as the band, I wanna see the original guys I saw in the video and in the magazines if possible.

21. RA is quite the musical change from Trixter. How did you get involved with those guys? And any future plans to record and/or tour?

Farley: The singer had reached out just before they got signed to Universal and he wanted to me to do some shows and essentially joined the band. But I had a lot invested with 40ft Ringo at the time and just couldnt leave. About eight months later he called again while on tour with Stone Sour and Powerman 5000 and had just fired his bass player, so I flew out the next day. I didn't know it then but that led to being in the band for the rest of its existence (five records and 10 years). No plans at the moment with them, but I'm always open to it. The singer has a lot going on in LA producing, etc, so I'm not sure if/when we will do anything.

22. How was the experience of playing and touring with Lita Ford? Was that before all the craziness started with her and Jim Gillette? Did you learn anything on that tour?

Farley: It was about a year before she left him. Jim was the guy I dealt with in the beginning. It was great working with someone of her stature and history. What I did learn was how much I can multitask because about a year or so in, I became her MD and Tour Manager so that was a fun challenge.

23. How did you get picked to perform with Jim Breuer at his residency? He is known for his spot-on impressions of metal singers – is that what you are doing as his band? How have the shows been so far?

Farley: Steve has been friends with Jim for awhile now and he had called him to put together a band for this year. This residency is basically developing a show that we will eventually take on the road and to other states for residencies. Its sooooo much fun! He really is one of the funniest guys out there, not to mention one of the best storytellers.

24. Another really interesting project for you and Steve was playing with the legendary Eric Martin. How did that come about? That guy has a magical voice.

Farley: We have known Eric since 1991. Last year he had a Japan tour booked that he needed a band for so he asked us to play with him. That was the seed because Japanese promoters and fans caught wind of it and we were asked to incorporate some Triter material into the show. From there it was a free for all. We did everything from Mr. Big and Eric's solo stuff to Trixter, as well as a 40ft Ringo tune and one of my solo tunes. It's very easy going and FUN!!

25. Any pressure knowing you were essentially replacing Billy Sheehan, who might be the best bass player of our generation (no offense!).

Farley: HaHa, replacing?? that term never entered my mind but I did step up my game in order to somewhat remotely come close to doing his parts justice (which is always a work in progress lol). No doubt an honor to play those songs and show my respect and admiration for Billy, I've been a fan of his since I saw him play with Talas in I think 87. The Japan tour with Eric was more about obscure pop Mr. Big tunes and less of the shred stuff but as we have brought it to the states we have included all the fun crazy stuff so its been a nice challenge.

26. Mr. Big has always been huge in Japan. Were those shows crazy like back in the old days?

Farley: Ya know, they were. It was actually amazing because Trixer hadn't been to Japan since 1994 and we met so many people last year that were actually at those 94' shows! Was soo cool to see. Eric and Mr. Big are absolutely a "BIG" deal over there so the shows were great.

27. What does 2018 and 2019 have in store for P.J. Farley?

Farley: I'm working on some new solo material, Breuer gigs all year, some more Eric Martin gigs. Maybe Trixter can fire back up again at some point. I love playing with different people so I'm down for anything really.

https://www.facebook.com/trixterrocks
https://www.facebook.com/pj.farley.52
https://twitter.com/Pjfarley1

Bruno Ravel
Danger Danger

Photo courtesy of Mr. Ravel's official Facebook.

1. The one question you must get sick of being asked! Did Ted Poley quit the band because he was intimidated by your vocals on Cherry Cherry?

Ravel: Could there be any other reason? I'd quit singing too if I heard "Cherry Cherry!" =]

2. We all know about the craziness of the Sunset Strip. What was the East Coast scene like for hair metal bands back when you guys were breaking out? Was there a "strip" type area and scene?

Ravel: There wasn't a "strip" type scene here, but there was a very active club scene, and a lot of bands trying to land a deal.

3. Is there a band you guys played with or that you saw in their early days that you were sure would make it – but they never did?

Ravel: Not one.

4. What is your favorite kind of pizza? And what cities have the best – and worst – pizza?

Ravel: Don't really have a favorite, love all styles, if they're made properly! With the pizza craze that has been going on in the past 10 years, it'd be pretty hard not to find a good pizza anywhere in the U.S. But if I have to choose the best, the obvious contenders are NY, Chicago, Philadelphia, Boston, Detroit and San Francisco. I couldn't tell you which ones are the worst, but they're out there!

5. You are an extremely talented and versatile musician. If you could only be remembered for one thing, which would it be – or which avenue are you most proud of? Writing, singing, guitar, bass, producing?

Ravel: Thanks! If I had to choose just one, it'd be as a producer/writer.

6. How is Low Dice Records doing for you? How is the experience of running your own label?

Ravel: It's doing ok. There really was no "experience" running the label. It came out of necessity. In '95 when Danger Danger was scrambling to survive, and we "took a left" musically, we formed Low Dice in order to release *Dawn*. Believe me, we would have much rather released our records on a major, but by then the music scene was already bad, and we had no choice but to release it ourselves. It took us a year or so to figure things out but when we finally did, things ran pretty smoothly.

7. Which question do you get more annoyed by: how did you and Steve first meet, how come Ted Poley got fired, or questions about Bang Bang and Naughty Naughty?

Ravel: Definitely Bang Bang/Naughty Naughty!!

8. How has The Defiants experience been compared to work in your past bands? Has your age and experience made the "band" process any easier?

Ravel: The Defiants has been the best, easiest, hassle free experience ever, and yes, being older and wiser has made it possible, because we've rid ourselves of all the issues that cause band turmoil, and just focus on the objective at hand.

9. The debut album was recorded with the artists in different cities. How was that experience compared to the old days, when a band would hole up for a month in a studio?

Ravel: In a perfect world, I would have much rather been together holed in a studio, but trying to record a record within a very tight budget made that impossible. Having said that, using the technology that is present, like remote recording software, FaceTime, WeTransfer, etc, etc made it a really fun enjoyable process.

10. What did you think about Tony Harnell's time in Skid Row? It's understandable why they might not want to work with Bach anymore. But it's almost an impossible position for a singer to fill.

Ravel: I kinda knew it wouldn't work, but was hoping it would, for their sake.

11. Danger Danger reunited for a tour a couple years ago. How was that? You guys must still get offered to do festivals and shows – all the 80s/90s hair metal bands are doing it. Any chance you guys would do that if the money was right?

Ravel: Danger Danger is in a good place right now. We only surface when there is a good solid offer for a good show. We're not the kind of band that is going to rough it out in the clubs unless it makes sense financially and fits within our schedules.

12. What do you feel about the bands that are still touring with only one or two original members and that have had a revolving door of members? It's OK as guys have to make a living or at some point, the band name should be retired and a new and should be started?

Ravel: That's a tough question. I'll just say, to each his own on that one. All bands have to figure out what is best for them. It's not for me to say.

13. If Michael Bolton called you tonight and offered you a year long gig with his band…..what do you say?

Ravel: Ha! I'd definitely consider it!

14. Do you think it was grunge that killed the hair metal era or more of an oversaturation of "copycat" hair bands? Or a combination of both?

Ravel: A lot of things killed hair metal, but the main thing was mediocrity, and over saturation. Too many bands out there, and a shit ton of bad music created the need for something different…grunge.

15. Do you see any way that normal ands can start making money from albums or singles again? We grew up in a time where bands put out albums every year or every other year. Now, if lucky, bands put out an album every five years. It sucks as a fan.

Ravel: As for your question regarding new bands making money from albums and singles? Well, the whole business model for music has changed. It's now streaming and virtual product, YouTube, etc, etc. The old business model is gone.

16. What's the story on you and West doing backing vocals on the Warrant Cherry Pie album? It seems odd for a band to bring in a bass player and drummer from another band to do backup vocals. Did you get to hang out with Fiona or Bobbie Brown???

Ravel: We are good buds with the Warrant guys. We were between albums, kinda living in LA, writing *Screw It* and just went by the studio to say hi to the guys. They happen to be doing backing vocals that day, and invited us to sing with them. Yes, we've met and hung out with Fiona, and Bobbie Brown. Both very nice…

17. What kind of kid were you in grade school and high school?

Ravel: I was a rebellious kid, but a solid B+ student. Did well on the SAT's too!

18. Also, a friend of mine went to college together and drove from Alaska – through Canada – to Washington in 1989. I bought two albums for the trip – your guy's and Dangerous Toy's debut. What do you think of those guys, did you ever tour or hang out with them?

Ravel: Met those guys a few times over the years. From what I can remember, they were real down home good guys! I Never really connected with their music though.

19. What's the biggest difference working with Poley, Laine, Harnell, Tramp and Bolton?

Ravel: The all have LSS (Lead singer syndrome) in some shape or form. Some of them have it worse than others. There are many, many differences between them. Way too many to get into. Other than our well documented past rift with Ted that is history, I'd say that all of them are good dudes, and I had great times working with all of them.

20. If a label called and offered you several million dollars for an album and tour this year and they let you pick your band, who do you call? Westworld, Defiants, Danger Danger?

Ravel: The Defiants.

21. We read that you have done a lot of "jingles" for some pretty famous organizations – ESPN, Spike, Oxygen, Bravo. How did you get into that? Is it pretty profitable?

Ravel: I got into it out of the necessity to work, and create in the mid '90's. It can be profitable, but in the past few years has since turned into a super cut throat nasty business where you end up selling entire creations for pennies on the dollar, and it's super competitive. It wasn't for me, so I stopped doing it.

22. Whose going to win the NBA title this year?

Ravel: Warriors.

23. Thoughts on Philly upsetting New England in the Super Bowl?

Ravel: I'm a huge Cowboys fan, have been since I was a kid. The Eagles are my most hated team ever. Their fans border on criminal, so I was rooting for NE bad…ugh.

24. Did you and Bill Sheehan ever make-up over the t-shirt/Talas deal?

Ravel: We never did, and I couldn't care less. I'm sure he doesn't even remember it.

25. A lot of stars from the era don't like the term hair metal or hair band. Your thoughts? It's all rock and roll at the end of the day, those titles just help break it down to a specific type and time period of music.

Ravel: Do I wish it wasn't called Hair Metal? Yeah, but it is what it is… whatever!

26. We've compiled a list of the top 1,000 hair metal songs of all time. You guys have 16 songs on the list. I "Still Think About You" is the highest ranked, coming in at #39 on the ballad side. Do you remember writing that tune and was it about a specific girl?

Ravel: Ha! Steve is gonna love this question! Anyone who knows me personally knows that I detest most ballads. There are very few that I can stomach. "I Still Think About You" is one of those that I hate. It's

Steve's baby. He came to me with the song 3/4 written and I filled in the blanks and helped with the arrangement. I'm pretty sure it wasn't about a specific girl, but you'll have to ask him about that.

27. You also scored five albums in our top 200 albums of all time list. Does that seem like a pretty reasonable representation of the band's career?

Ravel: Thank you! I'm not really sure how to answer that, but sure,! I'll take it!

28. We also have a feature on the most underrated writers of the era. Example – people think of Skid Row and automatically think about Sebastian Bach and his magical voice. But Sabo/Bolan actually wrote all the songs.
Same deal with Danger Danger – a lot of people don't know that you and West were the brains/engine behind the band's success. We've got you and West on the list. How does that feel?

Ravel: It always feels good to be recognized for what you do. Thanks!

29. Thoughts on these duos, who also made the list:

Slash/Izzy: Awesome! Sure Axl was the focal point, but without Slash and Izzy… a very different outcome!

Bolan/Sabo: - Kinda the same as Steve and I. Without great material, a singer has nothing.

30. We've chosen Jungle as the #1 rock song, Love Song by Tesla as the #1 ballad, and Appetite as the top album. Thoughts? Agree? If you disagree, who would you have put at #1 on those three lists?

Ravel: Agree with GnR, but strongly disagree with Tesla's Love Song. Great band, but not a fan of that song. If we're talking straight "Hair Metal" here, I'd have gone with maybe *Every Rose* or *I don't Wanna Miss a Thing* or maybe a Bon Jovi ballad. As I said before… for me? Ballads? NO! =]

Mark Gus Scott
Trixter

Photo courtesy of Mr. Scott's personal webpage. Photographer: Rod Dunlon.

1. How did you get involved with the video game The Monkey King? Can you share that story?

Scott: I work with a film production company called Global Star Productions. We have a downloadable video game coming out. The Game is called, **"The Monkey King – The Adventure Begins"** based on the #1 family fantasy, martial arts hit movie out of China. The new game allows users to visualize a three-dimensional space and objects within it. Many, many applications. Nothing like this has ever been done before, particularly on a cell phone! I produced the music and sound effects for the game with Pete Loran. We are very excited about this huge release! I wrote and produced the soundtrack/music for the game and Peter and I produced the Sound Effects for the whole game.

2. You've paid a lot of respect and tribute to our armed forces. Why is it so important to you to support the military?

Scott: Playing for our veterans is something that started a very long time ago. Ever since I was in junior high school I would march in the Memorial Day parade with my high school marching band in my hometown of Paramus New Jersey. At the end of the parade, as the lead trumpet player, I would perform Taps as a salute to our fallen combat soldiers.

On Veterans Day, I would also perform Taps at the infamous George Washington Memorial Park Cemetery to honor fallen veterans. It all started 30 years ago. To me it's just natural to keep doing it. It's one of the few things I feel I an actually offer.

Trixter has always had a soft spot for our military and civil servants. One thing is for sure, when we played a military base on tour, there was no crowd that was more rocking! No crowd that appreciated seeing the show more. It is my honor to serve them. They are some of the people on this earth that get the least respect and deserve the highest. Play for them, I believe it's the least I can do.

3. The Christmas Miracle album is pretty fascinating. Can you share the story behind that? Are you playing all the instruments? Can you explain your association with Hope 4 Kids International. Tell us what its about, what role you play, and why it's important to you?

Scott: To tell you the truth, I really had no advanced plans to record a Christmas album. All the other guys were involved with ancillary projects. I was doing some soundtrack and special effect sound work for a video game called The Monkey King with Pete Loran, the singer for Trixter. Now, when you spend the better part of your day being creative in making sound effects, it will work your brain. So while we were taking a little break, Peter said, "Hey Gus, go get the trumpet from your car and let's see what this thing sounds like." He put up a couple of microphones in his two-story foyer and he recorded me playing for about 15 minutes. Cut. We sat down in the control room and he started to tinker with the sound.

After about five minutes of tinkering, we looked at each other and were surprised at how good it sounded. I had recorded trumpet in the studio in the past, (I actually played trumpet on A song called "Nobody's a Hero" on our second album *Hear!*), but never as a lead voice... always background.

So the question in my mind was, what the hell was I going to do with it?

More recently I was listening to many different versions of the song "Ave

Maria". It came to my attention because it was prominently featured in the TV show The West Wing as well as used in the video promotion of the movie Hitman. Being classically trained, I was always familiar with the song since youth but really starting to embrace it much later. The voices that we typically used in recording the song were very angelic. Lord knows I can't sing. But what the hell would it sound like if I play trumpet on it? So I built a backing track and laid the foundation with Pete. Then came the moment of truth. I had to use the trumpet to sing the vocal line over the backing track. First time ever did something like that. I recorded half the song and immediately told Pete to cut. I had to hear what this thing is gonna sound like. We listened back while Pete tinkered with the controls. After two minutes, we looked at each other and knew we were onto something.

But what the hell was I going to do with it? Pete said I should get some more songs together. I said, "by the time I get all of this material together, it will be Christmas!"

Ah-Haaaaaaaaaaaaaaaaa!!!

That gave me direction. One thing is for sure, there's no shortage of beautiful Christmas songs to put together an album for the greatest time of year with the greatest soundtrack. I played a majority of the instrumentation – Everything on "A Gift From God", "Silent Night (Reprise)", "Symphony for Christmas Eve" and "Little Drummer Boy" (except electric guitar – Pete played it).

100% of the proceeds from Ave Maria will be donated to Hope 4 Kids International. Since 1973, they have been providing aid for children all around the world that have been afflicted in so many ways. They dig wells around the world to bring fresh water to poor villages. They find families for children with lost their parents. They gather sponsors from around the world to support children in need. And 90% of the donations go to the cause. Truly amazing!

The staff at Hope 4 Kids aren't just office workers. They all support kids and sponsor them. They all take the trips to places like you Uganda, Mexico and the Philippines to meet these children and work with them face-to-face. A true investment in the cause. It is one of the most rewarding experiences I've ever been privileged to be involved with. What an amazing feeling to help a child in need and truly make the world a better place. I am truly honored to be their spokesperson.

4. You toured with Warrant early in your career. What was Jani Lane like back then before his addictions took over.

Scott: In the summer of 1991, Trixter had the honor of being a part of the biggest tour of the year with Warrant and Firehouse... otherwise known as the "Blood, Sweat and Beers Tour". I seemed to get friendly with the guys from Warrant, but most notably with Joey Allen and Jani Lane. I believe they were two more extreme individuals, similar to myself.

One thing I found truly amazing about Jani, he could smoke, drink and party all night, and he would be able to get on stage and sing and perform like a true pro, every night! Never complain, never worried, just got up there and kicked their ass every night! It was truly supernatural and amazing to see.

He's the guy that got me started drinking tequila. He would invite me on the Warrant tour bus on overnight drives and on occasion would buy me a hotel room at their hotel even against my insistence that I could pay for my own room.

On occasion he would invite me to take a limo ride with him and share his bottle of tequila with me and we would watch out the windows as the bodies of fans would slam against the car trying to get our attention. It was a very wild time and our dreams of rock-stardom were truly in full bloom.

He was very kind, generous and certainly loved to lead the party! It was very sad for me to see him unhappy later in life. Certainly gone much too soon. He is truly missed.

5. Who were some of the bands you most enjoyed touring with?

Scott: Poison, The Scorpions, Warrant, Firehouse, Stryper, Slaughter, Kiss, Great White, Winger.

6. What prompted the Trixter comeback in 2007 and then another return with New Audio Machine in 2012?

Scott: I remember flying home after leaving the band. I remember thinking to myself, this is a great start for the big come back. I think we all knew that one day we were going to put it back together and have a triumphant return. And that's just what we did.

Our first show back was at Rocklahoma and we literally brought the house down. A major storm struck the festival at the end of our set and literally brought the two side stages collapsing down to the ground. Thank God no one was killed. Sure did generate a lot of buzz though.

After a 13-year vacation, we all got back together to rock once again and enjoy what we love to do best...Play Live and Kick Ass! We got back together and played some big shows in 2008. We did a few outdoor festivals like ROCKLAHOMA, we opened for Poison, the band Boston, Cinderella, Scorpions, and Warrant – Awesome bands – Awesome times!

To do it all over again is such a rare privilege. We continued to play numerous festivals opening for bands like Poison and the band Boston, selling out big shows and playing hard! Selling out a big hometown show in celebration of our triumphant return was most gratifying. Lots of press. Lots of attention. It was nothing short of awesome. We were back with a vengeance!

As far as the new CD *New Audio Machine* goes, Steve Brown (guitarist) had some song ideas that he made demos of and we just started working on a new CD. Then, the weirdest thing happened. The more we worked on it, the better it sounded. It went from demo, to laying drum tracks, then bass, the guitar, vocals, etc..... Every time something else went down in the studio, it just sounded better and better. Putting out our first studio album since our return, *New Audio Machine*, debuted at #56 on iTunes. Trixter was back and we were coming to kick your ass! The idea that we got an opportunity so long ago to do so much was truly a gift from God. To do it all over again, there are no words...

7. We really loved The Coolest Thing. Were you proud of the way that

album came out?

Scott: Absolutely! Love *New Audio Machine*! Love the way it came out! "Coolest Thing" could really be something…..

8. *Human Era is our second favorite Trixter album. It's really great. How in the world does a band from the late 80s put out one of their best albums in 2015?*

Scott: That's a good question! I have a better question, "How do you put out 2 great Albums like that and not tour the shit out of them???" I wish I had a good answer for you.

9. *How is the writing/recording process different now than it was when you guys were young kids back in the day? Our favorite song from it is Rock to the Edge of the Night (which we also think is the fifth best Trixter song of all time!)*

Scott: It is amazing how the recording process has changed so drastically over the past 20 years. Even less now that I'm really thinking about it. The whole record industry has changed along with it as well. In the old days, the record company would give you a bunch of money to go record your record and devote money towards the promotion of that product. Money generated from record sales will go towards recouping the advance to record your album and 50% of the promotional costs.

With the amazing advances in modern technology and the creation of economical computer programs like ProTools, just about anybody can afford to turn their house into a studio. With a good engineer, you could produce your own album for next to nothing. And with the multiple avenues of social media and the Internet, you could promote those songs you make for free and reach a very wide audience.

New Audio Machine and *Human Era* we recorded in this fashion but had distribution through the front tears record label. The best part about the whole process these days is that we have the freedom to do what we want when we want to without the concern of added expense. We got to make the product just the way we wanted to and it was very satisfying and gave us a grade level of pride in our music and the way it came out.

***10. The music world is a fascinating beast. Those two albums are just
as good, if not better, than your first two. But those first two sold a
million copies and made you guys superstars. While the last two
probably didn't go Gold. As an artist, how does that make you feel?***

Scott: Well, there are a few things to consider here. First off, it was a
much different time. MTV truly fueled the success of this band and with
their support back in the day. It truly reaped great rewards.

Not to mention, these days, albums are not selling at the rate of frequency
that they did 20 years ago. That's just a statistical fact. Every
year, more and more people are converting to file sharing and on-demand
services to provide their music. Even in the financial sense, the artist is
not making the same kind of money that they were 20 years ago off
album sales.

You have to understand the business landscape before having a temper-
tantrum over the fact that albums today are not selling like they used to
back in the old days. That's life I guess. Very thankful for the fact that we
do have and the opportunities that we have to play live.

***11. Do you think rock albums will ever become a "thing" again? I
might be in the minority, but I miss the days when we fans PAID artists
for their creative work. I liked buying an album and supporting my
favorite bands – as opposed to what the internet did to the music world,
where people just take band's music for free.***

Scott: It's hard to say where records and album sales will be going in the
future. Quite frankly, I did not see it going in this direction 20
years ago. Did not really give it much thought and when something has
been around for so long you don't think it would ever change. I guess
I give it more thought now.

One thing I do see, is that artists are charging a lot more to go see them
play live. And people are buying! Perhaps that's the trade-off. Artists I
believe will continue to use the Internet in more creative ways ultimately
to get you a live show to increase capital expenditures. VIP experiences
as well truly lead to a successful bottom line.

12. We did a top 1,000 songs of all time list – broken down to 650 rockers and 350 ballads. The three highest ranked Trixter songs are: One in a Million…..Give it to Me Good…..As the Candle Burns.

Thoughts/memories/etc on those three brilliant tunes?

Scott: One thing is for sure, I truly believe that *As the Candle Burns* could be a major cross over commercial hit radio hit! I have a lot of faith in that song and I believe the world, if they heard it, it would truly embrace it on a big scale.

I think that whole album ought to be re-mastered and re-released. As far as *Give It To Me Good* and *One in a Million*, they were both long-running #1 Hits on MTV. Established Trixter as a bonafide international rock sensation.

It truly is one of the greatest things to see your band number one on MTV. Lots of radio play and getting the attention of so many people. Truly was an amazing time.

13. How great was 1991 for you? Number one song on MTV, album goes gold and makes the Billboard top 40, toured with Poison, Scorpions, Warrant, FireHouse. All at just 19 years old. You must have been on top of the world.

Scott: So many of my dreams have come true 100 times over. I always watched my idols play at the Meadowlands Arena in NJ and I would always say, "One day, that's gonna be me!"

In 1991 Trixter got to play there opening for the Scorpions and in 1992 we got to play there opening for the "Hottest Band in the World" Kiss! To play arenas and amphitheaters from coast to coast and around the world? It truly has been a gift from God.

The best thing I can say is "Thank you." To the person reading this right now I say, "Thank YOU!" We would be nothing without YOU! The Fan! The individual that waits in line, that buys the cd. When Mom and Dad tell you to keep it down, you turn it up! It's YOU - That pays too much for parking at the show. That buys the tickets and waits for the show to start. And when the lights go down and the band takes the stage, it's you that can be heard screaming your head off… because you love it. And Damn It… We love it too! We Love You! More than anything we do… We love to play for you!!! Thank you!!!

14. At that point, did you realize how fleeting fame was going to be? Along came grunge and MCA just started dropping every band they represented.

Scott: Very interesting how a series of events led to Trixter disbanding. Please bear in mind, it did not happen overnight exactly. It all started back in 1991. We had three number one videos on MTV. Our third video, "Surrender", was #1 on MTV for two weeks when MTV made a conscious choice to abolish dial MTV and the Top 10 countdown.

We were the last number one video ever to be played on MTV. As a matter fact, we were never played on MTV again. We went from 15 weeks at number one on MTV to no MTV airplay at all. What was even stranger to us was that we were on the road with the Blood, Sweat and Beers Tour (Warrant, Trixter and Firehouse), playing in places like the World Amphitheater in Chicago and selling it out to 33,000 people, but yet we were cut from MTV. It did not make any sense to us whatsoever. But apparently, MTV had a bigger plan in mind. They were going to take what was alternative and make it mainstream and take the mainstream and make it alternative. By 1994, Grunge was in full swing and command the airwaves and bands like Bon Jovi, Def Leppard and yes, Trixter, somewhat fell by the wayside. Subsequently, we lost our record deal, lost our agent, had no management and it was difficult for us to develop a plan to sustain. I quit the band in January 1995. The guys disbanded later that year. I would venture to speculate that there were similar instances in other bands as well. Things are hard enough to succeed when times are good. When times are bad, you better get on the ball.

15. Between Trixter, Poison, Warrant and FireHouse…..which band got the most trim?

Scott: OK, that's got to be one of the best questions I was ever asked! Ha ha Ha ha ha! It's almost like asking someone how much air did you breathe versus someone else. Very difficult to measure particularly in high-volume and over long periods of time. Great question though!

16. Touring with Kiss must have been a blast. Those guys are legends. But in retrospect, maybe it was showcasing you guys to the wrong audience. A Bon Jovi or Def Leppard tour probably would have been better for your career.

Scott: I will agree with you. But, you can't always get what you want. Touring with Kiss was a dream come true however. They were a very big inspiration. Having dinner with Gene Simmons three times a week was pretty awesome!!! Great Tour!

17. VH-1 ranked you guys as the 29th best hair band…does that seem about the right spot to you? That's a pretty good ranking considering you really only had two full length albums during The Day.

Scott: To be in the Top 40 is pretty awesome – and #29 sounds good to me! God Bless VH-1!!!

18. You shared a stage with Dokken in 2009. How much different was the vibe, the backstage scene, the chicks different in 2009 than your 1991 shows!

Scott: It's questions like this that get people in trouble! Haaaaaaaaaaaaa!!!!!!! Things were certainly crazier in the old days.

19. How was Don, he's rumored to be a bit grumpy at times.

Scott: I just hung out with Don last week. Always great to see him. We played a lot of shows together over a long span of time. Great storyteller! He's always nice to me.

20. You guys are one of the very select few bands from that hair metal era to have stuck with your core group lineup. What made your foursome so special and able to do that?

Scott: We grew up together even before becoming band mates. One thing is for sure, we are the same idiots that we were all those years before. I must say, I see differences in all the other bands that we played with back then. Seeing them today, I see a change in the individual members, their attitudes and how seriously they take themselves. I guess we got older and have grown as well. It has been a true honor and pleasure to experience friendship with these people and to see how they have grown as individuals throughout this whole journey. Truly a treasured experience that I hold close to my heart.

21. What do you think of bands like LA Guns, Ratt, GnR, etc that have stayed touring and putting out albums, but with a revolving door of musicians. Some of those bands have had two versions touring at once. Do you think that's OK – guys just making a living. Or do you think once it's down to one original member and four brand new guys, maybe it would be better to just start a new band?

Scott: I believe you have to look at it this way, if the alternative is to not play, then you have to move forward with what you can assemble. If you love it and your bandmate does not or has a problem in some way, then create a lineup that can agree and play. More power to them.

22. You've started hosting rock festivals. What brought that gig on?

Scott: The opportunities are there and I love having fun…. And getting paid for it???? It's a no-brainer!!! If it's Rock and Roll – Bring IT!!

23. What does 2018 and 2019 have in store for you??

Scott: Oh Shit, Got some things cooking….. certainly keep you posted. Going to launch **MyCockRocks.com!!! Really!!!!!**

24. Who do you consider to be the best drummers of the hair metal genre?

Scott: There's too many! Alex Van Halen, Jason Bonham, Robert Sweet, Simon Wright, A.J. Pero, Tico Torrez, Wild Mick Brown, Rod Morganstein…

25. What do you think of Guns N Roses reuniting and touring….but without Steven Adler!

Scott: I am friends with Steven Adler – Love Adler!!! I have no interest in GnR.

26. Are you a fan of Mike Terrana?

Scott: Mike Terrana is bad ass!!!!!

https://markgusscott.com
https://artistecard.com/markgusscott
https://www.facebook.com/trixterrocks

Stacey Blades
Electric Radio Kings, L.A. Guns

Photo courtesy of Mr. Blades' official Facebook page.

1. Can you tell us how Electric Radio Kings were developed? How did you choose the artists to work with?

Blades: Paul Christiana the singer and I have worked together for about four years now. We were the last two artists to work with the late legendary producer Andy Johns (Led Zeppelin, VH, Rod Stewart, Chickenfoot, Rolling Stones) before his untimely death in May of 2013. Paul wanted to do another project and recording session last summer and that's how this new band formed. We recorded in Las Vegas as opposed to Los Angeles.

2. You and Paul Christiana have worked together a lot. What is it about

Paul that hits home with you?

Blades: Paul and I have an amazing songwriting chemistry and great relationship.

3. The two single sounds like a late-80s Van Halen to me. The guitar work sounds like vintage Eddie Van Halen. Am I off base or can you hear that a bit as well? Hearing "Grabbing at a Distant Star" and "Sympathy For Me" has me jonesing for more. Can't wait to hear what the rest of your sound is like.

Blades: Wow interesting take?? Lol. Well I think it's more along the lines of GnR, STP and Foo Fighters. We are really going for a contemporary vibe with the band and our material but it has all the classic elements with a modern vibe.

4. Plans for a nationwide tour? More music videos? Full length album?

Blades: Yes, we are going to start doing more dates nationally this summer and we are going to be recording more material as well as shopping a record deal in the near future. The next single will probably be a killer track called "Round Go Mary" and a video to follow

5. If you could tour ERK with any 2-3 bands, who would you choose to go on the road with?

Blades: STONE TEMPLE PILOTS, FOO FIGHTERS, POP EVIL and GNR!

6. What the hell bro? When we saw that you wrote a book we immediately went to Amazon to purchase it. Part of our project is a ranking system of the top 30 rock books of all time. We pulled it up on amazon and BOOM: Paperback: $2,090.96. Used copies: $151.74. We love you man and are huge fans of your career. You are one of the best guitar players out there. But 2Gs for that book?

Blades: Wow that's nuts lol. I've seen a few used copies for way over priced listings. I took the book off the market a few years ago as I was shopping a new book deal. I guess the original copy is in high demand ;)

7. _Were you friends with fans of the band Slik Toxik? Their debut album Doin' The Nasty is pretty incredible. Were Fraidy Katt and Slik Toxik rivals?_

Blades: No not really, that was so long ago. I really don't remember them that much. There was a melting pot of great bands in Toronto in 90/91 much like L.A. in the late 80's. I do remember hearing of them getting signed when Fraidy Katt was rehearsing one day.

8. _Fraidy Katt.....interesting band name, did you come up with that? You guys sounded a lot like Faster Pussycat!_

Blades: Ya at the time we were really going for that LA Guns, GnR, Pussycat thing. Dirty street hard rock sound.

9. _How big was the hard rock scene in Canada – and did it mirror the American scene, where hair bands ruled for a couple year and then grunge took over?_

Blades: It was amazing, especially the summer of 90/91 when Toronto was turning into the next LA and was featured in quite a few American magazines stating that fact!

10. _How did Symphonic Slam come about? Was it a labor of love, how long have you wanted to do a pure guitar album?_

Blades: That was an amazing experience! Was released on Cleopatra Records in 2009. Yes had always wanted to do a guitar instrumental album. Adam Hamilton did an incredible job arranging and producing that record!

11. _Roxx Gang, how did you end up with those guys – Canadian guitar player with American band. Over the years, have ya'll been able to bury the hatchet and become friends again?_

Blades: They had an ad in Metal Edge Magazine. I responded to it, sent a press kit got an audition, flew down to Florida, kicked ass and got the gig

:)

No, not really. I'm actually contesting rights and percentages with Kevin for Sound exchange. It's ridiculous coz he's trying to claim 100% of everything, even stuff I wrote and co-wrote. It's a shame really but I have spoken to Wade and Roby recently. All good and all in the past

12. Supercool with Vik Foxx – another cool band you were in. What happened to them?

Blades: Was a cool project. We did some shows in LA back in 2001 and did a Japanese tour. Just didn't last, but was a cool band.

13. Smack was a cool band. More of a punk vibe? Junkyard is one of our favorite bands of all time. Are you a fan? How did you land Patrick Muzingo?

Blades: Smack was a great band. Ya, we made some noise in that scene in LA. We could never find a permanent drummer in that band lol so we were friends with Pat and he helped us out. We actually had interest from Nancy Walker at Island Records at the time and then the singer and bassist broke up the band.

14. We really liked "Hollywood's Burning" from Tales From the Strip. Do you have a favorite song or two from that album? Or can you share any memories from writing/recording it?

Blades: An amazing time in the band. Loved making that album from start to finish. "Love Skin", "Gypsy Soul", "Electric Neon Sunset", "Vampire", man that album is so killer!

15. We think Hollywood Forever is one of LA Guns best overall albums. In fact, we've got it ranked as one of the best sleaze rock album of all time (1981-2017) and as the band's fourth best album of their catalog. How was the experience working on that one? Our fav songs: the title track, "You Better Not Love Me", "Underneath The Sun" and "Queenie?"

Blades: Making that record was a struggle. We all worked separately during the recording. Then when did all get together in a room it was fights, disagreements and lots of arguing. I really enjoyed when I recorded with Andy Johns on my own and it was also fun when Kelly Nickels came in and played bass on one of my songs "Venus Bomb." The whole band was starting to fracture at that point and at the end of the year and tour for that album I left. Overall I think it's a good album but *Tales* is better IMO.

16. You were part of two legendary bands....but also two bands that have always had a lot of dysfunction. Two versions of each band, revolving door of members. As somebody deep in the music world, how do you explain that to fans that don't really know what goes on? Die-hard fans of those bands look at it and go "what the hell guys, why can't you get along. We want to buy a new album and see you on tour – but every month it's a new drama or controversy or new band member." Is it money, ego, what causes all that turmoil?

Blades: Ya, it's messy. I try to stay away from all that drama. It has a lot do to with egos and not being a team player. I can't really comment on all that coz it's not my fight. But in the long run it's the fans that get the brunt of it.

17. Blades/Donnelly Production – how did that get started and how's it doing business wise? Do you enjoy just going in the studio and creating sounds/songs/music?

Blades: I met Jason in L.A in 2012 and we started to do a ton of music cues and loops for various companies. Quite a few of our music cues have been featured in National Television shows like Duck Dynasty, Wahlburgers, shark week, Pitbulls and Parolees, etc

18. Let It Rawk had an amazing lineup. Why did you that sort of group together, how did you pick the all stars, and how much fun were the shows?

Blades: I hand picked all the guys, who were all good friends and amazing players. The three years we were together was a blast.

19. Is there one album or song that you've done that you feel like

captures the true Stacey Blades heart/soul the most?

Blades: I think the new stuff with Electric Radio Kings is some of my best work. I'm also very proud of Hollywood Forever.

20. At what age did you realize you had the talent to be a professional musician?

Blades: I started at a very young age on piano. By the time I was 10 I was performing in recitals and could read music and play like a champ. Once I got a guitar in my hand I knew this is what I'm going to be doing. It's more than just talent - it's drive, commitment, sacrifice and never stopping

21. What advice would you give to young guitar players?

Blades: Own your game and never stop learning different styles!

http://www.staceyblades.com
https://www.electricradiokings.com
https://www.electricradiokings.com
https://www.facebook.com/stacey.blades.1

Steve Blaze
Lillian Axe

Picture courtesy of Mr. Blaze's official Twitter.

1. We were fascinated to see that you are the main songwriter for Lillian Axe. I don't think a lot of casual fans know that. What are you most proud of in your career, your guitar work, vocal ability or songwriting skills? Which aspect do you enjoy the most?

Blaze:

I am proud of the dedication and love for this band from all members, past and present, and the love and support of our friends and fans all over the world. On a personal level, I am equally as proud of my guitar playing and my songwriting. Awards-wise, I am proud of the Louisiana Hall of Fame induction the most.

2. How does your songwriting process work? Lyrics first, music first, etc?

Blaze:

There is no method at all. Sometimes a song is written in 15 minutes, sometimes a year. It can start as a musical piece or as an idea. Usually music first, then lyrics, but the theme is created as the music develops.

3. We saw Lillian Axe last year at the Hair Metal Holiday festival in Austin Texas. Do you remember that gig? If so, how was it for you?

Blaze:

I remember it well. We had a blast! Great venue, lots of great bands. We had a great response.

4. You and Michael "Maxx" Darby are the only original Lillian members to still be in the band. Why have you two been able to stick it out whereas the other guys couldn't/wouldn't?

Blaze:

Lillian Axe is about the songs and the music. Over our 34 year career, there are members who have moved on to other facets of their lives, always with no hard feelings,only well wishes. As in all relationships in life, people change their goals and their situations. We keep it going because it is in our life's blood to make music to influence people for the better.

5. Robin Crosby produced your first album. How did you guys hook up with him and how was that experience? A lot of fans think he was the real heart and soul of Ratt, pretty tragic that he passed away so young.

Blaze:
Robbin saw us when we opened for them on their Dancing Undercover tour. He wanted to produce our album and we hit it off famously.

6. You guys have went through a few different singers. Do you think that has hurt the band in terms of reaching a certain level of success? Usually the singer is the most recognizable member of the band because of the vocals. Are you searching for a specific sound/singer?

Blaze:
If you look at a 30 year history of recording albums, Ron was the vocalist for 16 years, Derrick for seven and Brian for seven. That is really not a case of not being able to keep a singer. People change their priorities in life, and we roll with those changes. Our singers last longer than most marriages.

7. How come MCA originally dropped you guys after two albums? And how satisfying was it to go to another label and release a hugely successful album and top billboard hit single?

Blaze:
With MCA's track record, we were lucky to get two albums. The president who signed us left MCA before the ink on our contract was even dry. To move on with success was highly satisfying.

8. What are you memories of the creating/recording process of "True Believer?"

Blaze:
Honestly, no different than any other song. When I wrote it, I wanted to create something powerful, melodic and upbeat. I wanted a song about the power of faith and belief in something, that unwavering strength you feel when you are fully committed to something or someone. We knew from the start that it would become our anthem.

9. We also liked the ballad "See You Someday." Any story behind that song?

Blaze:

This song , although sad by nature, is meant to give hope to those who suffer the loss of a loved one. The deepest hurt we can as human beings can experience is the loss of someone we love. I have had so many people tell me how this song has helped them through the worst times in their lives. It's quite humbling when you have the opportunity to reach someone in that capacity.

10. Which is your favorite Lillian Axe album? Or was there one that really captured your true vision the best?

Blaze:

I don't have a favorite, so to speak, but Psychoscizophrenia and Days Before Tomorrow stick their necks out a bit higher as the most representative of the Lillian Axe message.

11. How much did it mean for you guys to receive the Jackson Indie Music Week Icon Award last year? And, to become the first hard rock band to be inducted into the Lousiana Music Hall of Fame?

Blaze:

Both of these accolades were so amazingly appreciated and humbling. There are many ups and downs in this industry, so when any recognition of your hard work is celebrated, it is incredibly received.

12. What's the status of The Forgotten Art of Melancholy? Will it be full of your own ballads or covers of famous ballads?

Blaze:

We have decided to refrain from doing that and concentrate strictly on the next studio album. We released a single for download called "The Weeping Moon." It's available now.

13. How did you end up with the band Angel? Where they still wearing all white when you joined!

Blaze:

Gordon Gebert was playing keys at the time for Angel, and he interviewed me for a book he was writing. We talked about Angel, and he mentioned they were auditioning guitarists, and asked if I would like to do so. Being a huge Angel fan I jumped at the chance, flew to NY and nailed the audition. We were all black at first, but soon after, they decided we needed to go all white.

14. You first started playing guitar at seven years old – that's amazing. Electric or acoustic? And did you just start messing around with it or did you have lessons? When did you realize that you were one of those one in a million talents?

Blaze:
I was actually six! My parents bought me an acoustic guitar and immediately put me in lessons at school. Within a few months, the teacher told my mom that I had exceeded the class's abilities, so I started classical and flamenco lessons. I knew I loved it and was blessed with the talent, but I never view this with anything other than a gift from God.

15. Near Life Experience is pretty crazy. You guys kick a lot of ass. NLE is way heavier than Lillian Axe. From Angel to Near Life Experience….that's quite the difference! How did this great band come about? We were surprised by how heavy you guys are. What are the future plans for the band?

Blaze:
NLE is a unique band, started up by me and my brother Craig, who drummed for Black Label Society for about 10 years. I never viewed it or wrote for it with any precognition other than to write powerful great songs. I wrote a lot of songs at that time, several which have gone on to Lillian records. NLE recorded two great records which were ahead of their time.

16. When (and why) did you become involved in the paranormal world? Did you have an experience yourself with a ghost? How is the experience of working on Through the Veil?

Blaze:
I started my fascination with the paranormal when I was a child. I saw and experienced things no one else did. About six years ago, I decided to put a group together of the best in the field here in Louisiana. We have

done many investigations, and we are currently preparing for our TV show called Through the Veil. More details soon.

17. What would you rather have occur in 2019. Write and record a top 10 album….or capture definite non-debatable proof of a ghostly spirit?

Blaze:
Write a Top 10 album. I have already done the latter.

18. Singing, songwriting, guitar playing, ghost hunting, building and designing guitars, rock 'n' roll clothes design….lol, is there anything you can't do?

Blaze:
Yes, cooking, dancing and fixing a car! When it comes to these things, I am useless.

19. Do you have a positive Jani Lane story you can share with us? Such a talented artist, shame he could never get ahold of his demons. He is one of our favorite singers of all time.

Blaze:
Jani was almost Lillian's lead vocalist when our first deal in 1987 was evolving. He flew to N.O. and spent three days hanging with me. He and I both were chiefs of our own tribes, so we went different paths, but he was a great guy, a sweetheart. The demons have claimed some of the best, e.g. Robbin Crosby.

20. What is the story of the MCA label? Almost every artist I've interviewed that was under MCA has nothing positive to say about them.

Blaze:
Irving Azoff signed us. He left. We did 2 records. MCA did nothing. Rumors are true. End of story.

21. You guys were an old fashion rock roll band that just got lumped into the "hair metal" era because of timing. Does that label bother you at all? Sebastian Bach recently turned down our interview request saying it was an "embarrassment" that we included him in the hair metal genre. Does it bother you to get attached to it?

Blaze:
I have much bigger things to be concerned with than whether someone calls us a hair band. It is what it is. I am still here.

22. For us, it's just a name that helps narrow down a specific era. Hair metal, hair band, sleaze rock, arena rock, cock rock....at the end of the day, we are just trying to celebrate and give praise to the bands we grew up loving. I wish we could come up with a titled that everybody loved.

Blaze:
Although we have never received what I believe we should have, we have been amazingly blessed for many years with fans all over the world. The stories are never-ending, concerning the lives we have touched and have been touched by. All blessings.

23. If a label offered you a blank check for an album and tour in 2019 – what band are you putting together? And what supporting band are you taking with you (money is no object)?

Blaze:
Lillian Axe, with Saigon Kick and Muse!

http://steveblaze.net
https://www.facebook.com/lillianaxemusic
http://www.lillianaxe.com
https://twitter.com/BlazeSteve

Ted Poley
Danger Danger, Bone Machine, Tokyo Motor Fist, new album with DegreeD

Photo courtesy of Mr. Poley's official website.

1. Let's start off with the question you probably get tired of being asked. But let's get it out of the way right off the bat. If there had been a tennis tournament featuring Jane Lane, Brett Michaels, Vince Neil, Sebastian Bach, Axl Rose and Jon Bon Jovi and yourself, who would win?

Poley:

I would. I was a varsity tennis player in high school. I still have my varsity letter. Maybe I will sew it on the back of one of my stage vests, ha ha!!

2. How did Tokyo Motor Fist come together? Crazy name, but it's virtually an all star band and that album is really great. Is that group going to tour?

Poley:

That is Steve Brown's baby. I was asked to sign and was honored to rock out with some of the best musicians on the scene. Steve is in Trixter and works with practically everyone. Greg is the bassist for Ted Nugent and also currently is playing in Tyketto. Chuck is Billy Joel's drummer.

3. We know that you've been heavily involved and raised a lot of money for animal shelters. How come that area is so important to you?

Poley:

I love animals and can't stand to see them suffer. I have several rescues myself and since I don't have room to save every cat and dog I support Forgotten Felines and Fido's of Germantown, PA.

You can visit my Facebook page and scroll to find my donation post and donate there.

4. Believe it or not, we actually met back in 88 or 89. Our very first concert was a show in Seattle with Warrant and Danger Danger. You guys were standing in front of the tour bus and chatting with a small group of fans. Surely you remember us! Lol. How was that tour? How was touring with Warrant, did they treat you guys well?

Poley:
Yes, of course I remember you! Haha. Warrant was my first tour through Canada and some U.S. states. They treated us great. Jani used to put me up on his shoulders for the last song of their set and we would sing together. He was friggin' strong!

5. I read an interview where you referred to Jani Lane as a "dick." What's the story behind that? We're read a few interviews from people who say he was a super nice guy, and a couple saying he had a huge ego. What's your take?

Poley:
I didn't know him that well yet. They were already known when our record came out so I was sort of intimidated by him when we toured, so I kept my distance. But he was a very cool guy at that time. Certainly he was nice to us and I absolutely never heard a bad word from a fan about him when we were touring. Warrant actually taught us how important it was to be cool to fans. They were always cool to their fans.

6. What is your secret to keeping your voice at such a strong level? So many of your peers are still out there touring, but their voices have clearly lost several levels of strength. You sound just as good today as you did 25 years ago – how is that possible? What's your secret?

Poley:
I sing all the time. It's like working out. You have to keep it up or you lose it.

7. Is true that DD let you go from the band back in the day via a letter? Hopefully over time some apologies were given over that!

Poley:

No Comment. ;

8. How do you feel about bands that have a constant revolving door of musicians? Do you think that's OK or is there a time when a name should be retired and a new band/name started?

Poley:
If it has the original singer and more original band members than not….it's OK.

9. Your quick thoughts on:

Bone Machine: The coolest band ever!

Melodica: A swing and a miss.

Prophet: My mentors, awesome musicians. Taught me structure and trained me in the ways of Prog.

Pleasure Dome: Super awesome album that didn't get the attention it deserved due to a bad album cover.

10. You use to sell antique toys? How did you get involved in that and are you still doing it?

Poley:
Yes, I have been collecting, buying and selling antique and collectible toys and trains for 30 years. If you have something cool to sell or trade – contact me!!!

11. How do you feel about the state of the music industry today in terms of releasing music? Because of downloading – and people being able to basically "take" music without paying for it – bands don't put out music like they use to. When I was a teen, bands put out an album every year or every other year. Now it's every 5-6 years, which sucks for a real fan.

Poley:
I try to release something new at least every other year. It keeps me alive

as an artist. I don't do it for the money…there is none, ha ha!!! I do it for the art. I am an artist. I make and release music. It's what I do. I don't just sing old songs, lol.

12. Is the future really just digital releases and bands self-releasing everything?

Poley:
Probably.

13. What was it like growing up a huge Kiss fan to then actually touring and hanging out with them?

Poley:
It was a dream come true! Amazing to hang out with those guys. Just amazing.

14. Do you think it was Grunge that killed off the hair metal / sleaze rock era? Or a combination of grunge and over-saturation of hair metal bands? I really think that if we could have just kept the top 40 hair metal bands out there, the genre could have lasted for several more years.

Poley:
Grunge was the new trend. Everybody sorry now? Haha. What a batch of crap that was. I am glad it's over.

15. How good of a drummer are/were you?

Poley:
Not so good anymore. At one time I was pretty good.

16. When did you start playing and when did you know you wanted to become a musician for a living?

Poley:
I started on piano at age four. Drums later on. I always wanted to do this. My aunt was a famous musician in the 1930s. She was a singer and piano player and had a lot of hits with people like Lena Horne and Cab

Calloway and others. I loved her! She was married back then to Jerry Arlen, bother and bandleader for Harold Arlen who wrote all the music for the Wizard of Oz – including "Over the Rainbow." That was my aunt, in the middle of that scene. She told me that I would be a famous musician when I was small. ;)

17. What tour format do you enjoy more? Playing at rock festivals in front of 10,000 fans but on a bill with 10 other bands. Or playing to 250 people in a seedy little rock club up close and personal.

Poley:
Playing to 10,000 at a festival is much more fun! No matter what anyone says. Clubs are still fun though. Sort of, ha!

18. Any Danger Danger shows/albums in the near future? Or maybe another Poley solo album? Or Poley fronting a brand new band?

Poley:
Just got back from Sweden where I recorded my best album ever. It's a new solo album that I did along with a Swedish band called Degreed. They are amazing musicians and songwriters and the album is the best sounding I have ever recorded. It will be released on Frontiers early in 2019.

19. You always stay extremely busy and have put out more albums than we can even keep track of! What do you do for fun that isn't music related?

Poley:
I go to Jamaica and relax. Otherwise I work 12-14 hours a day doing stuff like this interview, which took an hour or so to type out…lol.

I own and run other businesses to. I am up by 5:30 AM and still working at 8 PM. Europe stuff early and USA stuff later in the day.

20. What's your favorite venue and city to play?

Poley:
They are all good. I have no favorites.

21. Did DD have to do the Sunset Strip game? If so, got any crazy stories to share and what bands were your main competition?

Poley:
Nope. We were from New York/New Jersey. We never did a single live show before we got signed by Epic Records on the strength of our demos alone. Those included some songs that made it on to the first CD: "Rock America", Don't Walk Away" and "Naughty Naughty."

22. How do you like the Monsters of Rock cruises? Is it cool to be so close and personal with your fans? Are you a guy who chills in his hotel room or by the pool or are you out there chilling with your fans?

Poley:
I love the cruisers! Monsters of Rock is the most fun you can have if you are a music fan. And I am probably the most visible guy on the ship. They call me the captain!

23. Frontiers is giving a lot of the classic guys/bands a chance to release music now. How have they treated you?

Poley:
I have been with them since practically the beginning of the label. They have always treated me like family. I love those guys!

24. You covered "Hands of Love" and mentioned that The Blonz also covered it. You said they were a "cool band." Did you know those guys back in the day?

Poley:
Nope. I really didn't give a shit about the Blonz and never really heard their whole version. I was actually surprised that someone had covered it by the time I thought of doing it. But I loved that song since it was submitted and ultimately rejected for the first D2 album back in 1988. I recorded it because I had always loved the original demo that was recorded by my friends Joe Lynn Turner and Tony Bruno.

25. Tony Harnell did backing vocals on Ghost of Love from the Revolve

album – how did that come about?

Poley:
No idea. And I never even knew that. Probably because he has been a friend of ours and might have been doing some other work with Bruno at the time. I have to go listen now and see if I can hear him!

26. Screw It is such a fantastic album, full of some really Great songs. But…...Slipped Her The Big One? Horny SOB? Do you look back at those songs with pride, or do you laugh and shrug the shoulders!!!

Poley:
It was the style at the time. And I didn't write the lyrics!

27. We've got DD at 60 and Screw It at 65 of all time on the album chart. Sound about right? That's pretty good for a 30-year period of thousands of albums.

Poley:
I appreciate it very much. Thank You!

28. Were you a fan of Dangerous Toys? My buddy and I drove all the way through Alaska to Canada to Washington to attend college. I bought two CDs for the trip – yours and the Dangerous Toys debut. We must have listened to them both about 100 times that week.

Poley:
Nope. I didn't listen to anything of our genre back then. But I like them now that I play festivals and cruises with them. They are cool guys and they certainly still rock.

29. We've been doing tons of research trying to get a real strong timeline of the era. Lots of people like to say Come On Feel The Noise is the first song of the era. But Def Leppard and Motley were around before that paving the way. Dokken released Breaking the Chains before QR hit it big. Whitesnake was going more mainstream. You can even start going back to Led Zep or even further back to Buddy Holly!!!! And all the glam bands. It's almost an impossible task. BUT we've traced the lineage back and have came up with the song that

we feel is the "baby" that birthed the Hair Metal era.
What would your thoughts be if we said Boston's More Than a Feeling
was the first song of the hair band/hair metal genre???
The riff. The chorus. The melody. The anthem chorus, singer hitting
the high notes. Put that song on in a bar and 90% of the customers will
start singing the chorus.

Poley:
The first thing that I heard that rocked "hair band" style was either Ratt's
"Round and Round" or Autograph's "Turn Up the Radio" around 1985
when I was in Los Angeles recording the first Prophet album. I was in the
middle of recording an album and living in Los Angles and driving to the
grocery store when Autograph's first song came on the radio. I was
stunned by the cool guitar chunks and big snare drum sound in the
beginning. So I pulled over and listened to the whole song and then got
bummed out because I knew that the new prophet album "just wasn't as
cool" as Autograph.

30. Is there anything else you would want me to mention or promote?

Poley:
Yes, please support a local No Kill Animal Shelter near you! Thanks
everybody, see you on the road or at sea!!!!

https://ted-poley.com
https://www.facebook.com/Ted-Poley-123851607689228
https://twitter.com/tedpoley

Terry Dunn
Banshee

1. You are the only original member to be in Banshee since the beginning. Are you still buddies with the three original guys?

Dunn:
Unfortunate no, we are not friends, there is a lot of resentment and jealousy from them that I am still moving forward with Banshee, Sad.

2. Why have you stuck with this band for so long, through so many ups-and-downs, new members and really - kept this and alive since 30-plus years?

Dunn:
Banshee has always been my baby, I founded the band in 1986 so I figure who better to carry the torch forward for the band then me. There has always been a supportive fan base and demand for more Banshee music so why not?

3. How come the original Banshee broke back in the day (after the third album)?

Dunn:
We had been black balled by Atlantic because of Tommy so no one would touch us and we could not stand each other by that time so we decided to break the band up

4. What are your thoughts on Tommy Lee Flood. Some of those high notes he hit were off the charts, especially on songs like "Cry in the Night!" How come he wasn't involved in the 2012 regrouping?

Dunn:
Tommy had a awesome voice and his screams were second to none, By 2012 our relationship was damaged badly and he also was having a lot of trouble with his voice and could not hit those notes anymore.

5. Some reviews said you guys softened your sound a bit on Race Against Time from your debut album? True, false, just the band evolving? How come the label dropped you guys? Atlantic was a pretty big deal. Banshee was respected, you had the singer with a magical

voice, you personally could absolutely shred on the guitar. It seemed
like you guys were close to breaking out? What did the label tell you?

Dunn:
Atlantic tried to mold us into a commercial band which we were not, yes
race against time was a bit lighter compared to what I envisioned the band
to sound like. We were dropped and blackballed from Atlantic because
Tommy slept with the head of A&RS girlfriend, the guy who signed us
and it had a devastating affect on the future of the band, we were pretty
much done

6. Take 'Em By Storm was your third and final album. Same question
as before. Your first two albums seemed a bit like a heavier Judas Priest
and Iron Maiden. Balls to the wall metal, but with a melodic sound –
like Halford/Dickinson. On Storm, it seems like you guys went full-scale
hard rock. Still harder than most rock bands, but not as heavy as the
prior two discs. Was that the plan, just an evolution of the band, trying
to break into the more mainstream rock side, etc?

Dunn:
Take 'Em by Storm was material we had left over after the Atlantic
release and yes it was heavier and we released it on our own, it has done
very well and I think it was a example of the direction we wanted to go
before getting sidetracked by Atlantic

7. What was the story behind the reunion shows? Who put them
together, how was the attendance, was it all the original members?
Were they just one-off shows?

Dunn:
The first reunion was in 1998 and Americas Pub in KC and it went over
well, Kent would not play the show so my good fried and drummer Kevin
Lear played and did a awesome job, we did another show in 2004 at the
Uptown Theater in KC as well and Kevin played that show as well, Bill
Westfall played bass on both shows

8. Do you remember writing "Missing You" and the story behind it?
We've got it in our top 1,000 songs of all time list.

Dunn:

I had the music for missing you and Tommy wrote the lyrics and it came together pretty fast, it was a typical love ballad which Tommy loved to do almost as much as much as he loved praising himself lol, it turned out to be a pretty popular song

9. What song/s are you most proud of or that you feel define you as a guitar player?

Dunn:

Actually I'm most proud of the new record *Mindslave* and the writing and music on it, it was the record Banshee should have done after the EP *Cry in the Night.*

10. What have you been doing since Banshee originally called it quits? Fans always wonder what musicians do once their popular bands break up. Did you stay in the music industry, start/play with any new bands, etc.

Dunn:

I was just living life and dealing with a lot of loss - that being the loss of my parents and my sister. I moved to Michigan to kind of start over and it was a good move. I started teaching guitar and getting my life together not really worrying about a band or the industry.

11. Which guitar players did you look up to or that influenced/inspired you as a young man?

Dunn:

Oh there were many, Randy Rhoads was one who I loved, Van Halen, Michael Schenker is awesome.

12. Was there a band back in the day that you thought would be huge – but they didn't make it?

Dunn:

Yeah Savatage has always been one of my favorite bands who had a short lifespan after there guitar player passed away in a car crash, I loved those guys.

13. Can you share any crazy or funny stories about your time with Banshee – touring, band interactions, etc?

Dunn:
Yeah at the begging of our Race Against Time tour we had put all the guitars in the bathroom of the RV and some in the bathtub. Well we stopped to get something to eat and one of the cases had shifted and turned on the bathtub faucet filling the tub up and soaking all of our guitars, we spent three days trying to dry them out and dry the cases…it was a mess.

14. What advice would you give young guitar players today trying to break into the music business as a career?

Dunn:
We in some ways its easier to get your stuff out there with the Internet and media but its different now with respect to labels and bands getting signed, it's much harder now.

15. Who are your desert island bands?

Dunn:
Oh wow. Ozzy for sure, Kansas, Michael Schenker for sure.

16. Is there anything else you'd like me to mention or to promote for you?

Dunn:
Yes a new Banshee record is coming out this summer called The Madness and we are excited about its release, WE have a new website we are working on but you can got to https://www.facebook.com/BansheeRocks to keep you updated.

https://www.facebook.com/terry.dunn.14

Tod Howarth
Frehley's Comet, Loudness, Ted Nugent

Photo courtesy of Mr. Howarth's official Facebook page.

1. What were you doing before joining the band 707?

Howarth:
I had moved up to Los Angeles in late 1979 to pursue a real music career and was playing with a few members from San Diego that had moved up there with me. I eventually left those bands and stated to play with guys in LA that would eventually lead me to Cheap Trick. I saw 707 at The Starwood early on and thought 'I could be in that band' even though I preferred heavier music. Later friends told me that they were looking for a keys/guitar guy.

2. That Mega Force album was really solid. Kevin Chalfant sounded like more rock version of Steve Perry. Was that the first major album that you were a part of?

Howarth:
Thank you! We thought the LP was killer at the time. Kevin was, is a great singer and yes he had a 'Perry' quality in his timbre but oddly enough back then, I really didn't hear him that way, his voice sounded, yes rougher, more Steve Marriot like of whom is one of my vocal heroes. 707 had recorded 'The Bridge' first but it got shelved so the next LP turned out to be MEGAFORCE- and yes that was my first major release.

3. A great band, an album that charted on Billboard and you guys had some pretty major tours. How come the band disbanded after that? It seemed like you guys about to take the next step up the ladder?

Howarth:

Our best tour was right after I joined the band – still a four piece then – when we toured and opened for REO Speedwagon on legs of their Hi-infidelity tour. We thought then that we were on our way then…ha! Not so much. With personnel changes, record label disasters and then firing of our managers 'things' went downhill in many directions and eventually in the end we were a four-piece again with Kevin and me sharing lead vocals.

4. 707 toured with the Scorpions, Rainbow, Ted Nugent, Loverboy, REO Speedwagon for that album. Did any of the bands stand out (in a good or bad way) for a young musician in terms of learning how the business works, how you wanted to perform and present yourself?

Howarth:
I never really paid attention to 'how the biz' functioned. I should have because then I would've had the real fire under my ass to make things happen quicker. I had not developed my lead singing abilities and my 'look' was dreadful…however I did see from other bands that there was a clear pathway to where I wanted to be, writing songs and playing with great players to make a group solid as a whole. Most all of the BIG bands that we toured with had something or someone that would stand out in a positive way for me but none that were indelible at the time.

5. How did you get the job in Frehley's Comet? Did you have to audition or did Ace just call you up out of the blue?

Howarth:
Through John Regan. I met him when he was playing bass for John Waite on the 'Missing You' tour in 1986 and I was playing with Cheap Trick - we were doing tours together here and there. I used to listen to John Waite's band's sound check and thought 'Holy shit the band is good, heavy, solid rhythm section and that bass sound, wow!'

I finally introduced myself to John and he said yes I've been watching you. I told him what I could do, sing, write, and play more than Keyboards. His response was, 'Hmmm, I have a project that I'm working on that just might work for you but I can't say at the moment.' We exchanged info and about four months later or so he calls and tells me who and what the project was. Frehley's Comet.

6. How was that experience – you joined a major band, with one of the most popular guitar players in the world…and you got to play guitar, sing lead vocals on some songs, and even write songs as well!!

Howarth:
Truthfully? It was a business move. I was not overly thrilled about the music as I was a heavier, darker type writer then and was not 'hooked' by much of Ace's material. The band? KICKASS! Ace's Leads? KICKASS – not my style but ripping! I felt VERY lucky that I got to sing, write, play keys and guitar (and a few leads myself) because that's all I ever wanted in my own band. I am eternally grateful to Ace for what he let me do and contribute.

7. Do you have a favorite album with the band?

Howarth:
No. The first one had power with Anton on drums, the second LP had half of my songs with solid pocket Jamie Oldaker so I'm split. Come to think of it 'Live plus 1' was probably a favorite because it's so raw, mistakes and all!

8. How come that band ended up breaking up?

Howarth:
After I left – yes I left despite the rumors that I was 'let go or fired' John stayed with him for a bit and drummers changed, Richie was back in the band – a great player entertainer but the whole ordeal faded with the onset of grunge and I would imagine that didn't help. I left the band because after the failed completion of the IRON MAIDEN tour, I was told that Ace should probably 'write' and 'sing' the entire next LP. I thought 'Ouch…. okay, so what do I do for income? If I can't write songs there's no publishing money coming in and plus it was a slap in the face, 'three steps backwards…..and I'd had enough of being many bands 'hired gun'.

9. How much fun was the recent reunion with the Comet? It looks like a huge crowd.

Howarth:

It was a lot of fun, as sloppy as it was - but I think way more fun for the KISS/COMET fans there in Indy. I was happy for them and the look on their faces, priceless!

10. Do you still keep in touch with or follow Ace's career? While a living legend, his live performances haven't exactly been highlight reels. In fact, we were at a festival he headlined last year and we left about halfway through his set.

Howarth:

Not a bit. Not on purpose nor spite I just don't. I've so very many musical endeavors of my own that require writing, staying in shape, self rehearsals for FOUR BY FATE or solo recording – all the instruments and then working in the real world because no one else finances my musical 'quests.' And I really don't have to keep an eye on him as fans always report to me on how well or bad he's doing – even when I hadn't asked. I know his patterns, he is a great guitar player, an icon and an image marketing genius of the day, that is human and can have bad nights like us all. I have always had to try so very hard to get anywhere with my music and then work even harder to keep it going, so I have very little empathy for those who think that it'll rain cash forever. It doesn't. I believe he's somewhere in the fluctuating middle there.

11. Ted Nugent was still a pretty big star in 1984. You sang some background vocals for Ted Nugent on the album Penetrator and then for the Loudness album Hurricane Eyes? How did those jobs come about? Were you friends with the bands and they just called you up to come jam a bit?

Howarth:

Nugent! Always the consummate entertainer. When 707 was doing all the big festival tours in the early 80's we did some shows with Ted. He liked the band because of its Michigan roots and we ended up 'keeping in touch' for various reasons. Eventually he and his manager wanted and did, manage us in 1983 but we were fading fast. In the end 'we' helped Ted record his *Penetrator* LP at The Record Plant in Sausalito, SF and he wanted 707 to sing backup vocals on the record. Kevin Russell and I did.

LOUDNESS came about through me being with Ace at the time and Eddie Kramer was involved with them as a producer. He asked me to 'ghost write' some lyrics/melody for them. Love that band, they kicked ass!

12. _What music aspect do you feel you are the best at and which one do you find the most fun and entertaining? Vocals, guitar, keyboards?_

Howarth:
Good and tough question. What I'm best at doing and what is most fun/entertaining are two different things. I'm best at songwriting and melody. My guitar playing is fat and solid from the rhythm base and my keyboard playing is structurally colorful in a dark, esoteric manner – I come up with inverted chords – like I do on guitar (check "The Way to Pahrump' off of my COBALT PARLOR solo CD…or the whole CD for that matter) .

While recording I feel I'm best at delivering the emotion on everything.

Live….I like to make people happy or experience the depth of my compositions by way of expression. Singing lead and playing guitar makes me more fluid, doing the same behind the keyboards is a bit more restricting BUT when singing deep emotions into 'It's Over Now' or 'Amber Waves' THAT kills!

13. _Who came up with the album cover design for Sillhouette??? Lol – shirtless, on a beach, with a beautiful naked woman in front of you…how come you are scowling!!!_

Howarth:
I did, thank you very much lol! Silhouette was an album full of tunes that reflected my direction, past and present (Then) – including a few that had been penned for the next COMET LP – as I toured with Cheap Trick at that time. I would tour with them then come home and work on this CD. I play drums but didn't have a set at the time so I had to program the drums on my KORG keyboard which took on average, 40 hours to solidify to my standards for each tune!

The 'scowl' was not intentional, it just was. The shot was taken in La Jolla California and the hot naked babe was an ex-girlfriend that agreed to do the photo. The shot was taken by a friend of mine who was a photographer/tattoo parlor owner then and now about to be released from prison for murder! (Long story) Mike – the photographer – also lent me his drums for the recording of 'COBALT PARLOR' and 'OPPOSITE GODS'

14. "Far Cry From Heaven" is a great song! Sounds a lot like Sammy Hagar Van Halen prime era. Any story behind that song?

Howarth:
I thank you! Again, all drum machine but I got the point across. Sammy! Love that singer – and I redid 'Rock Candy' a few years back with my old COCOA BLUE cover band from the 70's.

The song is about my ex-wife. She had, shall we say, many fucking issues. We had two kids together and they've turned out exemplary adults but back then I left her in late 1988 and the tumult will be in my book. We were finally divorced in 1990 but the damage and shit she put me through is and was unforgivable, hence the song.

15. It was interesting listening to your solo albums. You seem to have went the opposite route of a lot of musicians. Instead of mellowing out as you got older, your sound seemed to get heavier on the later albums! Was that a conscious effort or just a natural progression of your sound?

Howarth:
Epic observation, thank you! I had my guitar player from COCOA BLUE (my 70's cover band) say the very same thing to me years ago after meeting up with me once I had 'made it'

As I said previously, the COMET was not heavy enough for me overall, neither was Trick (even though their early stuff was kickass!) nor Ted. Here's the deal, I love deep dark esoteric melodies and orchestrations…they grip the inner, hidden emotions of the listeners – even though they may not know it.

HOWEVER, on the flip side, my easy listening genre of acoustic, keyboard oriented writings I thrive on even deeper emotions combined with gut wrenching lyrics and melody passages. At this point in my life I'm back to the hobby aspect of recording – I will continue to do what I want and what I feel. HEAVY rock then adult contemporary easy.

16. I know you are proud of all your solo efforts, but is there one that you are most happy with or that you feel like captured your sound/vibe the best? Also, of all your songs, do you have any that you'd consider to be your favorite 2-or-3 tunes?

Howarth:
'COBALT PARLOR' is my favorite. It is the first complete solo CD where I played everything including real drums (finally). The songs 'MISGIVINGS' and 'THE WAY TO PAHRUMP' are my favorites off of this CD. The songs are about a woman that I almost married in 1996 but had my reservations…she lied about 'things' and then she wanted kids…I had three, I was not bringing anymore into the world at my age back then.

The third tune would be 'JIMBO'S BUNK' off of 'OPPOSITE GODS' about my best friend who survived a horrible Harley accident in 2001 which left him a paraplegic for years. I wrote it for him when he was alive. He committed suicide three years ago. I cried for three days. Still not over it.

17. You've performed with Cheap Trick a few times over the years. How did you become associated with those guys?

Howarth:
I was with them 1985/86 then 1990-96 then 1999/2000 off-and-on in 2008 for the 'Live at Budokan' 30-year anniversary show.

When I had moved to LA 79/80 I ended up playing with some 'cool cats' of the day that had ties to Cheap Trick as they were from the Illinois area as well. Pete Comita, Jon Brant were playing with a guy named Miki Free in LA – another Illinois transplant. Both Pete and Jon would end up playing bass for 'Trick' even though Pete was a guitar player. In the course of things they had mentioned that I could be a great 'hired gun' to do keys and vocals.

18. You were an active musician in the late 80s and early 90s. What did you think of the "hair metal" music scene that dominated LA and then took over the world for a few years. From GnR to Warrant to Bon Jovi to Poison and all the bands in between.

Howarth:

Well, I had tired of some of the 'formula bands' that gained prominence then, even though many were flat out great musicians. The dichotomy was that I had joined The Comet that I felt wasn't anywhere near as cool as some of the bands I was bored of! I was all about Van Halen from the beginning and I saw them in 1979 here in San Diego - one of the only bands that had real balls in the heavy rock genre and was from California. GNR was great – they opened up for us, CHEAP TRICK in 1986 and then Mike Clink who was an assistant engineer for John Stronach (Joe Walsh and many others) ended up producing their BIG breakout record 'Appetite for destruction'

There were a few more 'hair' bands that truly kicked ass back then. Skid Row, Warrant, Ratt (a few locals dudes that I've played with)

19. How did Four By Fate come about? You put together a pretty powerful lineup for that band. Have you guys done any touring? Plans for 2018?

Howarth:

John Regan and I had been trying to get Ace to do a 25 year reunion show for The Comet some years ago but Ace, then was all about his solo band(s) and wanted nothing to do with it. So John and I - with help from friend/fan Mitch Lafon of Canada suggested we do a KISS/Comet thing and recommended guitar player Sean Kelly. Another major help that would become a 'manager' of sorts was Danny Stanton, he recommended WASP drummer Stet Howland to handle the skins. We assembled the band, polished it up a lot and did some shows

20. Relentless is a pretty solid and interesting album. Was it an easy writing/recording process as you'd worked with a lot of the band before?

Howarth:

Thank you...Easy? Yes & No. John and I have obviously worked well together 31 years ago and once we amped up after all those years – it was even better.

I had a few songs written and prepared for my solo album that I just applied to the FOUR BY FATE initial recordings. The tough part came when Stet Howland had the misfortune of a car accident the weekend of the first recordings where we had to scramble (because of reserved and spent recording money – along with the fact that I had flown out already to do as such) to find another drummer, thanks to Danny Stanton, AJ Pero of 'Twisted Sister' was suggested and found. Wow what a powerhouse! Then after the first six songs tremendous guitar talent Sean Kelly bowed out because he to paraphrase, would say 'I really had no idea FXF would be this 'heavy' We of course respected his decision and to this day remain very good friends.

Enter Pat Gasperini! Singer, Songwriter, epic guitar player to say nothing of his lead abilities! He had written and previously recorded a song titled 'FOLLOW ME' with John Regan on bass. John brought the song to me prior to the initial six songs being recorded and I LOVED it! Heavy, BIG rock sounding as the man is a great songwriter. So when we needed to fill the lead guitar player spot he was such an easy fit for us.

Then poor AJ passed away after recording the first six songs. More sadness along with of course the dilemma of finding a fit. Through Pat and a few others comes Rob Affuso, SKID ROW and he completes the next six recordings to complete the CD.

20A. If you could take Four By Fate on the road this year, and could pick ANY two bands of your choice to tour with.....who would you select?

Howarth:

It's a trick question RUN!!! Nice....well of course I'd like to pick bands that would complement FXF or at least be somewhat similar in genre AND then again there's bands that I personally love but are probably too young for our 'audiences' LOL!
It's probably safe to go with relevance from the late 80's CHEAP TRICK comes to mind – but only so I could mess with them, but maybe...hmm,

beneficially STYX, FORIEGNER, there are many others but I'm drawing a blank…

21. What bands/musicians were your main influences while growing up? Are there current bands out there today that you would pay to see?

Howarth:
Man you are asking one Hell of a lot! 'Growing up' hmmm. Well The Beatles were the first – yes I'm that old. Then I got into Black Sabbath, Humble Pie. THEN, Steely Dan, KANSAS, STYX, FOREIGNER, Jeff Beck (THE BEST) Aerosmith, Rick Derringer, Cheap Trick, Van Halen – and then we leap into – Alice in Chains, Stone Temple Pilots, Soundgarden (this all after the Comet of course). There are very few bands that I would pay to go see and tolerate being part of the crowd. STP, 'Chains and Velvet revolver were a few. I would pay now to see Greta Van Fleet.

22. At what age did you realize you were going to be a musician for a profession?

Howarth:
'Realize' A very good word here. At 18. In my High School yearbook – POINT LOMA HIGH – at the back of the book where everyone is listed and quoted in saying most anything including 'Future' mine said one thing. MUSIC.

23. When not doing music related things, what do you like to do for fun?

Howarth:
I have mechanical abilities so I rebuild/restore old cars. I do off Road activities – quadrunners, sand rails, I love water sports as we have a boat - Wakeboard / water ski, winter sports LOVE to SnowBoard/snowski, summer exercise as in
Roller/ice rink/inline skate. I'm a canvas artist, acrylic paintings of cars/motorcycles – chrome reflections are a favorite. I read extensively, I write short stories for fun…(for now).

24. How is the rock scene in San Diego right now?

Howarth:

You know, I've no idea truly – I mean I don't go out very often to the local digs as I still spend a lot of time in my own studio, working on another solo CD and then rehearsing for Four By Fate shows when they come up so the last thing I want to hear after all that…is more noise! But the times that I have gone to see anyone, they're pretty damn good. I would guess that there is a lot of young talent kicking ass out there, even locally here.

25. We just took a trip to the San Diego Zoo. Pretty amazing place, kids really loved it. But holy cow - $9 for a hot dog, $9 for a bottle of water, $21 for a bottle of sun spray, it was pretty insane. What do you love the most about living in San Diego?

Howarth:

Best Zoo in the world – and you pay for it! Yes, sorry – the prices here are insane but so is the housing and rents I hear, cost of living etc.

The best thing about living in SD is the weather of course, fairly epic, I grew up near the beach and now live even closer to the beach but not only that, closer still to Mission Bay. I'm in the Point Loma area where I went to Junior High and High School. Weird after all the years of moving to Los Angeles first, then San Fran, then spending time in Michigan, Rockford, Ill and New York…I end up back home.

I'm also close to the sand dunes (three hours with the motorhome and trailer) and then Big Bear mountains where my family has a cabin, two and a half hours away (no traffic).

The one thing I am concerned about is the construction and increased density. It makes for miserable local traffic anywhere – like LA and then the homeless issues. But that's another discussion as I'm on the Midway Planning board here because of our family business real estate.

26. What do you have planned for the rest of 2018 and 2019?

Howarth:

Besides working my ass off I am doing the basic tracks to my next solo CD where again I'm playing everything – electric drum set this time for expediency,
FOUR BY FATE will be doing everything possible to continue to bring our music out and about. I will be revamping my website www.TodHowarth.com in a big way in the next few months.

27. Is there anything else at all that you'd like us to mention or promote?

Howarth:
I wish to thank everyone that has followed and enjoyed my music, career and even my FACEBOOK life as it is. Keep an eye out for FOUR BY FATE events and my new website as there will be item to purchase that I'm creating personally...

I WILL be starting my book on my life and doing some paintings of Americana as I stand for this nation.

28. THANK YOU for taking the time to share your thoughts with us!!! We really appreciate it.

Howarth:
THANK YOU for asking! The very best of luck on this and in life!!

https://www.facebook.com/tod.howarth
http://www.todhowarth.com

Tony Cardenas Montana
Great White, Shadow and The Thrill

Photo courtesy of Tony's official Facebook page.

1. Shadow and The Thrill recently opened up for the legendary Lita Ford. Was that your guy's biggest show so far?

TCM:
I will answer this from a different perspective, in that, I feel the biggest show we played was the very first one! It's all gravy from here on out, now we learn, and grow.

2. What's the story with this band? Why and how did it get put together, any chance of an album and more touring?

TCM:
Shadow & The Thrill is basically me and my dear friend, and amazing musician, Brentt Arcement. I played all guitars, bass, vocals, and he did all drums, percussion and keys. We played almost everything and co-produced almost everything. We work so well together.

We will be releasing our album that was recorded in New Orleans and Los Angeles in late July, 2018. This is straight off of our one-sheet, which I will send to you as well.

"Shadow & The Thrill is a modern blues infused, groove laden, hook filled melodic rock band that comes from the streets of Los Angeles and New Orleans bringing you songs of salvation to soothe the soul! Their debut album, SUGARBOWL, was mixed by the certified multi-platinum, and Grammy Award winning, Sylvia Massy (Grammy: Johnny Cash). "

3. You played on a couple of Great White's most successful albums! How was the experience of playing with them in the 80s when they were one of the biggest rock bands in the world?

TCM:
Well, we certainly had a successful run in the 80's and early 90's, and I appreciate the comment, but, we were still developing when the whole genre came to a crashing halt.

It was really hard work. We were all very focused, and although much is said and written and reported about the partying and fame side of it, the truth is, is that it was a brutal exercise of touring/recording/appearances/writing/press and such. There was SO much pressure to really take advantage of the moment. We did our best, and we did a pretty good job. The fact that we still go out and play a lot of that music is a testament to the hard work from all of us back then. Quality work for the most part. I'm very proud of it all.

4. Was there a lot of pressure to replicate the success of Once Bitten when you guys went in to write/record Twice Shy? And was the band happy with how Twice Shy turned out?

TCM:

Of course, the pressure was immense, and a lot of that was on my shoulders as the "new guy." I certainly did not want to be the reason that Twice Shy was LESS successful than Once Bitten! So, I think we did a pretty good job all the way around. I'm pretty sure the band and management were not expecting me to become a writing force as well, and that was a very pleasant surprise for all of us too.

5. Great White is a great hard rock band. But seemed to have a great ballad or two on every album. What was the inspiration or what was it about you guys as songwriters that enabled great rockers to hit their soft side so effectively?

TCM:

Yes, that seemed to be a tradition from the genre at the time. We're all just romantics at the end of the day I suppose.

6. I know you weren't part of the writing process, but did you enjoy playing "Save Your Love live?"

TCM:

I still enjoy playing "Save Your Love", which was co-written by my dear friend, Stephen Williams, who passed away in 2015. Stephen is the reason I ended up in Great White in the first place. So, this song has a special place in my heart.

7. Hooked was a great album. Very underrated in our opinion. How was the experience of writing, recording and playing that one? And do you have a favorite song or two from it?

TCM:

That was a good piece of work, it is what it is and let's face it, it came out just a little before the genre crashed and Seattle took over. It was hard work, we were burned out a little at that point, 5 years of touring and such... "Afterglow" was a good choice for a cover.

8. I know it's a cover. But your guy's version of Afterglow is actually our favorite Great White recorded song.

TCM:

Ditto

9. Which of the two albums did you enjoy writing/recording the most?

TCM:

I have some personal reasons for enjoying the recording of Twice Shy much more than the other things we did. Exciting times!

10. You only wrote a couple songs for each album – but, coincidently, you co-wrote one of the best songs on both albums!!! With that amount of talent/success, they should have let you write more!!! But was that your deal – you came in hard and heavy on a great song or two – rather than a guy who just wrote a ton and then you weed through and pick out the gems?

TCM:

Yeah, like I mentioned earlier, it was a pleasant surprise for all of us, that I was able to contribute in that way. We played and rehearsed A LOT, so, we did get to jam and try to make things happen spontaneously too.

11. "Call It Rock N' Roll" and "Mista Bone" are both awesome. One is a flat out rocker and the other a cool groovy jam. We've actually got "Mista Bone" as the fifth best Great White rock song in their entire career. Can you share any insights or memories of writing/recording that bad boy?

TCM:

Well, Bone emerged out of a jam session, really. I was working on this heavy riff, and the guys just started grooving along. It was fun to play, and we needed something that "felt" good to perform. It serves that purpose to this day in the live set. It's a musician thing.

12. Do you prefer being a singer or playing bass or playing guitar? Which one is more fun and which one do you think you are better at?

TCM:

I have always just wanted to play guitar, but as soon as I opened my mouth, in any band I've ever been in, I get put into the lead vocal thing... oh well... Obviously in Great White we had one of the greatest voices in the biz, so I got to just play, which is what I do for the most part now in Jack's version of Great White. Jack has me sing a little on the live show. It's fun. He's very generous that way.

I did a stint with my Australian friends, TwentyTwo Hundred, where I was a front man, and sang on a UK tour opening for Slash. All the big arenas in the UK. I really enjoyed that, it certainly is a great feeling to address and perform to crowds of that size. I like it.

So, I prefer to play my guitar mostly. Short answer.

13. Jack Russell is such a legend and has that magical voice. What's it been like working with him? It's amazing how – at his age and after all he's been through in his career, that he still sounds so amazing live.

TCM:

Yes, I'm blessed to be able to work with him and to LEARN from him. I basically learned much of what I used on my own album and with TwentyTwo Hundred, from Jack, and from listening to Jack all these years. Some would say, that my first solo album, *Tombstone Shuffle*, sounds a LOT like Jack. It makes sense.

14. How did you end up on Jack Russell's 2017 album He Saw it Comin'? We personally loved that album, and have it ranked as the third best rock album of 2017.

TCM:

Honestly, I was not involved on the album to a great degree. I had one co-write, with "Sing of the Times", and that was it. I didn't really play much or write much on it. The guys did a great job though, and perhaps I'll be more involved on the next one.

15. Did you have a good relationship with Mark Kendall? What are your thoughts on him as a guitar player and band mate?

I loved Mark, as I loved all the guys. Now that I have had to meticulously learn many of Mark's things for performing on guitar, and similarly, I have had to learn much of what Lardie did as well. I have immense respect for them both as players, writers, and producers.

16. Can you tell us what you were doing and how you were selected for Great White? And conversely, why you ended up choosing to leave?

TCM:

I was introduced to the band by Stephen Williams, co-writer of "Save Your Love" and auditioned as they were having difficulties with Lorne Black. I think at first, they just wanted someone that looked like Lorne and could play. So I fit the bill there. I think they got much more than they bargained for as time went on.

17. How did the Platinum Master's Monster Circus come about? You've gotten some huge stars to play in it – from Dee Snider to Fred Coury, Bruce Kulick and John Corabi. How have you been able to get such major players to be involved?

My partner, Peter Merluzzi and I decided to bring our show concept to life, brought in some other partners, and took it to Las Vegas. We did one showcase and were offered a contract from the Hilton before the first show. It was exciting. All my dear friends loved the idea and came to play. Rudy Sarzo is truly one of my dearest friends in the business, and one of my mentors. He was such a huge influence and contributor. John, Bruce, Dee, Fred, Bobby, all... I owe them such gratitude.

18. How does playing it compare to playing rock shows? Which one do you enjoy more?

TCM:

I LOVED my show in Vegas, and I will do it again somewhere in the world. I would say that I love the stage show aspect of Monster Circus because it had to be precise, very regimented. I love playing in other band situations, and live, where I get to improv a little. That is the greatest feeling of all to me. Stand and deliver, on stage, in the moment.

19. How has the Anna's Brother band been going? That's an unusual name – what's it about? How would you describe your style of music and what plans do you have for the band in the near future?

TCM:

Anna's Brother was really about me starting to play music again. I had basically quit music to start and raise my family. I had changed careers, and entered into the high-tech world. Eventually, conceiving and founding an Internet e-commerce company. My dear friend, Al "Bax" Baca pushed me to start playing, writing and recording again. Anna's Brother was a great band of local friends. We recorded an EP with Sylvia Massy, and those tracks are being shopped for media placement. Great songs, there are a few videos out there. I would love to play with those guys again, loved 'em all.

20. A few years back you toured with Slash during a world tour. How was that experience? How was it working with Slash, who is regarded as one of the top rock guitar players of our generation?

TCM:

Well, he's amazing. Pure and simple. I learned A LOT from working with him in that short time. We did a live in the studio iTunes Sessions album that I'm so very proud of. We did several live albums in Australia for EMI's Abbey Road Live label as well, that are awesome. Myles Kennedy was a great friend and teacher as well…what a voice. Wow.

21. What did you think of him (and Duff) going back with Axl Rose in Guns N' Roses for the reunion people thought would never happen!

Their tour absolutely killed it financially, one of the top grossing of all time.

TCM:

I think we all saw that coming. I have friends that work on the tour, and I saw the show. Amazing.

22. As a rock fan, what would you be more interested in hearing. A new GnR album featuring Slash/Duff....or a new ACDC album with Axl Rose on vocals?

TCM:

Honestly, what I think is inconsequential. I'll wait to see like everyone else, and I'm sure it'll all be great!

23. What bands and musicians inspired you as a youngster? And what bands/musicians are out there today that you really enjoy listening to and you really respect?

TCM:

I was amazed by their skill when I was a child. Later, Van Halen, the Jimmie's, Blackmore, Derringer, the Schenker bros, etc. Now I realize that the music I grew up on was mostly early rock and R&B influences. I am leaning back on Elvis, Little Richard, Stevie Wonder, Earth Wind and Fire, etc.

I really am a huge Frank Sinatra fan too. I can listen to that stuff all day long. What amazing arrangements, so rich musically.

24. Is there anything at you'd like us to mention or promote????

There will be a Jack Russell's Great White album out soon with acoustic versions of all the Once Bitten songs. Look for that.

I will be releasing Shadow & The Thrill's "Sugarbowl" in July, so that will be announced soon. I will be doing some dates with S&TT in between my shows with JRGW in major markets. I hope folks find S&TT on Facebook, and keep an eye out for shows coming their way!

Tony Harnell
Starbreaker, TNT, Skid Row, Westworld

Photo courtesy of Mr. Harnell's official Facebook page.

*__1. The question you probably get tired of answering! Let's just get it out
of the way right off the bat. Are we ever going to get a
Poley/Harnell/Sonic reunion album/tour?__*

Harnell:
Nah, I doubt it:) but I never say never about anything!

__2. How did you get involved with that franchise?__

Harnell:
Ted and the producer Jun Senoue asked me way back in 2000. I really had
no connection to it at all, the popularity took me by surprise and I got a lot
of new and young fans from those songs.

*__3. I read your 10 albums in 10 days on Twitter. And in your interviews,
you've mentioned growing up listening to all the normal bands: Beatles,
Zeppelin, Queen, etc. Are there some lessor known bands/singers that
have inspired you over your career?__*

Harnell:
I guess my list is kind of typical. But yes I love Francis Dunnery, Jeffrey

Gaines and tons of unknown singer/songwriters and bands. Also a big Alanis fan and I love Glen Campbell!

4. You give online vocal lessons. How has that experience been? Is it mostly young kids trying to train their voice….or guys who are already top-notch vocalists who just need some fine tuning?

Harnell:
Both! It started back in the early 90's with singers coming to my house and just kept going from there. I love it and can work with people all over the world!

5. How did a surfer-skater boy from San Diego initially hook up with a Norwegian metal band?

Harnell:
Long story!! Well documented! lol

6. You seem to have a special connections with Michael Sweet. How did that friendship start and how come you guys have formed such a bond?

Harnell:
We toured together in 1987 and remained friends since, Robert too. Both great guys and great musicians. Oz too!

7. We've done a year of research listening to every hard rock song released from 1981-2017 for the hair metal / sleaze rock genre. We took the early 80s Motley, Dokken, Ratt, Whitesnake, Twisted Sister, Quiet Riot and then went backwards to try and nail down the song that really started the genre. Come On Feel The Noise punched it over – but it wasn't the song that started it all. Zepp/Queen/Slade was where it all started taking shape. SOOOO we finally mixed all that together and came up with the song that we feel birthed the genre. It's a song that is close to your heart.
The opening guitar riff. The high pitched vocals. The chorus that everybody has to sing when it kicks in – no matter where you are. The prefect stadium anthem. You know what song we are talking about? If we told you that More Than a Feeling was the song that birthed the entire Hair Metal genre…..thoughts?

Harnell:

I could believe that:) makes sense. It's a blend of styles. TNT mixed metal with a smoother Journey type melodic approach and I that was kind of a natural accident based on our different influences:)

8. What do you have planned for the rest of this year and 2019?

Harnell:

Well Starbreaker is almost finished so that will be released this year and maybe another project but my goal is to start releasing what I hope will be a series of new albums, finally, as a solo artist and possibly a steady new band as well!

9. Besides TNT, you've jumped around a lot between various bands. What is it about that style of career that you enjoy? Would you be bored playing with the same group of guys for 30 years and having to play the same songs a million times?

Harnell:

I don't like jumping around at all, it just worked out that way for better or worse. And it wasn't a lot of bands it was two:) If I could change a few things I would but I don't like to dwell on the past or hang onto regrets. I've made my peace with all decisions and have moved on and so have the other parties involved.

10. Early in your TNT career, you guys toured with Twisted Sister, Stryper and Great White. How did those three heavyweight bands treat you? Any fun – or bad – memories?

Harnell:

They were all great and I only have positive memories and have remained friends with all the bands!

11. After the Intuition album dropped, you guys really broke big in the United States. How was that major success different than being big overseas?

Harnell:

Well for me it was good cause it was home. But fans everywhere have one thing in common - they love the music! The American headline tour we did was a lot of fun though and it was amazing to get out there on our own and see how many fans we had in the US!

12. "Tonight I'm Falling" and "End of the Line" were our favorite songs from TNT. Any special memories about writing/recording them?

Harnell:
I barely remember but I know I did! Lol.

13. How was that 2014 reunion with TNT? A sense of closure or just fun to go jam with the old fellas?

Harnell:
2014 and 2017 were both good touring years for us overseas. 2014 was probably more successful and more fun.

14. How did you meet up with Bumblefoot and how was it working with him? He gave us the nicest rejection letter ever for this project. He apologized for not having the time to answer our questions and then wished us a happy Easter. Is he as nice and humble of a guy as he seems?

Harnell:
He's an awesome person and extremely talented. We met years ago in the early 90's and reconnected at NAMM in 2013 and started working on music almost immediately! He's become a good friend and I hope to work more with him in the future:)

15. That Tony Harnell & the Wildflowers featuring Bumblefoot album was amazing. Probably our favorite thing from your glorious career.

Harnell:
Wow thank you! That was fun to do and was done at all of our home studios!

16. Your mom was a well-known opera singer. Do you think genes had a part in your remarkable 4-octave voice? As a kid, were you already tearing it up? When did you know you wanted to be a singer?

Harnell:
I always sang and I'm sure my mom had a lot of influence on that. She was very supportive of anything I wanted to do. I guess I was 16 or 17 when I decided to do this for real.

17. Do you ever regret hanging up the skateboard and becoming a singer? You could have been the next Tony Hawk!

Harnell:
I do sometimes yeah but more than that I wanted to be a pro surfer! But I guess fate would have me do something else:)

18. Are we ever going to get a Jackals reunion???

Harnell:
Haha no!

19. Westworld had a really cool sound. Our second favorite Harnell album. How did you hook up with Bruno Ravel? Were you a Danger Danger fan?

Harnell:
A friend of ours kind of put that band together and it really worked! We created some really special albums together! I loved that band!

20. We loved Starbreaker. A couple of your bands/projects were a bit mellower. Starbreaker seemed a bit heavier than most of your stuff. Was it fun to get in there and sing that style?

Harnell:
Yeah I just love drawing on all my influences and letting loose so I'm at home with Starbreaker or mellower stuff:)

21. *"One Way Ride" is our favorite solo Harnell song. Do you remember writing/recording that one?*

Harnell:
I do. I was in Sweden I think it was 2007! It was a fun and creative time for me:)

22. *Did you ever work with Jani Lane back in the day? Thoughts on him?*

Harnell:
I think Jami was a really talented guy and I would have loved to have written with him but I never met him.

23. *What advice would you give to young up-and-coming musicians who hope to make it as a professional in today's music environment?*

Harnell:
Learn everything. Learn an instrument, play live as much as you can and know your ability level, that's really important and surround yourself with a very small circle of people you trust.

24. *What would you rather hear in 2018 – a new GnR album featuring Slash/Duff back in the band or the new ACDC album with Axl on vocals?*

Harnell:
GNR.

25. *Is there anything else that you would like us to mention or promote??*

LOOK FOR A NEW STARBREAKER ALBUM COMING THIS YEAR! Probably late summer or fall!

http://tonyharnell.com
https://www.facebook.com/pg/starbreakerofficial

Danny Vaughn
Tyketto, Waysted, Vaughn

Photo courtesy of Mr. Vaughn's official Facebook.

__1. In 2007 did a two-man acoustical act opening for Journey, how much fun was that? What do you enjoy more – doing an acoustic set, playing in a seedy club in front of 100 Danny Vaughn fans….or playing with a full band, rocking out in front of 10,000 fans?__

Vaughn:
I don't think it's fair to say that I enjoy any of those one things more than any other. They are all different. They create a different type of emotional reaction but, in the end, I've gotten to do what I set out to do in life all of those years ago, which is to make and perform my own music. It's the journey that is most gratifying. And speaking of Journey, yes, opening for them was an experience of a lifetime. And I owe that all to my good friend Jeff Scott Soto

__2. You played Lancelot for Gary Hughes's rock opera Once and Future King Part I. How did you get involved in that and how was the experience?__

Vaughn:
You have done your homework! That happened in the early days of file sharing and being able to work collaboratively over the Internet. Gary reached out to me because he had written this opus and he was looking for a variety of singers for the various roles. He sent me the two songs set aside for Lancelot and gave me some good guidelines and I did my best to match up to what he wanted.

3. Looks like you've released almost 20 albums worth of material in your career. Is there any one or two albums that you are most proud of or that you really feel capture your sound/essence the most?

Vaughn:

That's tough to answer because each thing I've been a part of has captured at least a piece of who I was and what I was doing at the time. "Soldiers & Sailors On Riverside" comes to mind because it was the first album I made after quitting the music business for five years. It was raw and organic and made in the company of good friends in a studio locked away from distractions in a very quiet, country setting. So I have very fond memories of that one. Coincidentally, that makes it very similar to the conditions in which we recorded "Reach."

4. No matter what happens, Tyketto seems to always come back for an album or tour. What is it about that band and group of guys that is so special to you?

Vaughn:

It's my first gang. That band represents the first time I, and some dear friends, decided we were gong to try and do things "our way" and make the music that we wanted in the way we wanted. That has remained true in its various forms over the years even with the changes in band members. Not everything we have done has been great but it was the best of what we had at the time and its success or failure, stylistically, rests solely on our shoulders. There is a great deal of satisfaction in that.

5. Do you like the process now of recording as opposed to how it was done back in the day. Now, people live in different states and Skype back and forth, send ideas through the email. The old days, guys would get together and spend months together at seedy hotels and studios. There is ease and convenience to how it's done now....but it seems like you lose some of the bonding and grittiness of working in a room together.

Vaughn:

I agree completely. Tyketto wrote all the songs for "Reach" from a distance and there were many times where that process was tiring and stressful for each of us. You can get so much more done in a room all together bashing ideas about. But we're smart enough to know that at some point you need to get into a studio together before anyone presses the record button and really work the songs through the old fashioned way. We did that to make certain that the songs we had created through technology would hold their ground in the real world. And some changes were made and not ever song got to see the light of day.

The recording process was something that I wish every young band still finds a way, and gets the budget, to do. Locked away in the beautiful Welsh countryside we had one agenda each day and that was to make an album. No distractions from home or work. And that's one of the reasons why we feel it's one of the best sounding pieces we have ever made.

6. If you had to choose, which option would it be?
You could write/record/produce a solo album that you felt was absolutely perfect. You poured your heart and soul into and it came out exactly how you wanted it. And people you respect – as well as the rock critic world - called it a masterpiece. But then it only sold 147 copies. OR….a Disney teen actor wants a music career, and their manager came to you and said "give us ten songs, as clichéd as possible, hit the common themes, we just need songs that 12-year-old girls will think are cool." You literally spent one day throwing together a group of the cheesiest songs you could find. Songs about Instagram, songs using words like "woke" and every silly cliché out there. Lyrics that make no sense except that they rhyme. And for that, the label will give you a check for $500,000.

Vaughn:
Can I do both???? Hahaha! What a crazy question. At this point in my life I think it's a safe bet that no one is going to come to me and ask me to write songs that 12-year-old girls will identify with. So I will continue to struggle to achieve the first option. And I won't use the word "woke" in a song ever. "Wok" maybe…but "woke", no.

7. As a musician/singer, what gives you more satisfaction – putting on an A-plus live show or putting out a quality album? Would you rather be known as a top-notch live band or album band?

Vaughn:

I'm glad that I don't have to choose between the two. I've always worked very hard to be both and I get equal amounts of satisfaction from both endeavors.

8. Do you think albums will ever become relevant again like they were 20 years ago? When we were kids, our favorite bands put out albums every year or every other year. Now, because every album is immediately downloaded for free on the Internet, bands rarely release music anymore. Which sucks for us fans. GnR was billed to be the next Rolling Stones at one point....Stones have over 50 albums, GnR has 5 studio albums. I would gladly give up YouTube and the ability to download albums for free if it meant that my favorite bands would release music more often. Is there any way to change the trend now or are we stuck here?

Vaughn:

I think trends and methods will continue to fluctuate. My greatest concern with how things are done now is that we now have a whole generation of young adults that have never paid for music. This creates apathy and entitlement in the listener. They will accept anything because it cost them nothing to obtain it. If you paid 15 quid for a cd and it sucked you were raving mad and perhaps you wouldn't but anything from that band again.

Now, people expect musicians to work for free and, sure, we want to express ourselves and will always do so, paid or not. Real players don't have a choice. But to ask us not to expect to make a living at our craft, something many of us have studied and worked hard at for years, is pretty unfair.

On a personal note, I have never really understood the deification of GnR. For me, they made one good album and not much else. (just my opinion, folks, no hate mail please) and I don't feel they represent the greatness that bands are capable of the way The Stones or Zeppelin or King's X do.

9. You toured with Iron Maiden. How were those guys on the road? Did they treat you well?

Vaughn:

You could not have hoped to work with better people. Unlike many bands out there, they are completely confident in what they do and who they are. They were generous and unafraid to have the opening band do well. Many bands want the opening band to fail so that they look even better. Maiden's philosophy is that if the opening band kicks ass then they get inspired to work even harder. And nobody works harder than those guys live.

10. What would excite you more as a music fan. A new GnR album or the proposed ACDC album with Axl on vocals?

Vaughn:

Ummmmm neither, thank you.

11. How does your song writing process work? You just wake up, pull out a guitar and see w hat happens? Or you get an idea, hear a phrase, etc and then sit down and try and write a song about it?

Vaughn:

Each song has a different genesis. There's no one set method for me. I do keep a scrap book of words, phrases and ideas that can occur to you at any time and when the time comes to work on a song I will sift through the ideas and see if some of them hang together to make a complete story.

Sometimes the music comes first, like in the case of "Letting Go" on the _Reach_ album, and the music just inspires a certain mood almost telling me what type of song I want to write. The best times, however, are when the new ideas seem to pop into your head almost fully formed; story, words and music.
It's like taking dictation. Those don't happen often but when they do they are often the best songs you make. "Standing Alone" was one of those.

12. Do you remember the first time you heard one of your songs on the radio and saw your video on MTV? What were those experiences like?

Vaughn:

I wish I could say that I remember it better than I do. It's lost in the mists of time now. I do know that it's a very exciting feeling.

13. How was it performing with Eric Martin? That guy has a magical voice. How did you end up with him on stage singing Mr. Big songs on an acoustic guitar?

Vaughn:

I have always held Eric and Mr. Big above almost all the rest of us. I think he is a remarkable talent and has a quality to his voice that makes him someone you can listen to singing anything. I was intimidated singing with him but he recognized me as a peer and treated me very kindly. Singing with him was a real joy.

14. Can you explain how the tour with Dan Reed came about? I'm So Sorry is one of our favorite songs of all time.

Vaughn:

I only met Dan in 2014 when Tyketto and DRN both played the Download festival. I had been wanting to put together a singer/storyteller duet with someone from our side of the tracks for many years but could never quite make it happen. I knew that Dan played a lot of acoustic shows on his own so when I approached him with the idea he was really enthusiastic about it and within a couple of months, the first "Snake Oil & Harmony" tour was launched. We just did our third one this year and we are looking forward to making an album together soon.

15. You've done tribute shows featuring Queen and The Eagles. If you somebody wanted you to do a tribute tour for a month this year, and you got to pick any band in the world, who are you choosing?

Vaughn:

I'm one of the co-founders of The Ultimate Eagles. I think we're the best Eagles tribute band in the world and part of the reason for that is how much we love the music that we're doing. I'm sticking with the Eagles. But, if I had to do another show I would love to try a Crosby, Stills and Nash show!

16. Did you enjoy the Monsters of Rock Cruise experience? Was it more fun hanging out with all the old rock stars that you ruled the world with back 25 years ago? Or more fun to be up close and personal with your

fans? Are fans pretty respectful on that cruise – like if you are eating lunch, do people come up and start talking, etc.

Vaughn:
People do come up and talk to you during lunch but you know what? That's what we're there for! I don't see how bands can get upset at interacting with the fans on the cruises. In my experience the fans are all very respectful of your personal space. Nobody has come banging on my cabin door while I'm trying to use the bathroom or anything like that. Part of the cruise allure is that you can get time to meet and chat more personally with the musicians you follow. I love the whole experience.

17. We read in an interview that after Tyketto broke up you "went back to work at a factory." Can you expand on that? What kind of factory or what kind of work it was? And then how long did it take before you gave that up and got back into singing?

Vaughn:
I worked in an auto part distribution center in Nashville as a forklift driver and order picker. I also worked in the shipping department for a company called "Sealed Air". They own the patent for bubble wrap. I gave up anything to do with music for about five years.

18. You see multi-singer groups in country and other genres. Old-school rock had CSNY and The Traveling Wilburys. Why do you think no hard rock group has done this? I would love to hear a hard rock version of the Wilburys. Say you, Eric Martin, Axl Rose and Tom Keifer. Would you be up for that? If you got offered a gig like this, what three singers would you want to bring along?

Vaughn:
Yeah, I'd love it. I'm not sure if hard rock allows for that kind of subtle interaction between voices but it would be a great thing to try. Managing all those egos, however, would be an unenviable task! Hahaha!

19. The six highest Tyketto songs on our top 1,000 list are: Standing Alone, Scream, When You Walk Away, Forever Young, I Need it Now and Dig In Deep.

Vaughn:
In my personal opinion, "Scream" is one of the greatest performance pieces we have ever done. It's hard to rank your own songs though and, while I do indulge in list making from time to time, I don't put much stock in it. It's an honor to be included in your all time list, though, thank you.

20. We really love Reach – it might be our favorite Tyketto album! It's amazing to see a band put out such a great album years after their so-called glory days.

Vaughn:
Thank you very much for the kind words about *Reach*. I happen to agree with you in that I think it's the best album Tyketto has ever done, including "Don't Come Easy'. I know for some fans that statement is sacrilege but hey, it's me, I can say what I want about my own work!

21. Quick Thoughts on the legendary singers from your era:

Axl Rose: Definitely a unique vocal stylist. I could never really get to grips with how I felt he has mistreated his fans, though.

Jon Bon Jovi: The guy we all wanted to be! Once the second album came out we were all on board.

Joe Elliott: Met him very briefly once and he was a super nice guy. His quality body of work speaks for itself.

Stephen Pearcy: I sometimes say that I hate the term "Rock star" but these days I think rock stars are in short supply. You know, the guys that are a bit larger than life and really live the whole life style? Stephen is one of those guys. He's for real and I wish we had more of him.

Don Dokken: Met him once. He wasn't very pleasant to me.

Sebastian Bach: Crazy boy!!! Again, another legitimate rock and roller. I went to club once to see Dee Snider's band Widowmaker. There weren't a lot of people there. Not like he would have gotten for Twisted Sister. Down in front was this guy thrashing his hair all over the place like a wild man despite the fact that everyone else was hanging back. He didn't give a shit, he was going for it. That was Bas!! And I thought, you know what? He's right.

Tom Keifer: Loved the Night Songs and Long Cold Winter. Tom Keifer is a great songwriter heavily influenced by the Stones. And that makes him all right in my book!

Eric Martin: As I mentioned, Eric is one of those voices that I can listen to all day. What he has is beautiful. And I'm pleased to call him a friend.

Steve Whiteman: The first rock star I ever met!! Kix were legendary right from the start on the East Coast of America and I got into L'amour one night to see them. I got back stage and ran into him and got to talking about vocals and technique and he was very kind and generous with his time. Flash forward 30 years later to the MORC and I meet him again and I'm still nervous. He not only has one of the most insanely good voices I've ever heard, on stage he is a combination of Mick Jagger and Bugs Bunny. A hero!

Mike Tramp: Mike and I have been friends for many years and I think he and I share this vision of our reality. We're both gypsies when it comes to our music. Go anywhere, play anywhere. We are both proud of the fact that, no matter what level we are operation at, we are managing to make our way through this world doing the thing we love most.

22. What is on your plate for the rest of 2018 and 2019?

Vaughn:
Tyketto will be appearing at M3 Festival in May, Rock Im Tal Festival in Switzerland and Stonefree festival in London in June, and then we are doing two very special performances in an atmospheric setting in Wales where we will be performing our music with a string ensemble, a horn

section, backing vocalists and special guests all to be filmed for a DVD release later in the year.

23. Is there anything else that you want us to mention? Anything you want us to promote?

Vaughn:
Just that right now we are all seem to be getting manipulated into being so polarized against anyone or anything that doesn't agree with our points of view. Facebook is a wasteland of intolerance, anger and cruelty. The only way we can change that is with our own efforts. Have a little more patience with each other and hear what we have to say even if we don't agree with it. We need more love in the world. Post more cat pictures!! Hahaha!

THANK YOU SOOOOOO much for sharing your thoughts with us. We really appreciate it. More than you could imagine.

http://www.dannyvaughn.com
https://twitter.com/dannyvaughnvox
https://www.facebook.com/Danny-Vaughn-49167339391/

Junkyard
We interviewed the entire band a couple years ago. This and the Jason McMaster interview are the only two that aren't from 2018.

Photo courtesy of the official Junkyard webpage.

David Roach - vocals
Brian Baker - guitar
Tim Mosher - guitar/vocals

Todd Muscat - bass
Pat Muzingo - drums

1. Dangerous Toys frontman Jason McMaster is from Austin, were you guys friends or did you know of each other? What did you think of Dangerous Toys?

David: Jason and I went to High School and worked together at a steak house, where I was a cook and he was a dishwasher. I was into punk rock and Jason washed dishes in the back while singing along to Saxon and Priest and shit...The Toys were cool. They had to separate us on tour because we were corrupting each other.

Pat: That was a pretty fun tour with them back in the day. I wanna say it was a few months? I forgot about us getting separated! Haha, from what I remember that didn't last long.

Todd: I'm not from Austin, so no I wasn't friends with them. Met them when we played a show with them in Oklahoma and that was the only time I'd heard them. They sounded good and they seemed like nice dudes.

2. How would you describe Junkyard's sound? A lot of reviewers called you guys Southern rock, but I always felt you were more of a pure rock-n-roll band with a touch of sleaze thrown in.

Brian: Lemmy Skynrd

David: I would call us a rock and roll band. I never understood what sleaze rock was. Everything about the music industry is sleazy.

Todd: I think a lot of reviewers are idiots. "They got slide guitar on that song so they must be a southern rock band." If I had to describe the sound it would be hard rock. I seriously don't know what "sleaze" means or the sound it describes.

3. Both your albums were great, chocked full of great songs. What excuse did Geffen give for dropping you after album number two? Was it before or after you handed in the third album?

Pat: Thanks for the kind words! I guess we may as well clear up the mysterious "third" record! After *Sixes* ran its course, according to the label (and you really can't blame them cause they spent a boat load on that release), we headed back in and started doing demos for a 3rd release, recording new songs (we really thought it was gonna come out) for the label to listen to. I recall 3 sessions where we went in and did some great stuff. We really wanted to go back to our punk roots on these recordings. We even recorded a few favorite covers of ours, Fears "I Don't Care About You" and The Clash's "Should I Stay or Should I go."

We also got to work with Tom Rothrock and Rob Schnapf (who went on to produce Beck, Foo Fighters, Motorhead, Elliot Smith, etc) who we were pushing to produce the "third" record.

After all the last batch of demos were recorded (I think it was "Tried and True", "Holdin' On", "All Those Bad Things" and a few more I can't recall?) were turned into Geffen our A&R guy was very happy. A few weeks later the rest of the label (really just one heavyweight at the label) simply said..."I don't hear any hits!" At that point we were released and did some shows around town to generate some money. We also had label interest but it was the same story (Grunge, Nirvana, etc) everyone else was hearing. At that time we knew grunge was going to be "the death" of the rock scene. We were never bitter about it like the other bands, I think they were all in denial but the reality was most of those bands had nothing to say in the 1st place. Musically and Lyrically (the bands complaining about grunge) weren't offering up anything new. It was really time for something new. In fact we were stoked to see bands like Alice in Chains, Soundgarden and Pearl Jam getting huge. They were all openers for us except Pearl Jam, who we knew from their old band Mother Love Bone and Green River.

I think I got off track a bit here! Haha, sorry. Basically here are the facts. The 3rd release had 2 tentative names. It was *Shinola*, in reference to "Shit or Shinola" an old 1940's colloquialism referencing Shinola shoe polish. The 2nd name was an inside joke in reference to *Sixes* 1st week record sales that were pre sound scan. If Geffen would have only reported the sales we would have entered the Billboard Top 200 in the top 20. Ya live, ya learn.

Todd: I guess we couldn't write that hit they were looking for. As I recall labels were dumping most of their rock acts unless you were wearing flannel. I don't blame them really. They're in the business of making money and fans were tired of having crappy hair metal power ballads shoved up their ass. I'm glad they blew it all up. You need a forest fire to make room for new trees. I know a lot of rock fans got butt hurt about Nirvana and Pearl Jam ruining rock. Whatever, so your favorite band got dropped because people got tired of lightweight over hyped bands with no balls or substance. As for us, I'm perfectly fine the way things worked out. Sometimes the baby gets thrown out with the bath water. We just went low profile and our true fans have been there all along. It is what it is.

4. All The Time in the World was your biggest billboard "hit" --but most fans still list Simple Man and Hollywood as your signature songs. What was the story behind Simple Man, Hollywood and Time? (In terms of writing them, did you instantly know they would be hits, etc).

David: All the songs on the first album were the band finding our sound, just cranking out songs and playing. We weren't thinking about hits. By the second album, there was pressure to write hits. I don't think "All the Time in the World" is the best song on that album, and I don't think any of us like playing it live.

Brian: The lyrics of all those songs tell the story behind them. Any traction on the charts was purely a coincidence.

Pat: I remember being at our rehearsal studio (early 87?) and "Hollywood" and "Simple Man" were presented to the band. The only thing that came to my mind about "Simple Man" was nice! I get a break! "Hollywood" didn't really strike any of us as a hit, even while we were recording it with Tom Werman. In fact it wasn't even being considered as the 1st single until it was mixed. I remember "Hot Rod" being the single track at one point. "Time" was different. The band had been sequestered/lock out at our rehearsal space in Hollywood after bouncing around town checking in and out of studios. We had some "Hi Tech" recording gear. By the time I was handed the tape of the song it was pretty much done except the bridge. I listened to it and liked the groove to it but my excitement was finally recording "Misery" and "Lost in the City" since they were older song. To me it was always gonna be "Misery" as the single..again once it was mixed the whole thing changed. "Time" had that chorus that people kill for at the time. We played it up until a few years ago and then we dropped it cause we just weren't feeling it anymore.

5. Who wrote Hands Off and was it about a personal experience? IMO, the third best song on your debut album.

David: Hands Off was written at the band house, "Texas West" in Hollywood. We were sitting in the living room and Nick Ferrari, from The Little Kings, said "A song that pretty needs an ugly title like, get your hands off my throat." It instantly reminded me of an actual event with an ex. SO yes, it's a true story. Everything I wrote happened.

6. Slippin' Away was a great ballad. How come you guys didn't do more slow songs?

Brian: Didn't write that many.

David: I don't know.... we just did what we did.

Todd: "Slippin' Away" was co-written by Steve Earle. Speaking for myself it doesn't make sense to set out to write a certain tempo of song. Whatever comes out comes out. I guess slow songs aren't where our heads were at.

Pat: I never looked at "Simple Man" or "Hands Off" for that matter as ballads, they were just slow songs. "Slippin Away" was a ballad for sure. I think we played that live maybe a dozen times? It's a good song to listen back to but we retired it a while ago. In the heat of our live shows, and we have to make a choice between "Slippin Away" or something like "Sonic Reducer" the faster more raucous songs are always gonna win. We do have our fair share of slower songs though. "Long Way Home", "Killing Time" & "Clean the Dirt" are all fairly slow but they are pretty damn hard edged.

7. Does it make you mad to get categorized with all the other "hair bands" like Winger and Poison when your sound is nothing like those bands at all. I put you in the GnR, Aerosmith, Cinderella, Motley Crue, Van Halen, Dangerous Toys, Tesla and Tora Tora level - and nothing to do with the typical hair band group.

Tim: There were a lot of bands lumped into the "hair metal" thing that weren't even close to it but that is a function of labels and media doing a shorthand of sorts and to be fair a lot of Junkyard fans like what are considered "hair metal" bands as well. That being said it's something we don't worry about too much, anyone who listens to what the band actually sounds like will know what we are about.

Brian: Just glad to be remembered

David: I wouldn't categorize us with any of those bands. I feel like we were always misunderstood. But, like Brian says, I am just happy to be remembered at all.

Todd: Doesn't really make me mad. More than anything it was disappointing. Americans have a hard time with labeling things they don't really understand. Were the N.Y. Dolls a hair band? GnR had some of the biggest hair in the history of rock. I mean if you think about it both Motley and Cinderella are "Hair". With Poison and Winger, their fans were never going to like us anyway we were too ugly. They were selling records to 15-year-old girls and dudes trying to fuck them. They were just crappy pop music.

Pat: We know that we have nothing to do with those bands, although if someone compares us to, say, Aerosmith... that's a compliment. The other "Hair Bands" not so much. "Hair Bands" are so funny, even now.

I have to agree with Todd about the "hair bands" back in the day. It was kinda gross the way they were treating people and women. If people need to categorize us as a "hair band" then chances are they really haven't listened to our stuff, which isn't all that hairy.

8. You guys appear to still be very successful overseas, even headlining major festivals. Why do you think the overseas markets love you guys, but you aren't as popular in the states?

Tim: I think overseas they value real rock n roll a bit more than in the states. That being said our US fans are the most hardcore.

Todd: I think Europeans got us and stayed with us because they have well-developed bull shit detectors. They seem to be able to be able to suss out what's real and what's fake. We went over there, no lights, no pyro or staging, just plugged in and blasted. A lot of Americans are into the "show" and spectacle. How else do you explain shit like the Kardashians and TMZ? If it's not being spoon fed to you here you're not going to get it.

Pat: I think I come in 2nd (I cant beat Brian! Haha) with the amount of tours I've done in Europe (with my old band Speedbuggy). Overseas is such a different vibe. They are true fans, they collect everything! I think they are just happy to have live music happen? There is so many forgotten pockets of Europe that when we (Speedbuggy) would show up and play in places like Croatia no one had a clue who we were, but there was 500 people there! Junkyard and Spain go together quite nicely. Our fans over in Spain just couldn't get over the fact that we would actually have a drink with them, or shoot the shit with them? I even asked them if most bands hide from their fans and they say yeah! We are always so excited to hit Spain that we will hang with anyone! Hell, we are on a vacation of sorts! We have done well in Switzerland and Austria and have yet to really hit France and Germany. We did tour England back in '92 (supporting The Almighty) and that was very successful! It was the 1st tour to promote the "Sixes" release and we couldn't believe how fast press was at that time! We did an interview and photo session with Kerrang and it came out the next week. We have yet to go back because, at the end of the day, we are going to go back there proper. I've heard of bands sneaking into the country, using the opening bands gear, etc. We aren't that way; we will sort out our Visas' and do it right.

9. You guys have always been regarded as a great live band. How was the reception to the 2000 live album?

Pat: Hard to tell? We were happy to have it out there; I think the fans dig it? As far as a real reception it wasn't marketed or promoted so it's a word of mouth release. It was interesting how it came about. We had a box lying around with stuff that Geffen thought we should have. There was a recording tape (ya know, the old analog way of recording) that looked like it was disintegrating. We took it to the studio where we did the "Tried and True" EP and had to bake the tape, then we listened to it and realized that it was a recording from a sold out LA show after our very 1st US tour. We have always been good friends with the owner of Cleopatra records and he said he would put it out. At any rate at least we got that elusive "live" release out of the way!

Todd: People seem to like it I guess?

10. We loved 2003's Tried and True. What is the story behind that album, which is only six songs long but hits 4-5 different sounds. The acoustic song, two songs that sound like heavy metal or hard core punk, a lovely mellow/ballad type song and an old fashion rocker that sounds influenced by 60s rock. The song Tried and True should have been a top 20 rock hit.

Tim: Tried and True was pretty simple- Let's do some new stuff. Constraints on time and budget kept it to EP length. It was a small label and sadly the song itself didn't get out there that much. Glad you like it though!

Pat: That was the 1st time we had been back in a recording studio since 1993? We had some song ideas and a few shows booked. Tim had a good friend who had his own studio and said c'mon in and lets track some songs. It was a strange time in the business with the indies not really knowing what they were up to, iTunes was still fairly new and didn't have the power of purchasing, bands putting out their own releases was few and far between. "Tried and True" was actually on our early 1992/93 demos and Tim had co-written it so we did a new version of that were it was less 90's ballady and more like a cool slow song. The acoustic version of "Simple Man" was basically to even it out as 6 songs, but boy did it work. It really showed that David is a singer, plain and simple, not a rocker/sleaze/genre pinned singer. The only reason it's an EP is cause it was meant to demo to the indies. Looking back it would have been great to have just 4 more songs!

11. Why the 12 year void of albums? Or, I suppose the other question would be, since you all were working with different projects, what prompted the band Junkyard to get back together and record an EP?

Tim: We play gigs now and again and recording was an extension of that really.

Pat: Was it 12 years?! Wow! We were all doing pretty diverse projects, touring and just plain working and creating careers and families. The big push for getting us back to playing together again has to out to the tour of Japan. As "Tap" as it sounds we got an offer to play 5 or so show's in Japan. It was totally out of the blue. The other thing is that we had always been in touch with each other after the band called it a day back in '93. We had been thru so much together, not just with Junkyard but also with our older punk bands in the early 80's. Japan was the kick in the pants that we needed to start playing again as Junkyard. The only bummer was that Tim couldn't make the tour but Jo from Dogs D'Mour filled in just fine.

I think the same month we got approached by The Supersuckers about opening for them at the House of Blues in L.A. That was such a brilliant package. We were fans of them already but we really didn't realize that they liked us back in the day.

As of late we are finding out just how much our releases have really stood the test of time. We've been told this by people that we would have never thought even knew about us. Its really cool when someone you listen to tweets ya back how much they liked one of the releases and we are like really?! Wow! It's a very cool feeling. I doubt bands like Tora Tora or Saigon Kick get props from big time Singer/Songwriters or bands like The Supersuckers, Buck Cherry, punk bands or even professional athlete's!

12. 2008 was a busy year for you guys. You self-released three albums worth of material. What is the story behind that? Why so much music all at once? How did it go, what has been the fan response?

Todd: We just put it out there to put it out. No real plan.

Pat: That actually was a busy year for the band? There was a huge amount of interest after we did co-headlined the 2nd night of the Serie Z festival in 2003 in the south of Spain. We had been going back and forth (with a great production company based out of Barcelona) on which year we were going to head over. Finally in 2007 we made the commitment to tour in 2008. For us touring is a difficult thing. Unlike other bands we all have pretty great careers and families but the production company worked with us so we could all use our vacation days to tour for a few weeks. The fan response, overseas, was so great! We couldn't believe how many people were coming to the shows and how far they were traveling to see us. Having done numerous tours over there myself I didn't even expect the turnout! We did get some backlash about the tour, mostly from people in the states who were upset we weren't touring the USA.

See, the thing about Europe is you can hit 5 countries in 2 weeks. In the states you could maybe do 5 states in 2 weeks? As of the last few years we have been getting offers to play mini festivals but we are really being picky about those. Some just don't really jive with what we are all about now. Its not that we are ignoring our "rock" past but even back in the day we didn't have a lot to do with "hair bands" or "sleaze rock" bands.

We really have more in common with Turbonegro then 80% of the bands that are on the US "rock" festivals. The Quireboys and Junkyard would be a more palatable show for all involved. As great as it is being asked to play the "revival" multi band shows we kinda look at it this way...why play a 30 minute set when we can play a 90 minute set in a dirty night club where we could literally hang out with every person who comes down.

13. Are you guys going to continue going the self-release method or would you like to hook up with a major label again?

Todd: Haha a major label!!! Who needs a major label any more. I never got into music to get rich. When I started all I wanted was to get some free drinks and get laid. My idea of the big time was opening for the Circle Jerks and having a bass that stayed in tune.

Pat: 2015 and 2016 are going to be exciting years and from how things are shaping up it will bring the band to the people in more ways then one.

14. What does the future hold for Junkyard? Another album? US tours? Are you guys going to play any of the big multi-band festivals that are so popular right now?

Pat: The future does look pretty damn good. The multiband festival is not very intimate and the revival shows don't really excite us much. It's great they are happening for the fans but some of the festivals are great for the "hair, or lack of hair" bands but for us to be on one it really needs to be way more diverse like the Riot festivals. We have wanted to hit places that we haven't done since 92 and those will happen in 2015. We just don't know when at this point.

Todd: Not sure. A US tour makes no sense unless we hook up with someone that can draw people and if that happens maybe 2-3 weeks. A more likely scenario would be to fly in and do a Friday in one city and Saturday in another within driving distance. Personally I have no desire to go play the nostalgia type festival, cruise, pool party. Ideally I want to play with bands I actually want to hear and hang out with.

15. I see your name attached to Guns n Roses a lot in various articles. Was there a relationship between the two bands? Got any crazy GnR stories for us? Did you have any interactions with Axl - was he different than the way the media represents him?

Brian: Not really, no and nope.

David: They came to see us at a club in Hollywood and we gave them some t-shirts. Axl liked the band and wore the shirt enough to get photographed in it, which was cool but that was the extent of our relationship. We opened for them once.

Todd: I spent some crazy nights with those dudes. Mostly Axl, Duff, and Steven. One night stands out in particular. Duff, Axl and I went to go see Johnny Thunders and soon as we walked in we got into a big scrap with some of Poison's crew. We got 86'd but snuck in by climbing up some pipes to a window on the 2nd floor and were able to catch the show. After the show Axl and I hopped into Johnny's limo and he had some chicks with him and wanted to go up and the see city lights from Mulholland after that things are a little hazy, I just remember waking up the next afternoon at the Chateau Marmont grabbing my coat and a beer and walked back to my flat.

Pat: We all have had different experiences with that band. Duff was the only band member who would travel to East Hollywood and hang with us. He knew our old punk bands and we knew of his punk band so it just made sense. It's a funny thing, with the punk scene your friends for life. Mostly cause it was about changing things, plus we were all fairly young and we were all outcasts. With the LA rock scene people were plastic and fake. Guns did help us out a few times. Todd (Muscat) and I used to hang out with Axl and Izzy a bit. Our old punk band "Decry" actually headlined a gig in Chinatown and we had Guns open for us. As far as Axl being insane I always thought he was a pretty mellow dude. Not a very jovial dude but fun to chat with about non rock stuff.

16. Speaking of GnR, what did you think of Chinese Democracy?

Brian, David and Todd: Never heard it

Pat: Looks like I am the only one who spun it once or twice? For as much time as they spent on it, it really didn't live up to the hype. I don't really know who played on it, or who wrote the material but it sounded, to me, like one of the many bands from the 1986 Hollywood scene. That was a confusing time. Bands really didn't think about the music as much as they thought about looking like Hanoi Rocks.

17. What bands did you have the most pleasurable experiences with while touring? Were there any bands or artists that were dicks to you guys?

Brian: Loved the Toys. Don't recall anyone being dicks.

David: Everybody we toured with was fun, I liked the Black Crowes a lot. Most people were cool.

Pat: Skynrd in 1991 were really nice. They didn't put restrictions on us. Also The Almighty was pretty cool. The Crowes tour was fun too. Getting to see a band break big time as they were opening for you was a trip. Early on we did a Wednesday show with LA Guns in San Francisco. At that time we had a pretty good following in the city that comprised of our old punk friends. Anyhow, it was the typical drum riser situation. LA Guns drummer was not moving his "shark cage" and there was no room on the stage with all their amps. Things got a little ugly and we pushed the riser back so David could have at least 4 feet in front of me. They had their rockstar tantrum (except the original guitarist) and everything went well...we never played a show with them after that. We did a few shows with Extreme and they were another band (well, really the singer) that were not so cool. Recently we did a festival show with Twisted Sister, we got booted out of our backstage room so the singer could have his treadmill in there. At the time we had just got off stage and they were getting ready to go on. In the end it worked out fine for us cause we really aren't the type of band that hides out backstage and changes into out Halloween costumes anyways.

18. Is there a band that you are really surprised didn't make it...........and a band that you are still surprised that they DID make it?

Brian: Us!

David: I am surprised Junkyard didn't "make it." Its a crap shoot and all the best music will never be heard by the masses.

Tim: There are always good bands that got lost in the shuffle . Like from the late eighties era - Flies On Fire, Broken Homes, Zodiac Mindwarp come to mind and there are always plenty of shit bands that get big but I don't begrudge anyone success so let's leave it at that

Pat: I have to go back into the vaults but its sad that our East Hollywood/Scream scene didn't get bigger? The clubs were there, the bands were actually making music but the businesses always wanted "The Strip" style bands. Later on around 94/95 East Hollywood finally got its due as it slipped into Silverlake. What did confuse me was how many bands sold so many records without having songs?

19. What current bands do you enjoy?

Brian: The Darkness, Lamb of God, NOFX

Todd: The Bronx, BRMC, Supersuckers, Riverboat Gamblers, Wildhearts, Red Fang, Off

David: I am out of the loop and always ten years behind the times.

Pat: It's a great time for new music, so many great musicians and bands. Turbonegro, Street Walkin Cheetahs, The Loud Ones, Dead Weather, Ryan Adams, Smash Fashion, Still love The Hangmen!

20. If you were stuck on a deserted island for the next 25 years, what five albums would you bring with you?

Pat: The Damned's "The Black Album" and "Machine Gun Ettiqutte",
The Who "Quadrophenia", AC/DC "If you want blood"
My Cat taxidermied into a turntable

Tim: Exile On Main Street, Never Mind the Bollocks, London Calling,
The Replacements- Let It Be, White Album.... lots of double albums!!

David: Elvis, Hank, Stones, Beatles, AC/DC, Motor Head, punk rock

Brian: Can I just bring a guitar instead? And 25 years worth of
strings?

21. What singers/musicians/bands inspired you during your early years?

Tim: Early early years- Beatles (and still for that matter), Stones, The
Who, Kiss, and then in my teens punk and new wave happened- Sex
Pistols , Clash , Damned, Minor Threat, Replacements, Elvis Costello,
etc.

Todd: Had to be the Ramones, DOA, Adolescents, Circle Jerks, Social
D, AC/DC, Motörhead Aerosmith, 999, Stiff Little Fingers, Ian Hunter,
those are some that come to mind.

Pat: For drummers its these 3 guys - Chuck Biscuits (DOA, Circle
Jerks, Black Flag), Rat Scabies (The Damned) and Paul Cook (Sex
Pistols). Bands when I was a kid are pretty much like Tim's. Recently I
got the same feeling watching Daru Jones (The Vultures) play that I
got when I was a kid watching Rat Scabies. Feels good to get inspired
again.

Brian: The Clash, The Damned, AC/DC, Iron Maiden

22. What Junkyard songs are you the most proud of? Which songs do you enjoy playing live the most?

David: I am most proud of "Hands Off" because of what people tell me
it makes them feel. I like playing "Blooze" and "Lost in the City" live.

Tim: I always love playing "Simple Man." From my view of the audience it seems to connect the most and mean the most to people.

Brian: "Hands off" and "Blooze"

Todd: "Blooze", "Hands Off", like when we do "Sonic Reducer" also

Pat: "Life Sentence" and "Blooze" pretty much sums it up although "Misery" is pretty fun live as well as "Lost in the City."

23. If you could choose any band to tour with, who would you choose?

Brian: Manowar

Tim: The bigger the better. Whoever that is.

Pat: We usually do well by ourselves. Its way more fun for the fans...but if we got an offer to tour with a "hair band" from back in the day I'm pretty sure we would pass unless it was Manowar.

https://junkyardblooze.com
https://www.facebook.com/junkyardhollywood

Jason McMaster
Dangerous Toys, Broken Teeth

Photo courtesy of Mr. McMaster's official Facebook page.

1. love the song Angel N U and feel it is one of the most underrated hair metal songs of all time. What was the inspiration behind it?

McMaster: We wrote the song in a 1990 sound check and the lyrics soon after. Working hard and playing hard is what the song is about. Too much is never enough, too nice, love hard, still not enough. That's pretty much it."

2. We also love Civil War by Guns n Roses. Are you familiar with Civil War, if so, your thoughts?

McMaster: It's a good song, I think that era of Guns is where they tried to spread out what they could do as songwriters in a sense of dynamics. And it paid off.

3. Screamin' For More is a great song that never got the recognition it deserved. What is the story behind that song?

McMaster: The first line in the song is influenced from a UFO song called High Flyer. Just a good balladeering rock song is what we were going for. Riffs influenced words and melody. Sometimes songs write themselves.

4. It was a bit of a departure from the normal Dangerous Toys sound, a bit more on the pop side. How did the band feel when you brought it to them?

McMaster: Scott (Dalhover, guitar player) had a part, it influenced me to write words an melody without judgments on style.

5. How is it that DT aren't thought of at the same level as the Skid Row, GnR and Motley's of the world? Unique and versatile voice, great guitars, hard rocking songs and power ballads. It sill amazes me you guys weren't bigger.

McMaster: Timing. First record should of come out about 1987.

6. What bands did you really respect from the era? Any that you didn't, or are amazed at the success they ended up having?

McMaster: Guns N' Roses are the last great band of that era. If you did not have any sort of clout, record sales, etc, you were going to be short lived . The popularity of that kind of hard rock switched over to a Seattle sound. Bad media slang ended up calling grunge. It's all still rock'n roll to me! But fashion, along with attitude, changed enough for people to throw away the wardrobe and switch out to what was hot just so they could fit in. I like a lot of the music from that class of 89, but there were only a few lucky enough to make a couple of records worth of material.

7. Axl Rose fans are obsessed with his "rasp" when he sings. You've probably got the most rasp of any rock singer out there. Do your fans harass you about using it too much or not enough? And how have you been able to keep it over all these years? So many singers from the 80s and early 90s sound terrible now live - how do you keep your voice so strong?

McMaster: Good living I guess! If people like it, great, if they don't like it, that's fine too.

8. The third DT song that made our list of best metal songs from the 80s is Queen of the Nile. We think it's the best song off of your debut album. Did you guys ever think about releasing it as a single?

McMaster: Yes, but the label was more into the idea that we had to get a second album release out though. They rushed us a bit.

9. What is the story behind the writing of Queen of the Nile?

McMaster: Obsession with Egyptian art and culture at the time of writing that record.

10. What are your 2-3 favorite DT songs (or which songs are you most proud of writing)?

McMaster: Promise the Moon and Transmission.

11. What songs do you love to perform live the most?

McMaster: All of them.... maybe Bones in the Gutter.

12. Have you heard Hardcore Superstar? If so, what do you think of them? (They sound like the modern day version of DT).

McMaster: Yes, we did a show with them in Germany, they were very nice and respectful.

13. Have you heard Chinese Democracy by Guns N Roses? What did you think of it?

McMaster: Yes, Axl sounded amazing on it. The record sounded new, and not much re hash.

14. All the bands from that era are doing the festival type shows now - would DT ever reunite and do the Monsters of Rock Cruise or any of the big name festivals that are pulling in the great bands from the hair band era?

McMaster: We have done the last two MOR Cruises. They were awesome.

15. What was the most fun/exciting or rewarding tour you've ever done. And/or with what other band?

McMaster: Operation Rock 'N' Roll with Judas Priest, Alice Cooper, Motorhead and Metal Church. Toured with idols.

16. You've fronted a Judas Priest, Kiss, Rush, Motley Crue, Def Leppard and Metallica tribute bands/albums. That's a pretty incredible range of singers to cover. How come you decided to do that? Did you have more fun on any one more than the others?

McMaster: I love rock n' roll, the world knows it! Sometimes the phone rings and you say yes or no!

17. Watch Tower was a heavy metal thrash band. What caused you to switch things up and go with a softer hard rock style like Dangerous Toys?

McMaster: Yes, and no . Progressive, fast, heavy, metal, jazzy, odd time signatures, way ahead of its time, and arguably a pioneering band.

Where do members of a band like that start? As fans of Rock n roll. To say that I switched styles is to ask why I switched bands. Opportunities to do new things is my best answer.

18. What do you think of all these old bands that have a revolving door of musicians now but they keep putting out albums and touring under the same name? Keep the name or start with a new name? Does it tarnish the legacy of the name, or do rockers not care about that stuff?

McMaster: Keeping the name to get paid is about all there is to it. Good or bad, ya gotta eat. I am happy that most of my bands have all same members.

19. How does a singer in a thrash band, hard rock band, and heavy metal tribute bands end up writing some incredible ballads. What can you tell us about Best of Friends and Promise the Moon?

McMaster: I didn't write Best of friends - Mike Watson did. Moon was one of mine. I like music, black metal, Elton John, and Sci Fi movie themes!

20. At what age did you realize you had an amazing enough voice to become a professional singer? If you hadn't made it in music, what would your 2nd career choice have been?

McMaster: I am a music teacher, but I've done food service, and construction, and didn't mind much. I've been into music my entire life. I started playing and singing at age 12 and I'm now 50! You have jobs so you can turn your hobbies or dreams into your job.

http://www.jasonmcmaster.net
https://www.facebook.com/Jason-McMaster-115362008494501

Tommy Rickard
Vain, Orchid, Eric Martin

Photo courtesy of Mr. Rickard's personal website.

1. How did you initially hook up with Davy and the rest of the guys to form Vain?

Rickard: We were from the same town, so I'd see Davy around, as well as seeing him playing in his bands. We met through some mutual friends. He was just starting Vain and was looking for a drummer, so I came down and jammed and never left. The rest of the guys and I all went to school together, so we just started piecing it together from people that we loved and always wanted to work and jam with.

2. At what age did you start playing the drums? When did you know you were good enough to do it for a living?

Rickard: I started playing when I was 13. From the first second I sat down at a drum set, I knew that, that was going to be job and career. My dad bought me a drum set for Christmas when I was 14, and that following summer was spent touring California. That was basically the beginning of my "career."

3. Steven Adler replaced you for a bit in the band. Kind of a big deal as he has a crazy career story. Did you have thoughts on that....or did you not care, since you weren't in the band anymore so you didn't care who they hired?

Rickard: Adler didn't replace me. It's funny that no one's ever cleared up that story.
Here's what really happened. Vain and Island records had parted ways and we were looking for a new label. Adler had always been a Vain fan, and loved Davy's voice. When he was ready to get his band, Roadcrew, off the ground he called and asked Davy to join the project. Vain were in kind of a funny place at the time, so it seemed like smart thing for Davy to check out. Eventually a few of the other guys joined Roadcrew, and I started Loaded with a few SF musicians that I loved. Of course it felt a little weird that your best friends and basically your family were now playing with someone else, but there were no hard feelings. I would even go to the Roadcrew shows and hang out with Steven and the rest of the guys.

4. We read one review that compared you to John Bonham. How does that feel and was he an inspiration while you were growing up? If so – or not – what drummers were you influenced by?

Rickard: I absolutely love Bonham. He was brilliant and revolutionized drumming. I also love Ringo, Matt Cameron, Tony Williams, and so many others. You can learn something from everyone, which is what I try to do.

5. Orchid sounds nothing like Vain! Complete opposites sides of the track. How did you get involved with them, and have you always been a fan of the heavier metal type music?

Rickard: I've always loved heavier, more aggressive, and more dynamic music. I've known Theo and Mark from Orchid for years. When I heard they were looking for a drummer, I was actually offering to help them find the right guy. Theo and I spoke a few times and we decided that we should get together and give it a try. It all happened pretty organically and felt really natural right away. We're working on songs for a new record right now. They're sounding great. Can't wait for people to hear the new songs.

6. From what we've read, Vain became popular really quick. What was it about Vain that separated you guys from the thousands of "hair metal" bands that were trying to break though in the late 80s?

Rickard: We did get a solid fan base pretty quickly. Honestly, I just think we had better songs, put on a better show, and everyone played as if their lives depended on it.... as if it may be the last show you ever play.

7. You guys were from San Francisco. Was there a version of the Sunset Strip there or did you guys have to go to Hollywood and battle on the Strip?

Rickard: There was nothing like the Sunset strip, but we did have a cool scene on Broadway in SF. There was also a cool thing happening in the Haight. Cool bands, bars, and some cool little clubs to play. We did play the Sunset strip. We had too. It was much easier to get people from record companies to come out and see you in LA.

8. No Respect is such a great album. Can you share the experience of what went into writing and recording it? Could you instantly tell (while in the studio) that you guys were creating magic?

Rickard: We knew we were making the album that we wanted to make. That was a raw, dynamic, passionate, and authentic to who we were, album. We had great songs and everyone played great. All we needed to do was capture what we were. We wanted to basically just convey what we were onstage on to this album. We didn't want to overproduce or smooth out our rough edges. There would be plenty of time to smooth things out on future albums.
Most of the songs were written and performed in clubs, during the year prior to us recording the album. There were a few that were written as it got closer to us heading into the studio. I think Icy and Beat the Bullet were the last two written for the album.

9. After such a successful debut album, how come the label dropped the band didn't release the follow-up album – that doesn't make much sense.

Rickard: A few members had some opportunities to try something new. Opportunities that may get them where they wanted to be in their careers. They chose to pursue those opportunities. There was, of course, lots of discussion re pursuing these opportunities. These weren't easy decisions. We were family but I totally understood and supported the decisions that were made.
As far as the label dropping us - Island had been sold to another larger "umbrella" company. This happened while we were out supporting *No Respect*. That new company wanted us to get in the studio and record an album for them, and had ideas about how they wanted it to sound, how they wanted to promote it, etc. We didn't always agree with these ideas, and the tension between company and the band just kept growing, until it finally reached the point of no return and we parted ways.

10. You guys also toured with Skid Row? How was that experience, they were a pretty great band back in the day. Was Sebastian Bach as crazy as he seems?

Rickard: That was a great experience and could not have been more perfect timing for both bands. Their debut album was doing really well and was probably at its peak as far as popularity. They were also doing their first headlining tour of the UK, and we were doing really well in the UK, so that tour sold out really quickly.
The bands all got along really well and had a great time playing together.
Sebastian was great. He was hilarious. When we first met, he asked me if I was a "Crueton." "Do you love Crue? I fucking love Crue!" I did love Crue, I just needed Bas let me know that my love for Crue had a cool name.

11. You came back to the band in 2009 – what brought that about?

Rickard: We had all continued to be friends over the years. Davy and I had worked together on a few projects and asked me to come to

Germany to record on the Delaney project. We had a great time. Soon after we discussed doing a European tour. It all just fell into place organically.

12. What were you doing during that 1991-2008 time period? Did you make enough money from No Respect to retire to the Bahamas for those years?

Rickard: I continued to tour and record with a bunch amazing artists. I worked with Linda Perry, Eric Martin and tons of other amazing artists. I always knew I wanted the freedom to play with a variety of musicians. I love playing and listening to a wide variety of musical styles. During that time, and still to this day, I continue to work with as many, creative, interesting and inspiring projects, as possible.

13. The last album is pretty incredible. We've got it rated as the second best rock album of 2017. How was it writing/creating/recording/playing with Davy/Jamie and Ashley in 2017 compared to being in your early 20s in the 80's?

Rickard: The main difference is that you're not in the studio rehearsing five nights a week, writing and rewriting songs and parts. You're also not out playing these songs in clubs and seeing how the people that like your band respond to the new songs.
I'd like to think we're better musicians by now as well, so things come together pretty quickly. Honestly, they always have. We've always had that chemistry.

14. You were part of the band that recorded the music for the song Beautiful by Christina Aguilera (written by Linda Perry). Did you get to hang out or spend time with Linda or Christina – if so, how were they?

Rickard: It actually wasn't a band. It was a bunch great musicians that Linda brought together to work on "Beautiful" as well as a few others. I've hung out with Linda a lot. She's the best. I LOVE working with her. She always gets the best out of me. I had briefly met Christina, but she wasn't around when the song was recorded. Funny enough, Christina didn't want drums on it.

15. You also played with Eric Martin, who had one of the best voices in rock music. We've heard he is a real sweetheart of a guy. How was your time with him?

Rickard: Eric is always great. Amazing voice and really fun and funny guy. I love working with him as well. He has such a great voice and such great groove and feel in the way he sings. It's a joy for a drummer to play behind.

16. Finally, you also toured with Scott Weiland. Was that a crazy time or was he pretty relaxed and normal on the road? It's a shame Scott could never overcome his addictions.

Rickard: I truly loved playing with Scott. He's a huge talent and a sweet, sweet soul, under the demons that he was unable to overcome. Of course some gigs were better than others. At their best they were truly amazing and inspiring as a musician, with Scott singing beautifully and writing songs on stage in real time. He would just ask me to give him some kind of groove, say a Manchester beat or something dark and swampy. Doug the guitarist would start playing some chords and Scott would come in, singing something totally unexpected but beautifully melodic. At their worst, Scott would show up two hours late, and be more than a little foggy, and not be at his best.

17. Can you share the story behind the Hard Road project? How did it come about, how has the experience been creating it, and how has the response been?

Rickard: The Hard Road is documentary style show is focused on artists that aren't household names who are pursuing their passions, and overcoming what can be life and death challenges, while still pushing forward, and creating brilliant and vital art. They're basically human interest stories that use art - mostly music - as the common theme. I had the idea while watching Anthony Bourdain's "No Reservations," and "Parts Unknown." He's a huge music fan, and often had musicians on these shows. I thought why not expand on the little things that he was just touching on. The idea is to travel and meet artists from all over the world and have them share their stories in hopes of inspiring even one person.

18. How did you get into the role of being a session musician for such a variety of different acts and genres? IE: How does a rock god end up drumming for Sean Kingston, Tone Loc and Naughty By Nature!!!!

Rickard: I've always been a fan of many different styles of music. I especially lean toward 70's Soul, 90's Hip Hop, 50's and 60's Jazz/Bop, as well the obvious, Rock, Metal, and Punk. I've been lucky enough to work with some people that produce events at NFL games, as well as corporate events in places like Vegas. These events will want to have celebrity guests at times and those celebrities don't always travel with their entire band. So the producers will hire musicians like me, that they trust to go in and be professional and do a great job. I've had so much fun doing these. Dee Snider, and Naughty By Nature have been two of my favorites. Kei$ha, Bret Michaels, and Tone Loc have also been great. Although I think I gave Bret a panic attack. I thought he was playing his songs a little on the slow side, so I wanted to push them a bit, but he REALLY likes playing his songs a bit slower these days. I guess my punk roots still haven't gone away.

Dito Godwin
Multi-platinum award winning producer
Motley Crue, Great White, No Doubt, Peter Criss

Picture of Mr. Godwin courtesy of his official Twitter page.

1. You were part of Reel to Reel productions in the late 80s focusing on Sunset Strip bands. What was that like? Was the Strip as crazy as us

fans have been led to believe? Can you share some crazy stories with us!!!

Godwin:
First (Real to Reel Productions). The scene on the Sunset Strip in the 80s was wilder and crazier then you can believe. I wouldn't believe it but I was there and part of it. The Whisky, The Roxy, Gazzarri's and the Central (the viper room) were the hot spots on Sunset.

The Sunset Strip was so crowded it was hard to walk from 9pm till 2am. Packed every weekend!!!!!!! Guys with big hair, spandex, the biggest of dreams and young beautiful girls dressed like you can imagine everywhere. I don't wish to share any crazy stories LOL. it was a great time, I was in the studio producing 4 to 5 times a week every week, big label projects and brand new bands just arriving in LA.

2. What bands did you work with?

Godwin:
Too many to name. From all over the world coming to Hollywood to make it happen. My reputation with bands in LA was strong, so I got a ton of fucking work.

3. From those years you must have witnessed hundreds of bands. Who were the most amazing ones to see live (back then, in their early days). And were there bands that you were surprised didn't make it......or that you still can't believe they DID make it big?

Godwin:
All of the above "YES" I produced No Doubt's first Interscope CD and it was no shock when they made it. I promoted Motley Crue *Too Fast for Love* in 1981, no surprise they made it.

4. Then you founded TnT records in 1991. Most successful bands/albums that you worked with?

Godwin:
I signed Peter Criss of KISS and recorded two CDs with him, one of which featured KISS legend Ace Frehley.

5. You've also taught Music business management and studio productions at several universities, including UCLA. Teaching college aged kids is a bit different than working with Motley Crue! How and why did you get into that line of work?

Godwin:

I had bad teachers my entire life so I decided to be a great teacher. I have been teaching
Music Business Management and Studio Production including, UCLA, SOU, University of Sound Arts and MI to mention a few. I've taught for over 25 years and love it.

6. You play multiple instruments, which do you enjoy the most and what are you the best at? Did you ever want to be a professional musician?

Godwin:

I have spent the most time playing guitar and bass. In my heart I'm a drummer because that's how I started in rock. Thank you Beatles. My friend and I walked home after seeing HELP The Beatles. On the way home I turned to him and said "now I know what I want to do." He agreed. We still make music together to this day professionally.

7. If a billionaire gave you a blank check and you could spend it producing/working with any 2-3 bands next year....who would you choose, or what bands would you choose to work with?

Godwin:
First Justin Bieber, Beck and Soilwork.

8. Would you be willing to tackle an Axl Rose/Guns N Roses album?

Godwin:
Bring it on!!!!! And they would love it!! Including Axl! No Doubt!

9. What was your involvement or connection with Black Sabbath? Your Wiki page says you toured with the band.

Godwin:

In the early 70s I played several festivals as an opening act for Black Sabbath. A great memory.

10. You founded EFM records in 2008. Is that your main gig today? What bands are you most proud of?

Godwin:
EFM records was a short-lived project distributed by Universal. It was great experience and I worked with some very talented artist. Including the late great Kevin Carlberg!!!

11. Can you share some thoughts on a few of the amazing bands you've worked with The good/bad/ugly/etc!

Godwin:
Great working with No Doubt. Great working with The KISS guys. Great working with the Great White guys. Incredible working with Jani Lane. There are so few bad or ugly projects that I have done that they are not worth mentioning.
Before I work with a client, we have established a relationship and we go into the studio focused and confident.

12. Jani Lane, Jaberwocky. Jani is our second favorite rock singer of all time. We love that you worked/recorded with him. Would love to hear any stories you want to share.

Godwin:
In the mid to late 90s I was working with Jani at a killer studio in North Hollywood "Jandermonium". We recorded four songs in three days. The last day I turned to Jani and said "we only have four hours of studio time left (on his way to Washington for a tour) and you haven't sung one song."

Jani said "Don't worry man I've got this" and in three hours sang his ass off on all four tunes including backing vocals. The tracks came out incredible!!! I was so impressed with Jani. At the end of the night Jani turned to me and said "Dito you blew my mind" That made me feel great.

We later worked together in 2011 our plan was to write for Jani and then sign him to my Universal deal and write for other artists as well. He appeared on That Metal Show and talked about working with me during the summer instead of touring. A bunch of my friends called me and said "Holy shit I heard Jani talking about you last night!"
How cool is that?!!!

13. You also helped break No Doubt, how was the experience working with that band?

Godwin:
I loved working with No Doubt, they were great even back then. Gwen was the most prepared artist I had ever worked with. Tracks from this self-titled CD have found their way onto five other No Doubt CDs through out the years. Producing this bands first cd changed both of our lives for the better.

COME SEE US AT:
www.facebook.com/hairmetalmusic
www.hairmetalmusic.com

Made in the USA
Middletown, DE
26 September 2018